Major General
Isaac Ridgeway Trimble

Major General Isaac Ridgeway Trimble

Biography of a Baltimore Confederate

Leslie R. Tucker

McFarland & Company, Inc., Publishers
Jefferson, North Carolina, and London

LIBRARY OF CONGRESS CATALOGUING-IN-PUBLICATION DATA

Tucker, Leslie R., 1948–
   Major General Isaac Ridgeway Trimble : biography of a
Baltimore Confederate / Leslie R. Tucker.
       p.   cm.
   Includes bibliographical references and index.

   ISBN 0-7864-2131-2 (softcover : 50# alkaline paper) ∞

   1. Trimble, Isaac Ridgeway, 1802–1888.
   2. Generals—Confederate States of America—Biography.
   3. Confederate States of America. Army—Biography.
   4. United States—History—Civil War, 1861–1865—Campaigns.
   5. Railroad engineers—Maryland—Baltimore—Biography.
   6. Businessmen—Maryland—Baltimore—Biography.
   7. Baltimore (Md.)—Biography. I. Title.
E467.1.T75T86   2005
973.7′452′092—dc22   2005012772

British Library cataloguing data are available

©2005 Leslie R. Tucker. All rights reserved

*No part of this book may be reproduced or transmitted in any form
or by any means, electronic or mechanical, including photocopying
or recording, or by any information storage and retrieval system,
without permission in writing from the publisher.*

On the cover: General Trimble (courtesy William Trimble); raid
at Manassas Junction

Manufactured in the United States of America

*McFarland & Company, Inc., Publishers
   Box 611, Jefferson, North Carolina 28640
      www.mcfarlandpub.com*

To William Trimble, with thanks
for allowing me access to the papers
of his ancestor, General Trimble;

to Dr. James Huston, with thanks for
his many hours of editorial assistance;

and most of all to my wife,
Dr. Phebe M. Tucker, with thanks for
all of her support through my endeavors.

Contents

Preface 1
Introduction 3

1. From the Wilds of Kentucky to West Point 19
2. Army Life: Toward a New Identity 35
3. A New Profession: Railroad Man 54
4. Becoming a Modern Businessman 68
5. A Time for Decision 91
6. Into the Valley 121
7. The Second Round at Manassas 145
8. From Gettysburg to Surrender 169
9. Unreconstructed Rebel 197
10. Conclusion 208

Bibliographic Essay 213
Notes 217
Bibliography 241
Index 255

Preface

Years after Appomattox a Rebel yell could be heard on a summer night as it rattled through the gingerbread Gothic mansion called Ravenshurst and invaded the peaceful Dulaney Valley of Maryland. This eerie sound told Minna Reynolds, great-grandniece of the retired Confederate major general Isaac Ridgeway Trimble, that he was once again reliving the moments when he led his division in Pickett's Charge at the Battle of Gettysburg.

His niece later recorded the awe she felt in his presence: "The general was rather overwhelming. He wore a frown most of the time and on weekdays he wore a 'peg leg' which made a hollow tap-tap sound when he marched down the boardwalk to the orchard to court martial us for eating green apples." Trimble had lost his leg as the result of a wound he received in that Pennsylvania excursion so many years before. "On Sundays he let Johnson, a fine 'body servant' during the war, buckle on his very best leg." The Sunday leg was "made of cork and strips of thin wood, and garter-like buckles with a most elegant boot on the foot."[1]

At first glance Isaac Trimble appeared to be the stereotype of the Southern elite. He lived in a 38-room mansion in the cool green Maryland countryside, graduated from West Point, and had family ties, by birth and by marriage, that suggested a place in the American aristocracy. A closer look reveals a much more modern man than one would expect. Trimble did not descend from the tidewater elite of Maryland and Virginia but from Pennsylvania Quakers. He had servants, but he did not believe in slavery. He did not pay for his impressive estate with the profits from a plantation but rather with his earnings as an engineer and business man, and in fact spent most of his adult life working for the driving force of American modernization, the railroads.

The objective of this study is twofold. The first and most obvious is to tell the story of Major General Isaac Ridgeway Trimble, CSA, which has not been told before now. The second is to use the life of Trimble as a case study to understand the relationship between the individual and his community. This relationship is an important aspect of mid–nineteenth century America, since an entire section of the country rejected the nation of their fathers and assumed a new national identity, which is the highest level of community. Perhaps the most unique aspect of this study is the use of psychology to understand the behavior of the individual and the role of the individual in the community and thus in history. The model that will be used is Maslow's hierarchy of needs, a model used by business schools as well as the social sciences for almost half a century but which has been ignored by historians. On occasion this study will shift its focus from the individual, Trimble, to the community he belonged to. This shift will help the reader understand the relationship between Trimble and his community.

Because this biography is only one man's story, it can offer only one perspective, but to delve deeply into one individual can give an indication of the immensely complicated motivational process at work. Life for nineteenth century Americans had become complex. They lost many of their European roots, and as a result they had to develop a new community identity. This biography will explore the complexity of the relationship between the individual and his communities, including his family, local community, state, and nation. In addition it will explore Trimble as he relates to several issues in nineteenth century Southern history. The first question to understand is why Trimble chose to fight for secession, especially when he came from a part of the South which remained with the Union. Related to the first question is whether Trimble could be considered a modern man and whether he supported or rejected modernization. The third question concerns Southern identity. The fourth covers Trimble during the period of Reconstruction and the notion of a "New South."

Introduction

This biography of Isaac Ridgeway Trimble, a Marylander who made the decision to cast his lot with the Confederacy, is a case study that demonstrates the complexity of community identity in nineteenth century America. Modernization brought about changes in the concepts of community, including that which is called "nation." Trimble, like other Americans, lived his own life, took care of his own family, and pursued his own personal goals, but he did so as a member of a community. The community is created by the individuals who live within it, but it also contributes to creating the individual. Trimble became a leader and influenced the direction in which his community moved, but the events in his community also shaped him.

It is important to understand that in the modern world Trimble, like other Americans, had various levels of community identification. The most obvious first level would be his family unit and the local community; however, fate provided stumbling blocks in his building an identity even at this basic level. In addition, he migrated between several states and did not have a firmly established state or regional identity. He finally became associated with the city of Baltimore and the state of Maryland. Late in life he abandoned his nation and adopted a new one, a fact that leads us to the key question: Why did he fight for the Confederacy? In addition to geographical communities, we find that he had bonds to professional communities; he was a West Point graduate, railroad engineer, and military officer. Trimble found that not only did his nation divide but the other communities that he belonged to divided with the nation. Thus he found himself at war with former friends and comrades.

For men like Trimble who were involved in the modern complex of American communities, the decision to join the Confederacy became exceedingly complex. The antebellum, Civil War, and Reconstruction years proved turbulent for all Americans, but especially for Southerners and especially for those who participated in the American identity. Historians have long debated the causes for the Civil War or why the South seceded. Many have tried to identify the one main cause for the American tragedy while others have recognized that numerous events came together at the same time and each contributed in some way to the resulting war. Each person who chose the side of the South did so in response to events beyond his or her control. All had their own reasons, or more probably a combination of reasons, which caused them to believe that they would be better off siding with the Confederacy rather than remaining with the Union. The most difficult aspect of trying to identify why Southerners chose the path to secession is that each had his own path; the South consisted of many individuals and thus there were many processes in the decision to join the secession movement.

This study of a single individual can also assist in understanding other broad questions in Southern history as long as we do not lose sight of the fact that what was true for this man may not have been true for others. As stated above, the first and probably most important question is his motivation for joining the South. Though his reasons differed considerably from those of a South Carolina fire-eater, he probably had much in common with others in the Upper South and border states. Second, and for some an explanation of the first, is the question of modernization. Trimble belonged at the vanguard of modernization, yet he identified with the "lost cause"—an obvious contradiction to the notion that the South resisted modernization. Third is the question of Southern identity and distinctiveness; at what point did the South come into existence, and who was included in this region? As Trimble searched for a community identity he did not give any indication of considering himself anything but American; he did not become a Southerner until the avalanche of events forced him to choose between the North and the South. He concluded that he belonged with the latter. It is evident that the war helped to create his identity as a Southerner. Some would question whether Trimble, as a Marylander, could be considered a Southerner at all. In reality the South consisted of numerous communities and sub-regions. Though the state of Maryland remained in the Union, it contributed many men no less supportive of the Confederacy than those from the deep South. Fourth, though he lived in a state that did not belong to one of the military districts, we find that he did experience Reconstruction and the "New

South." In some ways the fact that he came from Maryland offers a unique angle to historical questions about Reconstruction. After the war he lived in a community of former Confederates and he became the leading spokesman for those from Maryland. He became closely associated with the redeemer Wade Hampton and had much in common with him. He did not battle to restore Southern rule as Hampton did, but he contributed to securing for the Confederate soldier an honorable place in American history. Trimble did not support the notion of a "New South." He did not see the South as a land made new by Reconstruction. After the war he recaptured his economic and social position in the city of Baltimore. He resumed his life among the social elite. He found acceptance among the former Confederate leaders who, like Trimble, attempted to recapture their financial position. He continued down the same path that he had traveled before the war, and the city of Baltimore followed that same path under the leadership of former Confederates such as Trimble, as well as those who had remained loyal to the Union. Each remained respectfully silent as the other celebrated anniversaries or ceremonies honoring their respective causes.

Entire philosophies are usually based on a handful of basic assumptions that one accepts or rejects. This study of the life of Isaac Trimble is based on a few assumptions that need further explanation. First, in order to explore the question of modernization it is necessary to identify the differences between a premodern and modern society. Second, it is assumed that the main motivation for the behavior of Isaac Trimble, as well as those he lived and worked with, is based on the motivational model known as Maslow's hierarchy of needs. Third, the individual becomes part of a society, or community, and it is the role that he or she plays in that society that is relevant to historical questions; it is necessary to define that relationship. Fourth, it is assumed that modernization was a constantly evolving process related to the expansion of the market economy in which industrialization was a relatively revolutionary step. Fifth, it is posed that modernization and the expanding markets produced an increase in the power of the central government. Related to this, as the communities within the nation competed with each other, the central government often had to choose sides and thus the government itself became a source of conflict. It could be said that states' rights were really matters of self-interest, especially for those from the region that became known as the South.

First Assumption: Definition of Modernization

There are distinctive dividing lines between primitive, premodern, and modern man. Many of us feel, in varying degrees, a longing for the primitive way of life of the noble savage. For thousands of years men lived in tribal or clan cultures. They had little need for written laws since the groups were homogeneous. Everyone had a place in the society and each one understood his or her responsibilities. With the arrival of civilization life became more complex, and with the advent of the modern world, very complex.

In trying to define the South in terms of modern and premodern customs, it is critical to establish the turning point. Some argue in favor of the Enlightenment while others look to the industrial revolution. European historians see the Renaissance as the birth of the modern world, though some debate the exact date or even the century when the middle ages ended and the modern world began. Robert Hollinger offered one definition of the arrival of the modern era. Before the Enlightenment, Western society was largely rural and agricultural, authoritarian, religious, unpopulated, homogeneous, and the economy was definitely precapitalist. The modern world brought with it political and ethical individualism, various forms of capitalism, democracy, science and technology, massive population growth and concentration, growth of urban areas, and cultural, political, and religious heterogeneity.[1] The industrial revolution, on the other hand, occurred when a particular national economy reached a crucial moment in its development called the "take-off" stage by W. W. Rostow. According to Rostow, this occurred in America before the Civil War (1843–1860). Great Britain began the process (1783–1802) followed by France (1830–1860), Belgium (1833–1860), and then the United States.[2]

Another view of modernization involves a question of attitude rather than technical or economic progress. Richard D. Brown uses the term "traditional" as the opposite of a modern society. The first characteristic of a traditional society is stability. Whereas traditional society had an attitude of acceptance or resignation, individuals in modern society are the opposite. They have a dynamism, and change rather than stability becomes the norm.[3] Some of the modern personality traits identified by Brown include innovation and improvement, social and geographic mobility, belief in the capacity to improve the natural and social environments, openness to new experience, personal ambition, and increasing independence from traditional authority figures.[4] It will be seen that Trimble satisfies the definitions of the modern society put forth by both Hollinger and Brown, and thus it could not be said that Trimble fought for the Confederacy to preserve a premodern Southern society.

Second Assumption: Maslow's Hierarchy of Needs

This study makes use of psychology. This is not a "psychohistory"; it does not attempt to psychoanalyze Isaac Trimble. The use of psychology here is strictly for the purpose of understanding the motivation of Trimble and the relation of the individual to his community. Historians traditionally have avoided the field of psychology, even in the writing of biography. In the social sciences it is important to determine "whether there can be said to be a discernible pattern in the way individuals think and behave."[5] There is an overlap "as the convergence of social, historical, and political forces becomes more evident in the pattern of all the branches of study that are related to man" and it "takes on the status not merely of a desirable goal but of an unquestionable necessity." In this "psychology will play a key role."[6]

Abraham Maslow became the father of humanistic psychology and in the process provided invaluable material for other disciplines concerned with human behavior and motivation. For many years psychology lacked relevance to the general population since it concentrated on finding a cure for the ill.[7] Before 1950 there existed two main branches of psychology, behaviorism and psychoanalysis. Maslow discovered that "their greatest limitation has been the inadequacy of their approach to *positive* human potentialities and the maximal realization of those potentialities."[8] In 1961 the *Journal of Humanistic Psychology* adopted Maslow's formulations as its operative definition for humanistic psychology and recognized the human capacities for "creativity, love, self, growth, organism, basic need gratification, self-actualization, higher values, ego-transcendence, objectivity, autonomy, identity, responsibility, psychological health, etc."[9] By 1950 businessmen had already grasped the lessons Maslow had to offer as they sought practical application of the human relations movement. Douglas McGregor of MIT became an apostle and by the 1960s Maslow's ideas "were being put into practice by some of the country's most pioneering executives."[10] Since that time Maslow's hierarchy of needs has become a standard in the study of management.

Historians have also shied away from the term "human nature." However, a basic model developed by Abraham Maslow has enjoyed wide acceptance among psychologists and psychiatrists. Maslow said that human nature "is extremely malleable in the sense that it is easy for culture and environment to kill off altogether or to diminish genetic potential," although he pointed out that a culture cannot increase this potential.[11] Other psychologists have recognized basic human needs, but Maslow revolutionized thinking on the subject when he recognized that "human life will never be understood unless its highest aspirations are taken into account." He labeled these "self-esteem" and "self-actualization." He went on to add that "growth, self-actualization, the striving toward health, the quest for identity and autonomy, the yearning for excellence must by now be accepted beyond question as a widespread and perhaps universal human tendency."[12] He identified a hierarchy of needs, often diagramed as a pyramid, in an "attempt to formulate a positive theory of motivation that will satisfy the theoretical demands ... and at the same time conform to the known facts, clinical and observational as well as experimental. It derives directly, however, from clinical experience."[13]

The first of five levels he called "the physiological needs." These can range from the obvious, food and water, to the less obvious, such as a specific craving in what one eats to satisfy the body's need for salt, sugar, or protein. The second level is "the safety needs." Everyone needs security, stability, protection, and freedom from fear, anxiety, and chaos. In society this is reflected by a drive for structure, order, law, and limits. "Other broader aspects of the attempt to seek safety and stability in the world are seen in the very common preference for familiar rather than unfamiliar things, or for the known rather than the unknown." In an even broader context this can also explain "the tendency to have some religion or world philosophy that organizes the universe and the men in it into some sort of satisfactorily coherent, meaningful whole."[14]

The third level is the integration of the individual with society, culture, or community; it is the need for belongingness and love. Children seek affection and approval from family and the larger community that the family belongs to. As the child approaches adulthood he will seek a mate; this is a response to the third level of need. Maslow also stated, "we have very little scientific information about the belongingness need," though he recognized that "this is a common theme in novels, autobiographies, poems, and plays and also in the newer sociological literature."[15] He also identified this level of needs as the greatest avenue of disorientation as a result of industrialization, because of the tendency of people to desert their communities. In the modern world many end up with a feeling of not having roots or a point of origin, or a lack of feeling of belonging to one group, because people are often torn from their neighborhood or community and even their families. "In our society the thwarting of these needs is the most commonly found cause in cases of maladjustment and more severe pathology."[16]

As stated earlier, Maslow's greatest contribution is his recognition that the higher needs are part of human nature. The fourth level he called "the esteem needs." He classified these further into two subsets. The first is "the desire for strength, for achievement, for adequacy, for mastery and competence, for confidence in the face of the world, and for independence and freedom." The second is "what we may call the desire for reputation or prestige, status, fame and glory, dominance, recognition, attention, importance, dignity, or appreciation." The highest level is "self-actualization." This is a more abstract concept that centers around the idea that "what a man can be, he must be," that when all the other needs are filled there is a universal drive that will develop "unless the individual is doing what he ... is fitted for. A musician must make music, an artist must paint, a poet must write, if he is to be ultimately at peace with himself."[17]

According to Maslow there are certain conditions that are prerequisites for the satisfaction of the basic needs and this explains many trends we have seen in world history. Such conditions as "freedom to speak, freedom to do what one wishes so long as no harm is done to others, freedom to express oneself, freedom to investigate and seek information," are among these prerequisites. In addition the individual must have the "freedom to defend oneself, justice, honesty," and "orderliness in the group." If these freedoms are denied they cause the individual to react as if they have been threatened.[18] Though the founding fathers of the United States never knew of Maslow, they seemed to agree with him in that they attempted to fulfill as many of these prerequisites as they could.

The pyramid diagram so often used to define Maslow's "hierarchy of needs" leaves the impression that the lower level need must be satisfied before the next level emerges. Most people are partially satisfied in all of their basic needs and partially unsatisfied. "A more realistic description of the hierarchy would be in terms of decreasing percentages of satisfaction as we go up the hierarchy of prepotency."[19] He does offer examples of those who, when deprived of food, suddenly realize that love is not so terribly important after all. When one is deprived of a basic need, especially one as critical as food or water, all other needs are suspended as the individual strives to replace the loss. It is also important to understand that although these needs are human nature the individual is not always aware that this is why he does what he does. Hunger is a more obvious drive, but as people seek self-esteem or self-actualization they are unaware that Maslow has identified the reason for their behavior. They are certainly unaware that once one need is satisfied it will be replaced by another one equally important. The hungry person will think that all he needs is food, but once that food is acquired he will need something else. The young man in love believes that he will have eternal happiness if the object of his attention will only return his feelings, but of course after marriage he will chase a new objective with equal enthusiasm. "So far as he is concerned, the absolute, ultimate value, synonymous with life itself, is whichever need in the hierarchy he is dominated by during a particular period."[20]

To make the study of Trimble meaningful as a case study it is critical to establish that he behaved in a psychologically healthy or normal way. The characteristics of a "healthy human specimen" given by Maslow consisted of clear, efficient perception of reality, openness to experience, integration, wholeness and unity of person, spontaneity and expressiveness, a firm identity, objectivity, detachment and transcendence of self, creativeness, the ability to fuse concreteness and abstractness, democratic character structure, and the ability to love. In contrast, those failing to progress in their quest for the basic needs show signs of anxiety, despair, boredom, inability to enjoy, intrinsic guilt, shame, aimlessness, feelings of emptiness, and lack of identity.[21] It will be clear in this study that the former is the best description of Trimble.

Trimble often displayed aggressiveness and thus it is important that this behavior be understood, especially since individual aggressiveness is often contrary to the common good. For the purpose of this study Maslow is also accepted as the authority on the motivation of behavior. This includes not only the aggression that takes a man into battle, but also the aggression displayed in the struggle up the social ladder. In other words, there is aggression between groups and within groups. There is historical, anthropological, and clinical evidence of the prevalence of aggression in human life. The conflict between groups is related to the first two levels of needs, food and safety. It also serves as a means of controlling aggression within a group. To project one's aggression outwardly maintains internal harmony. The result is what we now call "ethnocentrism, prejudice toward outsiders, and intolerance of human differences." The second category of aggression involves dominance hierarchies and rituals of display. The latter rarely involves fighting that would produce serious injury.[22] Maslow stated, "aggression, we have learned, is both genetically and culturally determined."[23] He began his behavior studies working with primates. In these studies he found a dominant animal in every group, and that a new animal introduced will assume his status in the "dominance hierarchy" within a short time after his introduction. Maslow also noticed the same drives in his study of humans. In humans, dominants can have different characteristics. Some are protectors, some are tyrants, and yet others, called "individualists," do not express their dominance as long as others do not try to dominate over them. He also observed that among the broad sectional and cultural differences in the United States, most of the cultures studied had some relationship of dominance-subordination between individuals.[24] Dominance is also one of the traits he associated with the search to satisfy esteem needs. This will explain the aggression displayed by Trimble toward those who are on the same side that he is, whether that be a business associate or a comrade in arms.

Individual aggression contributes to the difficulty of modern men to establish a community identity. Obviously, extreme aggression within a group could result in the extinction of that group. In such a case the individual's ambitions for the sake of self-esteem could destroy the third level of needs, identity with a group. For primitive man, his social group or community became clearly defined by the tribe or clan that he was born into. The growing complexity of advanced civilizations produces a more confusing concept of community. This, no doubt, explains the longings most of us have for a simpler time. People have a need to have relations with others and thus find their places in society and the world. Primitive man found the work he did to be clearly defined. The modern production worker does not so easily comprehend his role in society compared to the primitive hunter. The hunter felt a secure oneness with the primary group rather than the emphases on individualism and self-reliance of the modern American. His identity as a hunter constituted his social role and total understanding of his maleness; his female counterpart had a clearly defined role and identity as a woman. For these reasons it is more difficult to define the concept of community for the modern.[25]

Richard Brown identified aggressive behavior as an example of the modern personality. He said that whereas the traditional personality shows passive and localist proclivities, the modern personality exhibits a significant drive for individual autonomy and initiative.[26] He identified as one of several traits "personal ambition for oneself and one's children."[27]

Individualism should not be considered contradictory to community, but rather in the context of community. The anthropologist Ruth Benedict reminded her readers that the individual and society need not be antagonists. The culture provides the raw materials from which the individual makes his life. Each man and woman finds opportunity and is enriched from the resources the culture has to offer. The individual likewise contributes to building the culture. No civilization has any element not contributed by some individual who is part of that culture, even if that individual is bringing in something borrowed from another culture. "The problem of the individual is not clarified by stressing the antagonism between culture and the individual, but by stressing their mutual reinforcement." The relationship is so close that "it is not possible to discuss patterns of culture without considering specifically their relationship to individual psychology."[28]

Third Assumption: Defining the Role of Community

In order to understand how Trimble related to his community it is necessary to define the assumptions made in this study. Historians, sociologists, anthropologists, and psychologists all struggle with defining community in the modern world. One researcher found 94 meanings given to the word in social science literature in 1955.[29] Modern man has found a way to fulfill the need for identity with the flexibility he uses in defining his group. It can be as simple as a network of family and neighborhood or as complex as that of the modern nation. Whereas the hunter knew most of those in his community, the modern does not. Modern man has established political boundaries which can be consistent with or divide communities. In the process Americans have became members in more than one community at a time. These can include family, both immediate and extended, neighborhood or town, state, and nation, as well as religious, occupational or special interest relationships.[30]

The first and most clearly defined community for most modern Americans is the family. In western European cultures the basic family unit has been the nuclear family,[31] and this has been the basis of early social organization. Families traditionally belonged to larger social units called bands, tribes, or in the case of extended family groups, clans.[32] Isaac Trimble did not differ that much from the primitive as far as family structure is concerned. The early death of his parents emphasized the extended family despite the fact that the nuclear family was and is the basic family unit in American culture.

The premodern community became more complicated, but essentially the individuals had little difficulty finding their identity. Those who first arrived in New England found community in the village they lived in. Such communities consisted of a group of like-minded people who wished to maintain a religious society. The early arrivals lived in an environment resembling that of primitive man in that they had a clearly defined sense of belonging, though it has been argued that this unity began to evaporate shortly after the founding of their "cities on a hill."[33]

Trimble came a century later and lived in a different region. By the early nineteenth century America became a nation on the move. Americans descended from people who had left their homes in Europe and over the first 200 years they had slowly moved west, but after the Revolution they began to migrate into the former Indian lands at a much greater rate. By 1800 people willingly left one community and moved to another. Trimble not only moved several times during his childhood, but his family had left their religious community, the Society of Friends.

When Americans moved to a new community they quite often did not start completely over, since they usually moved west in the company of relatives or neighbors from their old community. Once they arrived they quickly created a new community. They differed from late twentieth century Americans in that their community identity had not yet been replaced by national identity. De Tocqueville observed that local governments constituted a sort of republic, though the strength of town governments diminished as one traveled south.[34] Towns retained their own local values independent of national ones, while at the same time they developed feelings of American nationalism. Increased mobility came with the transportation revolution. Towns had two main population groups, one successful and permanent and the other less successful and likely to seek their fortunes elsewhere. Once successful, people typically identified with the town in which they found success. De Tocqueville's analogy is somewhat misleading. On one hand the local communities found themselves within political boundaries such as county, state and nation and developed some identity with a greater community. On the other hand local communities became divided by political parties, church affiliation, or other groups.[35] Americans proved to be quite adaptable in their struggle to find belongingness.

Western migration took many Americans into new counties and states as well as new local communities, and Americans abandoned their old state identity and adopted a new one. Isaac Trimble was born in Pennsylvania of parents who had just moved there from Virginia and shortly after moved to Ohio. While growing up, he lived in Ohio and Kentucky and when entering West Point he moved to New York; after graduation he lived in Maryland, Delaware, and New England. In the late twentieth century the states appear to be subdivisions of the nation, but in the early nineteenth century people often felt a greater loyalty to their state than the nation. Thirteen colonies existed before the United States. They created the nation, and until the Civil War the state constituted the most important political power beyond the town; however, from the time of the Revolution Americans became increasingly willing to desert their state identities.[36]

Some felt regional identification, mainly because of the similarities in lifestyle; however, regions did not exist as political units. A few men, such as John C. Calhoun, attempted to instill regional pride but the resulting organizations formed for such purpose lacked political teeth. Geographical similarities can often produce similarities in culture regardless of political boundaries. For example, the various nations of the Mediterranean have much in common because of their geographical similarities. The hot weather and long growing season gave the southern states something in common, but probably the most significant impact came with the routes of migration in the western expansion. Those in the South learned to grow certain crops which could only be grown in the warmer climates; therefore as they moved west they stayed in what is today the southern tier of states. The laws governing the expansion of slavery also helped to dictate migration patterns. As they moved west they retained some ties to family and friends who remained behind.

In studying Isaac Trimble we see a typical American greatly influenced by the western migration and the transportation revolution. It should be remembered that the transportation revolution did not necessarily cause the western migration but in many ways occurred as a response to the demands of the masses of people who wanted to move west. The British created the Proclamation Line of 1763 to avoid Indian troubles caused by the flood of white settlers into the Indian lands long before the transportation revolution. Trimble's family joined those moving west and in the process created a tradition of abandoning one community and adopting a new one. This is the most remarkable characteristic that Americans learned in their transient culture. Trimble retained his family ties, but beyond that Americans developed a greater flexibility as they would drop one community and adopt a new one — local, state, or national.

The aggression of Trimble proves perplexing in understanding group identity. As stated above, in the process of finding self-esteem Trimble often behaved aggressively toward those who belonged to the same community; according to Maslow this is human nature. What we also find in America is that local communities develop competitive attitudes toward each other as they fight for economic advantage for their group. Trimble's hometown of Baltimore became quite aggressive toward Philadelphia as each attempted to become the center for western markets. Maslow did not discuss what happens when one group develops an adversarial relationship with another group while both being part of the same larger group, whether that be county, state or nation. This is one of the great dilemmas of modern society and the greatest threat to the concept of nationalism. Once united, nations can quickly crumble when communities within the nation fight against each other. In nineteenth-century America a hierarchy of communities existed in which some more closely attached their identity to the national community while others remained tied to their local communities. Such a hierarchy of communities and the related aggression of those communities is not uniquely American; the situation is summed up quite adequately by the old Arab saying, "I against my brother; I and my brother against my cousin; I, my brothers, and my cousins against the next village; all of us against the foreigner."[37] The most difficult problem for large nations is to define clearly "foreigner."

In addition to the family and geographical communities, from local to national, we also find that the modern Americans developed other bonds that generated community identity. For Trimble this included the brotherhood he joined by becoming a West Point graduate. The bond between West Point graduates is legendary and resulted in great human drama as they faced each other on the field of battle in the 1860s. We also see in Trimble a man who attended West Point with the objective of becoming an engineer. In the process he developed a career as a civil engineer and railroad man, and also became part of another community—a business or professional community. The latter community consisted of many men from the former since West Point provided many of the trained engineers who built the railroads. In the nineteenth century most Americans moved to a new land and then found a way to support themselves. With the modern concept of "career" we find a breed of men who chose their residency based on career opportunity. We will see that such is the case with Isaac Trimble in choosing the city of Baltimore as his hometown.

Fourth and Fifth Assumptions: World Markets and Growth of Centralism

There are two assumptions in this study related to the importance of the market economy. The fourth basic assumption is that modernization was a constantly evolving process related to the expansion of the market economy. This began much earlier than thought by some historians and spread throughout the western world. The acceptance of this view would mean that the North and South were headed in the same direction but at a slightly different pace. The fifth basic assumption is that the expanding world markets produced a growth in centralism. The expansion of markets created a conflict about the role the state should play in the economy. The advantages in unification were clear, but at the same time reliance on government actively generated competition between individual communities for control of the government.

Isaac Trimble, like other American individuals, pursued his own interest, established a community identity, and as time passed found himself increasingly subject to the rules of the central government. Eventually Trimble saw the central government as a threat to his local community and he chose to resist its power. The growth of central government came about with the development of world markets beginning well before the industrial revolution; however, with industrialization nations became even more centralized. Southerners did not reject central government; they in fact created their own, thus suggesting that they feared that the existing government favored some sections of the country over others.

By the nineteenth century people increasingly looked toward the government in establishing economic policies or arbitrating conflicts between various local communities who competed with each other in attempts to gain a greater share of regional, national, or world markets. The role of government in the economy has been a question debated since the dawn of the modern world, and the debate continues today. A major problem for the United States involved attempting to formulate a plan that would equalize benefits without favoring a particular community or region. Trimble's life reflected this contradiction. Government support for the Baltimore & Ohio Railroad (in the form of surveyors) introduced him to that industry, yet he became involved in community competition during his career when he went to work for the Baltimore & Susquehanna Railroad.

The use of terms such as "industrial revolution" implies a suddenness that can often be misleading. In reality industrialization constituted only one step in the growing importance of world markets. Marxist historians especially tend to view the world as the product of revolutionary events, and thus they interpret modernization as the sudden replacement of the aristocracy by the bourgeoisie. The change was considerably less revolutionary than believed by many, and in fact came about rather gradually. Trade existed even in primitive societies, and there is evidence that a market economy existed in England prior to the great plague of the fourteenth century.[38] This market economy began to grow after the great plague increased the demand for labor and gave a larger portion of the population an opportunity to compete in the market place.[39] The turning point between the modern and premodern markets came with the expansion of a world market. Prior to the sixteenth century the European world market existed primarily in Venice, but this involved only the world known to Europeans. The expansion of these markets led to world voyages and eventually colonization and a true world market. The first center briefly thrived at Antwerp and then quickly shifted to the Netherlands. This growth in world markets also led to a need for protection by the merchants. They knew that the strength to enforce international contracts and to offer protection of property from pirates and thieves could come only from a central government; in the sixteenth and seventeenth centuries the needed central government came in the form of absolute monarchy. The Netherlands not only revolutionized the world markets but they created an alternative to absolute monarchy when they established a republic.[40]

With the development of world markets the English competed with the Dutch and eventually took the lead. The aristocracy looked for a stronger central government and left the local government in the hands of the gentry. The crown adopted an economic policy which affected the colonies, and in fact explained the need for colonies: mercantilism. This policy of the crown encouraged the growth of a native merchant marine, provided protection for English manufactures and English agriculture, and encouraged accumulation of hard money. The colonies helped to fulfill these goals by providing the mother country with raw materials, served as markets for English manufactures, and trade with the colonies was such that Great Britain benefited.[41]

The Enlightenment philosophers debated the nature of government and the role of government in the economy. Quesnay held a more traditional view in that he considered land to be the only source of real wealth, that landowners pay the taxes, and that the monarch was the chief landowner. He believed that agriculture was national economy and trade was international. The most long-lasting aspect of Quesnay's philosophy was that he discussed the nature of economy and established that there existed a relationship between economy and government. John Locke expanded the scope of the relationship with his belief that men entered into a society for the preservation of their lives, liberty, and estates. Locke went one step further in that he saw not only a relationship between government and the economy, but he believed economy to be the superior.[42] During the age of Thomas Jefferson and George Washington men talked about "political economy." At the time of the Revolution, influenced by Adam Smith, Americans believed economics to be a branch of science whose object was to "enrich both the people and the sovereign." In the late eighteenth century men did not separate economics and ethics. At this time commercialization itself is what made the distinction between the modern world and the past.

The Federalists and Republicans debated the proper role of government in the republican order. They valued land and property as a means to personal independence, not for selfish motives but for the basis of a more republican citizenry. The crisis of the 1780s brought about a more realistic grounding to republicanism because the people suffered from economic depression. The new constitution became a means of making the nation more industrious. By 1800 it became clear to Americans that there would be no simple formula, though the election of Jefferson represented a move back to the ideals of 1776. This was the America that Isaac Trimble entered in 1804, but by the time he went to West Point in 1818 the Jeffersonian ideal had faded. Uncertainty can be threatening to the second level of needs: safety and security. Jefferson himself began to realize that America depended on Europe as much as the Europeans depended on America.[43] During the 30 years before the Civil War, Trimble lived in an America in which communities competed for economic advantage, and Trimble often found himself at the center of these battles.

1

From the Wilds of Kentucky to West Point

In 1813 the nine year old orphan Isaac Trimble lived with his sister and her husband, Charity and James McClintick, in Chillicothe, Ohio. While there he attended a local school. James kept a horse that he allowed his young nephew to ride to water in the nearby Scioto River. In a time and place in which many men did not own horses for riding, little Isaac became the envy of some of the other boys who expressed their jealousy by throwing rocks at him. When he told James about the problem the uncle replied, "Why don't you thrash one of the boys and then they will let you alone?"

Isaac cautiously answered, "But if I got off the horse to whip one of the boys, what will become of the horse?"

"Never mind the horse," James said without hesitation, "he will come home to the stable."

Several days later the youngster came across his enemies who again began throwing stones at him. Isaac singled out one of the bigger of the boys and attacked. He continued until the others agreed to stop stoning him. Isaac returned home on foot, proud of his victory in what he described many years later as "his first battle." From that time on Isaac Trimble never hesitated to stand up for himself and in fact displayed considerable energy in the pursuit of his goals.[1]

The early life of Trimble seems almost irrelevant to Southern history since he had only slight ties to the South; however, it is significant in that he did become a Confederate leader. He was born in Virginia and spent some of his childhood years in Kentucky, but neither he nor his family indicated any strong regional pride, and in fact seemed to move without hesitation in search of economic opportunity. If anything, the Trimble family demonstrated a weakening of state pride and increased identification as Americans.

Trimble showed signs of adaptation to the modernization process, which is not a case of Southern modernization but is an example of a modern man who eventually identified with the South. Well before the industrial revolution, Isaac and the Trimble family met several of the criteria of modernization as defined by Robert Hollinger and Richard D. Brown.[2] They were Quakers living among the Scotch-Irish and Germans of the Shenandoah Valley and western Pennsylvania, a heterogeneous environment. They moved in search of economic opportunity. Though several members of the family moved together, they displayed individualism as they left the Society of Friends and ventured into the American frontier. This also demonstrated an openness to new experience, as well as a less dependent attachment on traditional values. Trimble's brother became successful in his economic and political endeavors, as did other members of the Trimble family. Trimble attended West Point, not in pursuit of training as a soldier but to become an engineer. He recognized the importance of getting an education to improve his future. Isaac and his family clearly demonstrated personal ambition and the dynamism so critical to the modern personality. The fact that he decided on engineering is an indication of a faith in the ability to change the environment, physically as well as socially. It also shows that he had an interest in science and technology.

Trimble had little to be concerned about as far as the basic level of needs defined by Maslow, and thus at an early age dwelled on the third level belongingness needs and even began to seek the higher level need of self-esteem. Frontier life may have generated occasional anxieties about the biological and safety needs of the first two levels, but there is no indication that such concerns existed for very long. Though his parents died while he was young, his siblings provided a feeling of family belonging. His brother David became firmly attached to Kentucky and spent the remainder of his life there as a community leader; however, this state identity did not spread to young Isaac. Though he did not develop any geographic loyalty he did join the community of West Point graduates. He established a professional identity with other West Point graduates, and he began the pursuit of the higher need of self-esteem with his academic performance.

The West Point that Trimble attended was a progressive institution and did not exhibit a militaristic resistance to modernization that some have assumed from that fact that so many Southerners attended the school. A slight digression from Trimble will demonstrate that West Point was one of the most modern schools in the United States at the time. The War of 1812 proved a need for military leaders in the new country; however, the early nineteenth century military had become technologically oriented. This resulted in making military education very compatible with the training needed to build a nation. West Point became a training ground for engineers as well as military leaders and Trimble became one of this new breed successful in both worlds.

Trimble pursued the hierarchy of needs as defined by Maslow, but he also developed an aggressiveness in his behavior which would help him find success in life, though it often resulted in conflict with his peers as well as his enemies. The fact that Trimble recorded the rock-throwing incident many years after the Civil War is an indication that it made a considerable impression on him. He learned that there would be times in life when he would have to take a stand for self-preservation. He entered West Point at a time when the new director had successfully taken command of the institution from a predecessor determined to retain control. Trimble did not mention these events but he did see an example in which men had to fight for success. He aggressively competed with his classmates to achieve his personal ambition while in school, though he did stay within socially acceptable limits. He fell short of graduating as an engineer, but he soon transferred to that corps after receiving his commission.

The family background of Trimble is worth consideration since it reveals that he came from a humble but hard-working family which became absorbed in the western migration. His ancestors came from various backgrounds, the Scotch-Irish of his father and the old Pennsylvania Quaker family of his mother. Quakers are one of the segments of the southern population that has received little recognition from historians. At the time that Trimble was born more Quakers lived in the South than in Pennsylvania.[3] One reason they have been so easily dismissed is that they are considered by some to have been an isolated population since they strictly enforced marriage from within their community. In reality this sent many of their community out into the general public as the Church disowned them. This is probably the single biggest cause for the diminishing numbers of Quakers throughout the nineteenth century. It is the reason that Isaac Trimble's family left the Society of Friends.

The Quakers took a strong stand against slavery, which along with more liberal land laws caused many to flee the Carolinas, Virginia, and Maryland and to head for the Ohio Valley.[4] With family on both sides of the Mason-Dixon, people of Quaker ancestry had a number of kinsmen who fought on both sides during the Civil War; for them the expression "brother against brother" had meaning. Trimble's family serves as a good example. His grandmother, Charity Beeson, was the daughter of Edward Beeson and Martha Mendenhall, from two old and influential Quaker families. Of the 101 Beesons who have been traced to the Civil War, 44 fought for the South and 57 for the North. Of the 39 Mendenhalls, 15 wore Gray and 24 wore Blue.[5]

The Trimble family followed typical Quaker migration patterns; they moved from Pennsylvania to the South and then to the West. Isaac's grandfather, Joseph Trimble, was born in County Antrim, Ireland, in 1711. He came to America at the age of 18 and landed in Chester County, Pennsylvania. He indentured himself to a Quaker man, William Brown, and it is assumed that he adopted his master's religion. Among his nine children Joseph had a son named John who continued in the Society of Friends. He married Katherine Wilson in Chester County in 1772 and they had three children. Ann, the eldest, was born in 1774 before the family moved to Hopewell, a village located just north of Winchester in Frederick County, Virginia. The meeting in Hopewell received John's family into membership on May 1, 1775. Samuel was born in 1777 and David was born in 1779. John's father, Joseph, and his wife, Katherine, died in the 1780s. While living in Hopewell, Virginia, John met his second wife, Rachel Ridgeway, and they married on April 10, 1788.[6]

John owned several pieces of property in Frederick County as well as two grist mills. While members of the Hopewell meeting John and Rachel had five more children, Sarah in 1789, Charity in 1790, Catherine in 1793, John in 1795 and William in 1797. In June of 1797, the family transferred to the Crooked Run meeting located about 13 miles south of Winchester. The Crooked Run meeting came from the Hopewell meeting and lasted until 1807. John began selling his land by 1796 and then took his family to Fayette County, Pennsylvania, where they joined the Redstone meeting on April 2, 1802. Many of the Quakers who moved into the Ohio Valley area after 1801 claimed that they did so because of their objection to the institution of southern slavery. It is more likely that the Land Act of 1800 had a greater impact. The Quaker rejection of slavery came gradually but the migration to Ohio came quite rapidly after the Land Act, suggesting that the economic opportunity provided more of a motivation.[7]

The Trimbles did not own slaves, but neither did they leave any indication of strong anti-slavery sentiments. The Pennsylvania Yearly Meeting of the Society of Friends chose to discipline its members for the buying and selling of slaves and in 1776 adopted a ban against the members owning slaves. In the eighteenth century many of the Quakers owned slaves and in those meetings where the slave holders dominated the acceptance of these policies came slower. It has been suggested that this contributed to the gradualist, segregationist, and paternalistic approach that the society took towards abolition and in turn influenced the policies of other American abolitionist organizations. As late as the 1780s much of the business of the various Pennsylvania meetings centered around the best way to deal with those members who had not yet freed their slaves. There is no evidence that John Trimble ran away from slavery. They moved directly from Pennsylvania and a part of Virginia which did not have slavery. Most likely he hoped to acquire some of the new lands opened up to white settlers.[8]

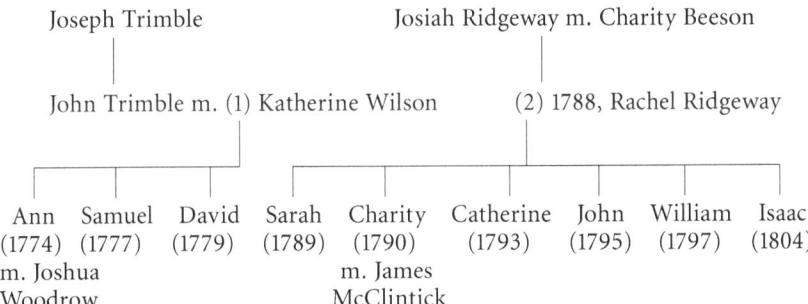

The Trimble family lived in the vicinity of the Redstone meeting for two years. It is possible that John had gone there with the intention of moving westward into Ohio as he anticipated reform of the much-debated land laws. William Henry Harrison helped to push through the legislation of 1800 which provided for more opportunities. Though the land available remained at two dollars per acre, Congress lowered the minimum purchase from 640 to 320 acres, thus reducing the total cash needed to buy land. This stimulated massive migration. Attempts to establish Ohio statehood followed rapidly after the passage of the new law, and in April of 1802 an enabling act authorized a convention to decide the desirability of statehood. This came about the next year. These events must have had a more direct impact on John Trimble in his decision to move the family to Ohio in 1806.[9]

Isaac Trimble was born in Virginia on May 20, 1804, while the family attended the Redstone, Pennsylvania, meeting.[10] They moved to western Ohio where the Miami Monthly meeting accepted them into membership on July 10, 1806. They lived there only a short while before moving to the Fairfield meeting in Highland County. Disaster struck soon after as John and Rachel both died from a fever in September of 1810 and were buried on the Kinikonick River. The young Isaac depended on his brothers and sisters for survival.

In a typical fashion the older children of John Trimble moved west, too. His eldest daughter, Ann, married Joshua Woodrow. This led to her being disowned by the Fairfield meeting in July of 1811 for "marriage out of unity," which meant she married someone outside the faith. Her sister Charity married another non-Quaker, James McClintick. Their sister Catherine joined another church in 1810. Thus, shortly after the death of John and Rachel, most of their family had left the Society of Friends.[11]

For the next four years after the death of his parents he lived with his half-sister Ann and her husband, Joshua Woodrow. They lived in Hillsboro, Ohio. While there he became attached to his niece, Elizabeth, from whom he "received the first rudiments of learning and ideas of gentleness and virtue." Years later he described her as "a very superior woman, and of great loveliness and character, and of winning deportment." He also became aware of the tribulations of war as the recruiting parties for the War of 1812 paraded past his sister's home. The boy became fascinated by the drums and fifes as the soldiers and would-be soldiers marched through the streets; he was so attracted that "the rod could not deter him from following the music." In 1813 he moved to Chillicothe and lived with his sister Charity. While living there he "had his first fight," the stone-throwing incident. At the end of the war he found a new male role model when his brother David decided to give him a home and education.[12]

David, the youngest son of John by his first wife, was born in 1779. In his youth he had "a remarkable fondness for books." He could not work and did "nothing but pore over his books," so John sent him to college. David attended William and Mary and graduated in 1799, studied law in Richmond under the Chancellor George Wythe, and became a member of the bar in 1801. Shortly thereafter he moved to Mount Sterling, Kentucky, where he lived when Isaac joined him. Isaac described his brother as he appeared in a painting that David commissioned when about 35 to 40 years old. At that time he had "full brown hair with sideburns, full face, ruddy florid complexion, brown eyes, arched nose." David did not feel restricted by his Quaker upbringing and their preaching against war. He fought the Indians in the Tecumseh uprising of 1810–11 and then volunteered in the War of 1812. He joined the forces of William Henry Harrison with the rank of major. His efforts in recruiting Kentucky volunteers and his heroism in battle won him the praise and friendship of Harrison as well as a letter of citation from the commander of the Kentucky reinforcements.[13]

He returned from the war in the fall of 1814, resumed his law practice, and soon after took Isaac under his wing. At the urging of his friend Henry Clay he ran for Congress two years later and won the election. His second campaign for Congress led to his involvement in a duel with his opponent, which produced the little song that his brother loved hearing as a child, "David Trimble shot McDanile: Oh, ha, oh — shot him with a silver bullet, Oh, ha, oh — shot him low the rim of the belly, Oh, ha, oh."[14] David served a total of five terms. After leaving Congress he had more time to develop his ironworks, the first blast furnace in Kentucky. David's business benefited from the tariffs, especially the 1828 tariff; however, the 1832 tariff sharply reduced the duty on semi-finished iron and caused the Trimble business to suffer severely at the hands of English competitors. David got hurt further because of Jackson's banking policies restricting credit. David's business used bank credit for sales payable on three to six month terms, and credit restriction crippled his ability to do long-term business.[15]

David felt an obligation to assist his siblings; he wrote, "It was my father's wish that I should take care of his children."[16] He saw that two of his brothers received a college education and one had a partnership in his ironworks. David enrolled his youngest brother, Isaac, in the Mount Sterling Academy, "in which arithmetic, Latin, Greek and Hebrew were taught by a thoroughly competent Irishman." Isaac "evinced a fondness and aptitude for study, reading history in the evenings and holidays of his own volition." When it came time for college he expressed an interest in West Point. David did not recommend his brother himself but rather solicited a nomination from his fellow Kentucky congressman and future vice-president, Richard Mentor Johnson. By the middle of June 1818 Isaac received notification of his acceptance at West Point and his orders to report to the superintendent at the beginning of September.[17]

Though Isaac was past his formative years when he moved in with his brother, there is no doubt that David replaced their deceased father as a male role model for the boy who was 15 years his junior. David promoted an interest in literature and education. He not only encouraged his younger brother to go to school, but he subscribed to the *National Intelligencer*, *Nile's Weekly*, *Franklin Gazette*, *Richmond Enquirer*, and the *Washington Gazette*. He kept himself informed by ordering copies of the president's messages, debates in Congress, the bills introduced, government pamphlets and speeches as well as atlases, maps, dictionaries, and French and German grammar books. His library included works on international, Constitutional and common law; American, English, modern European and ancient history; and other subjects such as religion, philosophy, logic, economics, commerce, industry, nature, mineralogy and military regulations. Isaac Trimble expressed the admiration he felt for his older brother when he wrote, "I think altogether he was the greatest man of his name from his liberal view, his exalted patriotism, his sound views on political economy and his sterling honor and integrity."[18]

Military education in the early nineteenth century represented modernization more than traditionalism, and in many ways proved more progressive than education at other universities. It is critical to clarify this point in order to reject the idea that Trimble and his fellow students went to West Point with the notion of preserving some militaristic premodern culture. The technology of the modern world provided weapons for its armies, and the military schools became centers for technological innovation. Leaders realized that a corps of engineers and artillery officers could defeat an army of saber-rattling romantics. These artillery and engineering officers "thought in the same terms as manufacturers, artisans, and businessmen, for like them they worked with machines that required exact knowledge."[19] The Enlightenment created a strange contradiction in that many intellectuals opposed standing armies, but at the same time the increasing technology created a demand for professional soldiers. Untrained noblemen could no longer dominate the officers corps. Louis XIV took action by establishing some cadet companies. Louis XV started the École Militaire, an idea suggested by an eighteenth century financier who made his fortune in war supplies. In 1751 Louis XV's founding decree stated, "It is necessary that the ancient prejudice which has instilled the belief that bravery alone makes the man of war would give place imperceptibly to a taste for the military studies which we have introduced."[20]

During the Enlightenment the military changed, just as other institutions did. The Jacobins replaced the Bourbon school with the École de Mars, motivated in part by a desire to unseat the aristocracy. In 1741 King George II founded the Royal Military Academy at Woolrich, designed to prepare "Gentlemen Cadets" for service in the engineers and artillery. Woolrich emphasized courses in algebra, geometry, fortification, mining, gunnery, and bridge building.[21]

The American Enlightenment leaders, such as Thomas Jefferson, George Washington, and John Adams, contributed the most to the founding of a military academy in the United States. The Enlightenment-era American Philosophical Society produced the United States Military Philosophical Society, founded by Jonathan Williams but which also included Thomas Jefferson, James Madison, John Quincy Adams, James Monroe, John Marshall, Benjamin Latrobe, Robert Fulton, and Eli Whitney.[22]

In many ways the West Point that Isaac Trimble attended provided a more progressive education than other American institutions. Before the Civil War the American college "was a stagnant, self-satisfied, superficial institution, dead and deadening." The core of the curriculum represented premodern thinking with its Latin and Greek. Students studied languages, but these languages only, for three years. They also studied a limited course in rhetoric and mathematics, natural philosophy, logic, metaphysics, and ethics. George Ticknor forced modern languages into Harvard studies, and Philip Lindsley attempted to develop more pragmatic studies at the University of Nashville, but such attempts at reform stagnated when Yale produced a faculty report in 1828. In that report the authors defined what a young man should study and this became the defense against reform for the next half century. Princeton agreed with the report and the two universities encouraged studies in classics, mathematics, and moral philosophy. Sylvanus Thayer moved beyond this stagnant thinking when he took command of West Point in 1817.[23] When Trimble attended West Point it could have been better described as an engineering school rather than a military academy.

The War of 1812 inspired reforms and with Thayer's leadership West Point underwent radical changes that made the school much more progressive; the transformation was still underway when Trimble arrived. Threats of war in 1794 stimulated Congress to authorize a Corps of Artillerists and Engineers, which became established at the garrison in West Point. In 1801 Jonathan Williams, who published results of some experiments he had undertaken with Benjamin Franklin in a treatise entitled *Thermometrical Navigation*, accepted Jefferson's appointment to head the cadets before the official authorization by Congress in 1802. Jefferson wanted to create a national scientific school, which he hoped to do under the guise of a military school. The law called for the Corps of Engineers "to constitute a military academy," and it specified 10 cadets for the Corps of Engineers and 40 for the artillery.[24]

By the beginning of the War of 1812 it became apparent that West Point had failed to provide the military leadership needed. On April 12, 1812, Congress passed a bill reorganizing the Academy and thus set forth the general principles by which it has been conducted and controlled to this day. It provided for a larger faculty and more graduates. A hasty graduation produced the officers needed for the war and left the commander, Captain Alden Partridge, and one lone cadet from which the new institution would grow. By the time of the treaty in 1815 Congress realized that the nation needed a corps of officers to lead in time of war.[25]

Just before the arrival of Trimble, a battle ensued that would not only change West Point but serve as an example to the young cadet of situations in which men aggressively protected their personal interest even when jeopardizing the good of the organization they worked for. In a way Partridge symbolized the inadequacies of traditional ways in a world of change, and the new commander, Thayer, would fight for progress as well as personal ambition. Trimble did not arrive until after settlement of the dispute, but he would attend classes with many who had been present during the struggle and no doubt the stories remained very much alive in 1818.

The first commander of West Point failed to provide the leadership that would meet the nation's needs. As a drillmaster and teacher Captain Partridge served well, but as superintendent and administrator he lacked judgment, leading to his replacement. When Thayer arrived on a hot July afternoon in 1817 the greeting given by the old superintendent, and former Dartmouth classmate, foreshadowed the transition. The old resisting the new, Partridge refused to surrender the superintendent's quarters. Thayer simply left and inspected the post. He found most of the cadets absent on an apparent unlimited vacation and five of the most prominent members of the faculty under arrest. Thayer did manage to move into his new quarters, but the situation came to a head the next month when Partridge demanded the right to reoccupy his former residence. Thayer chose to retreat for the moment. Soon after, Partridge ordered the corps paraded and stood by while Lieutenant Charles Davies read an order announcing that Captain Partridge was reassuming command. Thayer wrote a letter to the man who had appointed him, Brigadier General J. G. Swift, and found the support he needed to regain control. Though absent during the final departure of his adversary, he later heard about the cadets who had swarmed down to the dock, shouting and cheering Partridge and vowing that they could not wait until he returned. Behind them marched the post band, contrary to Thayer's direct orders.[26]

A new and modern curriculum had been implemented just prior to Trimble's arrival. Thayer began his reforms by asking the teachers for a detailed description of their courses, including the textbooks they used and what books they needed. He then demanded a general examination for every cadet and found that one-fifth of the current enrollment had serious academic deficiencies. He made discipline swift, and he ordered each cadet to submit the names and addresses of their parents or guardians. He also wanted to create a spirit of absolute fairness and made a great effort to not show favoritism to those with powerful friends and relatives. He passed his first test when he informed Thomas Pinckney of South Carolina, former governor, congressman, minister to England and Revolutionary War hero, that the resignation of his son would "be accepted to take effect from the date of this letter." He emphasized science and totally neglected the classics and the art of war, even before the issuance of the Yale report. He considered engineering the most important subject, especially civil engineering, and for a time West Point turned out better engineers than soldiers. He built his reforms on courses in mathematics and French, the latter considered to be important because many of the textbooks had not been translated into English. Thayer and Congress agreed that the primary peacetime function of the Academy would be to supply the nation with the trained men needed to build bridges, canals and highways, to dredge harbors and rivers, and to provide a reservoir of expert soldiers. West Point continued to be the only source for such men until the opening of Rensselaer Polytechnic Institute in 1824.[27]

The young Isaac Trimble set out for West Point totally unaware of the significant changes that he would be sharing in, but simply desired an education in engineering. Eventually Thayer would raise the age of entrance but these reforms did not come in time to prevent Trimble from becoming a cadet at the age of 14, one of the five youngest of the 140 plebes. He set off on horseback with a companion for a six-week trip over the Allegheny Mountains to New York City. The frontier in which he lived still posed the threat of Indian attack so he and his traveling companion did not build campfires until they got farther east. Once in New York he secured passage on the *Firefly*, one of four steamboats that traveled the Hudson River at the time. The new mode of travel did not find immediate acceptance. John H. B. Latrobe made the same trip and at the advice of a fellow New York hotel guest chose to travel upriver on an Albany sloop that promised to land him at the dock in time for breakfast. The 15 year old Latrobe, who ranked among the youngest himself, and Trimble would not only attend school together and be lifelong friends, but they would live to be the oldest surviving members of their class section. The young men arrived at Gridley's, a large two-storied wooden building a few steps to the north of the road down the river, and joined a crowd of newly appointed cadets awaiting examination. Latrobe recalled this as his first experience of sleeping three in a bed.[28]

Latrobe identified the reason for the strong bonds of community between West Point graduates. He and Trimble went through hardships considerably greater than most who attended the reunion of 1884, but all understood when Trimble began his speech by saying, "We meet to-day as comrades, who, under the influence of early sentiments, are united by the common heritage of love for the old Academy."[29] Though some had worn the Blue and some the Gray they all shared this brotherhood. No doubt the Spartan lifestyle and discipline of the school contributed to the loyalty that other schools could only dream of from their alumni.

Some cadets ended up in the North Barracks and some in the South Barracks. A typical room in the North Barracks, more pleasant than the South Barracks, would be 18 feet square divided by a wooden partition into two smaller rooms of unequal size. The smaller one held the cots, one in each corner. The cots consisted of no more than camp stools widened and lengthened to accommodate a person six feet tall. The larger room held a table, four or five chairs, and a gunrack with pegs above it for the accouterments. In a recess next to the fireplace they would find a woodbox and close by it the tinderbox. This tin contrivance, four inches in diameter with a close-fitting cover, contained rags burnt to tinder, a flint, and steel. It did serve its purpose in igniting the fire that the cadets huddled around, feet near the flames and wrapped in blankets, while the books in their hands kept their minds busy. The Hudson River provided the only bathtub.[30]

The cadets ate in the east end of the Mess Hall, both floors, in a plain environment. The interior held four long tables, with the commonest benches for seats. Tablecloths would not be introduced until long after Trimble left. They did receive plenty of good food. The bread proved especially delicious and they would often hide a piece in their caps, along with some butter, to be toasted over the fire in their rooms. They ate with two-pronged forks and knives, and when asked what part of the roast or boiled beef they preferred a common answer would be, "a big bit anywhere." That these primitive conditions provided the foundation for the community of West Point graduates is revealed by Latrobe's statement, "these were merry days, and the buttered toast, after 'taps,' was more enjoyed than many a feast which, later in life, it has been my fortune to partake of."[31]

The uniform Trimble wore did not change much until long after the Civil War. The coat, padding and all, and pants, with the exception of the black stripe on the outer seam, remained identical. In Trimble's day they did wear leather stocks, the shirt collar above them, instead of being turned over the collar of the coat. For a cap they had a "stiff leather cylindrical pot," with a very narrow visor, and in the front a brass plate with the arms of the Corps of Engineers. Behind the plate a socket of whalebone held the long black plume. Each plume had a tulip-shaped holder and a brass curb chain from the top of the cap on each side, attached to the plate. They also had cross-belts for cartridge-box and bayonet, and a waist belt.[32]

Trimble and his classmates lived in an ordered world. In those early days the Academy did not use demerit marks. They paid the debt for their sins by extra tours of guard duty or the loss of Saturday afternoon

1. From the Wilds of Kentucky to West Point

First known sketch of a West Point cadet appeared in *Analectic Magazine* in 1820. This is the style of uniform Isaac Trimble, class of 1822, would have worn.

privileges. If the infraction was serious enough the cadets experienced confinement in the prisons in the North Barracks. On Saturday afternoons squads of misdoers, with wheelbarrows, shovels, and brooms, policed the barrack yards. The fourth class looked up to the experienced cadets until they learned the drill, but then class distinctions disappeared, social class being more of a basis for friendships than the class at the Academy. In Trimble's day more "gentlemen's sons" found placement. Hazing did not exist in the early Thayer years.[33]

The cadets found time for amusement, but most of this time they spent with their comrades. Their world rarely extended beyond "Buttermilk Falls," and that required travel down a rough road. The famous "Benny's" had not yet come into being and instead they went to "Cold Spring." Though swearing could be heard as frequently as "the army in Flanders," and they smoked cigars ("very miserable ones"), the class of 1822 did not drink whiskey in excess. As stated by Latrobe, they had the understanding "that we were gentlemen; and it was this feeling that it was pre-eminently the wish of Colonel Thayer, himself the noblest gentleman, to instill into those under his charge." The cadets found few "humanizing influences" from beyond their own ranks. They occasionally visited the houses of the professors, and sometimes young ladies would attempt to catch a glimpse of an evening parade or attend the chapel on Sunday mornings in seats specially reserved for them.[34]

Regionalism did not have much of an impact on Trimble. He never mentioned the subject in the early years of his life. William Henry Harrison hinted at a bias that resided with David Trimble when he wrote to him, "if you fail in getting a Kentucky bride, do run over to Ohio and I will show you some fine Yankee girls."[35] Latrobe claimed that "Sectional differences were unknown at West Point in 1818," though he did concede that "to say there was no distinction between cadets from the slave holding and non–slave holding States respectively would not be true." Latrobe, who came from Maryland, clearly identified with those of the slave holding states, though he felt no contempt for the northerners, and in fact he boasted of the friendships he made with fellow cadets from Connecticut, New Hampshire, Massachusetts, and Pennsylvania.[36] Jefferson Davis did not have the same impression as Latrobe. Davis went to West Point just a few years later, well before 1831, and expressed some distaste for those from the North. He commented on their thriftiness when he said, "the Yankee part of the corps find their pay entirely sufficient." He also said that "these are not the sort I formed an acquaintance with," and added, "you cannot know how pitiful they generally are." His first year especially he associated only with cadets from the South who he felt lived a looser, freer, more expensive kind of life at West Point.[37]

No doubt the ability to survive contributed to the feelings of comradeship among these early cadets. Of the 117 in the first year, only 59 made it past the first screening, 48 the next, and only 40 graduated. Of those who did not finish, some resigned, some "turned back" to repeat a year, and some Thayer and his staff "found to be deficient altogether."[38]

During these years Trimble matured considerably. By the end of his second year his class rank fell to 53rd. He blamed his troubles on "lazy roommates, who thought more of clandestine 'suppers' in the room than of study," though he must have accepted some responsibility since he took steps to raise himself from the fourth and lowest section. He responded to his cousin, Senator William A. Trimble of Ohio,[39] who reproached him for neglecting his studies and "appealed to his pride" and reminded him of his brother's kindness, and that "he ought in gratitude to make better use of his opportunities." Isaac soon had the highest marks in the fourth section. When he did not get his promotion to the third section he went to talk to Colonel Thayer and said, "he was ashamed to confess that he had neglected his studies, but had resolved now to study hard, with the hope of getting up in his class." When Thayer informed him that Cadet Vinton had the same marks Trimble rebutted, "but why not transfer us both? I promise you that I will leave Vinton behind when we both get into the 3rd Section." He then added, "I will study harder than ever and go on until I get into the First Section; if not, there is no use in killing myself by hard study and but five hours of sleep at nights."[40]

Thayer did transfer both cadets, and Trimble returned to Thayer's office to thank him. He said, "Now Col., as I have a start, I mean to get the highest marks in this section and hope soon to get into the 2nd Section if highest marks will do it," and then he added, "if I struggle hard, I must be encouraged." His hard work quickly put him at the top of the third section, and again he approached the superintendent. "Colonel, if you have noticed the professor's returns for some weeks past you will see that I am the only Cadet in my section who has been marked 'plus 18,' and I hope soon to be transferred to the 2nd Sec." He confidently added, "I promise you that I will soon be first in that." Thayer responded by saying, "go on with your studies, and depend on having justice done you." A week or two later he received the transfer, leaving Cadet Vinton "somewhere about the middle of the 3rd Sec. in marks."[41]

He gained attention from the other cadets because of his progress. One cadet of the first section said to him, "You think to get into the 1st Sec. I suppose, or maybe aim to be among the 'first five' in the class." Trimble replied, "I shall certainly go into the 1st Sec. and will try to be at the head of that." The first cadet said, "Ha! ha! My boy, you will find that we of the 1st Section are 'harder nuts to crack,'" to which Trimble simply stated, "We'll see." When the time came for transfer he once again took the initiative by approaching Thayer. Thayer said, "but the professor has not recommended you for transfer, as is usual." Trimble recognized the politics involved when he said, "I don't think he will. The fact is, I can see, that he don't like to see me outdo 'his boys.'" He received his transfer.[42]

At such an early age Trimble learned more than the lessons of the classroom. He did not hesitate to display internal aggression when he needed it to achieve his goals. He also demonstrated an understanding of bureaucratic politics and the value of speaking up for himself. He often said, "That this accomplishment of a settled purpose, by hard struggles, filled his heart with more hopeful joy and pride, that he had ever known." He claimed that no other cadet at the Academy after falling near the foot of his class had ever risen from the lowest section to the highest. His valiant efforts came too late; he could not raise his grades enough to graduate an engineer. He finished West Point 17th in his class, and received a commission as 2nd lieutenant in the First Artillery (having first been brevet 2nd lieutenant in the Third Artillery).[43]

In his early years Isaac Trimble did not appear to be a Southerner at all; if anything, he would have to be called an American. He was born in Virginia, his family attended a Quaker meeting in Pennsylvania, he lived in Ohio and Kentucky, and went to New York to attend the Academy at West Point. Though he lived with his brother who had firmly established a community identity in Kentucky, Trimble did not appear to have inherited those sentiments, and in fact never lived in Kentucky after leaving for school. The cosmopolitan attitude reflected modern rather than traditional values, as did his personal ambition, desire for technical training, and adaptability.

West Point did not educate the sons of a landed aristocracy in premodern military traditions but rather in the technological skills needed to bring the new nation into the modern world. The new superintendent of West Point used modern education techniques rejected by the leading American universities of the day. This is the education that Trimble obviously had interest in. Though he failed to maintain the grades needed to join the ranks of the engineering corps he earned a commission in the next best field, the artillery, with the ambition of transferring to the engineers. While in West Point Trimble learned quickly to adapt to the bureaucratic world and displayed great ambition which at times in his life would prove to be a burden as much as an asset.

Trimble's behavior can be understood in the context of Maslow's hierarchy of needs. As a young man he did not have to worry much about the basic physical or safety needs. As for belongingness needs, he retained family ties which enabled him to get into West Point and produced the incentive to raise his falling grades. He also gained a new identity, not only in joining the brotherhood of West Point graduates, but in developing the modern concept of career. Any local, state, regional, or even national identity did not seem to impact his early decision making process. He made obvious advances into the fourth level of needs in that he sought personal satisfaction in advancing his class ranking, and may have even begun the process of self-actualization. As Maslow said, "self-actualization means working to do well the thing that one wants to do. To become a second-rate physician is not a good path to self-actualization. One wants to be first-rate or as good as he can be."[44] Trimble clearly sought personal fulfillment in his studies at West Point.

2

Army Life: Toward a New Identity

The morning of July 4, 1828, dawned refreshingly cooler than normal for Baltimore. The city bulged with a rapidly expanding population as throngs herded into town to witness an historic moment. Fifty thousand spectators prepared themselves for the planned spectacle. Amid banners and decorations they filled every window along Baltimore Street. Beginning at Bond Street to the east the audience stretched for two miles, unusually quiet and orderly for such a large crowd; no disturbance could be seen except for a mother or two searching for a lost child. At eight o'clock the procession began at Bond Street. The "good ship" *Union*, completely rigged on Fell's Point, sat on the extreme left of the line, and greeted the musical bands as a symbol of "our confederacy and navy." The parade headed for a large stone located in "a field two miles and a quarter from town, south of the Frederick Turnpike road, and near Carroll's upper mills, on Gwynn's falls," which they reached two hours later. Charles Carroll of Carrollton, the only surviving signer of the Declaration of Independence, headed the list of dignitaries that included the president and directors of the Baltimore & Ohio Railroad Company, the Army engineers, the mayor and city council, and the orator of the day. Guests in the pavilion included "the Speaker of the House of Representatives of the United States, Governor Coles of Indiana, the members of Congress and the Legislature, and the Cincinnati and Revolutionary Solders, Colonel Grenier and General Devereux."[1]

Forty miles away at Georgetown, President John Quincy Adams, long a supporter of internal improvements, participated in similar ceremonies for the rival Chesapeake and Ohio Canal, using a ribbon-bedecked spade. Adams' spade struck an unreceptive earth which forced three or four attempts before achieving its objective. Meanwhile, Carroll turned the first spade of ground in Baltimore to set the cornerstone for the first real railroad in America. "I consider this among the most important acts of my life, second only to my signing the Declaration of Independence," the old statesman declared. "If even it be second to that," he added.[2]

Isaac Trimble observed the proceedings as one of the engineers honored. His name appeared on the scroll, which along with a copy of the charter of the company, had been hermetically sealed for preservation and placed in a cavity of the stone. All of those present displayed an acute awareness of the importance of their project. That scroll described this new venture as "a work of deep and vital interest to the American People." The presence of the Revolutionary heroes served as a reminder of the newness of the nation. The founders of the railroad saw this new link of transportation as a means to strengthen the bond between the states. They claimed that "its accomplishment will confer the most important benefits upon this nation, by facilitating its commerce, diffusing and extending its social intercourse, and perpetuating the happy union."[3]

During the 10 years that Trimble spent in the Army he continued to seek fulfillment of his personal needs and in so doing acquired a new career, started his own family, and began the process of establishing a community identity. The changes in his life came about as much by chance as design. When he chose to attend West Point he knew that he wanted to be an engineer, but fate introduced him to railroads. He remained completely flexible to geographic preference, but the railroad brought him to Baltimore. While in Baltimore he met the woman he would marry.

While Trimble sought fulfillment of his personal needs, it is the third level of belongingness that created in him the desire to establish a community identity: at the same time America became a complex hierarchy of communities. His marriage and career contributed to his becoming part of a particular community within the city of Baltimore. By the time Trimble resigned his commission in the Army he had only begun to establish bonds with the city of Baltimore, but as time passed he became more firmly attached to this ever-changing and increasingly complex community.

The United States made early attempts at developing a policy for internal improvements, and this policy would change the direction of Trimble's future. The central government had become involved with transportation in the eighteenth century, but one of the first official steps came with the founding of the Corps of Engineers in 1802. In 1806 Congress

2. Army Life

The cornerstone of the B & O Railroad was laid on July 4, 1828, in a lavish ceremony attended by the young lieutenant Isaac Trimble. His name and participation in the project were hermetically sealed and preserved in a cavity of the stone. The stone is presently in the B & O Railway Museum in Baltimore.

authorized the first surveys for the National Road. In 1808 Albert Gallatin issued a "Report on Roads and Canals" in which he advocated extensive federal aid to internal improvements. He justified the need for federal assistance and even proposed the forms it should take. He saw a need to improve communications along the Atlantic seaboard as well as a link to reach the West. It would be difficult to maintain a bond between the states without communication. In 1817 the secretary of war, John C. Calhoun, advocated that the federal government's funds from the chartering of the Bank of the United States be used as a means to finance internal improvements. By the time Trimble entered West Point internal improvements had become a major concern, and the school became a training camp for the needed engineers.[4]

A promising advancement toward a national policy came with the passage of the General Survey Act of 1824. Major Isaac Roberdeau, head of the Topographical Bureau, stressed the usefulness of topographical engineers in public improvements. He believed that government should take an active part in the promotion of civil engineering and that the Union would profit from assisting transportation and communication, as well as finding advantages in national defense. West Point served as a starting point, but the cadets needed to receive experience. James Monroe also believed that Congress could finance internal improvements but could not establish control over them. The General Survey Act gave the president the power to secure surveys and plans for routes that he deemed of national value. The Act attempted to provide a means for funding nationally important roads and canals with federal subscription to stocks of enterprises; Monroe looked specifically to the Chesapeake and Ohio Canal as such a project. This Act had a direct impact as the new law increased the need for engineers. Because of this law Trimble finally achieved his goal of transferring to the Engineers in mid-1824.[5]

It is necessary to understand the power of localism in order to see its impact on Trimble. The competition between local communities had a direct influence on his career as well as his eventual choice of a local identity. These local communities competed for the skills of men like Trimble. Ultimately this competition would contribute to the temporary collapse of the central government in what we now call the Civil War.

The greatest obstacle to the successful development of a national plan for internal improvements came from local and state governments. Each individual community fiercely protected its own interest in developing trade, especially the rapidly expanding western commerce. Local communities challenged each other for control within states, but they often reached some compromise and used the state governments to maintain advantages over other states. Political unity did not characterize the scramble, but some consistency existed in the various regions of the nation. New England almost solidly opposed federal funding. Those states had developed good road systems on their own and they saw federal assistance as an advantage for their competitors. New Englanders feared they would lose more of their population if transportation to the West became a reality. New York and Pennsylvania gave the most support for the development of western travel since the most promising routes lay in their borders. Their representatives almost unanimously voted for the Survey Act. Shortly after the passage of that act, however, both found state funding for projects and began to turn away from seeking a national plan. Though Calhoun came from the South, he could not muster general support from the Southerners who believed that other sections would obtain more benefit from national funding than they would. In addition the needed funds would necessitate an increase in the already hated tariffs.[6]

Only the West gave continuous support for government involvement, but they too suffered from localism. The small farmers wanted to gain access to more and better markets as well as improved transportation to facilitate travel to the East. Those living in this region did not have access to as much capital as the eastern states and thus they tended to look to the national government for assistance. Despite a common objective, the competition between local communities to acquire their share of the markets interfered with any attempt at universal approval of particular projects. As the Baltimore & Ohio Railroad headed west, Wheeling competed for advantage over Pittsburgh as well as other Virginia cities such as Wellsburg, Moundsville, Sistersville, St. Marys, or Parkersburg. Madison, Indiana, made plans to become a railroad center and competed with the neighboring cities of Jeffersonville and Lawrenceburgh, which had similar ambitions. They filed grievances against Cincinnati and Louisville as the competition heated up.[7]

Localism finally destroyed the hopes of a national plan. For example, as word of the success of the Baltimore & Ohio spread, the demand for government surveying services increased. Each community demanded fulfillment of its individual objectives and thereby put the central government in the position of favoring one locality over another. In 1829 Major Abert recommended that the Topographical Bureau be increased in size and that it be made a separate agency within the War Department, becoming part of the Board of Internal Improvements. Despite Abert's efforts, the government failed to establish a system for financing major projects. By the early 1830s the federal government had lost any initiative in creating a national plan. The battles between local communities led to an emphasis on small scattered improvements as the engineers attempted to avoid favoritism.[8]

At first Trimble did not become part of the transportation revolution. He graduated from West Point in June of 1822. Because of his poor grades in his early West Point years he began his army career in the artillery. He was brevetted a 2nd lieutenant in the third Artillery; and commissioned as 2nd lieutenant in the First Regiment of Artillery. It is interesting to note that the date on both of these was July 1, 1822. After a traditional summer furlough he began his first assignment of ordnance at Fort La Fayette in New York Harbor. A year later he went to an artillery ordnance school in Pittsburgh. He continued at Fort La Fayette until June of 1824.[9]

The passage of the General Survey Act of 1824 increased the demand for engineers needed for surveys, plans, and estimates of roads and canals deemed to be of national importance. This no doubt led to the fulfillment in mid–1824 of Trimble's longing to be transferred to the engineers. This would then lead him to a new career in civil engineering.[10]

To many in 1824 the way of the future appeared to be canals, which led to Trimble's first assignment on topographical duty. The Erie Canal proved to be profitable and generated intense interest. By the end of 1819 the middle section of the canal opened up for a distance of 75 miles, and in the autumn of 1823 the Champlain Canal opened for business. They achieved final completion in 1825, shortly after Trimble's transfer. Other parts of the nation tried to copy the success of the Erie in stimulating trade. The city of Baltimore encouraged the construction of the Chesapeake & Ohio Canal which would follow the course of the Potomac River westward to connect with the Ohio valley and thus make the city a center for western trade. The government contributed to the building of canals and by 1860 had subscribed over 3 million dollars in canals, making the Chesapeake & Ohio the primary beneficiary. President Monroe wanted to provide financial assistance to the massive project and proposed the route be surveyed by Army engineers. In the end the states provided most of the needed funds. The Board of Engineers' attention to canals in its first year led to Trimble's first engineering assignment as a surveyor for the C & O.[11]

Some encouraged the construction of new roads, which took Trimble to his second assignment on topographical duty in 1825. New England had a well-developed network of highways by 1825, but New York and Pennsylvania, with greater distances to traverse, had the most mileage. The most ambitious project called for the construction of a National Road. This road started at Cumberland, Maryland, the western terminus of the Frederick Pike from Baltimore. Clearly, Baltimore would benefit greatly from the extension westward. It reached Wheeling by 1818 and by 1833 one could travel on it to Columbus, Ohio. By mid-century it went to Vandalia, Illinois, at which time the railroads rendered the project obsolete. Trimble worked primarily on the planned New Orleans extension of the National Road.[12]

Secretary of War John C. Calhoun took considerable interest in inter-

2. Army Life

A section of the C & O Canal as it looks today. This was designed to be the first canal to connect the Ohio River with the eastern waterways. This was one of the first projects that the army engineer Isaac Trimble worked on.

nal improvements, including a durable road that would connect Washington with New Orleans, the task that Trimble worked on. In his Annual Report of 1824 Calhoun discussed the projects of greatest national importance. First, he wanted to see a canal connect the Potomac with the Ohio and Lake Erie, as well as canals around the falls at Louisville on the Ohio and Muscle Shoals on the Mississippi. The first canal to connect the Ohio with the eastern waterways would be the C & O. His second objective called for canals to connect the large navigable estuaries along the Atlantic coast. His third, the road between Washington and New Orleans, would provide benefits for defense, commerce, and improved postal service. The opposition by Andrew Jackson eventually led to the desertion of the C & O project, but long before that Trimble got transferred to survey the National Road.[13]

During his time on the National Road, Trimble, still in his early 20s, traveled extensively. Under the chairmanship of General Bernard, the United States engineer who had been one of Napoleon Bonaparte's favorite officers, Trimble explored possible routes for Calhoun's proposed road to New Orleans. He traveled on horseback through the capitals of Virginia,

North Carolina, South Carolina, Georgia, Alabama, and Mississippi. He returned by a second route east of the Blue Ridge Mountains along the Piedmont. Calhoun directed that a third route be explored. Bernard assigned Major Poussin and Lieutenant Trimble to that task. They started in Washington in May of 1825 and crossed the Blue Ridge at Rockfish Gap. They followed the Shenandoah River to Knoxville and then continued southwest toward New Orleans, where they arrived in December. There Trimble spent the winter drafting his report. He seized the advantage of being in a different culture and took French lessons. His studies at West Point taught him to read French, but not to speak it. He returned to Washington in the Spring of 1826. In a little over a year he had covered more than 6,000 miles on horseback.[14]

While working on the National Road he established a relationship with a man who would change the course of his life, Lieutenant Colonel Stephen H. Long. Long graduated from Dartmouth in 1809 and entered the United States Army as a second lieutenant of engineers in 1814. He taught mathematics at West Point for two years. Long had a far-ranging view of America and its rivers. He led the third major government expedition to the West, after Lewis and Clark and Zebulon Pike. In the summer of 1819 he piloted a steamboat of his own design, the *Western Engineer*, farther up the Missouri River than any steamboat had ever gone before. He armed the boat and built it to resemble a sea serpent in an attempt to impress the Indians. In May of 1826 he was assigned as an assistant in the Nashville to Buffalo segment. Trimble worked with Long in the summer and fall of 1826 when they considered another scheme for the National Road between Washington and Buffalo. In the winter of 1826–27 Trimble prepared their report for that assignment and assisted in the final report for the road to New Orleans. Just before being transferred to the Baltimore & Ohio Railroad survey, Long worked with Trimble on another government road survey from Ohio to Alabama. When Long went to Baltimore he took Trimble with him.[15]

It is important to understand the complexity of Baltimore society in order to understand the environment in which Trimble would eventually make his decision to join the secessionist forces. Since the Revolution the city had grown rapidly and in the process had become more diverse. With the growing diversity, competition for control of the city administration increased. The city also gained greater influence in state politics. Civic leaders in the 1820s responded to economic competition with other communities by building the nation's first railroad. Because of this Trimble's career became specialized. He also met and married a daughter of one of the prominent families of that city. This marriage and new career began to draw him into the community of the Baltimore elite. By the time Trimble resigned his commission Baltimore had begun a period of change that accelerated as it came closer to 1861.

During the years that Trimble established his ties with Baltimore, the city grew to dominate the state. Maryland had four major regions within its borders. As the nineteenth century progressed the eastern shore and western shore of the Chesapeake grew apart. This manifested itself in feelings of distrust between the two sides of the bay. Later, distinctions developed between the counties in the north and those in the south as the former leaned toward Pennsylvania and the North while the latter looked toward Virginia and the South. The southern and eastern parts of the state had soil and economic conditions similar to those of the South. The northern and western counties identified more with the North. Sectional animosity accelerated as the economic center of the state shifted from the south to the north. The city of Baltimore, geographically located in the middle of the regions, rapidly gained dominance.[16]

A pre-industrial and unspecialized merchant elite ruled the city in the last half of the eighteenth century; Trimble's in-laws came from this segment of Baltimore society. The society resembled European seaports with a mercantile community, "sedentary, deferential, aristocratic, and with social relationships fixed in a hierarchical order with the merchants at its top." The more numerous lower levels of society had virtually no economic, political, or social status identity. All members of the elite had common interests so that the only political conflict centered around differences in opinion of how to best achieve their objectives. They came to power by capitalizing on changing needs and sought vertical integration by handling all functions of their business.[17]

As Baltimore grew it became more diverse. The city, which became a leader in the fight for American independence, changed considerably by the time of the Civil War. In Baltimore, located not only on a dividing line for the state but for the nation, a variety of contradictions could be found—industry beside slavery; numerous religions including African Methodists, Baptists, and Roman Catholics; and many ethnic groups—yet "all contributed to Baltimore's development in intriguing ways."[18]

The financial prosperity brought about by the Revolutionary War served as a catalyst in changing the nature and leadership of the city. During this time Baltimore surpassed Annapolis as the leading port on the Chesapeake. Two entirely new groups appeared, the manufacturers and the merchant-millers. These two groups had interests divergent from the old city aristocracy. By the end of the Revolution a new group of families emerged in Baltimore's aristocracy, a mixture of merchants and landed gentry, as well as Quaker millers and manufacturers. They helped to create a more diverse economy as well as greater specialization. This group grew in power and influence through the Federal period and the War of 1812, and then they seized control of the municipal administration. They used the city government for their own advantage and used new technology in various production and transportation methods which brought the railroad and Trimble.[19]

Some division existed in the new leadership of the early nineteenth century over the question of nationalism. Most of the new elite had supported the Constitution, but a division began during the events of the 1790s. Both groups continued to support a strong central government, but they disagreed when the interest of Baltimore conflicted with national interest. The first group, mostly lawyers and merchants, sided with the federal government whereas the second group, which consisted of a few highly influential merchants, defended the position which proved best for Baltimore. The second group believed that national policies should reflect local interest. "Their point of view was not localism *versus* nationalism, but localism *and* nationalism; they believed that what was good for Baltimore was good for the nation, and that things should also work the other way around."[20] This second group assumed leadership and became the municipal officeholders and thus better known with those men influential in the everyday life of the city, including master craftsmen and tradesmen. The families leading this alliance included those who had been part of the Scotch–Irish immigration from northern Ireland and who had settled first in Pennsylvania, including Presbyterians, Quakers, and Baptists. These families had moved from southeastern Pennsylvania in the 1760s and 1770s to take advantage of Baltimore's wheat trade. They formed the nucleus of those who had supported the Revolution. They also brought about the incorporation of the city. In the process the middle class gained greater power and used this power to further promote their own prosperity.[21]

Baltimore became more aggressive as the competition between communities within the region intensified. The greatest challenge to Baltimore came from the rival city of Philadelphia. Both cities struggled to control the trade to and from the Susquehanna Valley. They both looked to the farmers and artisans of the valley as producers and consumers. The settlers in the Susquehanna relied on roads for transportation to market since the river had natural obstructions. As early as 1791 Governor Mifflin of Pennsylvania realized that the river became a dividing line between those markets which belonged to Philadelphia and those that tended to go to Baltimore, and thus Pennsylvania adopted a plan for promoting the improvement of roads and navigation within the state. At that time transportation facilities often proved more influential than state governments, and thus Baltimore came up with its own plans to keep the valley within its sphere of trade. Philadelphia had an advantage in that it had considerable influence in state government, but Baltimore had the geographic advantage. Baltimore became more ambitious and also developed plans to gain control of trade with the West. They saw the C & O canal as well as the westward expansion of the National Road as a means to achieve this objective, but in 1827 they developed a more ambitious though more risky plan to compete.[22]

In the 1820s Baltimore became desperate in its attempt to increase its share of the growing western trade. During the years before and after the War of 1812 the port helped to make Baltimore the third largest city in the country. This prosperity suffered some setbacks in the 1820s that generated considerable anxiety among city leaders. New men with new ideas came into power and "created what would become the nineteenth-century sociopolitical framework for articulating community processes."[23] What they began would be expanded upon by following generations, but they started the free public schools and other public services which generated greater political democracy. There arose a conflict between those who responded more readily to prevailing conditions and those who tried to preserve the former way of life. This is the environment that the men worked in when they created the Baltimore & Ohio Railroad, which gained universal acceptance within the community.[24]

The Baltimore & Ohio Railroad emerged as that city's response to the increased competition. On February 12, 1827, a group of merchants met in the home of George Brown to create a plan for Baltimore to keep and increase its share of western trade. They discussed the advantages of canals and a new form of transportation, railroads. They appointed a committee to decide a course of action. On February 19 the committee presented a document which began by pointing out the efforts of Philadelphia and New York to gain the western trade. It also pointed out the geographic advantages Baltimore had by being 200 miles nearer the navigable waters of the West. They apparently did not see Washington D.C. or cities in Virginia as competitors, and only mentioned New Orleans as the greatest threat from the South. They presented a charter for incorporation to the Maryland legislature and received its approval on February 28. They elected the first board of directors on April 23 and the next day they formally incorporated. In that month they petitioned James Barbour for federal aid in the form of the survey work which drew Trimble into the scheme. Virginia gave its approval on March 8 after receiving guarantees that the route would stay north of the mouth of the Little Kanawha. Virginia could profit also from the railroad, but leaders there wanted to protect the route recommended in Gallatin's 1808 report which would be most advantageous for that state.[25]

The people of Baltimore quickly displayed enthusiastic faith in the adventure. The *Niles Register* reported the plan that had been adopted by "certain of our most intelligent, public spirited and wealthy citizens." Only a week before the *American* published an editorial in which they promoted the Pennsylvania Canal which would divert Susquehanna trade to Baltimore, but they quickly swung around to the side of the railroad.[26] The citizenry bet their money on the venture, "then came a scene which almost beggars description. By this time public excitement had gone far beyond fever heat and reached the boiling point. Everybody wanted stock."[27] Almost as many shares sold on the last day as the first, 13,387. The two mile long crowd that gathered to witness the laying of the cornerstone likewise reflected the enthusiasm of the citizenry.[28]

With our hindsight it is not so easy to appreciate the risk the people of Baltimore took. We may never know how much they owed to luck and how much to wisdom. Forty years later Latrobe, the former classmate of Trimble and one of the men deeply involved with the B & O from the early days, admitted in a lecture that "no one then anticipated the growth of the country beyond the Alleghenies." He also reminded his audience that "railroads were then not thought of. Canals were the means relied on." Latrobe implied that circumstance forced them to take the chance they did as the people of Baltimore began to consider rails to be the only viable means for them to compete. "It was a straw for a drowning people to catch at. It was a great faith; and it was the evidence, too, of the unseen," he continued, pointing out that "the people generally of the United States knew nothing of railroads but the name."[29] The people of Philadelphia reflected the thoughts of many when they offered to send Baltimore a supply of straitjackets for those with "Rail-Road Mania."[30]

Trimble did not actively seek assignment to work in the new industry but rather found himself among the pioneers by chance. In 1835 *The American Railroad Journal* proclaimed the Baltimore & Ohio as "the Railroad University of the United States," and Trimble would be in the first graduating class. Only two examples of rail travel existed in the United States in 1827, both of those used only for hauling raw materials a short distance. In Quincy, Massachusetts, a three-mile line ran from the granite quarries to the Bunker Hill monument on the Neponset River. In Mauch Chunk, Pennsylvania, gravity propelled coal nine miles on rails to the Lehigh River. The B & O would be the first true railroad line. The War

Department responded quickly to Baltimore's plea for help by sending three engineers: Dr. William Howard, Lieutenant Colonel Stephen H. Long, and Captain William G. McNeill. The Quaker, Jonathan Knight, joined the trio in June. Trimble's involvement came in July at the request of Long. As previously mentioned, the two had been working together on the road to New Orleans. A total of 10 hand-picked topographical assistants, several of whom had already worked on surveys, joined the company with the approval of the principal engineers. All but one had graduated from West Point.[31]

The topographical team worked fast and efficiently to accelerate the beginning of construction. The first stage called for them to explore all reasonable routes from Baltimore to the Potomac River Valley intersecting at any point between Harpers Ferry and Cumberland. The second phase called for one team to survey the first part while a second team did preliminary investigation of the route that would connect the Potomac to the Ohio. On each possible route the engineers had orders to note the ascents and descents in feet per mile. They also recorded the location of "valleys, hills, and precipices," as well as the elevations of any depressions. They observed the flow of all watercourses and "the character of the rocks, soils and aspect of the adjacent country."[32] They made such observations for the purpose of deciding where inclined planes might be needed and the availability of water that would be required to provide steam for the engines. Afterwards the most promising routes would be examined in greater detail.[33]

Though Trimble was one of several lieutenants, the principal engineers obviously had considerable faith in his ability, which resulted in him playing a significant part in this American adventure. In the first phase he went with a team which left Baltimore in a northwesterly direction to the Upper Patapsco Valley, following it to Westminster and then along the Monacacy Valley across South Mountain to Hagerstown. At first he acted alone in exploring the district from the Cumberland to the Ohio along the Cheat and Little Kanawha rivers. Initially the plan called for him to work with Long, but the latter suffered from fever which he had contracted while working with Trimble on the Ohio to Alabama road. At that time they feared the "fever season" along the rivers, though they did not realize that mosquitoes carried malaria and that the insects thrived in the warm waterways of the South. The country beyond the Cheat proved very rugged and at times the mountain laurel grew so thick that it almost prevented passage. Later Trimble received assistance from others. In eight weeks Trimble and Joshua Barney explored 38 different routes totaling more than 225 miles. In reconnaissance of the western extension he walked the entire dis-

Portrait by Samuel Bell Waugh of Isaac Trimble made during the years that he was an engineer in the United States Army (1822–1832). Courtesy the Maryland Historical Society, Baltimore, Maryland.

tance to the mouth of the Little Kanawha, but due to Virginia's determination to protect that route for its own purposes "he spent the winter of 1828–1829 exploring a possible alternative route between Cumberland and Pittsburgh." Trimble wrote the report of 1828 which became a star attraction during the "Grand Procession" of that July 4. He also became the only Army officer selected to participate when actual construction started later that month.[34]

While the construction of the first phase began July 7 the topographers did the actual survey work further west. In the survey work the team noted horizontal angles, the elevations, and the distances in their field books. From the field books they would translate the information into plans, producing three-dimensional representations of the railroad. Trimble's old classmate, John H. B. Latrobe, handled most of the legal work for the line. In May Latrobe and Long had headed out on horseback to secure right of way releases from the property owners. Meanwhile, senior lawyers anticipated challenges from the C & O Canal, a competitor, and thus decided that they needed deeds. Latrobe again headed west, taking Trimble with him to survey the land for legal descriptions. A third member of the team rounded up two justices of the peace who witnessed each transaction. Latrobe described this task as "wearisome work."[35]

One reason that other army personnel did not work on the construction is that the railroad began hiring the important players away from the Army. As early as April of 1828 they hired Knight as engineer at $3,000 a year, and Casper Weaver became the superintendent of construction at $2,000 a year. They hired Long at the same salary as Knight, and the next month they offered William Gibbs McNeill $1,500 a year. The Corps of Engineers finished their work for the Baltimore & Ohio in December of 1829. Early in 1830 the president of the company, Philip E. Thomas, "sent for Lieut. Trimble and earnestly besought him to remain with the Company and take the position of Chief Assistant to Jonathan Knight, who had been appointed Chief Engineer." Trimble would be trained to replace Knight, who "was growing infirm." He considered this "a tempting offer for a youth not then twenty-six years old," but decided that "at the time [he] did not wish to leave the Army."[36]

In 1830 Trimble, now an engineer with railroad experience, went to Massachusetts with Major McNeil. The response to the new railroad came quickly from other communities. McNeil had been loaned to work on the Boston and Providence and Boston and Lowell Railroads, and Trimble would serve as his principal assistant in the location and construction of the two new lines. By 1838 the Boston and Providence would be 41 miles long and have 10 engines. The Boston and Lowell would extend over 20 miles and employ six engines.[37]

Meanwhile, changes took place in the Army administration. The Academy clearly fulfilled its obligation in providing engineers for the nation and the process of resignation enabled West Point to continue as the national school for civil engineers as well as military engineers. Promotions came slowly and the Army not only tolerated but encouraged resignations. In 1831 the Secretary of War separated the Topographical Bureau from the War Department, and in the same year they started withdrawing line officers from duties not directly under its command. Of the 10 engineers who had worked on the B & O between 1827 and 1830, eight had resigned by 1832 and all 10 by 1837.[38]

Later in 1830 Trimble returned to ordnance duty. He was in garrison at Ft. Monroe, Virginia, from late 1830 to 1831. Three is no record of Trimble complaining about this move; however, it probably had some influence on his decision to leave the military. This may have been a temporary assignment until something else came along, but it may be that the Army tried to encourage him to leave.[39]

Another variable contributed to his final decision; he met his future wife, Maria Presstman, sometime around 1828. His brother David wrote to him on May 26, "you have my consent to marry whenever you please." David retained a fatherly role for his little brother and added, "I only pray you to marry a sensible, well informed woman of good family and good constitution." He also added, "I suppose some money would be of no disadvantage in furnishing a house."[40] Isaac and Maria became engaged a year later and married on July 4, 1831.[41]

Trimble's marriage to Maria Presstman brought him into an alliance with one of the old aristocratic families of Baltimore as well as a connection to an old South Carolina family. Maria's grandfather, George McDougall Presstman, "was born in Dumfries of Scotch-Irish parents and arrived in Baltimore from Londonderry in 1763."[42] He became one of the merchants that ruled that city at the time of the Revolution. He joined the Ancient and Honorable Mechanical Company, which had formed to protect the town from Indians during the French and Indian War. The mayor at the time, and the next six successors, would all come from that company. He worked with two other leading citizens in purchasing that city's first fire engine in 1769. His son, William, followed in his father's footsteps as a successful shipping merchant. In 1793 he married Anne Ferguson Cattell, daughter of Captain Benjamin Cattell of South Carolina.[43] The Atlantic coastal trade brought William Presstman and his wife together and thus created a connection between a leading family of Charleston and one from

Baltimore. Two young business partners, William Presstman and William Calhoun, met the two Cattell sisters, Anne and Lydia, at a St. Cecilia Ball in Charleston. Both men came from successful families; Calhoun was the son of Baltimore's first mayor. The two sisters moved with their new husbands to Baltimore but they maintained strong family ties to Charleston. The estate of their brother William passed to Anne and Lydia since he had no children. The families of the two Baltimore sisters retained an interest in their brother's "Oak Hill" plantation until 1846.[44]

Maria was born in 1802. Her family was "close-knit, affectionate and protective of one another." They lived in the vicinity of Old St. Paul's Episcopal Church where they regularly attended services. After learning the "three R's" at home she attended a private female academy where they taught her history, geography, composition, English literature, and natural science, as well as decorum. Her literary skills are reflected in the diary that she kept. Portraits were painted at the time that Maria became Mrs. Trimble. Isaac was a handsome young man of five foot eight inches and weighed about 140 pounds, "with high forehead, curly, very dark brown hair, sideburns extending to the chin, eyes of the same color and deep-set, aquiline nose and firm, well-shaped jaw." Maria, a scant 89 pounds, had "a rather long face, small mouth and chin, straight, slightly pointed nose, blue-grey eyes and very fair complexion," and "naturally curly, light brown hair."[45]

The couple lived in the North their first year together. After their marriage Trimble received a temporary detail to survey the route of the Mohawk and Hudson Railroad so they spent "many pleasant days" in the Catskills. Maria loved the "beauty of [the] mountain scenery." The impending birth of their first child caused Maria to long for home and family. Trimble got a 60-day furlough and in November they set out by sea for Baltimore.[46]

Though Maria enjoyed some aspects of her life in the North, her diary reflects her determination to return to Baltimore, her family, and her home. They left from Boston and ran into "a most dreadful storm" before reaching Providence. They then boarded a steamer for New York "but all description would fail to give the reader any account of what [they] suffered." Three times they tried to cross Point Judith and each time had to return to Newport, "all passengers sick, with very few exceptions." They finally reached New York and spent the night in the Clinton Hotel, but in order to avoid the influenza which "raged in New York," they left the next day for Brunswick. Trimble "engaged a Hack" for the trip to Philadelphia, which he felt would be more comfortable than the stage for his sick bride. After a night in the Heads Hotel of Philadelphia they headed south despite the rain; Maria's "anxiety to reach home was so great" that she "would not agree to stop any longer." She had promised to stop and visit her brother, Stephen Wilson Presstman, rector of Immanuel Episcopal Church in New Castle. After a night in the parsonage Maria insisted on departure in the rain, for by this time she felt "all impatience to reach home." A canal boat took them the rest of the way, but Maria felt too ill to meet with her family whom she had gone through such hardships to see. She temporarily revived and soon started receiving visitors, one after the other. She felt "too excited by seeing the friends who called," and she "relapsed and was not able to leave the house until Christmas Day."[47]

Trimble returned to Boston, but as he realized the attachment his wife had to her family and Baltimore and saw dim prospects for a future in the Army, he decided to resign. Their first child, David Churchman Trimble, was born on April 18, 1832. "Weighing but five pounds" he "was pronounced by everyone to be a handsome child." An extension of his leave allowed Trimble the opportunity to be in Baltimore for this joyous occasion, but he returned to Boston with the idea that his family would join him in July. Once again together, the new family took rooms in a boarding house at Number 22 Beacon Street.[48]

Trimble resigned his commission on May 31, 1832, to accept a job as the principal assistant engineer for the Boston, Massachusetts, and Providence, Rhode Island, Railroad. As previously stated, the Army had been encouraging people to leave and his future appeared to be more profitable in the private sector. In addition he now had a wife and family to support.[49]

What is clear about the military phase of Trimble's life is that he responded to the changing environment, yielding to the desire to fulfill his personal needs, and in the process developed an identity as a professional railroad engineer, and the head of a new family. The quest to fulfill his personal needs is not to imply that he had selfish motives. His desire to establish a family and belong to a community came from what Maslow called the belongingness needs. Though the drive comes as a personal need it usually results in a commitment of the individual to others with whom he establishes his identity. This can include the immediate family, the extended family, and the community. In Trimble we see the foundations for all three. In the case of the community we find him becoming not only a part of Baltimore, but also establishing himself in a career community: a railroad engineer.

It is also clear that he saw a future in civil engineering, but his railroad career came about by chance rather than any great desire on his part. He chose to be an engineer but he could not transfer to the Corps of Engineers until after the passage of the National Survey Act of 1824. He must have had some notion of the job he would be doing as an engineer, but the Army issued his assignments to the C & O Canal and the National Road; there is no evidence that he requested these projects. Army orders placed him under the command of Lieutenant Colonel Long, and Army orders sent Long to survey the new railroad for Baltimore. Long requested that Trimble assist him and thus he moved to Baltimore where he began his railroad career.

Trimble's attachment to the community of Baltimore began during this time, but it too resulted from chance rather than any ambition of his to be part of the state of Maryland or the city of Baltimore. The men of Baltimore responded to economic competition by building the nation's first railroad, and in the process they brought Trimble to their city by their request for surveyors. While there he met and married a lady of that community. Initially Maria accepted her duty to go to New England with her husband, but she clearly maintained a strong attachment to her Baltimore friends and family. Prior to 1832 Trimble never expressed any strong bonds to any community, town, county, or state. He had moved around as a child and moved around during his Army career. Though he still did not have a strong attachment to Baltimore or Maryland, it is clear that his wife and career helped to draw him into that community.

As of 1832 there is still no indication of any identity as a Southerner or Northerner. He did not reveal any hesitation to move to New York or even New England, and neither did his wife. The only reason either had a preference for Baltimore is that Maria's family lived there. The Baltimore community that Trimble became attached to had a traditional rivalry with the city above the Mason–Dixon, Philadelphia, but it also competed with Washington D. C. and the cities of Virginia. These conflicts did not reflect any strong regional bonds for the leaders of Baltimore, nor for Trimble. If anything the actions of both the community and Trimble reflected motives of self-interest.

3

A New Profession: Railroad Man

Isaac Trimble and his wife, Maria, boarded the packet ship *Independence* as it sat in New York harbor on August 8, 1834. After setting sail the crew discovered that many Irish immigrants had hidden in the hold. They had given up hope of finding a better life in America and did not have the funds to pay their passage home. "Poor creatures," Maria entered in her diary. "How I pitied them." The crew forced the poor souls into the pilot boat "in spite of their cries and prayers," and sent them back to the land they tried so desperately to leave. One hundred and sixty steerage passengers remained, men, women, and children, who could afford to pay their way. Some planned to fetch their families back to the United States, but many of them, "from want of exertion," returned to their homeland even poorer than when they arrived in the land of promise. A good breeze came up out of Sandy Hook, and they left "the high blue hills, the last scene of [their] native land, fading rapidly in the distance." Maria "had always suffered so much from being at sea," though she had taken only short voyages, and concluded that she would "have the same horrid feelings" and prepared herself for bed. To her astonishment "day after day passed without feeling at all sick," and during the entire voyage she had only one day of seasickness.[1]

America experienced great change during the nineteenth century, and that change was not always beneficial. Maria's description of their trip to England serves as a reminder of the turmoil which accompanied progress; Trimble set off to develop his new career traveling with Irish immigrants who had abandoned their dreams in the new world. The Irish had an especially difficult time being accepted in America.

During the decade of the 1830s both Isaac Trimble and the city of Baltimore began a process of change. Following his resignation from the Army, Trimble developed his career as a railroad professional. He continued to fulfill his personal needs by providing for his new family, increasing his self-esteem, and working toward self-actualization. He increased his skills and knowledge of railroads and the trip he took in 1832 helped considerably. He accepted several different assignments and positions to keep himself on the edge of a rapidly growing industry. Not only did he increase his technical knowledge but in the process he also acquired some management skills. He had been among the first graduating class that had worked on the Baltimore & Ohio, and thus many opportunities presented themselves; he received job offers in management as well as engineering. He faced minimal competition and therefore did not have extensive experience with the jealousies and fears that accompanied political jousting for promotions. Trimble continued to give little regard to geographical location in his choice of assignments but it became increasingly clear to him that his wife could not be happy if she lived too far from her family in Baltimore. In the end he took another step in establishing a community identity with the city of Baltimore by moving there, but he also strengthened his ties to the community of railroad professionals. The Baltimore & Ohio not only started a new career for Trimble, it also began a new age for the city of Baltimore. The city changed dramatically between 1828 and 1860, and the foundations for that change came in the 1830s. The divided Baltimore that rioted at the President Street Station on April 19, 1861, bore little resemblance to the united Baltimore that celebrated the founding of the Baltimore & Ohio Railroad on July 4, 1828.

Both Trimble and the city began the process of modernization. To understand Isaac Trimble, the Confederate general, it is necessary to have a basic understanding of the city that he lived in at the time that he made his important decision about national loyalty. He progressed from an orphaned Quaker boy on the American frontier to a business leader in the city of Baltimore; this metamorphosis reflected the changes the nation went through. Baltimore played a prominent role in the modernization of the United States and, like Trimble, the city would be forced to choose sides when the nation divided.

"An astonishing thing happened in Baltimore during the 1830s: all the historical forces that had been at work for more than a generation suddenly cohered."[2] Economic growth changed the city not only physically but culturally. As previously stated, the city prospered in the first two decades of the century and then floundered in the Panic of 1819 and struggled during the depression of the 1820s. The effort to revive, which brought about the construction of the railroad, payed off by 1831 and the economy grew. The inflation of the latter part of the decade exaggerated the feelings of success, but they fared considerably better than in the previous decade.[3]

The city fathers would have liked to have claimed responsibility for the improved economy, but two of the contributing forces of change came from outside of the United States. Great Britain changed its economic policies from mercantilism to free trade, and thereby took the lead in an emerging world economy. Previously localized eighteenth century seaport economic centers, such as Baltimore, participated in this new world economy centered in Liverpool. Baltimore hoped to profit from its relatively more convenient location to the English city, and its new transportation links to the west which could help to make it a vital center in this new world. Yet they could not compete with New York. Advantages for New York included established ties with Liverpool (two or three fewer sailing days closer) and better links to the increasing western trade. The flow of goods and ideas came from Liverpool to the United States by way of New York. Baltimore, like other cities on the American coast, found it more economical to buy British goods from New York than to buy them directly from Liverpool, and thus they became increasingly dependent on that city. A second boost to Baltimore's economy came from British investment capital which began to flow on a large scale to Baltimore among other American cities. Numerous British investors sought new opportunities in America.[4]

The changes begun in the 1820s formed clear patterns during the 1830s, and these changes brought about the passing of the old order. They included increased immigration, institutionalization, and industrialization. The misery of the immigrants recorded by Maria occurred in New York, but immigration also increased in Baltimore. This new population brought with it new expectations and demands. The private and individual old-order attitude did not meet the needs of the new population. Education, fire and police protection, and charity became increasingly institutionalized, and as they did Baltimore became more urban and less like a village. The old families, such as the Presstmans, could either change their objectives for the city or lose the role of leadership to those who could satisfy the new demands.[5]

Though the local community of Baltimore became increasingly fragmented it also became increasingly less isolated from other American communities; it became more cosmopolitan. The forces creating change in

Baltimore appeared in varying degrees in other communities and in some ways the concept of nationhood changed and grew. Between 1815 and 1860 the population of the United States increased four times, but the value of manufactured products increased eight times.[6] As communication and transportation improved, communities shared more ideas and experiences. When Baltimore found success with its railroad, other cities realized the necessity to build their own if they hoped to compete, and thus they coaxed men like Trimble to assist them in their projects. By its communication developments Baltimore became increasingly part of the larger national development; but at the same time local communities fought bitterly and selfishly for trade advantages while increasing the need for better communication and cooperation.[7]

Changes spread to the countryside. It is important to remember that no great architect created the design but rather it came despite self-interest. Though one individual can do little to change his community, the community is the sum total of all of the individuals who live within it. They required better communication and cooperation between communities on both the state and national level, but at the same time wanted to protect their own interests. Baltimore did not strive to become part of a national project but continued to expand its three traditional market areas: the Susquehanna Valley, the west, and southern Maryland and the Washington D. C. area. As the transportation and communication links spread from the city they carried the forces of change. In the decade of the 1830s Trimble began to assume a leadership role on behalf of Baltimore as the city competed to expand its markets.[8]

By 1840 the physical appearance of Baltimore reflected the organizational, political, and cultural changes due to modernization. In the city "the Jacksonians pushed municipal services away from private ownership or operation toward municipalization." Not only did city services expand but they became "more uniform, regular, and efficient."[9] The physical boundaries of the city expanded as the population grew, and as the city expanded different communities grew up within the city limits, and thus generated a competition for control of the city government. Police and fire departments became more bureaucratic as they grew to accommodate the physical spread of the city. The needs of the various communities resulted in the city services becoming more political. This can be seen in the municipalization of the Baltimore Water Company.[10] These changes probably appeared more obvious to Trimble since he left the city for extended periods of time. What might not have been so readily apparent is that "the real authority of the aristocratic, personal, private, and individual old order had been broken in the process."[11]

Trimble had begun a new "profession as civil engineer." He recognized that he had skills "attained mainly through the instruction received at West Point."[12] He enhanced these skills and eventually specialized in railroads during his 10 years of service in the Army. In the end he had joined a new professional community.

Though the Trimbles returned to Baltimore, largely at the urging of Maria, Trimble continued to display little reservation at abandoning his geographical community in pursuit of his career goals. He returned to Boston following the birth of his son David on April 18, 1832. He accepted a position as principal assistant engineer for the Boston, Massachusetts, & Providence, Rhode Island, Railroad. His wife soon joined him in Boston and they took some rooms in a boarding house at No. 22 Beacon Street. In March of 1834 Maria gave birth to twins, but they lived only two days. They were buried in Mr. Appleton's vault, under St. Paul's Church, Tremont Street.[13]

The trip to England in 1834 came about when he accepted a job offer to buy "iron and locomotives and other machinery." He represented three different Boston railroad companies: in addition to the railroad he worked for he also represented the Boston and Lowell, and the Massachusetts and Western. They gave him considerable authority, "with an unlimited credit on the Barings to pay for what he ordered." He also had the task of obtaining information on the construction of locomotive engines for Lowell Manufacturing. The Trimbles left their son, David, with his grandmother in Baltimore and then headed for New York where they caught the *Independence* to Liverpool.[14] They left New York on August 8th, and on the 25th "the Steward announced the joyful tiding of having caught a bird." Maria expressed her awe and frustration as they sat near the great British financial center: "on Thursday the 28th we anchored, the tide being against us. This is tantalizing, being in sight of Liverpool; however, in the afternoon a small Steam Packet was sent down for the Mail and the passengers all went up to Liverpool in it." They reached the dock at 5 o'clock, and "it was raining hard. [They] got into a little carriage which was drawn by one horse, ... called Hire Cars; and drove to the Adelphi Hotel," which Maria called " a splendid house." They enjoyed their "repast and retired for the night."[15]

The trip to England proved to be a great opportunity for Trimble to expand his expertise in his new career while fulfilling his obligations. Liverpool manufactured the most advanced locomotives of the day, and he soon placed orders for "many of them." He also visited the iron works at Birmingham, Leeds, and Newcastle-on-Tyne to procure "thousands of tons of rail, ... a planeing machine for iron," and other equipment. He also observed railroads under construction in Ireland, Scotland, and Wales, and made at least one call on George Stephenson, the father of British railroading.[16] In 1822 the directors of the Stockton and Darlington railway initially planned to use "animal traction" until Stephenson persuaded them to use steam. When the railroad opened September 27, 1825, Stephenson's "Active," later renamed "Locomotion," pulled the first public passenger train in the world.[17]

After London, Trimble spent a week in Paris to familiarize himself with French railroad construction, operations, and the proposed nationwide network. While there the Trimbles toured the city sights. He added to his collection of scientific books,[18] but they also made some personal purchases which included eight or nine oil paintings as well as a set of china costing 331 francs. Maria enjoyed Paris, where they visited Notre Dame, the churches of St. Roch and St. Etienne-du-Mont, the Pantheon, the Palais du Luxembourg, the Palais Royal, and the tomb of Abélard and Heloise.[19] They attended an Italian opera "where the music was delightful." Maria did not see France as more progressive than the United States. She described the villages of the countryside as "nothing but poverty and the greatest want, not only of comfort, but of cleanliness." She went on to say "although my opinion of France is a miserable, dirty, unprepossessing Country — never was I more delighted on landing at Dover that I was again on English land." Though she found England more pleasing she did describe distressing scenes of industrialization. While taking a trip to the Drury Lane Theater they "walked around the Saloon and beheld the most shocking scenes." She wrote, "My heart grieved to see human nature so depraved, especially among young females."[20]

Maria generally enjoyed touring London and Paris, but she suffered considerably in the early part of the trip when her husband took care of business. While he traveled about the foundries and railways she remained behind in lodgings at "Miss Eaton's boarding house on Percy Street." She rarely left the boarding house except to attend Anglican Services, which she did at least three times and as many as five times per week. Her loneliness and homesickness generated physical symptoms so that in early January of 1835 she wrote, "Dr. Bickersteth called again, this making 17 visits in all." She did show rapid signs of improvement as soon as her husband returned and they began touring.[21]

They arrived back in the United States in March of 1835,[22] and Maria's undeniable attachment to her family in Baltimore once again drew them toward that city. The proliferation of railroad building in America, along with the expertise Trimble gained, generated offers of employment. The Massachusetts and Western and the Baltimore & Susquehanna both tried to entice him to work for them. It is clear that he had reservations about accepting the Baltimore offer when he wrote that he "was aware of the disadvantage to himself professionally of separating from the large capitalists and enterprises of the Northeastern States."[23] This one statement reveals several different aspects about Trimble at this point in time. First, he did not demonstrate any great regional loyalty. Second, he showed an understanding of the importance of investment capital. Third, he revealed the dedication that he had to his wife in that he made a final decision based on her needs over his own.

With his acceptance of the position for the Baltimore & Susquehanna Railroad Trimble became involved in a classic example of the fierce trade rivalry that existed between cities in early nineteenth century America. At times local, state, and national identities became confusing, especially when a course of action created a conflict of interest at the various levels and thus forced the individual to decide which side to take. Communities such as the Susquehanna Valley, Baltimore, and Philadelphia became aggressive in protecting their own interests. Individuals within communities each pursued their hierarchy of needs and they selected leadership based on common objectives. Those with the power wanted to see leaders who could protect their personal interests. The population of these three local communities gave priority to their local interests over state, regional, or national interests. Those living in the Susquehanna believed that they could profit more by allying themselves with Baltimore rather than Philadelphia, even though the latter not only lay within the boundaries of their state but occupied a leadership role in Pennsylvania politics. Philadelphia demanded state loyalty from those in the Susquehanna Valley, while Baltimore pretended not to see the importance of state boundaries. After the opening of the Baltimore & Ohio, "there developed a sort of metropolitan mercantilism in which railroads, rather than merchant fleets, were the chief weapons."[24] Philadelphia entered the war shortly after Baltimore and they quickly mobilized. By 1840 Pennsylvania had more railroad mileage than any of the other states.[25]

State governments became involved with railroad projects because of the power the states had to grant corporate charters. Due to the large amount of capital required to build a railroad, as well as the considerable risk involved, the founders established corporations. The general population tended to view corporations as monopolistic devices, but they tolerated them in the case of internal improvements. Before 1860 corporate charters required special acts of state legislatures. State legislatures became a means to control the power of these companies, and they often reserved the right to purchase the road from the owners. In hopes of encouraging railroad development the states often gave sweeping privileges of eminent domain.[26] Even before Trimble participated in the Baltimore & Ohio Railroad ceremony of July 4, 1828, others made plans to build a railroad which would secure the trade of the Susquehanna. They received their charter from the Maryland legislature on February 13, 1828, for a line that would run from Baltimore to York Haven. The problem came in securing a charter from the state of Pennsylvania.[27]

Those living in southern Pennsylvania, especially in York, gave immediate support to the road.[28] The builders of railroads made their plans with their own profits in sight, but they quickly gained support from others in the community because of the tremendous multiplier effect a railway had on the local economy. Farmers, manufacturers, and mine owners increased profits, consumers got more for their money, and real estate values increased. "The community gains, the advantages resulting to those who were not actually investors, often greatly exceeded those which accrued to stockholders."[29] The *York Gazette* wrote, even before Maryland granted the charter, "Baltimore Must and will be the Great Central City of the Union." Thus they accepted the claim by the Baltimore sponsors that "the prosperity of Baltimore is tributary to the prosperity of the interior of Pennsylvania," and that the road would give those southern Pennsylvanians "the benefit of a safe, cheap, and certain communication to a market for their produce."[30]

Philadelphia took a stand for states' rights as it attempted to protect its own interest. The corporate management doubted that the Pennsylvania legislature would deny a charter for their portion of the road simply "because it happened to be beyond the imaginary line which separates the two States." Those in Philadelphia claimed to defend the interest of the state of Pennsylvania. They said that Baltimore would benefit from the diversion of trade that resulted from expensive state canals and railroads. *The Pennsylvania Gazette* argued, "it may seem churlish and unkind, not to give permission to make a road, but the point is, if we do, we may give with it the whole trade of the state." Philadelphians claimed the right to the trade of the entire Commonwealth because of the large contributions made to the state treasury, which in turn paid for the internal improvements.[31]

Both sides resorted to aggressive name-calling campaigns, mainly through the editorials of their local newspapers, and in the process revealed the complexity of American identity with appeals made to local, state, and national loyalties. Pennsylvania appealed to state loyalties while Baltimore argued for the liberalism and brotherhood between communities within the same nation. They also pointed out that they asked for no financial assistance from Pennsylvania. The *Pennsylvania Gazette* wrote that granting Baltimore's request would be "repugnant to every principle of state pride and state policy." When Baltimore made their appeal to brotherhood the Philadelphians reminded them of their refusal to allow Pennsylvania to tap into the Baltimore & Ohio Railroad. The people of southern Pennsylvania continued to support Baltimore and the old sectional rivalries between the interior and the seaboard of the state reappeared. They resented their contributions to the state projects, such as the Pennsylvania State Works, which did not really benefit them. The *York Gazette* claimed that "among the important rights of a free people, is that of having unrestrained commercial intercourse with each other." They expressed self-interest when they went on to say, "we owe it to ourselves as a paramount duty of self-preservation to protect ourselves against the consequences of a commercial tyranny by guarding against the establishment of a commercial monopoly."[32]

The struggle to make the connection between the Susquehanna and Baltimore continued for several years, but the project finally came into existence. Emmett M. Doudel of York first brought the proposal to the Pennsylvania House of Representatives on December 20, 1828. They abandoned a request to charter a company which would extend the Baltimore & Susquehanna from the Mason-Dixon Line and replaced it with a request to grant the existing railroad the privileges and immunities of a Pennsylvania corporation. The legislature defeated that question in February of 1829. On April 8, 1829, they did win passage of an act to extend an old canal company that would require goods to travel over water and rail on their way to market in Baltimore. At one point York made plans to construct a connecting railroad without a state charter. Finally, a bill to incorporate the York and Maryland Line Railroad became law on March 14, 1832. The *York Gazette* reported, "Men, women, and children seemed to have but one wish, the wish of testifying to one another how deep, sincere and heartfelt was their joy ... the national flag was unfurled over our heads. The bells rang merrily and long. The cannon growled in the distance."[33]

The railroad progressed slowly even after they overcame the biggest hurdle. By July 4, 1831, they completed the first seven-mile division, but since they could not build in Pennsylvania they decided to construct a branch road to Westminster, Maryland. Enthusiasm increased in Baltimore once Pennsylvania granted the charter for the connecting line. They then had to face the lack of funds. The state of Maryland granted a million dollar loan to the company.[34] The city of Baltimore also found occasion to provide assistance to the railway.[35] Meanwhile, the Baltimore promoters objected to the York proposal involving the York and Maryland Line Railroad and on April 15, 1835, the Pennsylvania legislature created the York and Wrightsville Railroad Company. Five of the seven officials of this new company were Baltimore citizens, including Trimble who was chief engineer for that line from 1836 to 1838 (this was at the same time that he was chief engineer for the Baltimore & Susquehanna). Soon after the Anti-Masonic Legislature on March 21, 1836, incorporated a railroad from Wrightsville to Gettysburg, and the two lines merged to form the Wrightsville, York, and Gettysburg Rail Road Company.[36]

Trimble expressed an awareness of the intense rivalry between Baltimore and Philadelphia, but he also demonstrated a desire to see peaceable resolution and cooperation between the great cites of trade on the coast. In his first report to the Baltimore & Susquehanna management he referred to the "question so interesting to the city of Baltimore and State of Maryland." He made a comparison of "this route for transportation of produce, &c. to market at Baltimore, and those offered by the works already completed or contemplated in Pennsylvania, with a view to the market of Philadelphia." In 1837 he spoke of the route "calculated to promote the object of the stockholders and the interest of the city." He went on to say that the new line would benefit the citizens of Baltimore, and that "this road will confer upon them ... a direct avenue to the trade of the Susquehanna Valley and that of the Great West." He then added that the "commerce of these territories" was "almost unlimited and more than sufficient to feed the enterprise and employ the capital of 'many cities.'" He said that "New York and Philadelphia must, on the extension of this road to the Susquehanna river ... share with Baltimore." He thought that the expansion of this route would ultimately resolve the conflict of the past. "No Atlantic city can *ever monopolize* the trade of the west; and when this trade is ample to fill the laps of all with wealth, a liberal spirit will surely prevail, and concede to each other a fair competition."[37]

During his time with the Baltimore & Susquehanna Trimble displayed his engineering skills. He made reference to what he learned while in England. In the "Engineers Reports" of 1835 he cited *Woods' Treatise on Rail Roads*, and in his "Report of the Chief Engineer" of 1836 he referred to a situation on the Liverpool and Manchester railway.[38] Besides the difficulty with fund raising, the new railroad had to face difficult construction and engineering problems, but this gave Trimble a chance to do something that had never been done before. Though near the seaboard, the countryside exhibited an irregularity of outline with numerous high, steep hills and scattered narrow, rocky valleys.[39] Trimble began his work by surveying the country and finally presented a proposed route which would be adopted. His route called for passing over an elevation of more than 800 feet. Prior to 1837, in both America and the United Kingdom, railroads used stationary power for grades of more than 20 feet per mile, though this cost them time and frequently resulted in accidents. Trimble had a strong "determination to avoid the use of stationary power on the summit, at any reasonable cost." He used the tables computed by a French physicist to show a locomotive's tactile power at different gradients, and on the basis of tests at the approach to the summit, he determined the practicability of the rate of 84 feet per mile. The uninterrupted service and greater safety compensated for the reduced speed of the locomotives. He accomplished his objective in 1838 and so impressed the management of the Massachusetts and Western that they used his method to cross the Berkshires, and shortly after that other railroads followed.[40]

Trimble also began to reveal an awareness of the management issues involved in running a railroad, mainly related to cost accounting. They exceeded the planned expenses in constructing the road and he proceeded to analyze the problem. He said that "an increase in the price of labor and provisions was at the time looked for, but not to the discouraging extent which has been realized." He went on to say that "this increase has exceeded fifty per cent." The labor increase reflected the shortage of unskilled workers that resulted from the construction of numerous turnpikes, canals, and railroads. He also ran into difficulties in the "excavation of earth and rock." At this time men accomplished such massive earth movement with no more than a shovel and their backs. In reporting the extent of the problem he could only say that he had intended to present "a more detailed estimate of the cost of the road," but that "the great irregularity of ground on the numerous steep and rocky side hills, prevented the completion of the requisite calculations in time."[41]

He continued to develop his professional network. With the Baltimore & Susquehanna he once again worked with Major William Gibbs McNeill, one of those originally assigned to survey the Baltimore & Ohio. McNeill had been a consulting engineer and Trimble began consultations with him in May of 1835. Trimble encountered another familiar name, General Joseph Gardner Swift, who had been responsible for Thayer's command of West Point. Swift had been engineer with the Baltimore & Susquehanna before Trimble. Trimble would be closely associated with the general's brother a few years later at the Philadelphia, Wilmington, & Baltimore Railroad. He also established a first relationship with the Ewell family when he hired Benjamin Ewell as an engineer. Benjamin had worked as a teacher at West Point after graduation, but on September 30, 1836, he quickly resigned his commission to accept the job offered by Trimble. He received $2.50 per hour with guaranteed promotion, though he ended up staying in the railroad business for a very short time.[42]

A brief glimpse at the Ewell family at this time is worthwhile. It offers not only a background to Richard S. Ewell, who would become the superior officer, comrade, and adversary to Trimble during the Civil War, but also gives an opportunity to compare and contrast Trimble with another future Confederate general. Though the Ewells came from a different family background, they shared some characteristics with Trimble. Benjamin, born in 1811, was Trimble's junior, and Richard, born in 1817, was even younger. The Ewells owned plantations and slaves in tidewater Virginia and both sons went to West Point. Though a planter family in the eighteenth century, the first two generations of Ewells made bricks.

The Ewells had lived in Virginia since the mid-seventeenth century, but like the Trimbles, the family did not hesitate to change residency in seeking fulfillment of their personal needs. In a cosmopolitan fashion they migrated freely across the borders of the states. Thomas Ewell, father of Benjamin and Richard, attended medical school at the University of Pennsylvania in Philadelphia, later worked at New York City's naval yard, and then moved to Washington D. C.

Their family, on either the father's or mother's side, offered no more resistance to modernity than did Trimble's. The father raised his family in the environment of the American Enlightenment and associated with men such Dr. Benjamin Rush and Thomas Jefferson. He also published several books on his medical research, and "shocked the 'delicate and refined females' of that day by attributing their fainting fits, tears, and tantrums to illness of body and not to sensibility of soul." The Ewells' mother, Elizabeth Stoddert, came from an old aristocratic Maryland family. Her father, like the Presstman family, participated in the commercial economy of Maryland; he owned a tobacco export company. She too lived in Philadelphia and visitors to her family home included Aaron Burr, Henry Lee, Oliver Wolcott, and John and Abigail Adams.

Both Benjamin and Richard sought personal fulfillment through a career, and neither one gave undue consideration to any state or regional loyalties in the process. Though the Ewells had a more impressive family background than Trimble, their father did have financial difficulties and the immediate family struggled for survival; the boys could not depend on family fortune. Like Trimble, Benjamin and Richard went to West Point to prepare for a career. Richard continued in the military while Benjamin, after his try at a railroad career, ended up teaching at William and Mary. In pursuit of personal needs they lived on both sides of the Mason-Dixon Line. They did not appear to resist the forces of modernization but rather followed the path that appeared to them to offer the greatest opportunity.⁴³

Employment with the Baltimore & Susquehanna once again brought the young Trimble family back to the city of Baltimore. They initially took up residence at the Eutaw House, where the charge, including board, light, and fire, came to "$1,800 per an." Trimble lived there with his wife, son David, his wife's niece, Lydia, and a servant girl. Maria gave birth to a second son they named William, after his maternal grandfather. With the new addition the Trimbles decided to rent a small house, the first home of their own since their marriage. They passed the summers in Spring Dale in the vicinity of York.⁴⁴

During the 1830s Trimble also began to diversify his business interest. In addition to his employment with the Baltimore & Susquehanna he also directed construction of the line between York and Wrightsville, part of the Wrightsville Railroad Company. The Philadelphia and Reading Railroad hired him as a consultant on their Harrisburg extension. He worked as a consultant on three different railroads in the Carolinas. The mayor and city council of Baltimore hired him to prepare a feasibility study for a cross-cut canal linking the city to the Chesapeake and Ohio canal. In 1838 alone he earned salaries and fees in excess of $20,000.⁴⁵

In 1840 a group of Philadelphia businessmen persuaded Trimble to build an iron foundry in Pottsville, Pennsylvania. The citizens of that town wanted to capitalize on their deposits of anthracite coal. They claimed that they "could supply the present wants of the country for which we are now dependent upon foreigners."⁴⁶ Trimble worked on experiments for the smelting of iron from anthracite coal. Though Maria loved Newport she wrote, "I cannot describe my horror at the sight of Pottsville. Never before have I been at a place that was so dreadful to my feelings." Maria fulfilled her obligation to her husband — "business brings Mr. Trimble to this place, therefore tis my duty to be contented and I will at all events try to be so" — but she made it clear that if she should die that she "not be buried at or near Pottsville." She found some relief when her sister, Georgiana, and her favorite niece, Lydia Presstman, visited. She even found an occasion for joy with her husband's baptism and subsequent confirmation in the local Episcopal Church. Maria survived until the firing of the foundry's furnace in early January of 1841. The Trimbles moved to Wilmington, Delaware, in August of that year in anticipation of Isaac's new position with the Philadelphia, Wilmington, and Baltimore Railroad. Though not in Baltimore, they did live reasonably close to Maria's family and no doubt found many opportunities to visit.⁴⁷

He worked at different positions between 1838 and 1842, and continued to move freely about the nation. Neither he nor his wife expressed any resentment toward the states in the North, but rather judged each location on its own merits. He began with a two-year "respite" in Newport, Rhode Island, and stayed in what Maria fondly called "dear Rose Cottage." During the 1830s Trimble worked toward fulfilling his needs for self-esteem and toward self-actualization. He developed his skills and reputation as a railroad man. He found many opportunities during this decade of rapid growth for the new industry, and he faced little competition since the demand for skilled professionals far outstripped the supply. He recognized the level of his ability and patiently worked his way up to the position of superintendent which he accepted from the Philadelphia, Wilmington and Baltimore Railroad. He continued to lack a strong attachment to any geographical identity, but strengthened his ties with his professional community. He based his decisions to move strictly on career opportunity rather than preference for a particular location. Nonetheless, his wife continued to pull him toward her family and home in Baltimore and no doubt led to his accepting the job with the PW&B and his first long-term connection to Baltimore. Maria felt a sense of duty to her husband, but could not deny the love and attachment she felt for her family. She did not express any city, state, or regional bias toward the various places in which they lived, but her family lived south of the Mason-Dixon and she continued to have a strong commitment to her family. At times her separation anxiety became so great, such as during the trip to England, that she felt physically ill.

Trimble worked among the forces of modernization in the United States, and found no contradiction to his wife's ties to the old Baltimore elite. Neither Trimble nor his wife expressed any fear or resentment toward the new city with its changes, physical and cultural. His business associations showed no bias toward the new or the old, but rather an acceptance of association with those who had the power. In his 1837 report to the management of the Baltimore & Susquehanna he made an appeal for compromise in the war between Baltimore and Philadelphia. In summation, in 1841 he demonstrated no southern loyalties, though at this time intense regionalism had not yet become obvious. Between 1841 and 1860 the pace of change would accelerate for Baltimore and the nation, so that Trimble would be living in a significantly different society by April 19, 1861. The foundation for that change appeared in the 1830s.

4

Becoming a Modern Businessman

September 1848

This is now the third day that I have been in this house. I have been struck with the regularity and order, which reign everywhere. It is Uncle's mind that hath done this, for all strive to please him, and you know he is the perfection of neatness and order. I have never seen a family whose members were so devoted to each other ... Uncle and Aunt are very unlike. Yet what is wanting in one is found in the other. Both are very active, yet while he acts never without deliberation, she is the creature of impulse. Both are firm and decided, yet she arrives at her decision with wonderful rapidity, he by degrees. I should imagine Aunt to be oftenest in the wrong, yet her perception is so quick, her intellect so strong, that it would be strange if her errors were very frequent. I should take Aunt, when not shrouded in grief as she is now, to be very sprightly and gay.[1] Indeed she told me herself that usually she is a great talker. Uncle is more quiet. He has the Trimble tinge of melancholy and yet at times is very cheerful and pleasant ... I may be mistaken in all I have said, but that they love each other, I cannot doubt for a moment. Such tender anxious solicitude about each other's welfare as I have never seen before marks every member of the family from the youngest of the family up. Indeed, Mother, I think they love one another just as much as we do at home. Yet they show it so differently. We never kiss. They do often. We seem anxious to hide our affection, half unwilling to let it be known how very dear we are to each other. They are ever anxious to show their love and with so deep a sincerity that you cannot doubt it.[2]

Historians have thoroughly examined the events of the 1840s and

1850s in search of the causes for the greatest war in American history. What is most remarkable about studying the records of Isaac Trimble's life is the lack of any indication that he would not only join the fight for Southern independence, but that he would continue remain loyal to the cause until his death many years after Appomattox. Prior to the war he dedicated his life to the pursuit of his personal needs, as most people do. The lack of letters or autobiographical discussion of the newspaper events leads us to conclude that he did not invest a great deal of time or energy outside of his personal world. Nonetheless, he lived during a period of rapid change and in the process became buffeted about by national and local trends. He became molded by the events and contributed to them. His personal struggles are of interest in trying to understand this critical period in American history. In many ways he reflected national trends, but he also had his unique personal experiences. It is this combination of cultural and individual influences that create the challenge for social scientists and historians in trying to find dominant patterns from the larger picture. No two individuals are exactly alike, yet everyone has some characteristics in common with others. He had little in common with some Confederate leaders, but had a great deal in common with some others. It is this commonality which is of value in understanding the trends in the United States during its greatest ordeal.

By April of 1861 both Trimble and his community had survived traumatic experiences related to modernization which had some effect on the way they reacted to the events of national importance. On one hand, they had grown more willing to compromise in hopes of ending the violence which plagued the city just prior to the Civil War. On the other hand, some old wounds had not completely healed.

Trimble turned to his immediate family to satisfy his need to belong. Maslow's third level of needs, belongingness, can be satisfied in different ways, though bonds with community and family are the most common. William McClintick wrote the above letter to his mother while visiting his Uncle Isaac in 1848. It suggests that Trimble sought gratification of these needs within his household. He did establish a community identity in Baltimore, but that came in response to his wife's needs. He also developed a professional identity, but he often made career choices based on his wife's desires; he accepted the job with the Philadelphia, Wilmington, and Baltimore Railroad so that his wife could be closer to her family in Baltimore. He pursued his career and provided for his family. As he resolved any identity issues he proceeded toward the pursuit of self-esteem and self-actualization.

Trimble went through two major ordeals in the mid-1850s and these events would not only retard his progress toward self-actualization but would have considerable impact on his self-esteem and belongingness needs. A new president for the PW&B brought about the first event. Not only did Trimble lose his job with the company but faced charges of misconduct in his office of superintendent. Shortly after an inquiry into the charges Trimble lost his wife. Like the child so long before who stood up to the boys throwing stones at him, Trimble did not surrender to his anger or grief. He continued on his career path in railroads and soon remarried, but the scars remained.

During the antebellum period modern businessmen like Trimble became perpetrators and recipients of internal aggression, which in turn jeopardized the belongingness needs. As pointed out in the introduction, men practice two main types of aggression, between groups and within groups. The former serves to satisfy the basic needs of providing security and safety. The latter arises as individuals struggle to fulfill the higher needs and end up competing with each other. When an opportunity appears for promotion only one applicant can succeed. This type of aggression involves dominance hierarchies and rituals of display.[3] The increased competition in modern society weakens the more basic belongingness needs. Maslow identified this level of needs as the greatest avenue of disorientation. These feelings result from the process of industrialization, as people are torn from their roots and lose the feeling of belonging with their local neighborhoods or communities.[4] Conflict and aggression became more prevalent in response to the loss of community identity. Trimble became a victim of this aggressive environment within the corporation.

The growing world economy drastically altered Trimble's hometown, and these changes would have a direct influence on both Trimble and his community when the Union began to divide in 1861. Baltimore became unrecognizable physically as the economic boom generated rapid population growth. The city became competitive globally and was a leader in the South American trade. The British Corn Laws opened the grain trade to Americans in 1846. This provided greater opportunity for the Baltimore merchants in the world markets, but it also strengthened the food-producing western states. The city had to develop policies on how to deal with competition from not only other cities but other regions. It could not find universal agreement on the best battle plans.[5]

In many ways the development of the southern trade conventions, which Baltimore participated in, reflected the nature of the growing complexity of interregional competition. Some in the South saw the conventions as a means of developing the region's economic advantages. The first four of these conventions (1837–1839) aimed solely at the establishment of direct trade with Europe. They called attention to the profits made by modern cities and the advantage of keeping those profits in the South.[6] In the next three, 1845–1851, they concentrated on internal improvements.[7] The aims became more numerous and complex from 1852 to 1859.[8] Only in the last phase, after 1859, did they reflect extreme sectionalism.[9] Even the states attending the conventions changed over the years. In the 1849 St. Louis conference numerous central and western states attended, including Pennsylvania, New York, Ohio, Indiana, Iowa, Wisconsin, and Michigan. It could be said that St. Louis was not really a southern city, but the Memphis convention of the same year attracted delegates from New York, Pennsylvania, Illinois, and Ohio.[10]

The 1852 convention in Baltimore showed that some of the leading citizens had a regional identity, but also provides an example of the continued fierceness in economic competition between cities. As previously mentioned, representatives attended from several states that could not even be called border states, much less southern. Brantz Mayer read an address on behalf of the Board of Trade and assured those present that Baltimore was a southern city.[11] This may have been a strategy for some of the economic leaders of Baltimore to make the city the center of southern trade, an ambition shared by other cities of the region. New Orleans had always been suspicious of internal improvements as an attempt to divert her trade to Charleston, Baltimore, or Mobile.[12] Following the convention, the press of New Orleans claimed that Baltimore wanted to divert her trade. The *Richmond Enquirer* accused the opening address of making too many allusions to Baltimore, referring to Mayer's desire to make that city "the great central axle of trade," and "the central entrepot of the Union on the tidewater—the great receptacle of internal produce and foreign distribution."[13]

The political environment also contributed to the reaction of Trimble and Baltimore in 1861. Baltimore became divided politically, in part because of the increased population and increasing ethnic diversity. The city became a center for the Know-Nothing Party. It has been claimed that the national platform of the party found greater acceptance in border-state Maryland because the state lacked strong influences from either the growing antislavery sentiments of the North or the Deep South defenders of slavery.[14] Know-Nothings of Maryland tended to be former Democrats more than former Whigs, they found greater attachment to the nativist secret societies, but they felt more pro-American rather than anti-immigrant or anti-Catholic. Violence resulted from "tensions associated with partisan realignment and the intensity of ethnocultural issues, and was often initiated by Democrats." On the positive side, they did have a legislative record as creditable as that of other parties, they had a centralized organization unique in American political history, and they "served as a catalyst for political change in the 1850s."[15] In Baltimore many had a fear of immigrants. Their hierarchy of demonology put Roman Catholics on the lowest tier, followed by immigrants, politicians, and finally sectional zealots.[16] These fears spread to the Maryland countryside as the effects of the city's growth spread.[17]

None of the records available from Trimble or other sources reflect any keen political interest or action on his part. The modernization process made Trimble's hometown less harmonious, but also made life more difficult in his professional community. The maturing of the business environment had a more direct impact on Trimble. When he went to England he represented three different railroads in his research. There seemed to be opportunity for all in this new industry. As time progressed the industry became much more competitive and in the end altered the way the companies were managed.

Before the Civil War Trimble and the men who built the railroad industry laid the foundations for modern management. Railroads began to mature by the 1850s. It became clear that one could not simply construct a railway and wait for the profits to come flowing in; one could not find success in the railroad profession with technical knowledge alone. Railroads became America's first big business and began the development of the management profession. The top men in the corporate bureaucracy developed the new skills needed to manage a modern corporation, but they also began to realize the need for a code of ethics. The modern corporate environment proved profitable and grew, but in the process internal aggression increased as the new hierarchy became a new social ladder. Not only did the men within fight each other for the next rung up that ladder, but disagreements on the best way to run the company often turned into fights to gain control.

The company where Trimble went to work in 1842, the Philadelphia, Wilmington and Baltimore Railroad, came into existence as a result of the maturing of the industry. Immediately after the success of the Baltimore & Ohio numerous railroads sprang up around the nation. Soon one could travel by rail between major cities, but long distance travel often involved more than one company. In January of 1838 one could travel between Baltimore and Philadelphia by rail, but it took three separate lines to do so. The Philadelphia and Delaware County Railroad Company had been formed in April of 1831; this line connected Philadelphia with Wilmington. They later changed their name to the Philadelphia, Wilmington, & Baltimore (PW&B), which became the name of a new company. The Wilmington and Susquehanna incorporated in January of 1832; it went from Wilmington to the Susquehanna River. The Delaware and Maryland Railroad Company acquired a charter in April of 1835, and that line went from the river to Baltimore.[18] "It became evident that the permanent and indivisible combination of the three companies, as one corporation, would prevent the danger and discord of jarring interests and sectional prejudice." The men behind the unification of the three corporations recognized that they could "secure that harmony of action in their united efforts for the accommodation of the public, so indispensable to their mutual utility, existence, and advantage."[19] On February 15, 1838, the three separate companies merged to form the PW&B, thus connecting the cities of Philadelphia and Baltimore by a single railway company.[20]

Though unified, the new company faced several challenges. The PW&B had capital of $2,250,000, and the new board elected Matthew Newkirk, Esq., as president. They completed the final link between Gray's Ferry and Philadelphia, and reported to the stockholders that "the expenses of the corporation have been diminished, the revenue increased, and the advantages in energy, promptness, and unity of action ... have been, thus far, satisfactorily realized, and every assurance afforded of continued and increasing prosperity."[21] The problems they identified included poorly graded foundations, poorly laid track, few depots and water stations; they also needed more cars and engines. They required more than $4.5 million to implement the needed improvements, "in other words, the company found themselves with a new and incomplete road, and burthened with a debt almost equal to their capital stock."[22] Attempts to raise the needed funds in Europe failed. Their insistence upon declaring dividends to the stockholders only added to the burden. This is the condition that existed when Trimble started work.

In 1842 the company began to make the changes needed to survive and become profitable. A special meeting of the board of directors decided to execute two mortgages "covering nearly $3,000,000 of the indebtedness of the company, and securing an extension of demands upon it."[23] Trimble became superintendent and chief engineer in April.[24] Newkirk resigned the presidency and M. Brooke Buckley replaced him on June 1. Also in 1842 the company completed its depot in Philadelphia at Eleventh and Market streets. They found the track "to be unserviceable, in consequence of the nature of its construction, the pattern of lightness of the rail." It then "became necessary to make preparations to replace it with a more substantial one, between Philadelphia and Wilmington." Under Trimble's supervision they completed most of that by 1845. They also acquired additional rolling stock. In 1850 they completed Baltimore's President Street station.[25]

An 1849 handbill of the Philadelphia, Wilmington and Baltimore Rail Road Company.

4. Becoming a Modern Businessman

PASSENGER AND FREIGHT STATIONS, PRESIDENT STREET, BALTIMORE.

The President Street Station of the PW&B Railroad was built and opened in 1850, during the time that Isaac Trimble was chief engineer for that company. This illustration is from a guide published in 1850.

During these times top management experienced rapid turnover but Trimble survived. Buckley declined re-election and the board chose Edward D. Dale in January of 1846. Dale did some further restructuring of the debt. He resigned the office in July of 1848. He could not be replaced until the following January when the board persuaded William H. Swift to fill the vacancy.[26] Swift, the younger brother of General Swift, had crossed Trimble's path a few times in his career. He graduated from West Point in 1819, the year after Trimble began, and had been resident and constructing engineer of the Massachusetts Western Railway. He resigned his commission on July 31, 1849, to accept the presidency and thus began his civilian career.[27] Swift resigned on February 28, 1851, and the man who made the greatest changes, Samuel M. Felton, replaced him.[28]

Samuel Felton fired Trimble from the PW&B, and in the process the two men became enemies. Trimble might have harbored some resentment of the fact that his new boss entered the railroad industry 14 years later than he did, as well as being five years his junior. Felton was born in Newbury, Massachusetts, on July 17, 1809. He often boasted of the poverty that he grew up in, claiming that it helped to mold his character. He had to work to put himself through Harvard, graduating in 1834. After two years of teaching he began a career in engineering and did his first railroad work in 1841. Despite the improvements made since 1842 the company had serious problems and Felton began immediately to implement his solutions. During the years that Felton held the office of president, 1851–1865, the line did resolve most of its problems and become a prosperous company.[29] His "first efforts, were ... directed to making the road what its business required it to be, — a first-class road." To do this he had to relay track, purchase new rolling stock, and construct new stations and greatly improve the existing ones. By 1855 the number of passengers increased by more than 200 percent, up to 653,000 from 297,000 in 1850. The receipts increased from $583,924 in 1851 to $942,000 in 1855, a 61 percent increase.[30] Over the years "all these changes, with the reduced time of transit between the two cities, had the effect of fitting the road for favorable comparison with any other of the first class in the country."[31]

Professional management began in the railroad industry. As the railroad business became more competitive it became important to have good management, and though most of the changes came after the war, some started in the antebellum period. The top salaried managers became increasingly technical and professional with promotions based on training and experience rather than family relationships. Though some factories existed in America before 1860, the largest one, Pepperell Manufacturing company at Biddeford, Maine, exceeded an expense budget of $300,000 only one year during the 1850s. In addition to size, railroads had other characteristics that generated a need for professional managers. Compared to manufacturing, railroads had more employees, a greater variety of activities and facilities, and a greater geographical spread. This made it necessary for managers to control the activities of men they rarely talked to or saw, thereby creating a sophisticated bureaucracy. The management had to make more numerous and more complicated decisions. Factory managers might be concerned about the safety of their workers, but railroad managers had to be concerned about the safety of their customers. They had to make long-term decisions on the setting of rates and the determination of costs, profits and losses, thus increasing the demand for a more sophisticated accounting system.[32]

As superintendent of the PW&B Trimble had to learn about management in addition to the technical skills that had put him in the position. Though not the largest of the railroads, the PW&B had expenses that approached $300,000, larger than most manufacturing companies. When Trimble started as engineer in 1842 the PW&B exceeded many other lines in length, including the Boston and Lowell, the Boston and Providence, and the Philadelphia and Reading.[33]

The management of staff for the railroad proved to be complex and required sophisticated skills. Covering a distance of almost 100 miles, the company had a large geographical spread for that time, and with it came the problems of controlling employees scattered all along the line. Trimble had to get men to do their jobs even though he seldom saw them; he had to utilize bureaucracy. He understood these skills by the time he became superintendent. He displayed an awareness of maintaining good relations with the workers, regardless of rank. As mentioned earlier, the construction of so many transportation projects created a labor shortage throughout the nation which put the workers in a better bargaining position.[34] When Trimble began he had "instructions from the Board of Directors, both verbal and written, requiring the General Superintendent to retrench expenses in every possible way." He made the necessary staff reductions confident that he "neither oppressed nor [did] injustice to any, however obscure or respectable."[35] He had an understanding of bureaucracy including the potential cost savings that can come from restructuring. In his first year, to help generate the requested cost savings, he reduced the number of supervisors on the Baltimore to Havre de Grace road from two to one. By doing so "a saving was effected both in pay and in the number employed."[36]

Trimble's management of resources also became more complicated with the great geographical spread and the diversity of assets which the railroad controlled. He had divisions that paralleled the three companies that existed prior to the merger of 1838: from Baltimore to Havre de Grace, from the Susquehanna to Wilmington, and then Wilmington to Philadelphia. He based the remaining organization of his reports to the board of directors on the variety of assets: bridges, engines and tenders, passenger cars, wood (for construction and fuel), and oil. He also had to manage depots and even a ferry.[37]

As superintendent, Trimble had a variety of complex decisions to deal with. Safety became a primary concern. The PW&B maintained a good record, even during the years of financial difficulty. From its formation in 1838 to 1855 the company had no fatalities, "with the exception of a single individual, who, leaning out of a window, contrary to the regulations, came in contact with a bridge timber." Except for that one incident the company boasted of their safety record as a "source of the keenest gratification to the company," and that it "should inspire the public with an unusual feeling of security."[38] Another example of the variety of problems Trimble had to contend with came in 1849; the company exceeded its expense budget because of the "ice blockade in the Susquehanna river."[39]

Trimble had an understanding of the importance of consistency and accuracy in the accounting records of the corporation. In the early nineteenth century no organization had established standards for accounting. The American Institute of Certified Public Accountant, Securities and Exchange Commission, and Financial Accounting Standards Board remained decades off; no one made pronouncements that are now called Generally Accepted Accounting Principles. In 1842 Trimble recognized the importance of comparison in financial information when he said that it "is necessary to enable the Company to form a comparison between the last and former years," and that such a comparison would help to "correct such abuses and neglect as may be said to creep, almost naturally, into the management of a large work."[40] To make comparison more meaningful Trimble realized the importance of the classification of expenses, an issue in accounting regulations today. In the 1848 annual report he referred to the classification of expenditures, and in 1849 he urged the "adoption by all rail-road companies of one uniform mode of presenting facts connected with the construction of each road, its principle characteristics, and the arrangement of accounts exhibiting annual expenses."[41]

The accounting methods of the day failed to adequately distinguish between capital improvement and operating expenses, thus making it more difficult to analyze financial statements. The importance of cost control is basic, but the analysis of financial records to achieve that objective is more sophisticated. The adoption of an accrual accounting system over a cash basis system became more important. When discussing the finances of 1844 Trimble commented that "it will be perceived that a large amount of these expenditures [do] not properly belong to the ordinary cost of 'working' a Road, but has resulted in part, form a general and extensive improvement in the character of the Road and its machinery."[42] In the 1846 report he said, "In conclusion, I would again refer to the tabular statements of expenditures, to show that though large, a great proportion of outlays, as in the previous year, are of a character not pertaining to the ordinary working expenses." Though he understood that such cost did not belong with regular operating expenses he did not envision the amortization of capital accounts that is standard practice today. Trimble said that "many of these costly improvements should have been provided and paid for, years ago, out of the original construction funds, instead of coming, as now, out of the current revenue of the Road."[43] He did not provide the solutions, but recognition of the problem is the first step to finding answers. He clearly recognized the importance of good accounting records in the management of a large corporation.

Felton's success at turning around the PW&B suggest the incompetency of the earlier management, including Trimble, but this might be an invalid assumption. Though the railroad experienced growth prior to Felton's arrival it accelerated considerably after he took over. From 1838 to 1840, before Trimble started, the number of passengers increased fifty one percent, and between 1840 and 1850 it went up an additional 35 percent; however, between 1850 and 1855, the first five years under Felton, the number increased 120 percent. Likewise, revenues increased 56 percent between 1838 and 1851 but went up 162 percent between 1851 and 1855. It is clear that the company improved its operations after Felton took over, but this does not necessarily mean that the previous management lacked competency. First of all, they had already started many of the improvements which Felton completed, but their financial problems allowed for slow progress. Second, and more importantly, the changes that came with Felton represented a maturing of the industry. As stated in the guide published at Felton's request, "when the line was built and stocked, railroads were in their infancy; there were no men of experience upon the subject in the country, and all the roads then built were 'buying experience,' from which the more recent ones have largely profited."[44] Trimble survived in the company for more than a dozen years while several presidents came and went, suggesting that the board of directors found his work satisfactory. Felton apparently did not agree; shortly after he took charge he fired Trimble.

An analysis of the charges brought against Trimble not only reveals something about his experience and character during the time he served as superintendent of the PW&B, but it also reveals something about the nature of corporate business during this period. If it is assumed that Trimble and the witnesses did not lie, then it can be concluded that Trimble's problems represent a difference in philosophy about what constituted ethical behavior in the modern corporate environment. Just as business lacked any accounting regulations, it also lacked guidance in management and ethics. The men running the companies had technical training, such as engineering, and did not study business or management as businessmen and women do today. Trimble faced a total of 13 different charges of wrongdoing while he worked for the PW&B. The committee that served as jury found him guilty of some and innocent of others. The case did not revolve around simply a presentation and debate of disputed facts, but rather around defining appropriate behavior of a superintendent and the responsibilities of upper management.

The first four charges stemmed from a relationship Trimble had with a man named Philip Quigley, an employee of the company. First, they claimed that he had a partnership with the man "engaged in contracts off the line of the Road." The second charge said that Trimble permitted men working for Quigley to pass over the Road without charge, and then went on to suggest that Quigley received "unusual and extravagant compensation for work performed for the Railroad Company." Clearly this implied that Trimble used company funds to compensate Quigley for efforts extended to their private enterprises. The third charge said that they transported materials for this partnership without charge. The fourth claimed that Quigley utilized men on the PW&B payroll to do work for Trimble, and that they also used company materials.[45]

Trimble began by defining his relationship with Quigley and then explained the basic philosophy behind his actions. He said, "as early as the year 1844 I became interested by purchase in Howe's Patent for the construction of truss frames for bridges, roofs, &c.," and that "with the full knowledge of your predecessors as President, and also of others in the Board of Directors, I was pecuniarily interested under this patent." Quigley worked, on a contract basis, as supervisor of this enterprise "dividing his time between such work and that of the Railroad Company, —from which he received a per-diem allowance when actually at work on the Road." Trimble confessed to allowing Quigley's men passage on the trains, but justified it by saying that "they were frequently called to work on the Road and at all times considered themselves as Road hands, from having been so long in the Company's service." Trimble went on to say that "Mr. Quigley often desired to leave the Road, as he found work elsewhere more profitable," and Trimble believed retaining the supervisor to be critical since "his leaving the Road would have been regarded by me and others, as a great misfortune."[46]

In response to these charges he confessed to the first two, though he did not feel that he did anything unethical; he completely denied the next two. To the first he said, "it is proper to state that it is not unusual for a Supervisor of work on one Road, to be allowed to engage in 'planning,' or other business off the Road," and then he gave examples of other companies in which they had such a policy, including the Reading, the Baltimore & Ohio, and the Baltimore & Susquehanna. To the second charge he said that by issuing Quigley's men passes "I did no more than what I considered was for the advantage of the Road, and due to him for long and faithful service." On the third charge he said that "Mr. Quigley has always paid the regular freight on all materials sent over the Road." On the fourth he stated, "I can state that no person while paid by the Company ever worked for me, or on my property, in any instance, with my knowledge."[47]

The "Committee," appointed from the board of directors, did conclude Trimble to be guilty of some of these charges, especially since he confessed his guilt, but they did not express great concern over his actions. They gave "as short and succinct an answer to each of the proposed inquiries as they [could], consistently with a clear expression of their views." On the first charge they answered "affirmative," since Trimble made no denial of the charge. On the second they accepted Trimble's admission with no comment on the correctness of his actions, but they rejected the notion that Quigley received "unusual and extravagant compensation." On the third charge they considered the possibility that Quigley may have transported materials over the line, but they said "that they are not satisfied that Mr. Trimble knew the fact, or connived at the practice." In the case of the fourth charge they said that "the proof is clear" that Trimble "did, at different times, employ on his own business workmen in the general employment of the Company." They added, "it is also clear that, on occasions he paid these workmen out of his own pocket," but that "on other occasions, there is great difficulty in deciding by whom these men were paid." Similarly, in the case of the materials used they saw proof that Trimble paid for some but could not satisfy themselves the he reimbursed the company for all supplies used for his purposes. They did leave an opening for his innocence by ending with the statement that they "have not yet been paid for."[48]

The next three charges related to Trimble's relationship with a man named Joseph Brooks. The fifth simply established a relationship between the two men. The sixth charge said that Trimble permitted Brooks to transport materials "over the Road free of charge," and that he permitted Brooks "to take or use ... property of the Company, without making any compensation." The seventh said that Trimble "permitted the said Brooks to receive monthly pay while he was engaged in contract work for the Company, or in work for any other person."[49]

Trimble pleaded innocent to these three charges. He emphatically stated, "I had no connection on my own account with Joseph Brooks in any contract whatever" and added, "I have had no business transactions with him except such as belonged to the discharge of my duty as General Superintendent," though he did admit one exception which he proceeded to explain. He had an arrangement with Brooks related to the procuring of wood-ties, but produced receipts and evidence that he made this arrangement for the benefit of the company. On the sixth charge Trimble admitted that Brooks "was permitted by agreement, to bring feed from Baltimore to Stemmer's Run, free of charge." He then explained an arrangement made between the company and Brooks, and that the past presidents knew about and agreed to it. Trimble went on to say that he "considered this a privilege, from which the Company derived more benefit than Mr. Brooks, as it facilitated the delivery of cross-ties." On the seventh he denied knowledge of any company materials used by Brooks.[50]

The committee absolved Trimble of any wrong doing in the fifth, sixth, and seventh charges. On the fifth they stated that they did "not find any legal or reliable evidence before them, that Mr. Trimble ever was concerned with Mr. Brooks," with the exception of the procurement of wood for cross-ties. On the sixth they said they could find no proof other than those "acknowledged by himself, and for which, he states, he was willing to pay." On the seventh charge Trimble admitted to Brooks's name appearing on the payroll as supervisor of the road, and while so engaged he got cross-ties for the company, but that "this was done with the knowledge of Capt. Swift when president of the Road."[51]

The next three charges related to business arrangements between Trimble and Henry Wempe, or the previously mentioned Brooks. The eighth claimed a partnership which involved speculating in the supply of wood for the road. From this stemmed the ninth charge which stated that they "excited" hostility "along the line of the Railroad from Havre-de-Grace to Baltimore," and that by his action they refused the "community the same facilities for the transportation and storage of wood as enjoyed by themselves." Some filed complaints with the city council of Baltimore, and to the General Assembly of Maryland about "an unjust monopoly of the wood traffic on the part of the Agents of the Road, and for a general disregard of the interests and convenience of the public." The tenth charge claimed that Trimble used company men to do work for Wempe in the wood business.[52]

Trimble denied these three charges while offering explanation as to how the misunderstanding came about. He stated clearly, "I am not a partner with Joseph Brooks or Henry Wempe in wood business or any other," and went on to say "this whole business about the purchase and sale of wood, has been the subject of misunderstanding and comment without my being aware of it." He then explained the difficulty in getting sufficient cross-ties for the quantity of new rail expected in early 1851. The responsibility lay with Trimble to secure the needed wood. In the process Brooks, on Trimble's behalf, made an agreement with Mrs. Ridgely in which they could get the needed timber, but that Brooks must clear the remainder of the land and cut the felled timber into "cord-wood." Some assumed Trimble to be involved in this arrangement, which he denied. He presented evidence that the only wood transported over the line fulfilled the need for cross-ties, and that Trimble "had no benefit, directly or indirectly in any contracts made by Brooks, or work done by Wempe." He went on to point out that neither the city council nor the state assembly attached any importance to the complaints lodged with them. On the tenth charge he stated, "I have not authorized any person in the Company's service to work for Brooks and Wempe in the wood business, or in any other."[53]

The committee cleared Trimble in these three charges. On the eighth they found the evidence and records too confusing to make any definite statement. On the ninth they recognized that complaints had been made to the city council and state assembly, but they could "not find any evidence to implicate Mr. Trimble in the charge of speculating in wood, or of monopolizing the wood traffic on the Road, or that these complaints worked any inquiry to the Company, either before the City Council or the Legislature." On the tenth charge they agreed that men in the employ of the company did work for Wempe, but that Wempe used other persons to do their work in the service of the company.[54]

The committee accepted the eleventh charge, which said that Trimble allowed manure to pass over the road free, "or at unreasonably low rates."[55] Trimble admitted the shipment of manure to his place, but in April he "gave directions to have all manure, &c., sent to [his] place regularly manifested and charged to [him], and he produced receipts that he paid $171.88 of a bill for $865.90. He claimed the remainder to be compensation of the company use of a spring located on his property.[56] The committee stated "that some manure, marketing and other things for Mr. Trimble passed over the Road, on which no freight has yet been paid."[57]

The committee also recognized some irregularity in the twelfth charge, but Trimble did not see anything wrong in his actions. The charge stated that Trimble employed Henry Wempe to purchase lots of land belonging to the Canton Company, on his behalf. It also said that Trimble had been directed to purchase this land, "for and on behalf of the Railroad Company," and then went on to say that Wempe possessed some of the land not transferred over to the company.[58] Trimble admitted ordering the purchase in his name, claiming the he could get a better price that way. He also admitted granting permission for Wempe to make use of land not utilized by the company.[59] In their report the committee simply repeated the story told to them, recording that Wempe did in fact build a house on the land, but they made no statement on whether they considered this to be right or wrong.[60]

The committee completely absolved Trimble of any responsibility in the thirteenth charge. The final charge questioned the accounting of scrap iron from the relaying of track between Philadelphia and Baltimore during the years 1850 to 1852.[61] Trimble responded "the old rails taken up since 1850, have been sold by Captain Swift, Mr. Felton, Mr. Campbell and myself, at various times." He then claimed that proceeds from the sale "passed through the hands of the agents of the Road," and that they had been "received by them or the Treasurer of the Company."[62] The committee agreed that all of the scrap iron had not been accounted for, but stated "they cannot conceive that it would be right or just to hold Mr. Trimble responsible for the loss."[63]

These charges generally resulted from a lack of clear definitions of ethical business conduct. Today there are numerous laws that did not exist in 1854 as well as several professional organizations which express opinions on business ethics. In 1854 large business had few authorities to turn to with questions relating to conflict of interest and internal control. Felton turned to Benjamin Latrobe as an authority on business ethics.

Felton submitted into evidence the responses Latrobe gave to questions previously asked in writing. Latrobe occupied the office of president for the Baltimore & Ohio Railroad at the time of the hearing. Felton began by saying, "I ought to state, in justice to Mr. Latrobe, that he wished if I could consistently get along without his answers, that I would do it."[64] Felton asked Latrobe to reply to his questions without knowing the names of any of those involved, and Latrobe considered them "as abstract enquiries ... and without reference to individuals who may be concerned," and he said that under those conditions had "no difficulty in answering them."[65] It is hard to believe that Latrobe had no idea of the "individuals" concerned. He had known Trimble for years, worked in the railroad industry in Baltimore for years, and must have heard at least some rumors about the hearings despite the fact that they took place in Philadelphia.

Felton asked a total of 17 questions, and the first seven generally related to conflict of interest. Latrobe stated without qualification that "no agent, of whatever grade, should voluntarily place himself in a position which would give an interest in any way opposed to that of the Company he serves," and went on to say "consequently he should have no share direct or indirect, in any contract between that Company and another party."[66] Latrobe assumed contracts to be adversarial and that by definition the interest of one party stood opposite that of the other, and for that reason one man could not stand on both sides of the fence.[67]

Felton basically accused Trimble of thievery with the remaining 10 questions regarding the proper use or accounting for corporate assets; modern auditors now call this internal control. Most of these questions related to the specific charges already discussed, to which Latrobe responded as one would expect. He said that no individual working for a company should use that company's labor or materials for any activities not directly related to the activities of that company. Any exchange of assets between an individual and the company should be an arm's-length transaction. In other words, any such transactions should be properly accounted for. Many of Trimble's problems stemmed from the informal methods which he used in accounting for transactions between the company and himself or those he did business with elsewhere. Several questions related to the wood transactions specifically, to which Latrobe responded by saying that such activities would be wrong.[68]

Felton claimed to be completely objective in subjecting Trimble to the hearings. He submitted a report to the board of directors on November 8, 1853, in which he referred to "rumors of an unpleasant character . . . about our late Superintendent," and that "if true in any part, it should be known to the Board to what extent, that they may take the proper action." The board accepted the report and formed a committee of five directors to investigate "the alleged official misconduct of the late Superintendent."[69] Felton expressed reservations when he said, "I had frequently heard vague rumors of official misconduct," but "only when they became often repeated, that I felt it my duty to make some general Investigation into the matter." He went on to say, "I am not to be regarded as Mr. Trimble's accuser."[70]

Trimble saw the entire incident as a personal attack by Felton, and questioned the means by which he had conducted the inquiry. He objected to the manner in which Felton interviewed the witnesses "in private, without any notice being served ... of time and place." He claimed that "had Mr. Felton asked me information upon any specific point, as other Presidents had done, I could ... have removed any doubt from his mind." He pointed out that he no longer occupied the position of superintendent, and that "no interest can be served by this prosecution," and suggested that his "character has been assailed for some ulterior purpose not yet disclosed." He continued by saying that Felton had been misled "by the craftiness of certain men, who had ends to accomplish, or resentments to gratify, or whose enmity I have provoked by a conscientious discharge of my duty to the Company." He considered the attack on his character to be serious, and expressed the desire that Felton "not escape the issue of his inconsiderate or unfair course."[71]

It is possible that the "ulterior purpose" referred to above involved nepotism on the part of Felton. Trimble did not officially accuse him; however, a friend of Felton's wrote to him claiming that Trimble had made such accusations. According to this friend, Enoch Pratt, Trimble claimed that Felton wanted to get his relatives into the company's highest offices, and that by 1854 he "had done so."[72]

Trimble never expressed any undue concern about the hearings. It is difficult to accept that they did not impact him deeply. He did make it clear that he felt the charges to be unjustified. We can only guess as to how long he might have held a grudge against Felton, but it is possible that Trimble might have felt antagonistic toward the Union when Felton took such a strong stand for it in April of 1861.

The period between 1854 and 1861 proved to be one of great transitions in the life of Trimble, which made the years just prior to the war a low point in the fulfillment of his personal needs. He had strengthened his community identity by a more extended residency in Baltimore, but he suffered some setbacks in his professional identity. The circumstances of his departure from the PW&B must have struck at his identity feelings of belonging as well as his self-esteem and self-actualization. He resigned his position as superintendent in June of 1853, left the PW&B altogether in January of 1854, and faced the hearing in December of 1854. The next few years he moved about as if searching for a new home, professionally. He formed a company based on one of his patents, he went to Cuba in 1857, and finally in 1859 became superintendent for the Baltimore and Potomac Railroad.

Trimble lost his wife shortly after his troubles with the PW&B. He clearly made numerous sacrifices in his career for his wife, which gives credence to William McClintick's description of the love and dedication Trimble felt for Maria. No document reveals the feelings or reasons behind the decision he made to marry Maria's sister, Ann Calhoun Presstman, a short time after Maria's death. It is difficult to speculate. On one hand, if the sisters had shared characteristics it would make sense that he would be attracted to Ann as well as Maria and therefore could have loved her as well. On the other hand, it could be said that he sought a replacement for his first wife by marrying her sister. In either case it will be seen that throughout the war he also had a strong attachment for his second wife.[73]

Trimble continued to prosper in the railroad community. He accepted a position as superintendent of the Philadelphia and Baltimore Central Railroad in 1854 and continued there until 1859.[74] He also had outside business activities. In 1855 he established a manufacturing company to capitalize on one of his inventions. In April he received a patent for a "wooden splice-piece for railways." This provided an improvement in the splicing of adjacent rails. He worked out plans to manufacture his invention in partnership with a man named William Huston. Huston, a machinist, had a business of his own prior to the joint effort with Trimble. They chartered the company, Trimble & Huston, in Delaware for the manufacture of this product as well as bolts, nuts, and all fixtures used in the splice.

The company sold its products to the Baltimore & Ohio, and the Philadelphia, Wilmington, & Baltimore, as well as numerous other railroads, and offered references from some of the leading railroad men of the day including Benjamin H. Latrobe and Trimble's old boss, W. H. Swift.[75]

In 1857 Trimble went to Cuba to work on railroads and there are at least hints of the level of compassion and dedication which he could feel toward the men under his command. As early as 1835 McNeil, the former B&O engineer, recommended Isaac Trimble for assignment to Cuba, though no record has been found to show that he went to Cuba at that time. He did respond to open solicitation by the Cuban government seeking foreign contractors to build a stretch of railway between Santiago and Havana. They accepted Trimble's bid and he set up a field camp to conduct his operations. Yellow fever invaded Trimble's camp. He "stayed in camp day and night, provided physicians and every comfort for the men," and personally "administered medicine and nursing, until the fever had run its course."[76] He did so at great risk to his own safety.

He took his last railroad job before the war when he accepted the position of superintendent for the Baltimore and Potomac Railroad in 1859. He established a relationship with that company shortly after leaving the PW&B when he surveyed the proposed route and issued a report of his findings in 1855. As previously mentioned, trade with the communities near Washington D. C. constituted one of the three main areas of interest for Baltimore merchants. The Baltimore & Ohio covered the western trade while the Baltimore & Susquehanna provided railway linkage to the Pennsylvania markets. The Washington D. C. trade remained open. The Maryland Assembly granted a charter for a new company "from some suitable point in or near the City of Baltimore, to a point on the Potomac River to be selected by the President and Directors of said Company."[77] Trimble continued in that position until the start of the war in 1861.[78]

Review of the report he published in 1855 offers a glimpse of what made the man tick immediately preceding the outbreak of war. It gives us some examples of his management skills, while revealing the extent to which modernization had affected him. He demonstrated an understanding of local, regional and national markets. Perhaps most interesting, his views and comments are completely void of any regional bias.

This report does not give a complete inventory of his management skills, but does give us some examples. He advised the stockholders that the line should be "thoroughly finished before being opened for use,"[79] thus avoiding some of the problems he had seen on the PW&B. He referred to the impact such a strategy would have on the stock prices and the importance of avoiding the "disappointment and loss of confidence"[80] that would come with a decline in prices. He referred to the effect on local real estate prices, stating that "experience has abundantly shown that every railroad has a prompt and decided effect to enhance the value of lands for many miles adjacent to its route."[81] He provided estimates of the probable sources of revenue that they would have when the line did open for business.[82] He also highlighted the importance and opportunity that would accompany completion of the 68-mile gap between a network of railroads to the north from Baltimore to Montreal, Canada, and to the south through Richmond, Wilmington, Charleston, and Augusta and then extending towards Mobile and New Orleans.[83]

In his 1855 report he promoted modernization and emphasized the part that railroads played in the new age. He said, "this *fast* line is a true representation of this *fast age*, and here as elsewhere, the railroad must supersede the coach and the steamer."[84] He had a firm grasp of his times when he told them "this is emphatically everywhere the age of progress." He realized that some remained critical of this "fast country," and that they believed this to be "a headlong recklessness," to which he responded "but when the extravagant conceptions of one year, regarded as purely visionary at the time, become the sober and useful realities of the next ... [it] fairly denotes the momentum of the country, and ceases to be an epithet of derision or reproach."[85] He then went on to say that railroads have "become in every country a necessity, and in the United States as elsewhere, it is the true index of commercial intercourse and measure of prosperity."[86]

Trimble recognized the importance of local commerce but placed it in the context of larger markets. He said, referring to the middle part of the proposed line passing through Anne Arundel County, that "every part of the middle district is without a ready access to market, for its heavy productions" and that the new line "would therefore contribute a large and profitable business to the road."[87] He also referred to the advantages for the commerce of Baltimore and how it would have "a direct commercial and social interest in expediting the trip from Charleston north, which this road will do much to promote."[88] Consistent with his previously stated sentiments about communities being willing to share in the prosperity he mentioned that "Richmond has also much at stake" in having railway connection to Baltimore and the northern cities.[89] He did not see a serious conflict between local interest and the development of national markets and instead emphasized that completing the network of railroads would be good for the nation. He said this line would complete the "link in the great chain of intercommunication along the Atlantic coast, passing through the great Commercial Emporiums of the country, from Maine to

Louisiana."[90] He even recognized the social responsibility of "those who take charge of the construction of public works," and how they should "protect the public from disappointment and loss" by resisting the "impatient wishes of the community."[91]

During this decade before the war, when discussions were heating up over the expansion of slavery, Trimble's report revealed absolutely no indication of regionalism, and he clearly saw the South as part of the modern age. He suggested that "the interests of Baltimore" might "be more generally and extensively promoted by a better connection with the South," but this statement is not intended to promote sectionalism but rather simply stated that Baltimore could find more opportunity to the south.[92] He spoke with equal enthusiasm of how the "chief sources of revenue" for the Washington branch "are found in the Northern travel to and from Washington."[93] It is also clear that he did not make any distinction between the North and South when talking about the role of railroads and the "age of progress." When talking of the national network of railroads his only reference to North and South is in terms of a directional relationship to the city of Baltimore. This national network would include 835 miles in the North, and nearly 1,200 miles of track in the South, extending all the way to New Orleans.[94]

During the decades of the 1840s and 1850s Trimble experienced professional growth and greater bonding with the community of Baltimore, but just before the war he had faced challenges which had a negative impact on his belongingness needs and self-esteem, as well as halting any progress in achieving self-actualization. Conflict and tension surrounded Trimble, completely unrelated to the growing national crises centered around the expansion of slavery in the territories and increasing sectionalism. All of these events set the stage for the drama that both the man and his city played in April of 1861.

Trimble did not make his decision to join the South independently, but rather as an individual from a divided community. The city of Baltimore, like Trimble, had become greatly affected by modernization. It had grown with the new economy and in the process the population became more diverse. Competition increased for control of the city government and the direction in which the community would grow commercially. Though they had been successful in reaching compromise, certain issues remained unresolved. The city exploded in 1861, producing the first battle fatalities of the Civil War.

Throughout the antebellum period Trimble continued to give no indication of regional preference. He strengthened his ties to the community of Baltimore, but he clearly relied more on his family to satisfy his belongingness needs. Even when revealing a loyalty toward his adopted home town he did not speak in terms of whether the city was northern or southern, but rather the role the city played in local, regional, national, and world markets. While with the Baltimore & Susquehanna he spoke with an attitude of brotherhood, and during the last two decades before the collapse of the Union he did not say or do anything to indicate a change in attitude.

Trimble experienced personal crises related to identity and belongingness. As the railroad industry matured, competition replaced the kind of cooperation which in 1834 had sent Trimble to England to shop for three independent companies. Not only did aggression increase between companies, but within companies men competed for control and promotion. Trimble came under attack from the new president of the PW&B which led to his dismissal as superintendent, eventual resignation from the railroad, and concluded when he faced charges before a committee appointed to investigate his activities as superintendent. No doubt this shook his professional confidence. He found love and security in his immediate family, but shortly after his professional crises his wife of 23 years died.

Trimble had always been a survivor. As a young child he became an orphan dependent upon the kindness of his siblings for nurture. He struggled at West Point to make up for the poor grades he earned his first year. He did not reveal any weakness during the late 1850s despite the accusations he faced from Samuel Felton and the loss of his wife. Nonetheless, on the eve of the Civil War there is little doubt that Trimble had just gone through one of the most critical periods of his adult life. He appeared to have resolved his personal issues before 1861, but it is difficult to believe that he had the same confidence which he had before the events of the 1850s.

5

A Time for Decision

On the night of April 19, 1861, Isaac Trimble, in command of 160 men, entered the Canton Engine House in Baltimore and seized one of the trains that belonged to his former employer, the Philadelphia, Wilmington and Baltimore Railroad. At the command of the mayor of Baltimore and the governor of Maryland they, along with another band headed by Marshal Kane, intended to destroy the bridges over the Back, Bush and Gunpowder Rivers. After crossing one of the targeted bridges they halted the train and Trimble and his men descended and stood in front of Mr. Bowman's house. Trimble announced his intentions to Bowman, the keeper of the bridge. Mr. Smith, the master carpenter of the road, Bowman's daughter Jane, and several armed men heard the proclamation. Though the men had been sent there to protect the bridge, none but Jane spoke up to Trimble. She called him a coward, and in a loud voice called on the others to do what they had been sent there to do, fight off the attackers. The men concluded that they were railroad workers, not soldiers and instead threw down their arms. Some ran into the woods while the rest hid in Bowman's house. Jane called on them to not run but to stand and show themselves to be men. When she saw that none responded to her pleas she picked up one of the guns that had been discarded on the porch and ran toward Smith. "Use it," she cried. "If you will not, I will." Despite the attempts by Jane to save the bridge, Trimble's men prevailed. As the fire consumed the structure Jane noticed one of her father's men trapped on the draw of the bridge. Again, she pleaded with her father or any of his men who remained to rescue the stranded railroad worker. "If no one else will go, I will," she screamed.[1]

The violence that erupted on April 19th produced the first fatalities of the Civil War. Young ladies such as Jane Bowman, as well as West Point graduates such as Trimble, took a stand for what they believed in. Following the election of Abraham Lincoln in November of 1860 the once-united nation began to break apart. The citizens of Baltimore and Maryland patiently awaited each piece of news. They watched their neighbors, friends, and relatives as they decided which side they belonged on, but they took no action until the dominoes began to fall in April of 1861.

The study of Isaac Trimble and the relationship between him and his community offers an example of the complexity involved in deciding to join the secession movement. His story, or that of Maryland, offers little if any insight into the processes involved with the fire-eaters and those who started the war, but the stories have much in common with the states of the Upper South and the other border states. Though the states of the Upper South did not secede until after the formation of the Confederacy, there is little doubt that the war would not have gone on as long without the support of those states. Maryland officially remained part of the Union, which raises the question of the southernness of the state; however, because of its strategic geographic location President Lincoln took extraordinary steps to insure that his nation's capital did not become an island in enemy land. If the assumption is made that southern nationalism did not exist until the Civil War, then the definition of the South before the war would be those states that had slavery. Therefore, Baltimore and Maryland were part of the South, each having their unique characteristics, yet at the same time having similarities to other communities within the region. Trimble decided to join the Confederacy influenced in part by his personal experience, yet he had much in common with others from the border states who made the same decision.

Several variables contributed to Trimble's final stand. As expected under Maslow's hierarchy, all progress in the achievement of his higher personal needs became suspended as he struggled with the question of identity. He, more than many, had learned to consider himself an American and had lived in many different communities throughout the nation. When forced to choose between sides in a house divided, he decided he was more Southern than anything else. What remains uncertain is motivation: personal or ideological. For some who have lived in many different communities the place of birth can become more important in the question of identity; Trimble was born in Virginia. There are no documents that exist from the time before April, or even during the riots, that reveal Trimble's sympathies, his decision was not clear until he headed to Virginia to volunteer for the Confederate Army. He would later claim that he felt that the people of the North hated Southerners, but he never made such statements until after he donned the Confederate uniform. He fled Baltimore as he heard rumors that many of the leaders faced arrest, which may have contributed to his final choice. The only thing known for certain is that once he made his decision he proved to be as loyal as any to the cause. His West Point obituary claimed that "of all the soldiers whom Maryland furnished to the Southern cause, General Trimble performed the most distinguished services, obtained the highest rank, and won the greatest name."[2]

It is difficult to evaluate Trimble's personal motivations, which he may have denied to himself as well as to others. During the mid-1850s he acquired a personal enemy who might have had a major impact on his final decision, Samuel Felton. At the time of his hearings with the PW&B, Trimble made it clear that he resented the accusations and considered them a personal attack. The accusations came from a man several years his junior and with fewer years railroad experience; this could have aggravated his feelings of self-esteem and his attempts to achieve self-actualization through advancement in the corporate hierarchy. In other words, Trimble probably felt some professional jealousies. Felton came out strongly in support of the Union from the very beginning, and some believed him to have threatened the peace of the community and to have added to the antagonism during that most trying time. The fact that Felton came from New England could have contributed to Trimble's belief that Northerners hated Southerners. Trimble may have simply viewed himself as the opposite of Felton.

It is necessary to study the actions of Baltimore in order to understand the reasons for Trimble's decision. Thus far it has been shown that Trimble had a firmly established identity with Baltimore. As events unfolded the community proved to be divided; however, in the end Trimble and many others concluded that they belonged with the Confederacy regardless of whether Maryland seceded or not. Of course many of them believed that Maryland would have joined the new nation if not for the actions of Lincoln and his Union Army.

There are four important issues that warrant consideration in trying to understand the actions of Trimble and his community in 1861. First, Maryland may have seemed as much northern as southern, but the fact remains that it was a southern state if the South is defined as those states that lay below the Mason-Dixon line and had slavery. Second, we must remember that each individual and each community had some characteristics in common with other Southerners and at the same time retained some unique qualities. Baltimore led the South in manufacturing and urbanization but these were characteristics of that particular community. These trends may have been more developed in Maryland, but the rest of the South had made some progress on these roads of modernization as well. Third, slavery became the main issue dividing the nation. Again, Maryland had its own unique brand of slavery and because of this the issue never weighed as heavily for them. Fourth, Maryland experienced political turmoil unlike that of the other states.

Relating to the first of these issues, it is assumed here that Maryland was part of the South. The definition of the South is as difficult today as it was in 1860. The 11 states of the former Confederacy are consistently considered to be southern, but a number of border states, including Maryland, are ambiguous in identity, giving rise to disagreement among authors. *The Encyclopedia of Southern Culture* stated the situation succinctly, "The South is at once both the most visible and most ambiguous of all American cultural landscapes."[3] The two states most frequently included in addition to the 11 Confederate states are Kentucky and Oklahoma, while the National Opinion Research Center's definition added Delaware, Maryland, West Virginia, and the District of Columbia.[4] A 1999 poll showed that only 40 percent of its population considered Maryland to be a southern state.[5] The southern identity of that state today represents a decline from 140 years ago.[6]

In the early days of the war Robert E. Lee vocalized the sentiments of many Southerners when he told the residents of that state that his army was "prepared to assist you ... in regaining the rights of which you have been dispoiled."[7] The actions of Lincoln and General Benjamin F. Butler lent credibility to this point of view, so that Lee imagined that his invasion of 1862 would encourage the citizens of Maryland to rise up and join him. Many of his countrymen changed their mind when this dream failed to materialize during the Antietam campaign.[8] Nonetheless, as will be seen, Lee encouraged Trimble to revive that ambition just prior to the Gettysburg campaign.

The slave states constituted the South, though each had their own unique character. Charleston differed considerably from Memphis, and Richmond did not look much like New Orleans. Compared to other states in the South, Baltimore was more industrialized, more urbanized, and had its own brand of slavery, but it was a southern slave-owning city and had been since the founding of the colonies. Likewise, the state of Maryland was below the Mason-Dixon line and had the peculiar institution.[9]

This brings up the second topic; Baltimore had some characteristics unique to its particular community, but this did not mean that it was not the South. Before 1860 the United States consisted of a multitude of communities. Though part of the same nation they retained their individualism. They often competed with each other in the growing market place. In the earlier chapters it has been shown that Baltimore likewise competed with other communities for trade. Sometimes the community interest crossed political boundaries, such as the towns in the Susquahanna Valley which allied themselves with Baltimore rather than Philadelphia. Baltimore identified with the South during the trade conventions when it attempted to become the leading commercial center for that region. When forced to choose, Trimble and many of the other residents identified with the South; however, Baltimore was in a border state and as such had a large segment of the population with stronger ties to the national identity, or the Union. Baltimore was part of the South even though it had its own personality. It bears repeating, the South, and the nation in general, were made up of many communities.

Maryland had considerably more manufacturing than the 11 Confederate states, but manufacturing increased in the region in the 1850s. Maryland had an average of $33.81 per person invested in manufacturing establishments compared to only $8.65 per person in the seven Deep South states. The Upper South states (here defined as the four states which seceded after Ft. Sumter: Virginia, North Carolina, Tennessee, and Arkansas) had considerably more invested in manufacturing with an average of $13.93 per person. The neighboring state and capital of the Confederacy, Virginia, came closest to Maryland with an average investment of $22.08 per person. Maryland led the other southern states in the amount of money invested in manufacturing, but the other southern states showed signs of following Maryland's lead. The amount invested in the seven Deep South states increased 70.3 percent from 1850 to 1860 and went up 61.6 percent in the four Upper South states during the same decade.[10]

Though Maryland had a larger urban population than any of the other states below the Mason-Dixon line, the statistics indicated increasing urbanization in the region during the antebellum years. As stated above, economic growth helped to make Baltimore a large city, which accounted for most of the 34 percent urban population for the state. In this statistic Maryland had more in common with one of the seven Deep South states, Louisiana, which helped to give the Lower South a larger urban population than the Upper South. The Upper South had only 5.1 percent urban population while the seven of the Deep South had an average of 7.3 percent urban. Georgia and Mississippi had less than three percent urban population, but Louisiana did not lag far behind Maryland with 26.1 percent; New Orleans caused this rate to be so high just as Baltimore distorted the Maryland statistics. The urban growth rate in the four border states had been 45.1 percent in 1850 and 44.1 percent in 1860, and similar rates existed in the seven Deep South states with a growth rate of 53.1 percent in 1850 and 39.5 percent in 1860.[11]

Despite these unique characteristics the people of Maryland had much in common with the other communities in the South, especially those of the Upper South. Trimble and many of his fellow Marylanders who followed secession did so only after the events in April of 1861. This is also true for the four states of the Upper South, which did not join the Confederacy until that time. These four states accounted for 43 percent of the new nation's population. In addition, 39 percent of those in the Lower South voted for John Bell, whose platform opposed secession, suggesting that many of those in the Deep South did not favor disunion until it became to late to turn back. It is quite possible that the majority of the population of the South became more dedicated to the Confederacy for the same reasons that Trimble and much of the Maryland population shifted their support. They would have preferred to remain with the Union, but by April of 1861 it became clear that they would have to fight fellow Southerners and they could not do that. In the case of Maryland, Lincoln and the Union gained control before the state could decide whether to follow Virginia to the other side, and thus we will never know for certain what their choice would have been.[12]

The election results of 1860 also showed Maryland to be typical of the four Upper South states—much more so than Kentucky and Missouri, even though these states were represented by the two extra stars on the Confederate battle flag. In Maryland 45.9 percent of the vote went for the States' rights candidate John C. Breckinridge, compared to 46.7 percent in the Upper South. Bell received 45.1 percent of the Maryland vote, compared to 45.2 percent in the Upper South. Virginia is the only Confederate state that had votes for Lincoln, but only 2.5 percent of the Maryland vote went to the Republican candidate. Only nine percent of Maryland's votes went to Lincoln and the Northern Democrat Stephen Douglas combined. In comparison, more than 24 percent of Kentuckians voted for the two Northern candidates, and a whopping 33.9 percent of the Missouri voters, with 12.6 percent going to Lincoln alone.[13]

The third issue that needs to be considered concerning Trimble and his community is the role of slavery. As national politics heated up over the issue of slavery a unique situation existed in Baltimore and the state of Maryland that produced infertile ground for both the abolitionist and fire-eaters. Maryland had slavery since early colonial days, but they also had an increasing population of free blacks. The city and much of the state had a growing distaste for slave labor, but they did not become abolitionist. As previously stated, even the somewhat moderate Republican platform attracted less than three percent of the voters.

The plantation economy, still existing in parts of Maryland, had used slave labor since its founding, but the state also had the largest number of free blacks. The 1860 slave population of 87,189 only slightly outnumbered the free population of 83,942. Within the state slavery tended to exist more in the agricultural southern counties and the Eastern Shore. The Eastern Shore had a greater variety of property owners with estates as small as $100 or as large $268,000. Demand for slave labor in the Eastern Shore declined as the region shifted to specialty crops such as strawberries and peaches. In total the slave population remained about the same in 1850 that it had been in 1830. The number of free blacks increased in the Eastern Shore, so that by 1850 blacks accounted for nearly one in every three free residents.[14]

The white citizens of the state and city did become concerned about the growing free black population, and it also became a source of unrest. In Maryland the number of free blacks grew by 20 percent between 1840 and 1850; Maryland had the highest ratio of free blacks to white population and the greatest number of free blacks, fugitives, and manumitted slaves in the United States. Many of them found their way to Baltimore. The residents of that city tended to fear those of foreign cultures regardless of color; much of the previous violence revolved around the immigrant population. The prospect of an increasing free black population increased anxieties about the future. The Maryland Colonization society was created in 1831 to return blacks to Africa. The state contributed $10,000 per year. Some of the new class of businessmen, such as John H. B. Latrobe, became leaders in the effort. The main support for this movement came from the parts of the state with the largest number of free blacks, the Eastern Shore and Baltimore.[15]

Despite concern over free blacks, the people of Baltimore did not become easily involved in the issues of slavery. They did not see slavery as a threat to free labor. The fact that both free and slave labor existed side by side in Maryland provided less fertile ground for Lincoln's concern over the expansion of slavery. Since a smaller percentage of the Maryland population owned slaves, Marylanders had less concern about the preservation of the institution. When it came to the slavery issue, Mayor George William Brown said, "it is not surprising that Maryland was in no mood for war, but that her voice was for compromise and peace."[16]

The fourth important topic in understanding the actions of Trimble and his fellow Marylanders in 1861 relates to the political environment of that time. Baltimore's diversity had created a volatile society during the

1850s, but Brown won the election with his promise of seeking peaceful solutions. Baltimore's numerous subcommunities caused the conflict. Most of the problems related to the ethnic population, but other groups further complicated the situation. The large free black population, immigrants, slave owners, manufacturers, and small merchants are only examples of the many groups that had their own ideas about what would be good for the city and state. They became more concerned about their local problems than about national issues. The political environment contributed to Maryland's attempt to remain neutral under the leadership of the mayor of Baltimore. Though the Whigs had disappeared some of their philosophy lingered on among the long time residents. The city's large population, industrial economy, and diversity generated political competition. Violence increased in the 1850s as the various groups struggled to gain power. By 1860 the city hungered for law and order.

In the 1850s the state of Maryland and the city of Baltimore had become Know-Nothing territory, but three main assumptions in the philosophy of the Whigs remained intact in 1860. The Know-Nothings grew as many citizens became concerned about the large number of immigrants, especially the Irish Catholics, but they operated under some Whig assumptions. Whigs believed that individual liberty could only exist if the corporate body of citizens were free, and that the virtuous citizen would be willing to sacrifice selfish interest for the good of the whole. They also believed that the strongest forms of government resulted from a natural and unavoidable division between rich and poor, though they also emphasized the importance of growing economic opportunity. They strongly feared a powerful executive "which posed the greatest threat to citizen virtue and corporate liberty," and would thus be "able to bribe the one and coerce the other through manipulation of public finance and public debt and the control of a mercenary army."[17] This fear left many of the citizens of Baltimore determined to prevent a mercenary army of a strong executive to pass through their city, which in turn led to the events of April 19.

The violence of the 1850s centered around politics. During the elections of that decade gangs of young men, under the cover of being firemen or in political clubs, became nothing less than street thugs who thrived on terror and violence; they had names such as Blood Tubs, Thunderbolts, Rip Raps, Red Necks, and the Plug Uglies. The police department, undermanned and sometimes encouraged by respectable politicians, failed to control the violence. In the election of 1856, the election mobs, armed with cannons and smaller arms, left 10 dead and 150 injured. Some tried to pin the violence on the Know-Nothing Party; however, the violence had began before their rise.[18]

The popularity of the Temperance Party is an example of how the citizens tried to find a solution to the problem with the political process. They believed the violence to be a byproduct of the urban problems which accompanied the industrial revolution. The party had been formed in 1844 but saw little growth until the 1850s. They believed that liquor caused the problems which included crime, violence, labor unrest, and domestic discord; "it caused the Irish to steal and the Germans to defile Sundays with beer fest."[19]

Mayor Brown and his reform party won the election of 1860 on the platform that they would put an end to the violence. The first reforms came in the fire and police departments. Many of the gangs came from the neighborhood volunteer fire departments, which Brown hoped to see replaced by a professional urban fire department which would exist for the sole purpose of fire protection. He also reformed the police department with the objective of making it more effective in maintaining peace in the city. Because of the great diversity of Baltimore's population the reformers avoided radicalism, whether it came from abolitionists or secessionists.[20] A correlation existed between the wards which voted for Brown as mayor and those that voted for Breckinridge for president, but this may have been due to their desire for reform rather than any strong secessionist impulses.[21]

As the nation moved through the election of 1860 and toward disunion, the city of Baltimore and state of Maryland, like other border states, remained divided in their loyalties for the North or the South. Pro-Union factions included the growing working class, manufacturers, and most large commercial leaders. The secession supporters included small merchants, young professionals, and Southern Democrats. The workers did lean a little more toward violence after October of 1860 when a financial panic led to all-out depression through the winter of 1860–1861. They became reluctant to listen to talk of secession.[22] Mayor Brown summarized his view of the situation in Baltimore, "her sympathies were divided between the North and the South, with a decided preponderance on the Southern side."[23]

One more thing is needed to set the stage for Trimble and Baltimore in April of 1861. It is important to understand the background of the four men who wielded the most power during that turbulent time of decision. They initially worked together for the main objective of maintaining law and order in the previously chaotic city. The key players represented the diversity of Baltimore, from the dedicated Unionist to the determined secessionist. George William Brown, who quickly became the leader, openly opposed secession, but in reality he straddled the fence. Governor

Thomas Holliday Hicks was clearly loyal to the Union, but he yielded his authority as governor and followed the lead set by Brown. City Marshal George Proctor Kane, a dedicated secessionist, took his orders from the president of the police board, Charles Howard. Howard's sympathies leaned toward the South, especially after the arrest made during Union occupation. Isaac Trimble also took his orders from Howard; he ended up in command of the civilian forces hastily organized in the midst of the turmoil. Though both Kane and Trimble took their orders from Howard, it is unlikely that Howard could have seized command of either the police or militia by himself.

George William Brown was born in Baltimore on October 13, 1812, the grandson of an Irish physician who had settled in that city in 1783. He entered Dartmouth College at the age of 16, and later went to Rutgers where he graduated in 1831 with highest honors. Shortly after his return to Baltimore he began the practice of law. He first took a stand against disorderly conduct when he joined the forces of General Samuel Smith to suppress the riots that followed the failure of the Bank of Maryland. Brown opposed secession and he did not believe in slavery, but in April of 1861 he stood up for his city and avoided taking a stand either for the Union or the Confederacy.[24]

Governor Thomas Holliday Hicks was born on a farm in Dorchester County, Maryland, on September 2, 1798. He came from a prosperous Eastern Shore family, and though the only one of the four leaders considered loyal to the Union, he was also the only one of the four to be a slaveholder. This serves as a reminder of how the historical trends have numerous exceptions. He received only a rudimentary education and worked on the farm until he began his political career. He started as a constable and then became sheriff at the age of 26. In 1830 he left his farm on the Choptank River to become a member of the state legislature, and in 1833 moved to a small town and engaged in the mercantile business. He started his political career as a Democrat, served in the general assembly as a Whig, and in the fall of 1857 won his election as governor with the American, or Know-Nothing Party.[25]

Marshal George Proctor Kane was born in Baltimore on August 17, 1817. His parents came from Northern Ireland. He received a liberal education and became a grain merchant. He aided the Irish victims of famine by sending food in 1846 and 1847. The people of Baltimore elected him to various local offices and President Millard Fillmore appointed him collector of the port. He received his appointment as Marshal of police under the reform government of Mayor Brown and Howard's reform Police Board.[26]

The last of the four players, Trimble, did not enter the picture until the end of the first battle. He was the only one not born in Maryland. He did not hold an office in either state or local government, but he apparently commanded considerable respect. He ended up with command of the civilian mob turned militia.

The road to disunion begin with the election of President Lincoln in 1860. As previously mentioned, the vote in Maryland came out very much like it did in the four Confederate states of the Upper South, with the exception that Lincoln won 2.5 percent of the vote. In the city of Baltimore the vote differed only slightly from the state. It appeared to be a little more radical, with Lincoln getting an additional .9 percent and Breckinridge winning 3.7 percent more votes. Perhaps more importantly the election of 1860 occurred without the violence that accompanied the election of 1856 despite the fact that tempers flared nationally. Baltimore had returned to peaceful resolutions and hoped to continue to do so.[27]

Mayor George W. Brown took command during the early days of April 1861. Brown commissioned Isaac Trimble as colonel of the local militia, and later issued him orders to burn the railway bridges into the city. Courtesy the Maryland Historical Society, Baltimore, Maryland.

As the Union dissolved, the people of Baltimore watched and waited. South Carolina started the chain reaction when it voted to secede in December of 1860. By February six more states followed South Carolina's lead and together formed the Confederate States of America. Still, the people of Baltimore and Maryland waited. As the mayor said, many "were watching Virginia's course, in order to decide whether to stay in the Union or go out of it with her."[28] Trimble could clearly be numbered among this group. A native of the dominion state, he talked about the "River, which only divides but does not *separate* Maryland from grand, glorious Old Virginia."[29] This attitude continued through April when James Ryder Randall read about the April 19th riots and wrote his song, *Maryland My*

Maryland, that would be popular with Maryland Confederates and in 1939 became the state song.[30] Randall wrote, "Virginia should not call in vain, Maryland my Maryland."[31]

Trimble's previous employer and antagonist, Samuel Felton, took some action in February of 1861 that had, in the words of Mayor Brown, "a sinister influence on the State of Maryland, especially on the city of Baltimore."[32] Felton convinced Lincoln that if he passed through Baltimore, as planned, that he would be assassinated. Felton, a native of Massachusetts, took a strong stand for the Union from the very beginning. Brown considered that Felton acted out of fears stimulated by his imagination, but he also said that Felton may have "in part [been] stimulated by the temptation of getting up a sensation of the first class."[33] Felton claimed the assassination plot to be part of a larger conspiracy which would conclude with the capture of Washington. He sent an agent to General Winfield Scott with news of his discovery in an attempt to divert the president's proposed route.[34]

In the end Felton succeeded in persuading Lincoln to sneak through Baltimore under the cover of darkness, though Brown, Marshal Kane, and Lincoln himself concluded that there appeared to be no foundation to the conspiracy theory. Marshal Kane "said he had thoroughly investigated the whole matter, and there was not the slightest foundation for such rumors."[35] Colonel Lamon, "a close friend of President Lincoln, and the only person who accompanied him on his night ride to Washington," after studying the documents, concluded "the conspiracy to be a mere fiction," and also "adds in confirmation the mature opinion of Mr. Lincoln himself."[36]

Lincoln listened to Felton, and both he and the city of Baltimore paid the price. Lincoln and his family made previous public appearances in 12 cities. It had originally been planned that they would go from Harrisburg to Philadelphia, through Baltimore and then on to Washington. Because of Felton's stories, they instead secreted him from Harrisburg to Philadelphia where they placed him on one of Felton's trains for a night ride to Baltimore. In 1861 the four major railroads which fed the city of Baltimore did not connect, so when Lincoln arrived at the President Street Station at 3:30 a.m. on the night of February 23rd, they disconnected his car and horses pulled it down Pratt Street to the Camden Station for the final leg of his journey on the Baltimore and Ohio. Later that day his family arrived in Washington from Harrisburg, and at 11:00 a.m. Mayor Brown and a strong police escort arrived to greet the President at the Northern Central's Calvert Street Station.[37] Colonel Lamon said that "Mr. Lincoln learned to regret the midnight ride. His friends reproached him, his enemies taunted him."[38] Baltimore also regretted the incident as "fearful

This etching by Adalbert Johann Volck shows Abraham Lincoln taking the PW&B between Philadelphia and Baltimore while on his way to be inaugurated as the 16th president of the United States. Trimble's former boss and nemesis, Samuel Felton, convinced Lincoln to sneak through the city under the cover of darkness, an action Lincoln later regretted. Courtesy the Maryland Historical Society, Baltimore, Maryland.

accounts of the conspiracy flew all over the country, creating a hostile feeling against the city."[39]

Despite the rumors and accusations and even the subsequent inauguration of Lincoln on March 4, Maryland remained firmly planted on the fence between the North and the South. Fate placed considerable power in the hands of Governor Hicks; the legislature had finished their business for the year and only he had the power to call them back into session. Mass meetings, called as early as February 1st, produced resolutions clamoring for action by Governor Hicks, who refused to call a special session out of fear that legislators would vote for secession. Pressure came from outside the state as emissaries from Mississippi, Alabama and later Georgia made efforts to persuade Maryland to join them. Governor Andrew G. Curtin of Pennsylvania sent emissaries to congratulate Hicks for not calling a special legislature. The governor refused to take any action and the cries of secessionists had little influence, at least until April.[40]

Even the firing on Fort Sumter could not stir the citizens of Maryland into action; that did not come until after April 16th. Determined to put an end to violence in the political process they initially criticized the people of South Carolina for firing on Fort Sumter. Then came Lincoln's call for 75,000 troops. This could have been aggravating to those who feared a strong executive. It also called for Maryland to take a militant position, thus ending their hope for a non-violent solution. As stated by Mayor Brown, "Immediately after the call of the President for troops ... a marked division among the people manifested itself."[41] Crowds began to gather outside two newspaper offices, one secessionist, the other unionist, as they eagerly waited for each little piece of news. Those watching Virginia knew what to do after they heard that the Virginia legislature voted for secession. Governor Hicks still refused to call the legislature. Missouri and Kentucky failed to secede but they refused to meet Lincoln's quota for troops. Even Delaware refused to send troops, though the governor excused his actions by claiming that they had no militia law in operation in his state.[42] Maryland would be the only one of these states that would leave the United States capital surrounded if it joined the new nation.

Brown and Hicks both still struggled to preserve the peace, and the governor fought to keep Maryland in the Union. Hicks went from Annapolis to Washington to visit the president and his secretary of war, Simon Cameron, to express his state's contempt for what he considered a coercive policy. Many in Maryland did not like the idea of taking up arms against another state. Lincoln and Cameron assured Hicks that any troops sent by Maryland would be used only in the defense of the nation's capital.[43] Apparently they convinced him and he expressed his loyalty to the

Union. On April 17th he issued a letter to Cameron stating that "the condition of affairs in this State at this time required that arms shall be placed in the hands of true men and loyal to the United States," and proceeded to request the arms needed for the four regiments.[44] Brown had more concern about maintaining the peace in his city; on April 17th he issued "a proclamation earnestly invoking all good citizens to refrain from every act which could lead to outbreak or violence of any kind."[45]

The situation worsened as the people learned about the intended transportation of troops across Maryland soil. Mayor Brown, who had tried to protect the trespassing 6th Massachusetts, later telegraphed the governor of that state and said, "Our people viewed the passage of armed troops of another State through the streets as an invasion of our soil and could not be restrained."[46] A prelude to the April 19 riots occurred the day before when a battery of United States artillery and several hundred Pennsylvania troops found "a great crowd of people at the station to meet them."[47] They attacked the state militia but did not bother the United States troops. They could accept the presence of United States army, but not that of a foreign state. According to Brown "an attack would certainly have been made but for the vigilance and determination of the police, under command of Marshall Kane."[48] Kane may have been a Southern sympathizer but he clearly gave priority to his duty to the city and its mayor.

In the beginning three of the four main players showed a united front in their determination to maintain order in Baltimore. Marshal Kane and Mayor Brown had already displayed this in their defense of the troops on the 18th. Governor Hicks arrived in Baltimore that afternoon and made a proclamation. "He assured the people that no troops would be sent from Maryland, unless it might be for the defense of the national capital."[49] He also promised the people an opportunity to chose between the Union and the Confederacy. The actions of Hicks appear to be somewhat inconsistent with his actions prior to the riots, and, as will be seen, after the riots as well. Evidence does not exist to prove his motives but it is likely that one of two possibilities, or perhaps a combination of both, guided his decision making. First, being a loyal Union man he undoubtedly felt under duress by the increasing display of Southern sympathies. Second, he understood Brown's dedication to peace and suspected that violence at this point would most likely carry Maryland into the Confederacy. Hicks encouraged Brown to make a similar proclamation and Brown "concurred with the Governor in his determination to preserve the peace and maintain inviolate the honor and integrity of Maryland." Brown could "not withhold [his] expression of satisfaction" at the governor's "resolution that no troops should be sent from Maryland to the soil of any other State."[50] On the same day they received news of the secession of Virginia.[51]

Meanwhile, Samuel Felton continued to act independently of both the state and civic leaders. Anticipating the disloyalty of those south of the Susquehanna and eager to protect company property as well as the Union, he organized a force of about 200 men including those that Trimble confronted on the night of April 19th. He planted them to guard the bridges and to act as a private regiment if need be. To appear inconspicuous he put them to whitewashing the bridges; the six or seven coats of whitewash also offered some protection in case of attempted burning.[52]

Tempers flared as the people learned that troops would be passing through Baltimore on April 19th, and the city began to appear more Southern. Felton continued to be uncooperative; Brown later complained that they could have been better prepared if the railroad had kept them notified of any planned troop arrivals on the PW&B. A crowd of 10,000 gathered in anticipation. They represented many segments of Baltimore society, from "substantial citizens" to "Negroes."[53] They began to display greater sympathy to the South, and "it seemed as if nearly every citizen wore a badge which displayed the Confederate colors."[54] Confederate flags appeared on the houses and on the people, and it appeared to both Southerners and Northerners that Maryland had taken a stand with the Confederacy. The United States flag disappeared and Unionists feared to restore it.[55] The 6th Massachusetts followed the same route Lincoln had taken in February, including the necessary horse-drawn connection down Pratt Street from the President Street Station of the PW&B to the Camden Station of the B&O. As the train cars proceeded down the street, rocks and bottle throwing escalated to gunfire. Brown believed the attack to be the "result of a sudden impulse, and not of a premeditated Scheme."[56]

Brown, Kane, and Hicks risked their lives in the attempt to minimize the violence of April 19th. Though fatalities occurred on both sides it would have been worse without the actions of these men. "The conduct of Mayor Brown in risking his life to defend the Northern troops was heroic."[57] Officers of the 6th Massachusetts praised the actions of Brown; the chaplain wrote, "his manly and heroic conduct on the eventful 19th of April secured to him the esteem and praise of every one of us."[58] Governor Hicks joined the effort to restore order and worked to appeal to the majority. He called out the state military to maintain peace, but he also telegraphed Washington to not send any more troops from outside of Maryland.[59] His speech to the crowds could have been the product of duress, or perhaps simply a shrewd political move. He said, "I bow in submission of the people. I am a Marylander; I love my State, and I love the

5. A Time for Decision

The 6th Massachusetts passed through the city on its way to Washington. Violence erupted on the streets of Baltimore on April 19, 1861, producing the first casualties of the Civil War.

Union, but I will suffer my right arm to be torn from my body before I will raise to strike a sister state."[60] The unyielding Southern sympathizer, Marshal Kane, stood beside the mayor and governor. He said that Brown "seemed deeply anxious that our laws should be respected and enforced." He also claimed to have "fought hard for their protection, at first almost alone but soon had the assistance of a part of [his] force who hurried from the neighboring beats."[61] Trimble did not arrive on the scene until after the first day of violence concluded. He "took no part in it whatever and was only present at its termination as an astonished spectator."[62] When he did join the other three he did so with the same dedication to terminating the violence.

The Baltimore leaders stood for localism, or States' rights, and in the end the only chance for order came when they took a stand for their state over either the Union or the Confederacy. In his speech of the 19th Hicks proudly stated, "I am a Marylander." Brown said, "Baltimore is the place of my birth, of my home, and of my affections." He then added, "no one could be bound to his native city by ties stronger than mine." After the 19th, men held meetings under the state flag of Maryland.[63]

Though the event was referred to as a riot, both sides sought particular targets rather than the random violence that the word riot suggests.

They appeared disorderly since the various participants had different objectives, and they lacked leadership until Brown and the others finally gained control. The violence began as the crowd attacked the train cars carrying the 6th Massachusetts. The troops had orders, "if you are fired upon and any of you are hit your officers will order to fire. Do not fire into any promiscuous crowd, but select any man whom you see aiming at you and be sure you drop him."[64] On the 20th and the 21st some Baltimoreans targeted the Germans. This might appear to have been a random attack of a minority group, but they did so because the Germans had volunteered to fill the four regiments demanded by Lincoln from Maryland. Many of the buildings sacked included gun stores as the people tried to arm themselves.[65]

Mayor Brown made the decision to destroy the railway bridges after the first day of violence. He first seized control of the telegraph lines and thus cut off communications with Washington. This did cause some problems because the only information received in the capital came from rumors. Though Federal authorities would interpret the destruction of the bridges as an act of terrorism against the United States, Brown and the others acted out of the desire to save their city and probably saved the lives of Union soldiers too.[66] Trimble later wrote, "his idea was that it would prevent further bloodshed; that if the troops kept coming through Baltimore, riot and bloodshed were inevitable, and if the bridges were destroyed it would prevent the transportation of troops through the city and thus save many lives."[67]

Governor Hicks approved of Brown's plans though he would later deny it. Marshal Kane and E. Louis Lowe reported to Brown's home and informed the mayor that he had received a telegraph that additional troops would be arriving on the Northern Central Railroad. Lowe, Kane, Brown, and his brother went to the bedroom in the mayor's house where Hicks slept. They convinced the governor that the only way to stop great bloodshed would be to destroy the bridges and thus prevent the troops from reaching the city and the awaiting mob. Hicks muttered, "it seems to be necessary," and when they asked if he approved "with great reluctance, [he] replied in the affirmative."[68] John Cumming Brown, Marshal Kane, and E. Louis Lowe all confirmed Brown's story to the General Assembly of Maryland.[69]

At 12 a.m. on the 19th Trimble received a request to report to Brown's office where the mayor announced the decision to destroy the bridges into the city. Trimble attempted to avoid the assignment as he feared that he would be suspected of acting out of revenge against his former employer.[70] Brown said, "no one else could be found at that hour to do it," and "that

The Gunpowder Creek Railroad Bridge was among those Mayor Brown ordered Isaac Trimble to burn in hopes of preventing United States troops from passing through the city and sparking further violence. Courtesy the Maryland Historical Society, Baltimore, Maryland.

no time was to be lost."[71] After asking if the governor agreed, Trimble accepted the task on the condition that he have the orders in writing. Within a few hours Trimble had damaged two of the bridges, 18 and 20 miles from the city, including the one which Bowman guarded. He made them impassable by burning the draw bridges, but limited the damage to the minimum necessary to prevent passage.[72]

The Union considered this entire action rebel activity and made every attempt to keep the roads into and out of Baltimore open. After Trimble's capture at Gettysburg, Cameron still considered him the rebel who had burned the bridges at the beginning of the rebellion. The attorney general considered the orders to be insurrectionary and hostile to the government. The Northern military leaders considered the railroad vital in their attempt to gain control in Maryland, and during these critical early days sought officers with railroad experience to accomplish that objective. Felton continued to communicate directly with the men in Washington, and Cameron advised him that Governor Hicks did not have any authority to prevent troops from coming to Washington.[73]

On the day of the 20th Brown again turned to Trimble to assist with his next objective, to gain control of the armed crowds gathering in the streets of the city. At the time the entire police department under Kane numbered 398 and they faced a crowd that began to exceed 10,000. Brown called for all men possessing arms to come to the defense of their city. The police board, under the president Charles Howard, appointed Trimble colonel of the impromptu militia. By taking this step he placed the potential troublemakers under local leadership which they could accept, and thus instead of causing problems they helped to prevent them. Trimble did not receive written orders until the 21st. The orders clearly stated that the militia existed to assist the police.[74] They also made it clear that martial music should not be played; "the sound of a drum at once collects crowds, and gives rise to the circulation of all sorts of rumors, calculated to produce unnecessary mischievous excitement."[75] Trimble had 2,265 men officially under his command, but at times the civilian crowds unofficially responding to his orders may have been as many as 15,000 to 20,000.[76]

The third objective required gaining control of weapons. Brown's call for armed volunteers brought many of the small arms in the hands of private citizens under the command of Trimble. In addition Trimble placed an order for 2,000 pikes from the machine shop of Ross Winans, the inventor of the steam cannon who would later be taken prisoner by the North.[77] In addition, Trimble's adjutant, Francis J. Thomas, went on a secret mission to Virginia to acquire additional weapons for "better defense of the city."[78] When Nathaniel Banks finally entered Baltimore he described the police headquarters as "in some respects a concealed arsenal."[79]

Once the preliminary steps had been taken to end the violence Brown next went to Washington to negotiate with the Federal government. He made the trip in the company of George W. Dobbin, John C. Brune, and S. T. Wallis and met with President Lincoln and General Winfield Scott. At this time he addressed the question of the bridge burning and convinced the president that he had acted solely out of the desire to maintain peace in the city.[80] Defending the actions of his constituents Brown told Lincoln that the citizens of Baltimore "regarded the calling for 75,000 troops as an act of war on the South, and a violation of its constitutional rights," and added "that it was not surprising that a high-spirited people, holding such opinions, should resent the passage of Northern troops through their city for such a purpose."[81] Lincoln finally agreed that in the future troops would pass around Baltimore, not through it. Scott said, "Mr. President, I thank you for this, and God will bless you for it."[82]

By April 26th Brown began to gain control of the city and he saw the end of the troubles by May 6th. On the 26th Trimble received orders to dismiss his command except for a guard at the armory. On April 27th Howard told him to release his command at his discretion. Unionists again showed themselves in public on April 28th when a ship crowded with men passed in front of Ft. McHenry, boldly displaying the same banner which had inspired the national anthem when it survived British attack of the fort in 1814.[83] On May 2nd, Howard sent written orders to Trimble to select from "among the Associations that have reported themselves to you, One Hundred reliable Men, who may be willing to volunteer to continue to give their aid to the City Authorities."[84] On May 6th Mayor Brown sent him a "request that the entire force which was organized for the defense of the City in the recent Emergency be disbanded as soon as possible."[85] When charged with the accusation that Baltimore had become a Confederate city, Brown insisted that it be described as "armed neutrality."[86]

Though Brown and the others fought for "armed neutrality," the Union took steps to seize the Maryland capital, and then turned its attention to capturing the state's largest city. Brown believed that "a large majority of her people sympathized with the South," but he recognized "that the larger and stronger half of the nation would not allow its capital to be quietly disintegrated away by her secession."[87] Even after the first day of violence when it appeared that Baltimore would be following the lead of Virginia, he said that "it was clear to all who had not lost their reason that Maryland ... would be kept in the Union for the sake of the national capital." He also pointed out that Maryland "lay open from the North by both land and sea," and that they would keep the capital safe "even if it required the united power of the nation to accomplish the object."[88] As Brown and the governor struggled to restore order in Baltimore on April 19th, General Butler arrived in the state capital, Annapolis. On April 20th the 7th New York arrived to reinforce Butler. Whereas Trimble and Kane destroyed railroad lines, Butler used the engineering skills of the 8th Massachusetts to restore railroad traffic.[89]

Even though Hicks had told the crowds in Baltimore that he would refuse to take up arms against another state, he did the most to keep Maryland in the Union. The Union apparently felt confident in his loyalty since they allowed him to complete his term as governor, and he then filled a vacant seat in the Senate. It is only speculation, but it seems likely that if he had been a Southern sympathizer the legislature would have followed his lead and voted to join the Confederacy. It is a fact that he refused to respond to demands that he call for a special session of the predominantly Southern-Rights Democrats Assembly. Finally, on April 23rd he announced that the Assembly would convene on April 26th, and the following day he moved the meeting site from Annapolis to Frederick; he believed that the sight of troops in the capital would produce a backlash vote for secession. When the legislature did finally assemble they reflected the confused state of affairs; the Senate voted that they could not act on secession, but in early May they passed resolutions declaring the war unconstitutional, and expressed a desire for the immediate recognition of the Confederate States.[90] When it finally became clear that the state government would not take the steps toward secession, "a large number of young men, including not a few of the flower of the State, and representing largely the more wealthy and prominent families, escaped across the border and entered the ranks of the Confederacy."[91] Ironically, as long as Maryland remained in the Union, localism, or "States' rights," worked against the South; even those who sympathized with the Confederacy "had no disposition to take arms against the union so long as Maryland remained a member of it."[92]

On April 21st Major General Robert Patterson received his orders of command and learned that it included the District of Columbia, Maryland, Delaware, and Pennsylvania, and immediately began to make plans to take control of Baltimore.[93] On April 27, he received orders in which Lincoln said, "you are engaged in repressing an insurrection against the laws of the United States," and that if "you find resistance which renders it necessary to suspend the writ of habeas corpus for the public safety, you personally, or through the officer in command at that point where the resistance occurs, are authorized to suspend that writ."[94] On May 5th General Benjamin F. Butler captured Relay, a junction of the Baltimore & Ohio Railroad. He then moved into Baltimore on May 13th, without official authorization, accompanied by the 6th Massachusetts, veterans of the April 19th attack. He found neither armed resistance nor brass bands on his arrival.[95] One observer claimed "the work of oppressing the citizens of Baltimore began as soon as General Butler had established himself."[96] Brown claimed that Butler entered a peaceful city "in the midst of a thunderstorm of unusual violence," and "took possession of Federal Hill." Brown went on to say that Butler received a promotion to Major General for "the capture of Baltimore," and that he "immediately issued a proclamation, as if he were in a conquered city subject to military law."[97] Though Brown had worked to restore peace in his city he ended up paving the way for Butler's occupation.

Armed with Lincoln's orders to suspend the writ of habeas corpus,

5. A Time for Decision

The interior of the outbuilding attached to Marshal Kane's Police Headquarters, Holiday Street, Baltimore. United States soldiers discovered cannon, muskets, and ammunition which they assumed to be intended for service to the secessionists. Courtesy the Maryland Historical Society, Baltimore, Maryland.

Butler quickly seized control of Brown's armory and began to make strategic arrests. He began with Ross Winans, the inventor of a steam-powered cannon. On May 21st he ordered Marshal Kane to turn over the weapons in control of the police. He dismissed Kane as marshal and replaced him with United States Marshal Washington Bonifant. On May 25th soldiers arrested John Merryman who had participated in the bridge burning. Chief Justice Roger B. Taney, a Marylander, challenged the arrest but learned that his authority could not stand up to Lincoln's army. On June 24th General Scott ordered the arrest of city officials, and before July 4th Marshal Kane, the members of the police board, and Mayor Brown found themselves under arrest. By September 17th the list included 31 state legislators.[98] Congressman Henry May of Baltimore described the city as "effectually under the heel of the tyrant as if the head of every man was in iron fetters." He said that "Federal troops are encamped in its squares and patrol its streets;

cannon are planted at corners, citizens are arrested for even breathing secession," and he claimed that "women are insulted with impunity, outrages are perpetrated that make humanity blush." He summed up the situation, "a reign of terror has been inaugurated which if not as cruel in results is as bad in principle as that of Robespierre when he enshrined a harlot as a goddess of liberty and bade the people fall down and worship."[99]

During his days in Baltimore Trimble waited at his home, "Ravenshurst." He heard rumors of his impending arrest. As a leader he would have been much more of a target than Merryman. It is not known if he had fled the city before the arrest of Merryman, but he did arrive in Virginia by May 25th, when he accepted a commission as a lieutenant colonel of Virginia Volunteers. Major Straw and Union soldiers under his command visited "the Castle," as neighbors called Trimble's Victorian mansion, to confiscate rebel arms that had been stored there. A thorough search of the estate, from the pigsty to the chimney, produced nothing but an ash-covered soldier. The boxes found in the house contained only Trimble's personal belongings, which he had packed but apparently could not find the means or the time to send on to his final destination.[100] As early as June 4th Trimble wrote to Robert E. Lee and said, "May I beg to remind you of my earnest wish to accompany the first force sent into Maryland,"[101] not knowing that the next time he saw his hometown that it would be as a prisoner of war.

Butler clearly intended to subdue any sympathy toward the South. The hostility Northerners felt toward Baltimore after the assassination conspiracy charges continued to grow. While in prison Kane said, "Scarcely a paper reaches us but what contains telegrams known to be false and libelous upon the motives and acts of those who by consanguinity and interest are identified with Maryland people."[102] Butler did not simply remove the prisoners for the sake of safety but clearly wanted them punished. On October 8th 74 of those taken from Maryland to Fort Lafayette in New York protested to Lincoln "against the inhumanity of their confinement and treatment." They said that "their condition could hardly be worse if they were in a slave ship on the middle passage."[103] When Kane returned to Baltimore 17 months later he addressed the citizens and spoke of his "arbitrary arrest." He charged Mr. Seward with the "flagrant violation of constitutional liberty," and said that he would "show that all that is bad in a man, unpatriotic in a citizen and corrupt in an officer finds itself concentrated in this individual."[104]

The events of 1860 and 1861 helped to create a firm community and state identity for Trimble, as well as creating a new national identity. As has been seen in the earlier chapters, Trimble did not seem to have a strong

As the United States Army, under the command of General Butler, entered the city, houses were searched and citizens were arrested. They also invaded the Trimbles' home, but unlike Mayor Brown and Marshal Kane, he avoided capture and arrest.

regional or community identity before the war. The actions of others led him to the position of being forced to choose. When forced to decide between being a Northerner or a Southerner he chose the latter. Once he made that choice then he felt that he had to protect his home. As the people of the South suffered, the bonds of their new national identity strengthened.

Trimble firmly believed that Northerners hated the South, and that they drove the South from the Union by their "bigotry & hatred of every thing southern." He said that the "Union was at variance with [Southern] feelings, tastes, pursuits, honorable aims & religion." He believed that only political interest had brought the two distinctive cultures together, and that the South separated as the only means to "self preservation and self respect."[105] Many years later he never retracted the claim that the North hated the South, but he softened his position when he said that "the great error of both sections of our country from the earliest times, was a deep prejudice against each other." He went on to describe it as "a prejudice founded in ignorance of the good traits of character in each." He did not record his hostile view until August of 1863, after his capture at Gettysburg. We have no idea exactly when he began to think this way. He did not express any such sentiments prior to 1861, so it seems likely that bitterness toward Northerners developed and grew as the war dragged on, further aggravated by the loss of a leg and imprisonment.[106]

As the foreign invader occupied his state, his city, his community, and his home he had to choose between yielding or fighting; he chose to fight for his home even though it lay within the borders of the other nation. The following lines are from a poem he wrote while a prisoner in Johnson's Island:

> To arms! Ye noble patriots brave,
> In firm array your bands!
> March on! March on! Polluted blood
> Shall drench our fertile lands.
> Ye children of a country loved,
> She calls you to the strife!
> Tyrants and slaves with Gothic war
> Assail your nation's life.
> Chorus.—Unfurl our flag, the Southern Cross,
> Shout loud the battle-cry,
> Of freemen's bold and clear huzza,
> For death or victory!
>
> We fight in holy freedom's cause,
> For homes and altar's fires;
> For sacred fames and equal laws,
> The gift of honored sires;
> For freedom's birth right won for us,
> Sealed with the blood of war,
> By men absolved on battle-field,
> To win or perish there.
> Chorus.—[107]

Even though he initially did not favor secession, once the process started he saw the North as a threat to his home and his people. In the above poem he spoke of the "home fires," and the "sacred fames and equal laws." He spoke of those things that they received as a "birth right." He said, in a speech, that he and his fellow infantrymen would "freely shed the last drop of ... blood for woman's protection and mother's approving smile."[108]

Trimble never spoke of being a Southerner before the war, but he realized that the "rivers of fire and blood" that flowed during the war served to strengthen and bind together the Southern nation. He spoke of the infantrymen men that he led and how they "marched together... fought together ... starved together."[109] He spoke of the war and "its effects upon that part of the country," and how "no home escaped its dire effects; its houses were deserted, or left with none but old men and powerless women to make them more desolate; its fields abandoned, or but small areas tilled for precarious subsistence." They also had "farming implements destroyed, horses taken for war service, cattle killed or driven away, labor disorganized and uncontrollable."[110] This no doubt inspired his cries to his former countrymen from the North, "the blood shed on Southern fields, will spring up in dragons teeth to revenge hereafter your wrongs & tyranny, and guard her borders from future desecration, long after you have carried out your boastful schemes of conquest or extermination."[111]

There is evidence that Trimble did not stand alone in his belief that the North hated the South. Brown certainly agreed with this view, "The Northern people had published invectives of the most exasperating character broadcast against the South in their speeches, sermons, newspapers and books."[112] The South had speakers who inspired the jealousy of Ralph Waldo Emerson, but the Puritan North had writers and through them acquired a more long-lasting cultural influence. Northerners began to see America as being the product of the values and philosophy established by their Puritan forefathers, while the South represented what was wrong with America. Though this influence strengthened with their victory over the South, the foundation was laid during the critical period between 1817 and 1865.[113]

The two greatest architects of the hatred that Trimble described, Wendell Phillips and William Lloyd Garrison, built their contempt on the hatred of slavery. Earlier anti-slavery Quakers visited the South and appealed to the slave holders. They did not hate the slave owner but rather the institution of slavery. Whittier, also a Quaker, never visited the South. Though he personally did not hate the individual slave owner, he created southern characters who other Northerners would have a hard time liking. Emerson admired some southern characteristics, but because of slavery he hated Southerners. Longfellow did not participate in organized anti-slavery activities, but he did write poetry condemning slavery. Thoreau took a more militant stance. In summary, the writings of these popular authors reflected the image of evil portrayed by Garrison and Phillips.[114]

Feelings of contempt or distrust of Southerners existed outside of New England; however, many Northerners did not share these views. Oliver Wendell Holmes agreed with the popular southern view of black inferiority and objected to violent abolitionists. Hawthorn did not feel hostility toward the South. Some magazines, such as the *North American Review*, *New England Magazine*, and *Waverly Magazine*, often printed articles sympathetic to the South. New York had strong economic ties to the South. As stated earlier, much of the trade between the South and England went through New York. They also profited from slavery with 30 to 40 percent of the price of cotton going to New Yorkers. Levi Coffin, who earned the name of "President of the Underground Railroad," understood the hatred and prejudice that many had toward the South, though he knew it to be unfounded. Once, when he planned a trip to New Orleans, his friends in Cincinnati "tried to discourage [him] from going down river ... saying that it would be at the risk of [his] life." Coffin, like Trimble, came from a southern Quaker background. He knew Southerners and he did not share the prejudices of his northern abolitionist friends. "This was no new advice; I had often been cautioned about going South, but when duty or business called me, I never hesitated, and through all my travels in the Southern States, I had spoken my mind freely on the subject of slavery." He went on and said, "I had endeavored to speak in the spirit of love and kindness, and had never been molested."[115]

One historian, Susan-Mary Grant, looked at northern nationalism as a source of the bloodiest conflict in North America. In her book *North Over South* she examined northern attitudes toward southern states and the development of northern nationalism. Whereas Floan concluded that the hatred of slavery united some Northerners in their contempt for the South, Grant concluded that it went beyond that. She claimed that "The North's attempt to define a national ideal was not, in and of itself, a destructive or wholly exclusive impulse, but over time it became so."[116]

It is difficult to separate emotionalism from statements such as those made by Trimble, but psychology can help in understanding the breakdown in conflict resolution which could lead to feelings of antagonism between one side and the other. By 1861 both Northerners and Southerners had reached the breaking point so that each side spoke aggressively about the other. The psychotherapist Joan Pastor did a study of organizational conflict which offers some insight into how the failure to understand each other could lead to the war. Regardless of the issues, it is the failure to resolve them which leads to aggression. Though the two sides united to fight a common enemy in the 1770s, the changing attitudes toward slavery brought attention to the difference in expectations that each side had regarding what the new nation would be about. According to Pastor, "the single greatest cause of conflict is differing expectations." This conflict comes in three stages. "The critical first step for preventing conflict is taking time to get to know one another." This is consistent with Trimble's view that the North and South both failed to do this. "If it turns out that our values lie on opposite ends of the spectrum, at least it's clear what the problem is." When it becomes clear that "something is not quite right," and "you are not getting along," then you have entered the first stage of conflict. At this first stage talking can resolve the problem. "If the problem is not handled at this stage, the conflict will grow until the differences in expectations become clear," which is the second stage; "it is harder to resolve." Conflict can be ended if both sides try to re-establish trust, but "if the conflict is not resolved at this stage, then it will move to a third and final stage." In that third stage, "you either start fighting or you start ignoring each other."[117]

Though some Northerners did hate the South and Southerners, thus justifying Trimble's stated reasons for becoming a Confederate, he did not admit some personal issues that may have had a greater impact on him. He had a personal conflict with Samuel Felton in the 1850s and because of Felton, lost a job he had held many years and then faced the public humiliation of a hearing. This same Samuel Felton acted completely independently of the city leaders and even the Unionist governor. The rumors he promoted as truth led to the president sneaking through the streets of Baltimore in the middle of the night and contributed to the hostility aimed at Baltimore by the Lincoln supporters. Felton added to the anxieties present on April 19th by having his own army and not communicating any plans of troop movement. When asked to set fire to the railway bridges Trimble at first requested someone else to do it "for private reasons,"[118] thus suggesting that he still had strong feelings about his past troubles. Trimble had lived in New England for several years without ever expressing concerns about conflict between the regions. It seems very likely that his sudden concern arose out of the personal conflict between him and his antagonist, Samuel Felton, a New Englander who did not identify or cooperate with the Southern native leaders that April in 1861.

Mayor Brown stated after the war, "and yet I feel that I am living in a different land from that in which I was born, and under a different Constitution."[119] Baltimore had progressed toward modernization before the war and some of the changes described by Brown had begun before Lincoln or the Confederacy. As conflict grew over the issue of slavery the still fluid bond between the numerous communities and states that made up the United States began to loose its adhesiveness. The people of Baltimore, including Trimble, had no strong commitment to either the preservation or abolition of slavery. During the 1850s they had experienced their own pain with the process of modernization and as the conflict grew violent they tried to maintain a neutrality. Finally, they could not maintain that position. When forced to choose, Isaac Trimble concluded that he belonged with the South. With the coming of war Trimble expressed an identity with the city of Baltimore, the state of Maryland, and the Confederate States of America. It will be seen in the following chapters that the war solidified his feelings of belongingness with the South, and that though he resigned himself to accepting the reality of defeat he never deviated from his new but firmly established identity.

6

Into the Valley

In the fall of 1861 Trimble faced only boredom in the early stages of the war. While in cantonment at Centerville, Virginia, the Confederate soldiers enjoyed good health, no shortage of rations, and only an occasional expedition against the enemy. The division commander, Major General Kirby-Smith, shattered the peaceful lull when he ordered all of his men, including the brigadier generals Arnold Elzey, Robert Taylor, and Isaac Trimble, to witness an execution. Two of the "Tiger Rifles" had "forced a guard" and resisted an officer; as a result they were given the death sentence. In a large field just south of Elzey's camp, at twelve o'clock, the regiments marched out in columns of companies, and in time to the tap of a drum took their places on three sides of a square. Trimble and his brigade stood in the middle, with Taylor on the left and Elzey on the right. In the center of the open space two white stakes awaited the condemned. A covered wagon entered the square chaperoned by two companies with fixed bayonets and loaded guns. The wagon stopped and the two men got out and sat on the two coffins that awaited them near the white stakes. They still wore the picturesque uniform of their company, "scarlet fez or skullcap, light brown jacket, open in the front, showing the red shirt, large Turkish trousers, full and fastening just below the knee, of white and blue stripes, white garters and shoes." A minister attended each man. After the wagon retreated two sections of their own company, in full uniform, marched in slow time down the center. Each section halted in front of one of the men and his selected box. The field officer of the day read the findings of the court and the sentences. The officers in charge of the squads ordered an inspection of arms. Another ordered the men to kneel, and tied their arms behind them and then around each stake. He then pulled down a black bandage over their eyes. The three brigades maintained such an oppressive silence that a single breath could be heard. The sun had shown on the condemned men for their last day on Earth. They heard, "Load at Will," closely followed by "Ready," and then "Aim." The final command of "Fire" sent a volley as if from a single gun. One man fell over on his face and the other on his side. "Such was the first military execution of the Army of the Potomac."[1]

The war involved human beings with the assortment of beliefs, emotions, and attitudes that make each one of us an individual. The execution that Trimble witnessed served the purpose of warning other men what could happen if loyalty alone failed to motivate them to obey the commands issued by their officers. This became even more important once the Confederacy made the decision to fill their ranks with conscripts. Though the events of April 1861 persuaded some, including Trimble, to follow the southern cause, others preferred to remain with the Union, or perhaps stay out of the fight altogether. The success of the new nation would be dependent on a degree of unity.

The individualism which accompanied modern society plagued the South, suggesting that they were not the pre-modern world envisioned by some. Not only did the privates question their reason for being there, but the officers often would disagree openly with each other. Sometimes they simply had personality clashes; other times they differed as to the best way to get the job done. Often the bitterness expressed by one officer toward another resulted from hotly contested bids for promotion. President Jefferson Davis observed men "who engage in strife for personal and party aggrandizement."[2] Trimble constantly griped about his peers and his superiors. At times he must have acted out of belief in what was best for the cause, but there is little doubt that some complaints came when men interfered with his own attempts at self-actualization.

Trimble quickly adjusted to his new environment in pursuit of his psychological needs as defined by Maslow. As a soldier the first two primary needs of food and safety became threatened, but there is no indication that Trimble dwelled on these. The third level belongingness needs strengthened as the war persisted and in the end he expressed feelings about being a Southerner which he had never displayed before the events in April of 1861. What is most remarkable is how rapidly he changed to seeking promotion in the Army as a means of fulfilling the higher needs of self-esteem and self-actualization. It will be seen that in the last years of his life he displayed his military success much more than any achievements during his 30 years as a railroad and business man. It is hard to say for certain when he began to look at military advancement as a prize, but by the end of the Valley Campaign (early June, 1862) hints surfaced which became more clear by the Second Manassas Campaign. Trimble displayed an aggressiveness toward his comrades as well as the enemy, a characteristic seen in other career officers who competed for promotion. As previously stated, this individualism is a typical problem in modern societies.

Despite the internal conflicts, the bonds strengthened between the men who served together, and this would help to develop the new national identity. Regardless of which state the men came from, they began to view themselves as Southerners. When they shared a victory they would share the credit. Praise from peers, commanders, or civilians would go far to reduce the strife among individuals. Trimble never expressed any regrets that he became a Confederate instead of a Union officer, or a soldier instead of a businessman.

The men he shared command with and the men who served under him considered him a fellow countryman regardless of his borderland background. He would often be referred to as a "Marylander," which no doubt contributed to strengthening his state identity. This is also an indication that the men from other states viewed those from Maryland as part of the new nation even though the state remained with the Union. Any conflict with other officers had nothing to do with the fact that he had been a big city businessman rather than a planter. Most of those who worked with him would be considered professional men rather than planters, and several came from Maryland or had Maryland connections.

Trimble had never served in a true military capacity prior to the war, but he quickly proved himself a capable military leader. He learned much from his early service with Thomas J. ("Stonewall") Jackson in the famous Valley Campaign. He realized the value of aggression in the business world, and he could see that this characteristic gave Jackson advantages in battle. Trimble adjusted well to his new profession, seeking advancement up the military ladder rather than the corporate ladder.

Trimble began his second military career as a lieutenant colonel for the Virginia Volunteers but advanced rapidly. At first he worked in his old profession, engineering. Within days the Virginians found themselves mustered into Confederate service and Trimble became a full colonel. General Robert E. Lee ordered him to take command of the construction of the forts and fieldworks for the defense of Norfolk. By August 9 he had been promoted to the rank of brigadier general.[3]

He did not give up hopes that Maryland would become part of the new nation. As previously mentioned, on June 4 he addressed a letter to Robert E. Lee and expressed his desire to accompany the first force to be sent into Maryland. He included with the letter detailed plans on how this first invasion could be accomplished. His arguments probably had some impact on Lee's dream of an uprising of Marylanders forced to remain in the Union, and he hungered for the projected 12,000 men who would join the Army.[4]

Trimble's first commander, Joseph E. Johnston, placed him in charge of constructing the artillery fortifications at Evansport on September 3. This would serve to restrict travel of U. S. boats to and from Washington, D. C. His command there included Walker's and Andrew's batteries, Swann's and Waller's cavalry, and Walker's brigade of infantry. He reported the first batteries to be finished and the guns mounted for service by September 29. Trimble complained of the lack of tools and the manpower furnished by slavery needed to do a proper job, but he did his best to fulfill expectations.[5] He claimed his work to be "scarcely less important than any now being executed anywhere in the South," and that "no efforts or risks should be wanted to insure success."[6] Though he had been trained for engineering and had not been in the Army for almost 30 years, he sought a battle command.

On November 16 he found his ambition fulfilled when Johnston gave him General George Crittenden's brigade. The regiments under his command included the 15th Alabama, 21st Georgia, 16th Mississippi, and the 21st North Carolina. He also had the support of Courtney's artillery from Virginia. His brigade remained attached to the division of Major General E. Kirby-Smith. He witnessed the execution of the two "Tiger Rifles" shortly after assuming his new command.[7]

While in camp in Centerville, Virginia, he won immediate respect for his command skills. He practiced the health care knowledge he gained while working for the railroads in Cuba when no less than 150 men of the 15th Alabama died from the outbreak of measles that hit his brigade.[8] Almost immediately upon assuming command he began to look out for his men, from seeking promotion for his aides to soliciting pay increases for the noncommissioned officers.[9] When not busy nursing his soldiers he "exhibited confidence as a commander with prompt obedience to orders essential to efficiency and the highest soldierly qualities."[10]

At the first signs of spring the army began to blossom into action. On February 21, 1862, command of the division went to Richard S. Ewell. By March 8 Johnston began to withdraw his forces from around Manassas and Centerville. He sent Ewell's division as far south as the Rappahannock to establish a line of defense, while the bulk of Johnston's command moved to defend Richmond from the assault of George B. McClellan at the start of the peninsular campaign. Ewell's orders included holding his position against any possible Federal attack and to help Thomas J. Jackson in the Shenandoah Valley if he requested assistance. Elzey's brigade made camp about a mile east of the Orange and Alexandria Railroad, while Trimble and Taylor took their brigades up river about a mile west. Through most of the month Ewell's division saw only skirmishing, some exchange of fire between pickets, or an occasional artillery burst. In April companies B and E of the 21st North Carolina became organized as the 1st Battalion of North Carolina Sharpshooters.[11]

Richard Ewell, brother of Trimble's former employee Benjamin, had some similarities to

General Isaac Ridgeway Trimble

his subordinate. As previously mentioned, Ewell, like Trimble, enjoyed the advantage of being part of a united nation and had lived and worked in several states along the Atlantic coast. He had become a professional soldier and continued in service after his graduation from West Point. He did not have a strong ambition for high command. He exercised his imagination most when using profanity. Like Trimble, he made every effort to remain in the Union and went with the Confederacy only when forced to choose whether to fight for or against his state. When he resigned his commission on April 24 he sacrificed 20 years of service. It took him four years with the Confederacy to earn what he made in a single year with the old army. When promoted to major general he acquired the resentment of those who expected the promotion, including Arnold Elzey, Jubal Early, and Jeb Stuart. He appeared rather strange in 1862, a balding 45 year old eccentric, whose beaked nose and the habit of cocking his head to one side reminded those he met of some sort of bird. He had heard so many bad things about his new boss, Jackson, that he immediately sought reassignment to any command — anyone but Jackson.[12]

One of the three brigade commanders that Ewell inherited from Kirby-Smith was Brigadier General Richard Taylor. The only son of President Zachary Taylor, he had never displayed an interest in a military career himself. He was born in Louisville, Kentucky, but he too, like Trimble and Ewell, had a rather cosmopolitan attitude about being part of the United States, and he felt free to cross state borders in pursuit of his personal ambition. Since he spent much of his childhood in frontier camps, he required tutoring. He studied in Lancaster, Massachusetts, then went to Edinburgh and later to France. He attended school at both Yale and Harvard. Initially a Whig he joined the Democrat Party in the 1850s, and attended the Charleston Convention where he fought to retain the unity of his party. He served in the state senate of Louisiana, and joined the Confederate cause after he saw no hope for peaceful resolution. When his brother-in-law, Jefferson Davis, appointed him a brigadier, he asked that the promotion be revoked to avoid the jealousy of his fellow officers. He liked books more than politics, and his study of military tactics combined with his native intelligence to make him a good general officer. He became respected for his wit, though he had a habit of stretching the truth for the sake of a good story. He got along well with his commanding officer, but each thought the other strange.[13]

Arnold Elzey ended up a brigade commander under the man whose promotion he had resented; he felt that he had earned that office as a reward for his service at First Manassas. Like Trimble, he came from Maryland, but unlike the former he came from an old planter family. He had chosen a military career; he served in the Seminole War, the Mexican War, and in peacetime. He commanded a United States arsenal in Augusta, Georgia, in 1861. Like the other generals in the division, he did not make the decision to join the Confederacy until after the fall of Fort Sumter. He brought his men back to Washington before accepting a commission as a lieutenant colonel in command of the 1st Maryland Infantry. He, too, possessed his eccentricities which would inspire some to refer to him as "crazy."[14]

Trimble completed the set of general officers in the division, and he also became known for peculiar behavior. General T. T. Munford described Trimble as "a gallant soldier of the old army in the olden times."[15] He became known for his fancy costume and his outspoken ways. Some expected him to be overly cautious because of his age, but they found him to be "as bold as any man."[16]

As the Fourth Division waited in limbo between Jackson in the Valley and the rest of the army on the peninsula, a plan developed which would place the handful of men in western Virginia in a starring role. The Union had approximately 180,000 men in Virginia, divided into four major armies. McClellan had his Army of the Potomac in the east, while Irvin McDowell's Department of the Rappahannock occupied the north-central part of the state. Nathaniel Banks's Department of the Shenandoah camped near Strasburg, and John C. Fremont's Mountain Department could be found scattered throughout the Alleghenies. It was the lack of a common command over the three armies in the west that proved to be the Confederates' best ally. Serving as Jefferson Davis's military adviser, Robert E. Lee recommended a diversion in the Valley that would prevent McDowell from reinforcing McClellan. The leader of this army would be Jackson.[17]

Thomas "Stonewall" Jackson had become a hero in First Manassas, but he had a reputation of being a much odder bird than Ewell or any of the brigadiers in Ewell's division. He wore an old army coat that he had worn in the Mexican War, and a broken-visored V. M. I. cadet cap. He had become as fanatical about his health as his religion. He believed that one side of him had become larger than the other, and would raise one arm in hopes that the blood would reduce its size and thus make him more balanced. When not sucking lemons for his health he would be on his knees taking care of his spiritual needs. He rarely made a command decision without praying over it. He descended from a large Irishman who had immigrated to Cecil County, Maryland, in 1748. The family prospered, but found greater success as professional men and politicians than as planters. Like Trimble, he looked to West Point as a means of beginning a career. He found greater satisfaction teaching at the Virginia Military Institute than he did in serving his country as a fighting man. Also, like Trimble, he did not like or profit from slavery, and he opposed secession. He accepted the constitutional right of his fellow Southerners to own slaves, and he also believed in the rights of the individual states, but he resisted leaving the United States until Lincoln's demand for 75,000 troops had forced his native Virginia out of the Union.[18]

The one characteristic that created the greatest wall between his subordinates and himself lay in his dedication to secrecy. Jackson felt determined to follow Lee's plans, but he kept from his officers "what he intended to do; where he was going; when he would move, and what he aimed to accomplish."[19] This caused the generals, as well as enlisted men, to question his orders. They failed to comprehend how he could accomplish his primary objectives. Ewell suffered the most as he often appeared ignorant to his subordinates when he could not explain to his men the reason for their actions. This led Taylor to say to his superior, "What, you, second in command, and don't know!" He went on to add, "if I were second in command I would know."[20] This would also create problems for Ewell when he found himself left stranded. He had orders from Johnston, but he had no idea where Jackson had gone, or what he had in mind.[21]

Some of the internal conflict experienced by Trimble and the other general officers resulted from the feelings of isolation as Ewell and his brigadiers waited. They would reinforce Jackson if called on to do so, but as time passed they grew anxious to fight. Ewell had learned to detest the "sour Presbyterian" which Jackson personified. He also became concerned when he heard of the defeat at Kernstown and the stories about the rough winter in the Valley. By April 16 the wait had swelled the division's ranks to 8,000 infantry, 500 cavalry, and 14 guns. Ewell had his men trained and they all had a strong desire to enter the fray, including Trimble. Lee and Johnston granted him permission to launch an attack against McDowell as soon as the Rappahannock River fell to the point that a crossing could be made. Just as they prepared to fulfill their dream Henry Kyd Douglas arrived with a dispatch from Jackson calling for assistance. A series of confusing orders from Jackson to Ewell sent the division to and fro, leading Colonel Isaac G. Seymour of the 6th Louisiana to claim that his division commander did not know his business. The division soon found itself near the Virginia Central Railroad where it could easily be moved toward Richmond or Fredericksburg if Lee should find that he needed them. By the end of the month things heated up in the Valley resulting in the first meeting between the two commanders at Jackson's headquarters on April 28.[22]

Jackson believed Banks to be too strong and feared making a direct attack to stop his march through the Valley. Of the three alternative plans presented, Ewell favored the one that called for striking Banks's lines of communications by New Market with the combined forces of Jackson and Ewell. Ewell and his men, including Trimble, had their desire for combat thwarted once again when Jackson finally ordered them to remain at Conrad's Store to check Banks's advance.[23]

The anxiety of these early days created more internal conflict than did personal ambition on the part of Trimble or any of the other officers. Indecision had damaged the relationship between Ewell and Jackson, as well as between Ewell and his subordinates, but the first days in the Valley further aggravated the relationships between the Confederate commanders. Ewell cursed Jackson for disappearing with no word of where he went, but a greater complaint revolved around the change in attitude that Jackson had shown. Before Ewell's arrival Jackson had treated him as an equal, but once Ewell entered Jackson's domain he became a subordinate. Captain David Boyd of the 9th Louisiana claimed that Ewell made a plea with Davis to replace Jackson. Meanwhile, Jackson had a victory at McDowell on May 8.[24]

Colonel Walker of the 13th Virginia began to question the sanity of all the southern commanders in the Valley. Ewell had asked him if he thought Jackson crazy, basing his claim on the circumstance of abandonment that he found himself stuck in. Walker had studied under "Fool Tom Jackson" at VMI, but could not admit him to be literally crazy. Later, Walker visited Elzey's headquarters where the latter accused Ewell of being crazy. While discussing the sanity of commanders, one of Walker's conscripts burst into the tent demanding permission to return to his home. He pushed a paper in front of the brigade commander to sign; in response Elzey lunged for a brace of pistols nearby and fired two errant shots at the fleeing soldier.[25] When he expressed his displeasure to Walker the colonel only laughed and said, " I was up to see General Ewell just now, and he said that General Jackson was crazy; I come down to see you, and you say that General Ewell is crazy; and I have not the slightest doubt that my conscript ... will report it all over camp that General Elzey is crazy. So it seems I have fallen into evil hands," he concluded, "and I reckon the best thing for me to do is to turn the conscripts loose, and march the rest of my regiment back to Richmond."[26]

Trimble finally witnessed some unity among his commanding officers. After two weeks of frustration and confusion, Jackson reunited with Ewell and the Confederate leaders began to work together. Ewell shared one important trait with Jackson; he had learned the value of rapid movement during the Indian wars. When he marched, his men used only flies instead of tents, and they took only the cooking utensils that could be carried in bags instead of chests. On May 13 he had received orders from Johnston that required the two divisions to attack Banks if he should head toward Fredericksburg. On May 14 he received word that Jackson had returned. When he got news of General Shields, one of Banks's division commanders, retreating from the Valley he felt compelled by Johnston's orders to follow. On that same day, May 17, he learned of Jackson's plans to attack Banks. Ewell now wished to join Jackson, but could only do so when he persuaded Jackson to counter Johnston's orders. Jackson realized that he had the perfect opportunity to fulfill his objective of distracting Banks in the Valley, but he knew he could not do so without Ewell's help. Trimble's commanding officers finally reached agreement in the decision to attack, and in the process began to establish a bond of mutual respect.[27]

After the weeks of confusion, for everyone except Jackson, and the related frustration and internal conflict, they prepared themselves for the first real battle that Trimble participated in, as well as beginning the military conquest that would come to symbolize Jackson's Valley Campaign. Jackson's army faced Banks at Front Royal on May 23. The battle began at 2 p.m. with the 1st Maryland Confederate attacking the 1st Maryland Union. Through no choice of his own, Trimble served in his first battle primarily as a spectator. The outnumbered Federals retreated and the conquered supplies helped the Union commander earn his nickname of "Commissary Banks." In three hours of fighting they had taken 700 men, 2 cannon, 800 small arms, plus more than $100,000 in supplies. More important, they had weakened the Union defenses of Winchester.[28]

While camped near Front Royal on the night of the 23rd Trimble revealed some interesting personality traits. Ewell kept his men busy into the night. Finally Captain Campbell Brown had closed his eyes to sleep when his black servant, Willis, warned him of someone stealing corn from his saddle bags. "Who is it?," asked Brown.

"It's General Trimble, Sir," Willis answered.

Brown nudged Ewell, "General," he said, "look at the old rascal stealing my corn."

Ewell and Brown watched for awhile, and then Ewell said, "Willis, go and give my compliments to that gentleman, and ask him to put back the corn he took from that horse."

When Trimble learned that the order came from Ewell he returned three of the nine ears of corn he had taken. Then, with Ewell and the others still watching he made up for the lost ears by removing some from the courier's saddlebags. Brown concluded that Trimble's horse had probably got the largest feed of any animal in camp that night.[29]

On the 24th Jackson pursued the retreating enemy toward Winchester, but Ewell's division did not see any significant action. General Ewell, with Trimble's brigade, the 1st Maryland Regiment, and the batteries of Brockenbrough and Courtney, had been instructed to move toward Winchester. At 5 p.m. Trimble's 7th Brigade remained about eight miles from Front Royal as Jackson detached Elzey and Taylor and took them with his division on the road leading from Strasburg to Winchester.[30] The men under Jackson encountered the enemy and might have made greater progress if Turner Ashby's cavalry had not "deserted their colors, and abandoned themselves to pillage to such an extent as to make it necessary for that gallant officer to discontinue further pursuit."[31] Trimble would have to wait one more day before becoming fully involved with the enemy.

The next day Trimble finally experienced combat. Ewell's abbreviated division marched down the turnpike between Front Royal and Winchester and stopped for the night about three miles from the city. At 6 a.m. on the 25th they arrived at a point one mile from Winchester, driving the enemies pickets before them. Jackson and his men arrived soon after dawn. The 16th Mississippi, 21st Georgia, and 15th Alabama, along with the six pieces of Courtney's artillery, reached a hill about a mile from town at 7 a.m. Soon after that the 21st North Carolina began the battle on the eastern side as they marched into town amid enemy fire that came from behind a stone wall. The 21st Georgia assisted Colonel Kirkland's North Carolinians and they quickly dislodged the enemy. The success of Trimble's brigade halted only briefly as a dense fog engulfed them for more than a half hour. By 8 o'clock the fog had lifted and the 16th Mississippi took a position on the east of town. Within a half hour a large part of the enemy force, supposedly their reserve, moved in the direction of the woods and disappeared from Trimble's view.[32] After the fog lifted, the battle between the Union and Confederate artillery continued. "For half an hour the fire exchanged between these two batteries was incessant and well directed on both sides, displaying a scene of surpassing interest and grandeur on that sunny but far from peaceful Sabbath."[33] Trimble had noticed a weakness on the Union left. He notified Ewell of his findings and requested permission to realign and attack. Permission denied, he continued with the original plan. Not long after, a cheer from the western hills of the town, where Jackson had been engaged with the enemy, signaled the retreat of the Union forces on their right flank. Trimble saw the flight of the broken Union forces move toward the Martinsburg Turnpike.[34]

Trimble had his first personal conflict with his commanding officer at the end of this victorious battle. In his report Ewell recognized the role Trimble played in the victory at Winchester. Not only did he record the heroic fighting of the 7th Brigade, but added, "I am indebted to that officer on more than one occasion for valuable counsel and suggestion."[35] The one bit of advice not followed included the suggestion that they pursue the fleeing enemy. Trimble recorded that he did finally receive the orders to advance on the Union flanks, but he added "had this movement been permitted half an hour sooner (prevented by causes known to you) the retreat of the enemy's reserve would have been completely cut off."[36]

The victories at Front Royal and Winchester went far to create bonds among the men under Jackson's command. They had worked together and sent the enemy in rapid retreat. The people of Winchester gave the Confederates a greeting that boosted the morale of the men, despite the bickering amongst themselves. Jackson recorded, "as our troops, now in rapid pursuit, passed through the town they were received with the most enthusiastic demonstrations of joy by its loyal people," adding that "for more than two months" they "had been suffering under the hateful surveillance and rigors of military despotism."[37] John W. Fravel of the 10th Virginia Infantry wrote, "In passing through Winchester we could hardly get along the streets for the ladies, who were so glad to see us." He went on, "they would actually hug some of the boys."[38] General Johnson captured the spirit in his description, "as the last Yankee marched down the main street of the town we were coming up a lane not three hundred yards behind them." He continued, "down the street we went, cheering like mad, and open flew doors and windows, old men, women and children rushed out, dressed and undressed in their Sunday clothes, and in their night clothes, hurrahing, crying, laughing, screaming." Any doubts about why they fought evaporated, "such an excited scene was never seen before or since — a whole people demented with joy and exhibiting all the ecstasy of delirium."[39]

Jackson had been more successful than he realized because he had attracted the attention of the potential reinforcements for McClellan. After receiving news of the battle at Front Royal, Lincoln made two military decisions. First, he ordered John C. Fremont to push eastward toward Jackson. Second, he ordered McDowell to halt his progress from Fredericksburg toward Richmond and instead to head for the Valley where he would crush Jackson's pesky army. Ignorant of Lincoln's orders, Jackson headed toward Harpers Ferry hoping to create northern fears of a Maryland or Washington invasion. He also hoped to divert attention away from Major Harman, one of Jackson's officers ordered to remove away from Winchester the massive stores captured in the battle. Trimble, as part of Ewell's division, followed Jackson in his pursuit of the enemy.[40]

On May 30 Jackson again demonstrated his skill at alienating his own officers. As General Winder warned Jackson of Union reinforcements gathering in Harpers Ferry, General Elzey advised that some long-range cannon had been positioned atop Maryland Heights. Jackson virtually accused Elzey of cowardice in his fear of "big guns," leaving the more aged subordinate flushed with silent anger. Jackson failed to recognize his breach of etiquette toward one of his generals in front of another. His attention became diverted toward the south as he received word of the advance of Fremont and McDowell's division commander, James Shields.[41]

Trimble once again found himself left out of the action. Jackson immediately fled for Winchester, leaving Ewell and his division to direct the slow-moving supplies on the start of a tortuous eight-day movement to meet the enemy. Confusion slowed Ewell as he mistakenly received information that the supply wagons had been lost. Meanwhile, lack of communication had left the 1st Maryland behind. June 1 also began one of the rainiest weeks in the war. The men had not received orders about their destination, and by the end of their first day of marching they had traveled 33.5 miles with no rations. The next morning the men received a barrel of crackers and continued on their way. Urgency had kept them away from the bounty of captured Union supplies, though Trimble's men had profited from the apparel. It had been reported that at Winchester 20 percent of his men fought without shoes, and they now solved that problem. By June 2 men began to straggle, wander off the road in search of food, hobble because of blisters, and collapse from fatigue. Anxiety added to the ennui of the long march when they received news of Johnston's wounds at Seven Pines. Commanders to privates now worried about the future of the army under a new leader. By June 6 they camped near Port Republic, in a position to strike either Fremont, Shields, or both. Since Shields lay about a day farther away Jackson decided to defeat Fremont first and then dispose of Shields.[42]

Ewell cursed the overburdened supply wagons on June 6 as the Confederates had their first encounter with the enemy forces closing in on them. The swearing teamsters struggled to extract the vehicles mired in the mud of the Port Republic road. General Ashby and his cavalry tried to hold back the blue tide on June 7 just outside of Harrisonburg. Trimble's brigade did not participate in that first encounter. Ewell felt pleased about the outcome despite the death of the loved cavalry general. Jackson mourned the loss of Ashby, even though he had problems keeping his men in line when they smelled loot or applejack.[43]

Ewell's division bivouacked on the night of June 7 near the battlefield where Ashby fell, and the next morning began the expected encounter. Jackson and the Confederate wagon train narrowly escaped capture by the Union cavalry in Port Republic. At 9 a.m. Jackson ordered Ewell to send his largest brigade to assist him in Port Republic. At 10 a.m. Fremont advanced toward Cross Keys. Ewell's division occupied a ridge, and in the center lay a field several hundred yards long where Ewell had posted four batteries of artillery. The Port Republic road passed thorough the center. Taylor supported the batteries, while General Stuart went to the left and Trimble to the right. Elzey remained in reserve. Ewell then received Jackson's previously mentioned request for assistance and responded by sending Taylor to Port Republic and moving Elzey to support the artillery. This left Ewell with fewer than 5,000 rifles, half as many as Fremont. Trimble then decided to move to a better position one-half mile in front of the main line, leaving the 21st North Carolina to support Courtney's battery. Trimble occupied the new position at 10:30, then the battle began.[44]

Trimble proved to be responsive, bold, and decisive during the battle at Cross Keys. At Ewell's orders the 15th Alabama had been left on picket one mile in advance at Union Church, and there became the first to engage the enemy. They barely escaped to join the rest of the division. Trimble ordered the remaining two brigades to hold their fire until the Yankees approached to within 50 steps of their line. They maintained order as the "enemy appeared above the crest of the hill [and] a deadly fire was delivered along [the] whole front," adding to which Trimble editorialized when he described "dropping the deluded victims of Northern fanaticism and misrule by scores."[45] After 15 minutes it became clear that the enemy would not advance, so Trimble attempted to capture one of their batteries. He proceeded by moving the 15th Alabama along a ravine; unperceived, they got on the enemy's left flank and in his rear. "The Fifteenth Alabama completely surprised the force in their front (the enemy's left flank), and drove them by a heavy fire, hotly returned, from behind logs and trees along the wood to the westward."[46] When he heard the sounds of heavy fire he ordered the 16th Mississippi and the 21st Georgia to move across the field toward the remainder of the Federal brigade. Trimble then received the support, at Ewell's orders, of Elzey's 13th and 25th Virginia regiments. Meanwhile the 15th Alabama had advanced to within 300 yards of the battery, to which Trimble gave the orders to charge. Trimble recalled, "upon reaching the hill I found it had limbered up and rapidly retired, having lost several horses by our fire." He added that "five minutes' gain in time would have captured the guns. This was lost by the Mississippi regiment in misconstruing my orders."[47]

Despite the failure to capture the battery, the enemy did begin a retreat, hotly pursued by Trimble. Another brigade of Union soldiers supporting the battery 200 yards to the left had advanced into the open ground, but the united efforts of the 15th Alabama and the two Virginia regiments forced them back. "After some minutes brisk fire by the enemy's sharpshooters their entire left wing retreated to their first position, near Union Church on the Keezletown road."[48] By this time General Taylor came to Trimble's assistance. Trimble discussed a renewal of the fight against the enemy now about a mile distant. Taylor agreed that they could "soon wipe out that force if it would do any good," but instead "proposed to return his brigade to camp, as he had that morning marched rapidly to Port Republic and returned, and his men needed rest and food." After Taylor's refusal to continue the contest he left at about 4 p.m. Trimble then disposed the three regiments in the woods about one-half mile from the enemy, "with skirmishers in front and on the flanks, sending word to General Ewell that the enemy had been repulsed on our right, and that [he] awaited orders."[49]

Trimble prepared himself to renew the attack. About a half hour after Taylor departed, Trimble received orders from Ewell to "'move to the front,' and that a force would be sent forward on the enemy's right to make a combined attack before night."[50] Too late to recall Taylor, Trimble proceeded with his own brigade to within 500 yards of the Federals. After a half hour of no word Trimble sent a courier to Ewell notifying him

General Trimble proved to be responsive, bold, and decisive during the Battle of Cross Keys. He did challenge the authority of his commanding officer, General Ewell, as he would do again at Gettysburg.

of readiness. A second courier went a half hour after the first. Soon after, he sent one of his staff lieutenants and said to Ewell "that if the attack was made on their flank, to divert their attention from my movement, I thought I could overpower the enemy in front, but that it would be injudicious to do so alone."[51] As he watched the Union soldiers light their campfires, draw rations, and prepare for a night's rest, Trimble knew he would have the element of surprise. After strongly urging a night attack he discovered that Ewell had headed toward Port Republic to assist Jackson. He briefly considered attacking alone but concluded that the possibility of failure would undo all that they had accomplished that day. He then withdrew, convinced that if he had not allowed Taylor to leave they could have been successful without involving Ewell in the decision to attack.[52]

Trimble finally confronted Ewell urging a night attack, and this led to a major conflict between the two generals. Trimble reported that he was "convinced that we could make a successful night attack and disperse or capture General Frémont's entire force—certainly all his artillery—I awaited General Ewell's return, and then urged more than ever the attack."

He went on and said that he "begged him to go with me and see how easy it was."⁵³ Ewell responded by saying that he would need permission from Jackson. Trimble then rode seven miles and obtained consent from Jackson for Colonel Patton's battalion to cooperate with him, and Jackson said, "to consult General Ewell and be guided by him."⁵⁴ According to Trimble, Ewell still declined to take responsibility. General Taylor joined Ewell in pointing out that even a partial failure could interfere with Jackson's plans for the next day. Trimble replied, "that we should have the army of Frémont pressing us to-morrow if not driven off, and that we had better fight one army at a time."⁵⁵ He finally abandoned hope for the night attack. Ewell revealed part of his reasoning in his own report when he recorded that "the commands of General Trimble and Colonel Patton were kept in position to hold the enemy under Frémont in check, and keep him from advancing upon Port Republic or taking any part in the engagement on that day."⁵⁶

On the next day Trimble gave little more than minimum support to Jackson at Port Republic. He took up his old position and remained there until 9 a.m. After the Union set up an battery to drive them out of the woods, Trimble retreated towards Jackson at Port Republic. He then received two messages in rapid succession to assist Jackson. After crossing the bridge he ordered it burned, which his men accomplished just before the arrival of the enemy. Jackson had already achieved victory before Trimble and his men arrived.⁵⁷

Trimble rarely praised his fellow general officers, but did not hesitate giving credit to the men under his command. He reported, "to the bearing of all the officers ... and the men I give most favorable testimony, and cannot withhold my highest admiration of their gallant conduct and fine discipline."⁵⁸ His recording of Taylor's refusal to attack the day before sounded rather matter of fact; however, his report on the failure of Ewell to allow a night attack fell just short of accusations of incompetency. Ewell, on the other hand, willingly gave credit to Trimble for their success at Cross Keys. He wrote, "Brigadier-General Trimble's, Seventh Brigade, had the brunt of the action, and is entitled to most thanks."⁵⁹ Ewell, in turn, received praise for his efforts throughout the Valley Campaign from everyone except his commanding officer, General Jackson.⁶⁰

Regardless of who gave whom the credit, the Valley Campaign of Jackson has often been recognized as one of the greatest military successes of the entire war. Ewell finally concluded that Jackson was not crazy but instead had "a method in his madness."⁶¹ With forces never totaling more than 17,000, Jackson defeated at least three times that number. He compensated for the shortage of numbers with speed and knowledge of the terrain. In just 48 days Jackson's men had marched over 676 miles, averaging 14 miles per day. At the cost of no more than 3,100 men, half of those captured, they inflicted close to 5,000 casualties, captured 9,000 small arms and so many supplies that they could not carry them all away. He had routed the enemy from the major part of the Shenandoah Valley, and in the process accomplished the main objective of distracting a large number of Federal troops from rendering assistance to General McClellan. But perhaps more important, the campaign had considerable effect on the morale of both armies; a good effect for the South, and a negative effect for the North. The men emerged a forged fighting unit. All of the general officers, including Trimble, became known and respected, and the men under their command came away with feelings of invincibility.[62]

Despite sufficient glory for all, a considerable amount of personal conflict remained in the wake. Trimble had some reservations about Taylor, and a definite lack of respect for Ewell. Richard Garnett had been removed from command and arrested by Jackson and blamed for the defeat at Kernstown. Ewell, Winder, and Taylor had all sought transfers from Jackson's command, and Turner Ashby and John Harman had submitted resignations. Several lower ranking officers had been placed under arrest, and several others complained. Jackson's penchant for secrecy sparked the spread of rumors, including a claim that when Winder appealed to the Secretary of War for a 30-day rest period, Jackson's stern opposition prevented the much needed recuperative period. Though some of his fellow soldiers accused him of acting out of ambition he probably believed it to be a matter of discipline. Jackson viewed fighting for the Confederacy as equivalent to fighting for God. Trimble, on the other hand, had a strong desire to be promoted to major general, and would eventually reveal his ambition to Jackson.[63]

As early as June 5 Lee considered recalling Jackson's army from the Valley, but the orders to move did not come until June 17. Robert E. Lee had been chosen to replace Johnston in command of the Army of Northern Virginia. His political strength lay in his ability to get along with President Davis. He sought advice from the president, and kept him informed on a daily basis. Lee knew that once the roads became dry enough for McClellan to continue his "battle of the posts" campaign that McClellan would start moving toward Richmond. Lee had the choice of surrendering the Confederate capital or fighting. He concluded that he needed Jackson to lead in the fight.[64]

Jackson ended up jeopardizing the reputation he had earned in the Valley by the poor job that he did in the Seven Days Battles, probably because extreme exhaustion finally caught up with him. He had become used to exercising ultimate command over his men, and now when faced with a subordinate position his commander, Lee, failed to assume the needed control. The Confederate army fought like independent divisions. Robert Lewis Dabney noted in later years that Jackson appeared to be thoroughly confused at Gaines' Mill. There had been a complete breakdown of communications between the Confederate generals. The problems for Jackson climaxed on June 30 when he reached his physical breaking point. Though no single explanation satisfactorily explains Jackson's lethargy, simple exhaustion accounted for much of it.[65]

Despite Jackson's personal problems, Trimble shared in the glory from the Valley along with the rest of Jackson's men. John W. Fravel, of the 10th Virginia Infantry, recalled a story which demonstrated the mystique that Jackson's army brought with them from the Valley. After they arrived in the east they waited their "turn to be put into action." Longstreet's men had captured some Yankee prisoners. Fravel and his friends taunted them with, "Hello boys! we are getting you, ain't we?"[66]

"Yes," they answered, "but Fremont and Shields are giving Jackson h___l in the Valley."[67]

They looked at the prisoners and said: "Do you see that man there on that horse? That is Jackson, and we are his men." They then pointed out that they had "done up" Fremont and Shields, and would "do them up."[68]

One of the prisoners threw his hat on the ground and said: "You will do it! It is no use to try to lick Jackson."[69]

Trimble again marched toward an unknown fate. Jackson maintained his traditional veil of silence as Ewell's division followed him toward the larger battlefields in the east. After a week's travel they reached the vicinity of Ashland, about 12 miles from Richmond, on June 25. Jackson rode ahead of his army and met with Robert E. Lee, D. Harvey Hill, James Longstreet, and Ambrose Powell Hill. After Lee explained the general objective he left the other men alone to work out the details; such a faith in his delegation of authority could explain the communication problem the Army of Northern Virginia had during the Seven Days Battles. Jackson returned to Ewell and the others even more exhausted after his meeting, but they set out the next morning.[70]

Lee's instructions moved Jackson's army of three divisions toward their first major encounter in the campaign, Gaines' Mill, also known as Cold Harbor. In addition to Ewell's and Jackson's divisions, Jackson also commanded Brigadier General Whiting's division which included General John Bell Hood and the Texas Brigade, and the 3rd Brigade as well as the batteries of Reilly and Balthis. Whiting took the lead on the morning of

June 26.⁷¹ Trimble recorded in his report that at 4 p.m. they could hear fighting "not more than 2 miles distant," and as usual second-guessed his commanders when he added, "in my opinion we should have marched to the support of General Hill that evening."⁷² They spent the night of the 26th near Hundley's Corner. Some skirmishing took place that night, but it did not involve Trimble or any of Ewell's division. The next morning Ewell led all three divisions in the continuation of their march. They drew a line of battle near Cold Harbor where the road they traveled intersected with the road leading from Mechanicsville to Bethesda Church.⁷³

Though Jackson did not shine brightly during the Seven Days Battles, Trimble performed well. At Gaines' Mill he led two segments of his brigade in two distinct and gallant charges. Ewell had ordered Trimble, along with the 8th Brigade, into the woods on the right of the road. After marching half a mile the front shifted father to the left. Trimble received orders to hasten to the front in the direction of the enemy fire. On approaching Cold Harbor the front shifted farther to the left. At Ewell's orders Trimble took the 15th Alabama down the road from Cold Harbor to McGehee's farm. After crossing the swamp he placed the Alabamians and the 21st Georgia in position to advance. In the process of moving into position for battle he lost contact with the 16th Mississippi and the 21st North Carolina. This is what created the opportunity for Trimble to lead two distinctive charges.⁷⁴

Trimble sent orders for the Alabama and Georgia regiments to advance, which they did despite the fact that they passed several other regiments retreating from the horrendous hail of shell and shot. They continued against "a perfect sheaf of fire, under which the killed and wounded were falling fast in [their] ranks." Trimble noted, "still the brave fellows pressed on, followed by a Virginia and Texas regiment, which took an active part in the action."⁷⁵ They fired their weapons until the guns became too hot to load. They exhausted all of their ammunition, and then consumed that of their fallen comrades.⁷⁶ Trimble, in a rare instant, did recognize the bravery of Ewell and realized that "his presence alone held the men in position for over an hour and a half under this terrific fire."⁷⁷ Not only did Trimble's men face the "combined fire of shot, shell, grape, and musketry,"⁷⁸ but also an early version of the machine gun. They captured two rapid-fire guns which could discharge 60 balls per minute. They consisted of a revolving cannon with hoppers into which they poured bullets.⁷⁹

Trimble left the two regiments under the command of Ewell and went to find his missing men. In his search he had the opportunity to do what he enjoyed, advise the other generals. He first ran into General Whiting near the Cold Harbor House. He "strongly advised him to meet the enemy half a mile or more to our right (north), so as to flank the force in ... front or encounter a separate body of the foe." He recognized his own brilliance; his advice allowed Whiting to meet "a reserved body of the enemy," which he not only defeated but captured their battery.[80] General Winder then asked Trimble where he should enter the field. Because of Trimble's recommendation to march well to the left, he "brought a timely support, in a perilous crisis, to General Elzey's and other brigades, which had been terribly cut up by the fire of musketry." In addition Winder captured the "well served batteries at McGehee's house."[81] The recording of such meetings and their related success might have been the product of Trimble's ambition. He came from Cross Keys confident to the point of being cocky, and may have been laying the ground work for his promotion to major general.

After finding his wayward regiments he led them in an attack where others had failed. He made the decision to enlarge the front which he had suggested to Whiting and Winder. At the word "Forward," Trimble "stepped off promptly." After a short distance they passed a regiment in gray on the ground. They then came upon an open field they would have to cross before reaching the enemy. Here the "balls flew thick and fast." After a steady advance they came upon a ravine or hill where the enemy awaited. They started to pass a second Confederate regiment, until the colonel halted them when he demanded, "where are you going?"[82]

"We are going to charge the enemy and drive them off,"[83] Trimble answered.

"You cannot do it," the colonel warned. "Four attempts have been made by different regiments, and each has failed."[84]

"We can and will drive them off," Trimble confidently proclaimed. "Forward boys, and give them the bayonet!"[85]

Some of Trimble's men shouted, "Get out of our way; we will show you how to do it."[86]

Trimble again declared the glory of the Confederate cause as well as praising the experience of his men when he recorded, "it would have required older and braver troops and those engaged in a better cause to have stood firm against an onset so rapid, so resolute, so defiant."[87] They swept the enemy from the hill. A hail of fire fell upon the fleeing Northmen. One entire regiment surrendered, while others escaped down a ravine toward the Chickahominy. Trimble, by chance, reunited most of his brigade when he came upon a captured Yankee battery held by several companies from the 15th Alabama and 21st Georgia. His brigade slept that night on the ground they had captured. Trimble recognized the magnitude of their accomplishment when he surveyed the excellent position the enemy had held.[88] He added to his report, "that it was done everywhere along the line by troops who had marched all day without food entitles the army to the name of 'The Indomitable.'"[89]

The charge at Gaines' Mill proved successful but costly for the Confederates and caused them to change their plans. Total losses on both sides exceeded 15,200 men, with more than 2,300 killed outright; the South suffered 8,751 killed and wounded. Ewell's division lost about 800 men, most of those from Elzey's brigade and Trimble's Georgia and Alabama regiments. Lee immediately informed Davis that the Army of Northern Virginia won its first victory; then he revised his plans. He shifted the troops by roads nearer Richmond and hoped to strike the enemy between White Oak Swamp and the James River.[90]

Trimble and the rest of Ewell's division saw little action between Gaines' Mill and Malvern Hill. Though Lee allowed most of the army to recover from its wounds on the 28th, by 10 a.m. he had Jackson send Ewell's division to advance down the north bank of the Chickahominy to Dispatch Station. They destroyed a portion of railroad track, but unfortunately an advance cavalry unit had burned the station and most of the supplies. Most of Trimble's brigade stayed in camp and tended to the wounded or buried their dead. Ewell then received orders to prevent the enemy from crossing Bottom's Bridge.[91]

Trimble appeared to assume the role of a major general. When they halted about 9 a.m. he sent a man up a tree, which the enemy had converted to an observatory. Trimble wrote a note to Lee and Jackson informing them that the officer could plainly see signs of Yankee forces moving southward, and certainly retreating. They held that position until 6 p.m. when Jackson had them return to Grapevine Bridge where they would follow his division. Lee responded that the enemy had heavy forces on the right, and that he had tried to reach them with artillery without effect. Meanwhile Trimble again wrote a note to Lee that he had seen other signs of retreat, specifically the burning of stores. They reached the York railroad near Bottom's Bridge about 2 p.m. After marching back and forth for several miles they halted about two miles from the bridge. Again Trimble called attention to dense clouds of dust which he interpreted to be signs of Union retreat. After 4 p.m., on finding a good place to cross the river, he finally convinced Ewell to attack what they anticipated to be a disorderly state of the enemy. Contradictory orders came from Jackson in time to stop the raid. Trimble documented his sage wisdom. He reported that it later became proven that McClellan did break up his camps in the locations Trimble had observed on Sunday, and that he had begun a rapid retreat. Ewell found nothing that day worthy of reporting.[92] Though Trimble may have been simply laying the groundwork in politicking for promotion, that night Jackson did discover "evidences of the hurried and disordered flight of the enemy ... now visible — blankets, clothing, and other supplies had been recklessly abandoned."[93]

They spent the night at Reynoldsville. On Monday the 30th they marched over the same road taken by the enemy 24 hours earlier. At Savage's Station some of Jackson's men captured an enemy hospital. About 2 p.m. Jackson's entire army exchanged artillery fire with the Union men. They reached White Oak Swamp about 4 p.m. Most of Jackson's army, including Trimble's brigade, spent the night at White Oak Swamp. The next day they would be in battle again at Malvern Hill.[94]

The Confederates closed in on McClellan's southbound army. Three roads led southeast below White Oak Swamp, generally parallel to each other and perpendicular to the Federal line of retreat. Benjamin Huger's division took the Charles City road, Theophilus Holmes's division traveled the New Market road, while A. P. Hill moved down the center on the Darbytown road. The plan called for them to intercept McClellan at the head and the flank of the column, while Jackson and Harvey Hill, rejoined by Ewell, would began to attack the Federal rear. Thus the Union army would have 45,000 Confederates on its flank and another 25,000 closing in on the rear.[95]

Trimble followed orders to march at sunrise on July 1, and his brigade crossed White Oak Swamp. They formed a line of battle on Poindexter's farm, opposite the Malvern Hills, at about 2 p.m., with his brigade on the extreme left, extending Whiting's line. At 3 p.m. Jackson again frustrated Trimble's aggressiveness when he rejected a request to surprise the enemy with an attack on his right. Thus they remained in that position for about three hours. One of his batteries had a 30-minute exchange of fire at 5 o'clock. At about sundown Jackson sent Trimble to support D. H. Hill to the extreme right where the battle had raged for two hours. One of Hill's officers guided them through dense woods in the dark, and for one and a half miles they became exposed to continuous and rapid fire from Union artillery. They took a position on the part of the field where John Magruder earlier had made a disastrous charge across an open field. Hill ordered him to remain in his position near the woods on the edge of the field. Trimble then felt compelled to advise Hill that the enemy would not expect an attack from his position, and that his brigade could approach undiscovered under the cover of darkness. After repeated refusal of his request Trimble had to hold his position. After midnight he bivouacked his brigade in the woods, disappointed by their lack of action.[96]

Bright and early the next morning, July 2, Trimble sought either Ewell or Hill to encourage renewal of the attack. He began to realize the hopelessness of the situation when he "found the entire army in the utmost disorder." As he rode through the camps he saw "thousands of straggling men asking every passer-by for their regiments." He found travel difficult with "ambulances, wagons, and artillery obstructing every road." He abandoned his eagerness to fight as he found the sights before him "altogether, in a drenching rain, presenting a scene of the most woeful and disheartening confusion."[97]

His brigade had not been involved in actual fighting, and by 6 a.m. they found themselves in good order and among the first to be ready to move out. Jackson ordered them to march to the church where they remained the entire day of the 2nd. On the 3rd Trimble received orders to move to the front, which he did. They encamped about eight miles from the James River, opposite Westover. On Independence Day they again went to the front, which had moved to about four miles from the river. This time they met some skirmishers and occasionally exchanged fire with enemy scouts. That night one of Trimble's regiments got called on for picket duty. They remained in that camp until July 8 when they received orders to move to the rear. On July 10 they camped only four miles from the Confederate capital, "scarcely able to march from the excessive fatigue and prostration, the result of constant fighting and marching in a country where air and water, were both impure, and rapidly breaking down the health of the army."[98]

As difficult as it had been on Trimble and his men, the Seven Days Campaign had been a grand victory for the South. The 30,000 men killed and wounded in the series of battles had equaled the number of the casualties from all of the battles in the western theater during the first half of 1862. They had established a pattern of greater casualties and harder fighting between the Army of Northern Virginia and the Army of the Potomac. The victor, Lee, had failed in his final effort to keep McClellan from the James River, or to deliver the crushing blow needed to force the North to peace talks. Jackson's lethargy had burdened him with enough blame to tarnish the glow that he had emerged with from the Valley. Longstreet especially had faulted Jackson at every step of the campaign, claiming that if he had been on time just once they might have succeeded in trapping McClellan's army. Longstreet concluded that Jackson could do well against the likes of Fremont, Banks, and Shields, but could not compete with the North's best. Complaints increased in Ewell's division as many of the officers tired of serving under Jackson. They considered him too demanding and too harsh. Some even appealed to Adjutant General Samuel Cooper to take command of the division away from him. Ewell himself had changed his view of Jackson, and began to recognize his military genius. As the Army of Northern Virginia recuperated near Richmond the rumors and feuds grew. A newspaper battle between Longstreet and A. P. Hill ended with Longstreet placing his opponent under arrest.[99]

Trimble had been involved with the war in a combat situation for a little more than a year. He had participated in his share of internal conflicts, from witnessing the execution of deserters to strategy disagreements with Ewell, the man directly over him in the chain of command. His constant attempts to second-guess the other generals began to suggest something more than a lack of sensitivity or excessive zeal. He carefully documented cases where he had made suggestions and where he felt that he had been proven to be correct. This may have been the beginning of his politicking for promotion to major general. He did on occasion praise other generals, as well as the officers and men who served under him.

Despite the clear presence of fighting among the ranks in the Confederate army, bonds had clearly been forged and gave them determination and reinforcement that they fought for a just cause. On two occasions Trimble had clearly mentioned that their success had come about because they were on the right side. The march through the streets of Winchester had boosted the men who had saved the civilians from the militaristic tyranny of the northern soldiers. Though many felt that Jackson had ruled with an iron hand, many of the men had grown proud of their association with the band who had played hell in the Valley. Not only had Trimble continued to reinforce his decision to join the Confederacy, but he had successfully transferred his identity to being a Southern officer. The suggestion that he sought promotion in the Army is an indication that he also looked to the Confederate army as a means to achieve self-actualization. He fought beside men who lacked complete unity, but they had worked together well enough to produce victory over their former countrymen.

7

The Second Round at Manassas

On the morning of June 8, 1862, near the end of the Valley Campaign, Thomas J. Jackson evaded Union capture. Just before the battle at Cross Keys he stood in the road enjoying the company of some of his men. One of them made a comment about "fancy soldiers." Jackson pointed to General Isaac Ridgeway Trimble sitting on a fence, wearing a black army hat, cord, and feathers. "There is the only fancy soldier in my command," he said. When told of the comment after the war Trimble only laughed; he knew that it was merely a joke at his expense. Jackson had great respect for the old general, respect he deserved. He proved it that very day in the battle that followed; Trimble's brigade swept the field. They approached to within musket range before being driven back, having given the order, "Don't fire until you see the whites of their eyes."[1] Trimble continued to serve under Ewell, who in turn remained under Jackson's command during the campaign at Second Manassas, referred to as Second Bull Run by the North. By the end of the campaign Jackson would recommend Trimble for promotion to major general.

Trimble had proven himself a capable military leader, offering invaluable assistance to both Ewell and Jackson. He continued to perform admirably during the next campaign, but his motivation became increasingly clear. He did not simply fight for a noble cause but rather had begun to look to the army as a means of finding self-actualization. One could only speculate that he actively campaigned for recognition while in the Valley, but as the Second Manassas campaign unfolded it became more obvious.

In a pre-modern society such promotion could be obtained by laurels won in the field of battle and thus winning the recognition of a prince; in a modern democracy such promotion involved political campaigns in addition to proving one's professional abilities. The internal conflict brought on by individualism continued through this phase of the war and in the case of Trimble it became clear that personal ambition motivated much of his contentious behavior.

It should be understood that Trimble did not suffer from an exceedingly abnormal selfishness but rather from a disease that existed on both sides of the front. Individual rights had become important to the American people; however, such self-centeredness can prove disastrous on a battle field. In the North political conflict climaxed when the former army commander, George B. McClellan, opposed the commander-in-chief, Abraham Lincoln, in the election of 1864.[2] As seen in the last chapter, the South also suffered from this side effect of modernization, whether that is the personal ambition identified by Richard D. Brown or the individualism of Robert Hollinger.[3] During Second Manassas Trimble not only criticized his competition, but became involved in a dispute with Jeb Stuart over who deserved credit for the most important single event in his bid for promotion. Whereas Trimble sought personal recognition, Stuart considered the conflict one of organizational jealousy: infantry versus cavalry.

By the summer of 1862 the romantic zeal that drove men to war dwindled considerably. Many of the men had grown tired and hungry. Officers fought personal battles. Nonetheless, the war had been put in motion and each one had to cope as best he could. They continued to fight for their cause, but their personal objectives often provided the incentive to make it through the next day, ranging from finding a ham to landing a promotion. Though Trimble had once struggled for personal fulfillment in the corporate railroad environment, by the end of 1862 he had become fully transformed into seeking self-actualization through military achievement.

Despite the fact that Trimble and his comrades had their personal objectives, the war continued to solidify their Southern identity. Trimble developed rivalries, and even personal enemies, but he never questioned the cause they fought for. His competitors criticized him, but they never questioned his loyalty nor considered him any less of a Southerner because he came from a border state that remained with the Union.

The campaigns of the summer of 1862 proved to be a time of opportunity for Trimble as well as some of his fellow Confederates, though in the end he emerged with a stronger Southern identity. It became a campaign of high stakes and of intense drama. The North could have won the contest, but the successful gambling of General Robert E. Lee and some disastrous mistakes by the North proved beneficial for the men in gray. This success demonstrated the genius of Lee to many Southerners, and also provided a stage for the emergence of Jackson and James Longstreet.[4]

At the time of Second Manassas the North responded to some of their problems by reorganizing. High command recognized the lack of unity between McDowell, Banks, and Fremont and how this had allowed Jackson so much success in the Valley. The unified Federal command became known as the Army of Virginia on June 26, 1862. John Pope replaced McClellan as the commander of the Union forces. Fremont refused to serve under the new commander. Pope did little to relieve internal strife since he had a habit of boasting about his successes in the West. In his first communication to his new

Stonewall Jackson looked at Isaac Trimble and said, "There is the only fancy soldier in my command." After the war Trimble laughed when he heard the story for the first time since he knew that Jackson respected his command abilities. Courtesy William Trimble.

army he told them how he had become accustomed to seeing the backs of his enemy. The Army of Virginia had three objectives: the first to protect Washington, the second to protect the Valley, and the third to draw Lee's attention so that George B. McClellan might take Richmond.[5]

The Confederate army also experienced some significant changes. Lee reorganized into two corps, one led by Longstreet and the other by Jackson. According to Ewell, much of the romanticism that had been part of the war had evaporated by the summer of 1862. He wrote to his wife that "some 100000 human beings have been massacred in every conceivable form of horror with three times as many wounded." He went on to describe the soldiers and how "the chivalry that you were running after in such frantic style in Richmond have played themselves out pretty completely," and that some now refused "to get out of the State to fight." He recognized that "such horrors as war brings about are not to be stopped when people want to get home. It opens a series of events that no one can see to the end."[6]

Ewell's division, which Trimble remained attached to, had undergone some major transformations. The once impressive army had been whittled down to 3,000 men. Jubal A. Early had been sent to replace Arnold Elzey, who had been shot at Cold Harbor. Richard Taylor received a promotion and returned to Louisiana; command of his brigade passed to Harry T. Hays of the 7th Regiment. Hays had been wounded at Port Republic and temporary command of the division went to Colonel Henry Forno of the 5th Louisiana. Forno maintained command during the brief period that Trimble remained with the division.[7]

Jubal Early, who had been wounded himself in May at the Battle of Williamsburg, reported to Ewell for duty. He was descended from Thomas Early, who had arrived in Virginia in the seventeenth century from Ireland. Early graduated from West Point in 1837. He fought in the Second Seminole War and earned a promotion to first lieutenant in 1838. Nonetheless, he resigned his commission to study law. He also pursued a political career beginning with his election to the Virginia House of Delegates in 1841. He did serve during the Mexican War, but then returned to his law practice. Like Trimble, Early had firmly opposed secession and joined the Confederate cause when his native Virginia seceded. In his early 40s he lacked any resemblance to the genteel and aristocratic image of the Confederate officer corps. He appeared to be at least 10 years older, chewed tobacco incessantly, cursed, and carried a canteen which most believed to contain "Old Crow." Jackson admired his fighting abilities but little else about the man.[8]

Ewell also received a new brigade under the generalship of Alexander Robert Lawton. Lawton commanded 3,500 rifles, the largest brigade under Jackson. He had been sent to assist Ewell at Gaines' Mill, but during Second Manassas became permanently attached to the division. He had been born in South Carolina in 1818. He graduated from West Point in 1839 but resigned his commission in 1841 and attended Harvard Law School. He settled in Savannah, Georgia, in 1842 where he practiced law, became president of the Augusta and Savannah Railroad, and a politician. After a term in the Georgia House of Representatives he became a state senator in 1860. Though he resembled Trimble in that he had lived in various regions of the nation and had worked for railroads, he differed considerably when it came to the war. Whereas most of the men Trimble had worked with had joined the Confederacy only after being forced to choose, Lawton had been one of the fire-eaters who had helped to create the chasm between the two sections of the nation. Though a professional man rather than a planter, he had supported a state senate resolution favoring immediate withdrawal from the Union. As a colonel for the First Volunteer Regiment, and acting under the orders of Governor Brown, he seized Fort Pulaski, thus committing the first overt act of war in the state of Georgia.[9]

Trimble also saw some change within his brigade. While in encampment at Strawberry Hill, near Richmond, they removed the 16th Mississippi as part of a program to have united regiments. Though his brigade still contained Georgians, Alabamians, and men from the Old North State, his fourth regiment left to join their fellow Mississippians. He would receive the 12th Georgia on August 27 as a transfer from Early's brigade, giving him four regiments once again.[10]

Following a brief period of recovery near Richmond, Lee's army came back to life in response to reports of Pope's advance. On July 13 Lee ordered Jackson, along with Taliaferro's and Ewell's divisions, to oppose Pope at Gordonsville. On July 14 Pope advanced with about 50,000 men, while the 90,000 under McClellan waited in threatening silence. Lee had only 80,000, but took advantage of McClellan's inactivity. At first Jackson had only 12,000 in Gordonsville, but Lee doubled the number when he sent A. P. Hill to reinforce him.[11]

Jackson, though praised after his death, continued to generate resentment from some of the men under his command, especially as the months passed and discomfort replaced romantic zeal. Generals and soldiers alike blamed Jackson for disrupting their rest. Taliaferro wrote his wife, "Jackson is never satisfied unless he is marching or fighting so that I have no hope of seeing you until the war is over."[12] Corporal Thomas Godwin of the 4th Virginia wrote to his sister, "it seems that we will never get to a stopping place," and also blamed Jackson, "for here we are again on our way to—where? If you want to know you will have to ask Genl. Jackson." He also complained about the discomfort of the train trip, "being very hot & the cinders filling our eyes & mouths. I had a seat between the cars where some one was continually climbing me all the time."[13]

Jackson's troops finally arrived at Gordonsville on July 19. Jackson had to guard the Virginia Central from Hanover Junction to Gordonsville, but he planned to attack the first enemy corps to arrive at that place. He would have to wait to put his plan into action. Lee ordered Pope suppressed on July 27. They advanced to Liberty Mills on August 2, and then towards Culpeper on the 7th.[14]

Jackson struck by ordering his men to move out on August 8 for what would become known as the battle of Cedar Mountain, also called Slaughter Mountain. Ewell took the lead, followed by Powell Hill's division, with Jackson's old division bringing up the rear. The initial advancement collapsed, in part because of confusing orders, but also because of the sluggishness of some of the officers. The excessive heat contributed. The next day, with the temperature still in the low eighties at 7 a.m., Jackson prepared to halt what he believed to be the advanced units of Pope's army. Jackson had 26 guns in position, 17 of those in the center of the line. He planned to unleash a double envelopment. Early would lead an advance along the Culpeper road, while Trimble and Forno passed over Cedar Mountain in an effort to turn the Federal left. Winder would support Early, but at the same time extend Jackson's flank until it overlapped the Federal right.[15]

Trimble's brigade saw action during the battle but suffered little damage. On the morning of the 9th he followed orders to approach under cover and occupied a pine thicket about three-quarters of a mile from the enemy picket lines, which they accomplished undetected by the men in blue. At about two o'clock Trimble received orders to advance through the woods on the right and to occupy a good position along the slope of Slaughter Mountain, which he found about 200 feet above the valley. He placed Latimer's battery by 3:30, and from that position did considerable damage to the union batteries. The cannons under Trimble assisted in an advance at 5:00 by distracting the enemy response. The 15th Alabama went out to meet skirmishers on the right, but Union artillery halted the planned attack on the enemy flank. The 21st Georgia and North Carolina progressed 400 yards from the battery on the Union left, followed by the 15th Alabama. The fire from his own cannon ended Trimble's plans to charge the enemy guns. By the time he halted their fire, the enemy had withdrawn. Trimble's brigade followed the rest of the army chasing the Federals, removing some ambulances and ammunition wagons abandoned by the retreating enemy. They bivouacked a mile to the enemy's rear.[16]

The South won the battle at Slaughter Mountain. The North had 1,758 killed and wounded, with an additional 622 captured, while the Confederates had only 1,283 casualties. Jubal Early gained hero status for his part in the battle. Trimble's brigade had only one fatality and 17 wounded. He attributed the low casualty rate to their ability to remain out of view of enemy guns through much of the battle. Jackson agreed to a Union request for a truce while they retrieved their wounded and buried their dead. Soldiers on both sides also seized the opportunity for friendly trade, while the officers exchanged opinions of the battle.[17]

Trimble followed Ewell's division as it drifted toward the next major engagement. They began to move on the 10th, but retreated back to the same position on rumors that the enemy had gone around the left. On the 11th they captured a Union brigadier general, several hundred prisoners, small arms, and six wagons of ammunition left on the field, ambulances, horses, and other miscellaneous supplies. Jackson suspended drill and other duties as he proclaimed the 14th a day of thanksgiving for the recent victory. They moved away to Liberty Mills on August 15, and then encamped at Clark's Mountain on the 17th through the 19th. On the 20th they crossed what Trimble called the "Rapid Ann," better known as the Rapidan River.[18]

Conflict in the ranks followed Jackson. Ewell challenged the accuracy of Jackson's reports when he praised Winder for his efforts at Cedar Mountain while ignoring Ewell's own accomplishments. Postwar writings revealed that Longstreet felt considerable jealousy and envy when dealing with Jackson. He had claimed that Jackson could only do well against second-rate Union generals, whereas the men under Jackson considered Longstreet's soldiers to be unproven units.[19]

Trimble did not become involved in the organization rivalries, but he felt increasingly convinced that he should be promoted to a major general. His successes in the Valley and the Seven Days Battles, followed by this capture of Yankee supplies, must have boosted his confidence. Since the first days in Maryland he clearly felt that he had the ability to lead, but he had kept his personal ambition to himself. Even his diary does not reveal his feelings on the subject. Then one night in August he made it clear to Jackson that he expected promotion and that he expected it soon. Dr. Hunter McGuire was present, and he felt that "the gallant General Trimble ... expected and thought he ought to be made a major-general, but when the appointments came out he was disappointed." Trimble knew Jackson, and he knew that the man did not approve of swearing. His frustration must have been great when he proclaimed, "By G__, General Jackson, I will be a major-general or a corpse before this war is over." Jackson did not reveal his thoughts, either about the swearing or Trimble's ambition. There is no record of Jackson pushing for Trimble's promotion until September 22, but it is clear that he respected Trimble's ability.[20]

The confidence that Jackson had in Trimble became obvious shortly thereafter. Dr. J. William Jones of Virginia recalled an interview he had with Jackson in late August. "General," he began, "are you aware that the enemy have crossed at the forks of the river, and are now moving up in the rear of General Ewell and between him and A. P. Hill's column?"[21]

"No! Have they?"

"Yes, sir, I have seen them."

"Are you certain they are the enemy?"

"Yes, sir, I am," Jones stated.

"How close did you get to them?" Jackson asked.

"I suppose about 1,000 yards," Jones answered. "I could plainly see their blue uniforms and the United States flag which they carried." He continued, "They shot at me, and cut the rear of my horse, as you see, and then I got away from there as fast as my horse would bring me."

Jones expected Jackson to send orders for new movements but instead received a response, "I am very much obliged to you, sir, for the information you have given me, but General Trimble will attend to them." Jackson continued by explaining, "I expected this movement, and ordered Trimble posted there to meet it."[22]

Jackson had put Trimble in the path of battle. While Lee continued probing up river for a place to ford, Jackson had parked his supply wagons near the shallow waters of Wellford's Ford, and placed Trimble there to protect them. At about midnight of the 22nd he received word that some Federals had surprised the wagon train and captured some ambulances and mules. Trimble immediately sent the 21st Georgia to recover the property and drive off the vultures in blue. His men returned with some prisoners who provided important information: the North had one or two brigades across the river, placed there to annoy them. Since Jackson's army had spread out, with Ewell's division five or six miles in advance, and Longstreet the same distance to the rear, Trimble decided to keep his brigade together and prepare for a defense.[23]

Trimble chose to attack the Union forces rather than to wait for them to make the first move. After General Hood arrived Trimble requested him to continue occupation of their current position and to be in readiness to offer any needed assistance. He then advanced toward the enemy, with skirmishers well in front. After the Union skirmishers retreated into the main force Trimble realized that they could easily be flanked on both sides. With the 21st Georgia and 15th Alabama covering the flanks, Trimble led the 21st North Carolina down the center. The enemy retreated to the hills on the river where they made another stand. "At this point, supported by their artillery on the north side of the river, they made an effort, by the blowing of trumpets, beating of drums, and cheers, to encourage their men to charge."[24] Trimble's men "boldly advanced with enthusiastic cheers and drove the opposing forces into the river and across it in great disorder."[25] The enemy sought protection in General Sigel's camp, which opened fire on Trimble's attacking men, but without serious injury. Trimble's forces continued in the chase and "slaughtered great numbers as they waded the river or climbed up the opposite bank. The water was literally covered with dead and wounded."[26] They took more than 100 prisoners and found one colonel among the dead. After an hour's occupation of the battlefield Trimble's brigade retreated unmolested and encamped one and one half miles away. They never needed to call on Hood for assistance. Trimble claimed that even though the enemy outnumbered them two or three to one, their killed and wounded outnumbered Trimble's men 10 to one.[27]

Lee came up with a plan which has been debated by military strategists for years, some calling it brilliant while others classified Lee as foolish but lucky. Though outnumbered by 75,000 to 55,000, Lee decided to split his forces, sending one half on a wide strategic envelopment to interfere with enemy communications. The next day the rest of his army would follow. Success depended on speed and deception; failure could be the total destruction of his army. Jackson would lead his forces on a march upriver beyond Pope's right flank, cross the stream where possible, and then continue on a wide sweep. His target would be the Orange and Alexander Railroad itself, not Manassas Junction. First, Jackson wanted to strike at Bristoe station since the destruction of the bridge there would cut Union communications.[28]

After the battle in which Trimble saved his wagon train, he followed Jackson in the great march toward Bristoe. On August 23 they stopped near Warrenton Springs. The next day they remained stationary and had a heavy artillery engagement with the enemy. That evening they camped near Jefferson. On the 25th they continued up the river, crossed it, and stopped at Salem, a total distance of 30 miles. The next morning they entered Bristoe.[29]

Jackson's army did a good job of destroying the communications and capturing Union men and supplies. Confederates got within 100 yards of the tracks before the Federals spotted them. Surprised and disorganized, the men in blue offered some resistance until Forno's Louisianans and Trimble's 21st North Carolina swarmed the half dozen streets of the small town. A northbound train escaped Confederate small arms fire and headed toward Manassas Junction where the soldiers would soon spread word of Jackson's presence to the Union soldiers to the north. Shortly after, Trimble's men heard a second train. This time Trimble's North Carolinians prepared themselves for a volley. The train slowly passed through the hail of bullets, glided past a derailing switch which had been thrown, and the engine and half of the cars tumbled down a shallow embankment. The victorious men in gray swarmed the train and its contents like buzzards. They reveled at the conquest of the train named "President," proudly displaying a picture of Lincoln over the cowcatcher. Almost immediately a third train with 20 empty boxcars entered the scene. After a Confederate with railroad experience signaled an "all clear," it plowed into the other train and magnified the wreckage considerably. As Ewell's and Trimble's men continued their plunder yet another train signaled its arrival. The engineer saw the wreckage, threw the train in reverse and headed south, where word of Jackson's presence would be spread in that direction. Jackson had put the Orange and Alexandria out of operation, but now he lost any element of surprise and would become the fox in a Federal hunt.[30]

Though Jackson realized that soon the entire Union army would have knowledge of his presence, he received information that would prove irresistible to him and provide a source of glory for Trimble. In addition to blocking Union communications and capturing supplies, Jackson's men had taken some prisoners. One civilian politician, after learning who had captured him, stared at the famous Confederate leader. He saw the crumpled coat and cadet visor adorning the rather plain looking man, then moaned in a tone of disgust, "O my God! Lay me down." The engineer and some of the other captives informed the unimpressive but capable commander that the main base of supplies for Pope's army lay about four miles up the line at Manassas Junction.[31] Once he learned of the treasure he "deemed it important that no time should be lost in securing [it]."[32] After puzzling over which of his exhausted troops to send on a mission so late at night, Trimble offered his "two Twenty-ones," referring to the 21st North Carolina and 21st Georgia. When Jackson suggested that two regiments might not be sufficient, Trimble responded, "I beg your pardon, General, but give me my two Twenty-ones and I'll charge and capture hell itself!"[33]

Jackson pondered the situation, and after Trimble had retired for the night Jackson made his decision. He sent for the aged but dependable brigadier. An aide-de-camp to Jackson entered Trimble's quarters and said, "if you choose, take Manassas Junction tonight. He leaves it to your discretion."[34] Trimble awakened his men despite the late hour and the fatigue which followed their 30-mile march. His dedication to the cause had always been obvious. His desire to do his duty had been equally obvious. He must have believed that the acceptance of the mission would also increase his chances for promotion. Jackson reported, "I accepted the gallant offer and gave him orders to move without delay." Jackson later decided to "increase the prospect of success," and sent Major General Jeb Stuart, without Trimble's knowledge. Jackson considered Stuart "the ranking officer, to take command of the expedition."[35] It is important, as will be revealed, that Jackson did not write his report until April 27, 1863.

Trimble received his orders to take the supply station at about 9 o'clock, "after a long and fatiguing march of the army from Salem to Bristoe Station." The "two Twenty-ones" had about 500 men in total. They halted when they heard an exchange of gunfire between some of Stuart's men and the Yankee pickets. Trimble recorded in his report dated January 6, 1863, "I informed General Stuart of my intention to attack Manas-

7. The Second Round at Manassas

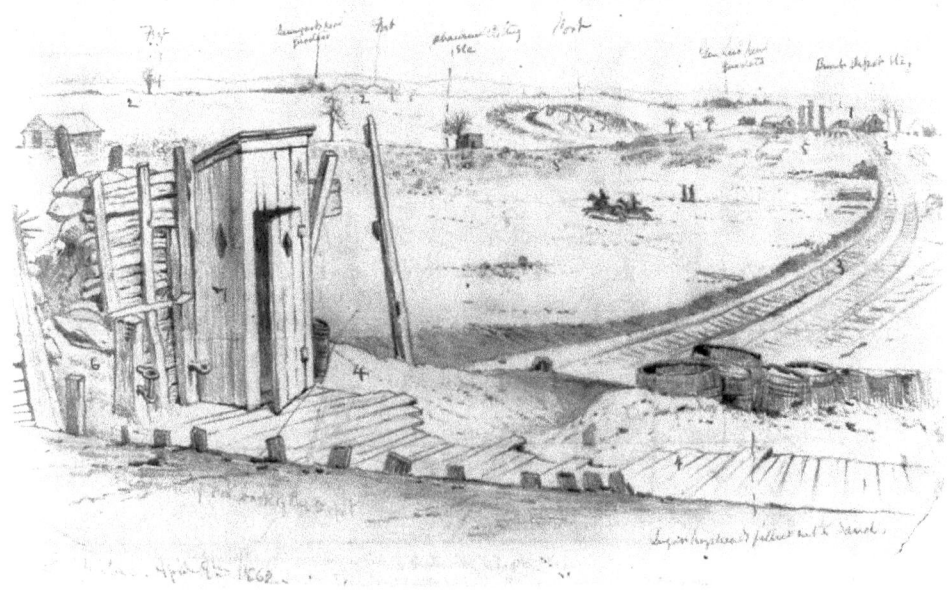

Some union captives revealed to Jackson that the main base of supplies for Pope's Army lay about four miles up the line at Manassas Junction. He called on Trimble and his "two Twenty-ones" to capture it.

sas Junction, and requested his aid with the cavalry which he had then with him." Trimble met no resistance until within a half-mile of the cluster of buildings. He sent men around the right and men around the left, and then advanced to within 100 yards of the batteries, "which continued their fire, one on the north and the other on the south of the railroad." He issued the orders to charge, and within five minutes his men held both batteries at bayonet point. The battle ended once they captured the Union cannons. Each battery contained four field pieces, horses, equipment, and ammunition. "Over 300 prisoners were taken, an immense quantity of commissary and quartermaster's stores, and a large train loaded with promiscuous army supplies, just arrived from Alexandria, and about 200 horses independent of those belonging to the artillery." In addition over 200 Negroes "were also recaptured." Trimble recorded in his January report, "I had no assistance from artillery or from any part of General Stuart's cavalry, a regiment of which arrived some hours after the attack was made and commenced an indiscriminate plunder of horses. General Stuart himself did not arrive until 7 or 8 o'clock in the morning."[36]

Once Trimble established control of the supplies, he sent a request to Jackson for some reinforcements as he knew about a large enemy force at

Centerville, and he expected more to arrive from Alexandria. He kept his men under arms throughout the night. He placed guards over the buildings and cars containing supplies. After the arrival of the fresh troops the plundering began. He clearly stated that his men did not participate, "I must, in justice to the officers and men of the two regiments, express the high admiration I entertain for the good conduct and gallantry which they displayed throughout the whole affair."[37] Jackson immediately praised Trimble and tickled his ambition, "Permit me to congratulate you upon the brilliant success with which God has blessed you; you deserve promotion." He also told Trimble that "the 12th Georgia and the 15th Alabama Regiments have been ordered to you this morning."[38]

Though Trimble vainly tried to protect his captured booty from Confederate pillaging, the long months of battle climaxed by the rapid march of Jackson's men generated uncontrollable hunger for the Union delicacies. Throughout the day of the 27th Trimble's brigade occupied three of the old batteries and redoubts at the Junction. They had resisted some attacks of enemy infantry and cavalry, but Jackson and Ewell both realized that they could never cart off all of the supplies and sent their men to the trough. Trimble reported, "it was with extreme mortification that ...

Stonewall Jackson referred to the raid at Manassas Junction when he recommended Trimble for promotion to major general. *Opposite top:* Though Trimble tried to protect the supplies at Manassas Junction, the men could not pass up looting the Union stores. *Opposite bottom:* Trimble and the Confederate troops had to abandon the supply depot, but they destroyed what they could not carry away.

I witnessed an indiscriminate plunder."[39] Jackson and Ewell both realized that what their men could not eat or carry away with them would be consumed by fire. The poor cracker-fed privates ate foods they had never heard of before, and then burdened themselves with new shoes and clothes.[40] John Ware of Tennessee recalled many years later, "They had amazed their inner beings with things undreamed of in their simple scheme of things as Confederate soldiers."[41] He also claimed that "tied on somewhere to nearly every man was a small sugarcured ham, a novelty and a promise of at least one more good meal in his life."[42] Edward McGrady said, "weak and haggard from their diet of green corn and apples, one can well imagine with what surprise their eyes opened upon the contents of the suttler's stores, containing an amount and variety of property such as they had never before conceived of."[43] He went on to say, "it is said that our friend, General Trimble, was very indignant at this sacking of the stores he had captured the night before and had guarded until our division camp up."[44]

Jackson realized that it would be dangerous to remain at Manassas Junction. With Pope on one side and McClellan on the other he could be cut off from Longstreet and crushed between the two Union armies. On August 28 Stuart's cavalry burned the depot and the infantry continued down the long confused road. Trimble wandered off twice, though Jackson's vague orders had left Hill and Taliaferro also confused. On his second wayward adventure Forno and Lawton both followed Trimble. By noon Jackson had the army heading in the right direction, past the old Manassas battleground, and then near Pageland, where Pope's army attacked.[45]

The main battles of the campaign began on the 28th at Groveton and continued for the next two days. In an effort to prevent Pope from gaining defensive advantage Jackson engaged the enemy at Groveton on August 28. In the beginning Pope had 62,000 men, which he hoped to use to capture Jackson's 20,000 before James Longstreet could arrive with his corps. Longstreet hesitated to attack once he arrived on the 29th, and thus may have avoided a complete route of Pope's army. When the battle reconvened on the next day Pope remained unaware of Longstreet's arrival. He sent his forces against the Confederate left. The defenders proved to be stronger than expected, and the North suffered defeat; however, they held Henry House Hill long enough that most of their army escaped across the river and avoided destruction by the Confederates.[46]

Trimble's brigade had become the left wing to the attacking force at Groveton. John Ware recalled that day which would be so costly for Trimble's brigade, and how the "ground, [was] stained with the blood of patriots, blue and gray." He reflected on the realization that what "was a moment ago the drowsy sound of the crickets and katydids is now a distant scattered rattle of musketry."[47] On Jackson's orders Trimble led the 21st North Carolina into combat. They suffered heavy casualties. Ware described comrades that day, and how he could "see only their faces, and they are not the faces of the soldiers of novels. They are sunburned and dirty and pinched, their eyes do not blaze with the lust of battle, as the novelist makes them do." He continued, "on the whole, they are rather calm eyes, but there is a tensity in this calm that rather chills you, and you feel uncomfortable."[48] At 8 p.m. Trimble received orders to continue the attack. The 15th Alabama did not hear the orders and so remained stationary as the 21st Georgia and 21st North Carolina became exposed to heavy front and cross fire of the North. Nonetheless they held their ground until the 15th Alabama finally began to move, followed by the newly acquired 12th Georgia. Though it appeared that the Yankee position could not be taken, neither did Trimble's brigade yield any ground. As the evening wore on, the Federal forces withdrew to a new line farther back. Trimble's brigade slept the remainder of the night before the commencement of Second Manassas the next day.[49]

The battle had been costly. Ewell received a serious wound which resulted in the amputation of a leg. Some men in Trimble's 15th Alabama offered to carry him from the field, but he barked, "Put me down, and give them hell!"[50] Lawton assumed command of the division. The battle also took a high toll in Trimble's brigade. Trimble said, "I have never known so terrible a fire as raged for over an hour on both sides. The dead and wounded bore next morning melancholy evidence of its severity."[51] On the 29th the 21st Georgia had only 69 of the 242 men who had answered the roll call on the 28th.[52]

The next day proved as devastating to Trimble and his men. The morning light revealed what William Oates of the 15th Alabama described "the carnage of the field," which they held. He went on to call it "the most sickening of any I ever beheld. Our dead and wounded were terribly lacerated by the explosion of the balls that struck them."[53] As the men stood around a fire the next morning the smoke attracted an enemy conical shell. "It struck the ground about fifty yards off, ricochetted and fell in [their] little fire, with the fuse burning as it whirled around and around, knocking the fire in every direction." As Oates lay close to the ground "the men in the group sprang to their feet and ran away, and the shell exploded and wounded two of them."[54]

Later in the morning Trimble led them into battle, and by order of General Lawton he placed them on the left. He selected a line near the railroad excavation and embankment and waited. Trimble recorded, "I expected

After the raid at Manassas Junction, Trimble went on to participate in the Battle of Second Manassas where he was "wounded on the 29th in the leg by an explosive ball which broke the bone and inflicted a bad wound." He spent the next several months recuperating and campaigning for his promotion.

a heavy force of the enemy to be hurled against our small body, not three hundred in all, but the men resolved to fight to the last."[55] Fearing that the enemy would outflank them, Trimble rode rapidly to the top of the hill himself, since he had no staff officers left, so that he might observe the field. An explosive ball hit his leg. He reported, "with great pain I kept my horse, rode back, and was carried from the field."[56]

Command of the brigade fell to Captain Crown of the 12th Georgia, the highest ranking officer in action. Jubal Early reported, 'I believe his brigade was not engaged during the day."[57] The casualties suffered by the brigade also indicate that they saw little action in the main battle, but it must be remembered they had very few left.[58]

Trimble did not report on the activity of that day, which had been limited for him. He wrote in his diary, "I was wounded on the 29th in the leg by an explosive ball which broke the bone & inflicted a bad wound — was carried to a Mr. Foote's & thence to Front Royall, where we passed a month most pleasantly in the family of Mrs. Cloud, a lady and her daughters of great dignity & loveliness of character."[59]

Trimble did not follow the army to Sharpsburg, and in fact spent the next several months convalescing. On October 15 he left the Cloud family and Front Royal and went to Staunton, where he stayed with the family of Mr. Opie who lived a mile from town. On November 16 the bone of his leg had knit and the wound nearly closed, but he became plagued with boils on his ankle. The boils prevented him from using his crutches. He wrote, "My chief trouble now is biles [sic] which form on the ankle & the lancing of which is the acme of pain — perhaps more so than amputation, as some surgeons declare." He left Staunton for Charlottesville on December 17. His family had joined him while in Staunton; when he left, he paid Mr. Opie $100 per month for himself, his wife and two sons. At that time Dr. Garnett recommended laudanum and lead water for his leg, "which has become much inflamed from the calf to the instep." He settled in with Mrs. Carr in Charlottesville.[60]

The heavy loses at Rapidan and Sharpsburg opened up opportunity for a promotion to major general. Lee had five good men that he considered worthy; in addition to Trimble, he evaluated Jubal Early, Edward Johnson, Harry Heath, and Arnold Elzey. The seriousness of Trimble's wounds served as a stumbling block for him. Jefferson Davis had a policy not to promote officers who could not physically take command; however, he refused to retire some who had become invalid. Lee recognized the injustice of not promoting a worthy man who had been wounded, but he also realized that the troops needed permanent commanders. The first command given went to Elzey on December 4, 1862. Trimble surrendered to his personal jealousies when he wrote to Adjutant General Cooper and mentioned Elzey's love of liquor.[61]

Though Jackson recommended Trimble for promotion, the aged commander took exception to the wording of the recommendation. Jackson praised Trimble but stated that he did not consider him a good disciplinarian. In his letter to Cooper, Trimble defended himself; "my Brigade had fewer stragglers; burnt no rails, committed no thefts in the country, was more often drilled both by regiments and in evolutions of the line by myself, than any other in the Army of Jackson."[62] He later wrote to the secretary of war, "If any disparaging representations have been made to the Department to counteract this testimonial [Jackson's recommendation for promotion], in justice to me I should be informed of their nature and be allowed to correct them." He went on to make it clear that his wound would no longer be a handicap, "If however it be considered proper by you, that the promotion shall take effect, I feel bound to observe that if my services are deemed important to the Government they will probably sooner be obtained by making the promotion at once." He then claimed, "as my recovery from a painful wound is probably retarded by the suspense in which I have been kept for some months."[63]

Though Trimble had openly challenged Ewell's decision making, he did not hesitate to solicit a recommendation from his former commanding officer. He wrote to Ewell, "I beg you to pardon any allusion to my own conduct." He went on to add that "I do covet your favorable opinion so far, as to be gratified with a recommendation for promotion from you."[64] He went on to remind Ewell of how Taylor had been promoted to major general after a single battle, but Trimble had proven himself at both Cross Keys and Gaines' Mill, mentioning only those battles in which Ewell had direct knowledge. Ewell never recorded why, but he failed to provide the requested recommendation.[65]

Jackson provided further assistance to Trimble in his quest for promotion by encouraging him to return to work. On January 1, 1863, he asked, "Do you not think you are well enough to sit in a comfortable room and give orders for a division, so long as it is in camp." He went on to advise, "it is important that we should have permanent commanders. If the division should march or go into action, then another could for a time discharge your duties. As soon as you report for duty I think you will be promoted."[66] On January 10 Trimble recorded in his diary, "reported for duty in consequence of a letter from Genl. Jackson." He went on to comment, "my wound not well, but I can sit up all day & write, read & converse."[67]

In a modern army, as with other bureaucracies, politics plays a role in any bid for promotion; Trimble covered the bases politically. On October 22, 1862, Jackson recommended Trimble for promotion, which Robert E. Lee passed on to President Davis on October 27. On January 19, 1863, that promotion became official. The orders simply stated that he would command a division of the Second Corps. The only recorded objection to the promotion of either Trimble or Early came from Brigadier General W. B. Taliaferro. As the senior brigadier in Jackson's division he felt that the next opening should have gone to him. He let it be known that he would try to transfer to some other theater of operations. Trimble left town for the army on January 28 and reached General Jackson's headquarters on the same day. On February 1 he assumed command and issued an address to his men.[68]

In the Confederate army, as in the Union, such promotions required further political savvy and approval by the legislature. In Trimble's case Louis T. Wigfall had offered opposition to President Davis by threatening to block his recommended promotions. As chairman of the Senate Military Committee, he saw an opportunity to curb what he believed to be executive despotism. He also had a personal grudge against Trimble.[69] Trimble heard of the final stumbling block to his long sought after promotion and "wrote a statement to Honble [sic] Boteler of my intercourse with Wigfall at Dumfries and showed him to be actuated by private malevolence, not considerate of public good." In response "Mr. Boteler replied that he would see Senators, give them facts & be prepared to defeat the designs of Wigfall which he thought easy."[70] Trimble received Senate confirmation on April 23, 1863.[71]

Trimble eagerly assumed his new command. Though he had reported to duty and frequently rode among the men, he did not participate in any significant military action. He performed his duties, and took care of the need for improved roads and proper care of the division's horses, though he did not see combat. The early part of 1863 became a time for rest and recovery. Many of the officers and men took extensive furloughs. Some took furloughs without permission; the desertion rate increased. Trimble attempted to solve the problem in late February and early March. He encouraged severe punishment for deserters, making sure that they served as examples. On March 28 he approached Lee with a plan for a surprise attack of Union forces. He attempted to solve the nation's problem with a plan to collect edible wild plants such as dandelion, poke sprouts, curly leaf dock, and watercresses. In such ways he served his division and country until a recurrence of his health problems on April 13. His illness began with a cold and then he developed erysipelas, and finally osteomyelitis.[72]

Trimble's relapse kept him from the field where Jackson died, Chancellorsville, but he ironically ended up with the fallen hero's old command in the Valley. Though he assumed command of his division in January, as previously stated, his promotion did not receive approval by the Senate until April 23. On April 27 he decided to leave headquarters and traveled to Richmond, where he stayed with his old friend J. W. Clarke. His division went to the battle at Chancellorsville without his leadership. By May 18 he continued to improve. He went out riding daily, starting out at six in the morning. Though illness plagued him after lengthy rides, he continued to improve. On May 20, 1863, Lee wrote to Trimble, "I have a proposition to make: it is that you take command, if able, of the Shenandoah Valley ... You will have all the Maryland troops, which I hope you will be able to organize and build up into something respectable. Their organization has been a failure so far."[73] On May 28 Trimble received orders from W. H. Taylor, Assistant Adjutant General, "You are hereby assigned to the command of the Shenandoah Valley and will proceed to Staunton, and assume command of all the troops in the Valley. You will report your arrival there to these headquarters."[74]

In the spring of 1863 a conflict developed between Trimble and Jeb Stuart. The controversy centered on the interpretation of the events that took place during the raid at Manassas Junction back in August. On April

10, 1863, Trimble wrote to Colonel O. J. Faulkner, Assistant Adjutant General, "I have received your communication dated yesterday calling my attention to a seeming discrepancy between your (my) report of the capture of Manassas Junction on the night of August 26, and that of Major-General Stuart, together with the extract from his report."[75] It sounds as if this is the first time that Trimble became aware of the problem. Trimble wrote his report on January 6. The discrepancy between them came on February 28 when Stuart finally filed his report of the actions during the campaign. Perhaps one of the most important discrepancies centered on the order of events. After discussing the awareness of the large stores at Manassas Junction, Stuart wrote, "As soon as possible I reported to General Jackson, who desired me to proceed to Manassas, and ordered General Trimble to follow with his brigade, notifying me to take charge of the whole." In this original report filed by Stuart little else is mentioned. He made initial contact with the enemies' pickets, as reported by Trimble, and awaited the arrival of the infantry. He next reported, "as it was too dark to venture cavalry over uncertain ground against artillery, I directed General Trimble upon his arrival to rest his center directly on the railroad and advance upon the place, with skirmishers well to the front." Stuart continued, "he soon sent me word it was so dark he preferred waiting until morning, which I accordingly directed he should do." According to Stuart the depot was taken as soon as daylight broke. Thus he recorded the events as he saw them, at the time with little concern as to whether Trimble recorded them the same way.

Trimble stuck to his story of the events and specifically disputed what he considered to be errors in Stuart's report. In the previously mentioned letter dated April 10 Trimble said, "I have carefully read over my original report, dated Charlottesville, January 6, 1863 and have to-day had a conference, thorough my staff, with numerous officers who took part in the transaction." He clarified that he had "not a word to alter, that report stating correctly the main facts, but not all the circumstances, which I shall now briefly relate." He said that he had no idea that General Stuart had gone on ahead. This difference could simply be a matter of awareness. He distinctly disagreed with some of Stuart's statements. "I received no orders from General Stuart as to the disposition of my force in its advance," clearly contradicting Stuart's report that he issued orders to Trimble. He added, "General Stuart is entirely mistaken in his statement that I soon sent him word it was so dark I preferred waiting until morning." He in fact had suggested to Stuart that a night attack be made. He asked Stuart to "assist with his cavalry in any way he judged proper." According to Trimble, Stuart did not use his cavalry at all during the night, and did not arrive until "two and a half hours after the capture had taken place." Of course at this point it may be that Trimble discouraged Stuart from joining in the attack so that the brigadier might assume all the credit. If taken at face value and entirely avoiding the temptation to speculate at such motives, Trimble made it clear that his infantry captured the supplies with little or no help from Stuart's cavalry. He said, "I am embarrassed by a difficulty in applying the compliment to myself or to him, but will generously give him the benefit of the doubt, and admit that it was taken without difficulty so far as his exertions contributed to its capture."[76]

On April 25 Stuart responded. He quickly stated, "I lay no claim to infallibility, and I am very far from imputing to the veteran General Trimble any improper intention or motive in what he has said." As to the discrepancy relating to the arrival of the cavalry, first of all he claimed that the depot did not fall until 2 a.m., and that it may have been later than that. He added, "I was in plain view all the time, and rode through, around, and all about the place soon after its capture." He insisted on his presence at the time of the attack, but explained that he spent considerable time looking for General Trimble but did not find him until 7 or 8 o'clock. As to the message that suggested they wait until daylight to attack, Stuart said, "while my recollection is clear that I did receive such a message, and received it from General Trimble, yet, as he is so positive to not having sent it or anything like it, I feel bound to believe that either the message was misrepresented or made up by the messenger." He also suggested the possibility that the message came from General Robertson whose sharpshooters had been previously deployed. Stuart emphasized "that he was under my command on that occasion." In reference to Trimble's report sounding as if they had discussed and agreed to the battle plan, "I was a major-general, he a brigadier; I was assigned specially to this duty and notified that General Trimble would report to me." Later he stated, "and even if General Jackson had not specially entrusted me with this command, as a major-general on the spot I was entitled to it and would have assumed it as a matter of course, in accordance with the Articles of War."[77]

Trimble and Stuart both sought third party confirmations of their stories. Major Thomas C. Glover, commander of the 21st Georgia, submitted a report dated April 10, apparently at Trimble's request, and stated "We attacked and captured Manassas Junction about 12 o'clock." They secured the ground and placed pickets to guard the approaches. "About sunrise Stuart's cavalry arrived in the town." He then added, "We had not previously seen them nor any other troops, except those of our own brigade."[78] At Stuart's request Surgeon T. Eliason, who accompanied Stuart, sent a report. He confirmed the arrival at night, and the first skirmishes between the cavalry and the Federals. He then stated that they heard more shots near daybreak, and that "we rode into Manassas almost simultaneously with the infantry, who had not full possession of the place, as the enemy were in full view at its eastern side. This was just after full daylight."[79]

The entire controversy seemed to have ended in April, with no action taken against either one of the generals. Since no reprimand resulted from the disagreement it might be dismissed as unimportant. It does, however, serve to show the controversy that officers can be involved in even though they fight the same enemy. Both Stuart and Trimble possessed egos and ambition, which no doubt served to fuel the heated exchange of reports and letters.

Jackson did not clarify his orders to his two subordinates, which could explain the problem. He wrote his previously mentioned report April 27, after the letters written by Trimble and Stuart. In that statement Jackson seemed to avoid addressing the disagreement between the two men. He did state that he had sent Trimble to the junction, and then later sent Stuart. Neither of the generals knew what directions Stonewall had given to the other, a chronic problem for those who served under Jackson. James Longstreet recorded the event. He stated, "The gallant Trimble, with five hundred of his men, volunteered for the service, and set out at once on the march. Stuart was afterwards ordered to join Trimble with his cavalry, and as ranking officer to command the operations of the entire force."[80]

Apparently the disagreement between the two came about as an honest difference in interpretation. It is also apparent that Trimble deserved credit for the capture of the enemy supply depot. After volunteering for the duty he had apparently dozed off. As previously mentioned, he received his orders from an aide who made no mention of Stuart. Once Trimble discovered Stuart's presence he attempted to coordinate their efforts, and in fact stated in his January report that, "he requested his aid with the cavalry which he had then with him."[81] He did not appear to recognize or accept that Stuart had been sent to take charge of the operation. Neither his early report nor his diary reflected any doubt that he deserved the credit for the victory. On August 26 he wrote in his diary, "I with 2 Regts. Captured Manassas junction and 8 pieces artillery — vast stores &c."[82] Stuart admitted that he arrived after daylight, as did Eliason, though the latter insisted that the enemy was still present.

Though Jackson appeared to avoid the controversy he clearly gave Trimble credit for the operation. On his letter of August 27 he congratulated Trimble and mentioned promotion. He officially recommended him for promotion the following month, which reached headquarters in October. Trimble entered into his diary, "On 22nd Sept. Genl. Jackson recommended me for promotion-stating that 'the capture of Manassas by two small regiments after a march of 30 miles was the most brilliant exploit of the war.'"[83] This entry in the diary was not the product of Trimble's imagination. Jackson wrote to the Adjutant General, "This charge resulted in the capture of a number of prisoners and 8 pieces of Artillery. I regard that day's achievement as the most brilliant that has come under my observation during the present war."[84] It is clear from this letter and the recommendation for promotion that he felt that Trimble accounted for the success of the action, regardless of who had command.

Stuart and Trimble did not have a history of conflict, and neither did they compete for promotion. Stuart had no reason to report facts other than what he genuinely perceived them to be. He did see two possible reasons for Trimble to be biased in his reporting. Both reasons represented points of traditional conflict within the Army. Early in his report he said, "I attributed these omissions to a certain jealousy of authority, which officers older in years are apt to feel toward a young superior in rank." He later said that "I am not in the habit of giving orders, particularly to my seniors in years, in a dictatorial and authoritative manner, and my manner very likely on this occasion was more suggestive than imperious."[85] This in fact may have added to Trimble's confusion under the circumstances. If Stuart did not emphasize his command, then Trimble would have been more likely to assume that he had control of his own forces. Later in the report Stuart indicated that the conflict might be more in the nature of a cavalry versus infantry contest. "There seems to be a growing tendency to abuse and underrate the services of that arm of service by a few officers of infantry, among whom I regret to find General Trimble."[86]

There is no indication that Trimble resented the cavalry. Neither his reports nor his diary contained any derogatory comments about that branch of the army. His advanced years, especially considering that he was a West Point graduate and one who had performed well since the first days of the war, might have created in him a hesitation to accept the authority of another officer, even one who possessed higher rank. Trimble's actions not only indicated one who had ambition for promotion, but one who had his own ideas. He even suggested military strategy to Lee. Some of the highlights of his months of service show him to be outspoken, aggressive, and one who not only had his own ideas but acted on them.

During this period Trimble did not lace his reports with expressions of Confederate patriotism, but he did offer some statements that indicated that such feelings had not disappeared despite the internal conflicts. On

December 1, 1862, he recorded in his diary, "war in its mildest form is a perpetual violation of humanity & justice."[87] He had no one to impress with this entry so it clearly reflects a melancholic view of the war. In his report on the battle of August 22 he said, "I can speak with pride and admiration of the admirable spirit displayed by the brigade, which went into action with that determined valor which had often before aided to secure victory."[88] In this he noticed that the men had some inner strength that they drew on that allowed them to enthusiastically attack. He recognized this same enthusiasm at Manassas Junction when despite their long day of marching "every man set out with cheerful alacrity to perform the service."[89] Trimble also revealed an admiration for the patriotism demonstrated by the fallen Lieutenant General Fulton who requested "in his last moments that the Confederate flag he had himself borne should be displayed before his failing sight."[90]

As the war continued Isaac Trimble became more aggressive in seeking personal fulfillment by promotion. The nearly 30 years of working for railroads had faded into the background as he struggled for advancement up the bureaucratic ladder of the Confederate army. This modern world promotion came about through political activity as well as military process. Trimble had displayed aggressive tendencies throughout his life, from his childhood challenge to the boys who threw stones at him to the hearing brought about by Samuel Felton. Nearing 60 when the war started, he had not changed his habits. He understood how to fight bureaucratic battles as effectively as military battles and finally succeeded in becoming a major general. There is little doubt that the issues that had divided the nation continued to be important, but Isaac Trimble, as other individuals, had his own personal goals and objectives. Many simply struggled to survive; Trimble struggled for self-actualization.

8

From Gettysburg to Surrender

>Monday, May 18th '63 — Continued to improve rapidly, riding out daily — started at 6 a.m. for Shocco Springs, Warren Co., N. C. and reached Warrenton at 7 — a long journey for an invalid & rather too much for me — however I felt refreshed by a sound night's sleep & started at 6 for the Springs by stage — arriving at Breakfast, which was eaten with a good appetite and probably too much — ate dinner at 2 — probably before breakfast was digested, for at 6 p.m. felt sick & threw up undigested food, at night had some fever, but it passed off by morning — It may be that the sudden stopping of my iron & quinine, which was left in Warrenton, had some effect on my stomach.[1]

In the final years of the war Trimble's personality did not change, but rather proved to be multifaceted as he adjusted to his continually changing environment. He continued to display his aggressive personality, but he showed this to be his nature regardless of the promise of personal advancement. He also continued to draw on the skills he had developed as a businessman as well as his military training.

During the last months of the war Trimble remained outspoken, not only for personal gain but in defense of causes that he found worthwhile. He became quite aggressive in his quest for promotion, but he remained rather contentious even after he became a major general. His conflicts before Gettysburg, such as the one he had with Jeb Stuart, may have been motivated in part by his desire to secure new office, but after the invasion of Pennsylvania he had different objectives. During the Gettysburg campaign he again served with Richard Ewell and quickly resumed his rivalry with him. He may have been setting the stage for further advancement but his pursuit of the issue after the end of the war suggests that he fought simply to prove himself right. He also campaigned after the war in defense of the North Carolinians who had followed his lead in Pickett's Charge. As a prisoner he used his aggressiveness to pursue better conditions for his men and to make plans for their escape.

While a prisoner he had his best opportunity to demonstrate his strength and resolve, often depending on the skills he had developed as a businessman as well as his martial training. He created a functional prisoner bureaucracy by dividing the labor according to the task to be accomplished. Just as he had combed the countryside seeking materials needed by his railroads, he faced even harsher restrictions as he assisted his command in accumulating weapons and other materials needed for their planned escapes. He utilized his networking and political abilities, both with his underlings and those who controlled his world. He endured physical and psychological stress as he led his men, but he often obtained concessions from their northern masters while constantly plotting the return of himself and his men to the South.

In summary, Trimble continued the pursuit of his hierarchy of needs. While in prison he must have felt the first two levels of needs, food and safety, in jeopardy; however, these did not repress his third level belongingness needs and the higher needs of self-esteem and self-actualization. Since he never expressed undue concern about the welfare of his family, his third level needs revolved around the question of community identity. He quickly adapted and became the leader of the temporary community of the prison camp, but at the same time continued to solidify his identity as a Southerner. As during the earlier part of the war, no one hesitated accepting him as one of their own or questioned his right to command just because he came from a border state. He and those around him knew that he was a Southerner.

After having his promotion confirmed by the Confederate Congress, Trimble had a relapse in his health which again took him out of circulation. In mid-April of 1863 he caught a cold which led to an attack of erysipelas "which came near being fatal."[2] On April 27 he tried to reach Richmond but found his path blocked by Yankee cavalry. His companion, Frank, fell into enemy hands and he lost all of their horses. He finally arrived at Richmond and stayed with his old friend J. W. Clarke. He remained there until May 18 when he decided to seek the healing powers of the waters at Shocco Springs in North Carolina.[3]

Even while planning his voyage of recovery to North Carolina he began to solicit work from Lee, which led to his being given Jackson's old command in the Shenandoah Valley. Trimble wrote in a letter dated May 15, "I am so near recovery from the severe attack of camp erysipelas, that my return to duty is looked forward to with much eagerness." He went on to add, "I therefore respectfully ask to be placed in some command in your Army of Northern Virginia, where I may, in your opinion, be most useful to our cause."[4]

In response to Trimble's request, Lee seized the opportunity to revive his old dream of bringing Maryland into the Confederacy and also demonstrated the faith he had in Trimble's ability. Lee wrote back on May 20 saying "I have a proposition to make: it is that you take command at Staunton." He explained that Colonel Davidson currently commanded these troops, with General Jenkins offering cavalry support. He told Trimble that he would "have all the Maryland troops." He began to reveal his dream when he told Trimble that he hoped he would "be able to organize and build [them] up into something respectable." He cautiously added, "their organization has been a failure so far." He explained that Trimble would have "general supervision of operations there," and that he would form the left wing of the Army of Northern Virginia. He must have recalled how successful Trimble had been at Manassas Junction when he said, "supply us with commissary stores and take Maryland as soon as you can." He concluded by saying, "Let me know when you will be able to enter on your new command and I will issue the order."[5]

Trimble quickly accepted the challenge, though he had doubts about finding enough new recruits in Maryland to create an army. On May 25 he wrote "I thank you for the honor you would confer."[6] He must have expressed some reservations about being able to succeed in raising an army of new recruits from Maryland, because he asked for the 400 to 500 Maryland troops already in service, to which Lee responded on May 30, "I cannot recommend [it], as it only opens the door to such as may be dissatisfied with their commanders, and will tend to promote dissatisfaction and desire of change." He went on to clarify, "I hope you will be able to increase the Maryland Battalion speedily to a regiment, without this auxiliary."[7] Trimble received a letter dated May 28 notifying him of his assignment to the command of the Shenandoah Valley.[8]

Trimble never had to pass this test. By the time he arrived at his new command, his troops had already left for Pennsylvania. On June 7 Lee wrote a letter to Trimble explaining that he had issued orders to the officers temporarily in charge of the Valley. Trimble did not leave for Staunton until June 19. When he arrived on June 22 he discovered that "all the forces in the Valley had moved or were under orders for Maryland."[9] He immediately set out on horseback to find Lee.[10] While en route Lee wrote a letter to Trimble dated June 23, "I am very glad to hear that you will be in Winchester to-day, and restored to health." He then proceeded to make one last push for Trimble to recruit Marylanders, "I have no objection to your going into Maryland, but would rather desire it." He went on to say, "if you can raise a division of Marylanders, I will give you all the aid in my power."[11]

On June 24 Trimble finally caught up with Lee near Berryville. After a courteous exchange of greetings Lee said, "You are tired and hungry, if you will step down to the mess you may find some remains of a fine mutton which kind friends have sent us, and after eating come up and we will talk."[12]

Lee customarily dined and finished before his staff. On returning to Lee's tent, after getting his fill of the mutton, Trimble said, "Well General, you have taken away all my troops what am I to do?"[13]

Lee kindly replied, "Yes; we had no time to wait for you, but you must go with us and help to conquer Pennsylvania." Lee went on to boast, "We have again out-maneuvered the enemy, who even now don't know where we are or what are our designs. Our whole army will be in Pennsylvania the day after tomorrow, leaving the enemy far behind, and obliged to follow us by forced marches." Lee optimistically added, "I hope with these advantages to accomplish some signal result, and to end the war if Providence favors us."[14]

Lee then changed the subject by saying, "[I have] received letters from many prominent men in the South urging retaliatory acts while in the enemy's country, on property, &c., for ravages and destruction on Southern homes." Lee turned to Trimble and asked, "What do you think should be our treatment of people in Pennsylvania?"[15]

Trimble answered, "General, I have never thought a wanton destruction of property of non-combatants in an enemy's country advanced any cause. That our aims were higher than to make war on the defenseless citizens or women and children."[16]

Lee rejoined with the solemnity and grandeur that Trimble later described as being so characteristic of the man, "These are my own views, I cannot hope that heaven will prosper our cause when we are violating its laws. I shall therefore, carry on the war in Pennsylvania without offending the sanction of a high civilization and of Christianity."[17]

There is little doubt that Trimble truly admired Lee for this position and the order he issued shortly after their conversation. Trimble wrote many years later, "I was never so much impressed with the exalted moral worth and true greatness of Robert E. Lee, as when I heard him utter with serene earnestness the words I have quoted, and beheld the noble expression of magnanimity and justice which beamed from his countenance."[18]

The noted primatologist Frans de Waal, professor of psychology at Emory University, published studies which showed that primates exercised compassionate behavior. Relating this to human societies he pointed out that as soon as the immediate threat to survival is removed, members of our species take care of kin and build exchange networks with fellow human beings both inside and outside their group. He qualified this by saying that "in practice human kindness and cooperativeness are spread thinner the farther we get from kin and community."[19] This conversation and the subsequent order suggest that Lee and Trimble maintained a level of compassion for their former countrymen.

The next night, perhaps inspired by Lee, Trimble had an opportunity to prove his ability to live his philosophy toward civilians. By the 25th the whole army, with the exception of Jeb Stuart, had crossed the Potomac. They followed the route taken by General Ewell some time before, and Trimble observed that the inhabitants occupied their homes and tilled their fields as if they saw no enemy. Trimble later wrote, "There was no indication anywhere of the abuses of war, and not a fence rail had been used at the camp fires as far as could be seen."[20] On that first night in enemy territory Trimble and his staff asked permission to stay all night in a farmhouse near the woods where the troops had bivouacked. At first the owner objected, even after being offered payment. Trimble mentioned the protection that they could receive from having a general officer stay in the house. The owner consented to lodging and a good supper. The next morning, after observing the family's doleful faces, Trimble asked why they appeared so distressed. They answered, "much protection you have afforded us, look at that garden. Last evening there were twenty bee hives on them benches, and now not one is left."[21]

Trimble, embarrassed and surprised, responded, "Well, my friends! I am very sorry, but the North Carolina boys never can resist the temptation of a bee hive. Had I noticed them last evening, I would have asked for a guard. Have you missed anything else on the place, anything wrong at the spring house?"[22]

"No," said the woman of the house. "I think not but what will we do for honey next winter?"[23]

"Well," Trimble began, "it is hardly worth while to look for the honey now, but I will do all I can for you. Your hives are worth a dollar each I suppose." He anticipated their concern when he added, "but as I have nothing but Confederate money, I will pay you two dollars for each, and if the money turns out good for nothing, I will redeem it in Baltimore after the war, if alive, you will find me there." They seemed to be satisfied with that arrangement and a good breakfast ended Trimble's stay.[24]

On June 26 Trimble suggested a raid of Baltimore. He met Lee in Hagerstown and volunteered to lead a brigade into the city and thus embarrass the enemy. Lee asked A. P. Hill if he could spare a brigade for that purpose. When Hill responded that it would reduce his force too much Lee rejected the proposal.[25]

Lee called for Trimble's advice later that afternoon. They had stopped for the night and Lee had his tent pitched near the road. He called Trimble to where he had seated himself, and asked about the topography. He stated to Trimble, "As a civil engineer you may know more about it than any of us."[26]

Trimble described the country and said, "Almost every square mile contains good positions for battle or skillful maneuvering."[27]

Lee responded, "Our army is in good spirits, not overfatigued, and can be concentrated on any one point in twenty-four hours or less. I have not yet heard that the enemy have crossed the Potomac and am waiting to hear from General Stuart." Lee depended on Stuart's reports and had become concerned at losing contact with the eyes of his army. "When they hear where we are, they will make forced marches to interpose their forces between us and Baltimore and Philadelphia. They will come up, probably through Frederick, broken down with hunger and hard marching, strung out on a long line, and much demoralized when they come into Pennsylvania." At this point Lee made it clear to Trimble that the overall plan called for aggressive behavior, "I shall throw an overwhelming force on their advance, crush it; follow up the success, drive one corps back on another, and by successive repulses and surprises before they can concentrate create a panic and virtually destroy the army."[28]

When asked his opinion Trimble said, "I never knew our men to be in finer spirits in any campaign."[29]

Lee beamed, "That is, I hear, the general impression." As the conversation continued Lee laid his hand on the map over the town of Gettysburg and said, "Hereabout we shall probably meet the enemy and fight a great battle; and if God gives us the victory, the war will be over, and we shall achieve the recognition of our independence." He then concluded, "General Ewell's forces are by this time in Harrisburg; if not, go and join him and help to take the place."[30]

On June 28 Trimble met Ewell at Carlisle as a volunteer aide to his former commander; after an initially warm greeting he became dismayed at the lack of action in light of the general plan as Lee described it to him. He succeeded in convincing Ewell of the advantages of capturing Harrisburg when Ewell received a dispatch from Lee. The enemy had crossed the Potomac and Ewell should march "to Cashtown or Gettysburg, according to circumstances."[31]

Ewell complained of the vagueness of the order, but once they heard that the enemy occupied Gettysburg it became clear to Trimble that they should head there. On June 30 Ewell set out from Carlisle with Rodes's division, Early being away at York. They reached Heidelburg before sundown. Early caught up with them after dark. Ewell then called for a meeting with Early, Rodes, and Trimble. He reported to them that the Union 11th Corps had been sighted in Gettysburg. Trimble understood the aggressive plan Lee had divulged to him and indicated to Ewell that they should head toward Gettysburg rather than Cashtown. When Ewell continued to debate the appropriate target Trimble finally convinced them to not lose any more time by heading toward Middletown. Being on the route to either alternative they could send a courier to Lee for clarification. Ewell agreed to follow Trimble's advice. By 10 o'clock on the morning of July 1 they received orders to continue on to Gettysburg. Rodes's division immediately set out and arrived about 12 o'clock, forming a line of battle on the north side of the road.[32]

Ewell's men quickly seized the moment. Guided by Trimble they rapidly advanced to a point commanding the town at the northern end of Seminary Ridge about a mile from the town. They occupied the Union right flank which had already become involved with the men under General Hill directly west of town. Rodes attacked with his infantry on the right and his batteries opened against those in front. Ewell ordered one of the brigades into the low ground towards and beyond the Mummasburg Road. By 2 p.m. Hill and Rodes had driven the enemy on the right while General Early reached the field on the extreme left driving them back in confusion and heavy loss. Trimble could see a mile and a half from one flank to the other, "and noticed that the whole space in open fields was covered with Union soldiers retreating in broken masses towards the town from [their] own and General Hill's front."[33]

Trimble rode with Ewell and in passing a body of Union prisoners he said to an officer, "Fortune is against you today."[34]

"We have been worse whipped than ever,"[35] the Yankee replied.

Trimble saw this as just the beginning of things to come. As they were riding through the streets, a shot passed through an open window in one of the houses, barely missing Ewell. At that point he chose to ride out to a farmhouse near a hospital. Trimble detected uncertainty in the face of the commander. "Well, General," Trimble began, "we have had a grand success; are you not going to follow it up and push our advantage?"[36]

Ewell replied, "General Lee had instructed [me] not to bring on a general engagement without orders, and [I] will wait for them."[37]

Trimble said, "That hardly applies to the present state of things. We have fought a hard battle already, and should secure the advantage gained."[38]

Trimble took upon himself to further explore the situation. He rode off to the north of the town and observed a hill, which he learned to be Culp's Hill, with an elevation that would allow them to observe the country for miles around each way and that overlooked even Cemetery Hill where the enemy had gathered. At about 3:30 to 4:00 p.m. Trimble returned and found Ewell "still under much embarrassment,"[39] and said, "General if you have decided not to advance against the enemy and we are only to hold our ground, I want to advise that you send a brigade with artillery to take possession of that hill," pointing toward Culp's Hill. "It commands Gettysburg and Cemetery Hill."[40]

Ewell asked, "How do you know that?"[41]

"I have been there," Trimble answered. "And you know I am not often mistaken in judging of topography, and if we don't hold that hill, the enemy will certainly occupy it, as it is the key to the whole position about here and I beg you to send a force at once to secure it."[42]

Ewell coldly replied, "When I need the advice from a junior officer, I generally ask it."[43]

Trimble ended the discussion with, "General Ewell I am sorry you don't appreciate my suggestions, you will regret it as long as you live."[44]

It appears that Trimble's prophecy came to pass. At the time, Trimble spoke the loudest and most clearly among the other Confederate generals who approached Ewell, including Robert E. Rodes, Harry Hays, Jubal Early, and John B. Gordon. Before Trimble's departure Ewell had sent James P. Smith to find Lee and pass on the desire to advance further. Just as he had decided to begin to advance, Smith returned with word from Lee: Ewell should take Cemetery Hill with his 2nd Corps alone since Lee could offer no further support. This convinced Ewell that he should not attack. After Trimble left he investigated reports of Union activities and finally returned to the possibility of taking Culp's Hill. After Edward Johnson arrived near dark Ewell finally made the decision that Johnson should seize the hill if he found it unoccupied. In a meeting with Lee at 10 o'clock that night, Ewell operated on the assumption that Johnson had occupied Culp's Hill and that they would be in good position to remove the enemy from Cemetery Hill. What Ewell did not know is that during the long period of hesitation the Union army had occupied Culp's Hill. The Confederates lost many men during the next two days trying to take the ground that Trimble had immediately recognized as a valuable piece of real estate.[45]

Some historians have defended Ewell's actions. One Ewell biographer, Percy Hamlin, pointed out that Ewell truly believed he had direct orders from Lee to not attack. He had also heard reports that more Union troops had been spotted close by. Hamlin also pointed out that James Longstreet and H. J. Hunt both agreed that Ewell had acted appropriately under the circumstances. Edwin B. Coddington, in addition to recognizing that Ewell felt that he followed Lee's orders, pointed out that the same city streets which had caused problems for the retreating Yankees also halted the advance of the Confederates. He also recognized that the men had become tired and many busied themselves rounding up and guarding prisoners. Donald Pfanz recorded the events that happened after Trimble left and gave the impression that perhaps Ewell did learn to regret his failure to capture Culp's Hill.[46]

For years after the war, Trimble and others identified Ewell as a major cause for the Confederate loss at Gettysburg. John B. Gordon wrote, "As far down the lines as my eye could reach the Union troops were in retreat." He concluded that "it was only necessary for me to press forward in order to insure the same results which invariably follow such flank movements."[47] Douglas Southall Freeman simply stated "that the new organization of the Second Corps was operating very clumsily."[48] After the war Trimble concluded that the loss at Gettysburg resulted from "adverse circumstances; disobedience of orders by his commander of cavalry, and want of concerted action and vigorous onset among his corp commanders at critical moments in the assaults of each of the three days."[49] It is clear that he considered the failure to advance toward Cemetery Hill, and especially the failure to seize the unoccupied Culp's Hill, to constitute the critical moments of the first day. Trimble recalled after the battle that a Union general approached him in the hospital and asked him why they did not push their success of the first day. Trimble responded, "Well, General I would like to know myself, but I do not." The Union general stated, "if you had advanced and pushed us vigorously, I fear our whole army would have been dispersed by night. We were strung out between Gettysburg and Emmitsburg, hungry, weary ... and you would not have had a brigade to oppose you at any one place."[50] Trimble recorded in his diary, "This was a critical error, for had we continued the fight, we should have got in their rear & taken the Cemetery Hill & Culp's Hill."[51]

Lee again made use of Trimble's engineering skills on the second day, but after that Trimble remained in the background. Lee arrived at Ewell's headquarters. He first met Trimble and expressed a desire to view the countryside and the enemy's position. Trimble recommended the cupola of the almshouse near by. From there they could see Cemetery Hill, Round Top, Culp's Hill, and the adjacent country. After a while Lee said, "The enemy have the advantage of us in a shorter and inside line, and we are too much extended." He then confirmed Trimble's opinion of the failures of the previous day, "We did not or we could not pursue our advantage of yesterday, and now the enemy are in a good position."[52] Lee repeated these words over and over throughout the morning as they met "Early, Rodes and others."[53] Later that day Ewell, with Johnson's division, suffered considerable losses trying to capture the elusive Culp's Hill.[54]

Trimble assumed command of W. D. Pender's division on Friday, July 3. On hearing of the loss of a general, Trimble requested and received the command by noon. Trimble relieved the acting commander, Brigadier General J. H. Lane, and acted under the orders previously given to him: "General Longstreet will make a vigorous attack on his front; General Ewell will threaten the enemy on the left or make a vigorous attack should circumstances justify it; General Hill will hold the center at all hazards."[55] The famous charge began with a two-hour hail of artillery. At the end of the cannonade George Pickett's division moved forward. At the same time Heath's division advanced under J. J. Pettigrew. The two brigades under Trimble formed a second line behind Pettigrew.[56] With the deliberation of men in drill, the two brigades of North Carolinians marched with purpose and accuracy. As they approached to within 150 yards of the Emmetsburg road, "they seemed to sink into the earth under the tempest of fire poured into them." At that moment someone on Trimble's left sang out, "Three cheers for the Old North State."[57]

Both brigades sent up a hearty shout and Trimble said, "Charley, I believe those fine fellows are going into the enemy's line."[58]

They reached the road and drove the enemy from the line, but Trimble began to realize that no one could withstand the destructive fire they faced. He became curious about the state of the other divisions and glanced in the direction of Pickett's men. He saw that the fire on Pickett's division had diminished as the gray tide retreated. Trimble remained seated on his horse though a bullet had passed through his leg and his beloved Jenny. He then concluded that it would be a useless sacrifice of life to continue the contest, and therefore did not attempt to rally the men as they began to fall back from the rail fence that had blocked their advance. When they reached the road the terrific fire came down in their faces and they began to melt away. Charley Grogan said, "General, the men are falling back, shall I rally them?"[59]

"No, Charley," Trimble answered, "the best thing these brave fellows can do, is to get out of this."[60] At some point he had dismounted to survey the wound that he and Jenny shared.

With Grogan's help Trimble remounted his horse and they walked back in an orderly fashion despite the increasing discharge of grape shell and muskets which caused Trimble to question how many would escape wounds or death. As they reoccupied their pre-charge defenses Trimble said, "That is right, my brave fellows, stand your ground, and we will presently serve these chaps as they have us."[61] The anticipated counterattack never came. Trimble left the command to General Lane, and as he left he muttered, "If the troops I had the honor to command today couldn't take that position, all hell can't take it."[62]

The fact that the charge became known as Pickett's Charge, rather than Trimble's Charge or Pettigrew's Charge, suggest a favoritism toward the role played by Pickett's Virginians. Though Trimble reacted more enthusiastically in his criticism of Ewell on the first day, he later participated in defending the honor of the North Carolinians who served under him and Pettigrew. In 1882 he said that on the third day they participated "in Longstreet's charge,"[63] a more appropriate name since Longstreet commanded all three divisions. The year before Trimble wrote a letter in which he said that:

> both Northern and Southern descriptions of the battle of Gettysburg ... down to the present time, give not only most conspicuous prominence to General Pickett's division, but, generally by the language used, have created the impression among those not personally acquainted with the events of the day, that Pickett's men did all the hard fighting, suffered the most severely, and failed in his charge, because not promptly or vigorously supported by the troops on his right and left. It might with as much truth be said that Pettigrew and Trimble failed in their charge because unsupported by Pickett, who had been driven back in the crisis of their charge, and was no aid to them.[64]

Such impressions continued well into the twentieth century. The first successful attempt at speaking out in support of the role played by Trimble and Pettigrew came in the 1950s from Glenn Tucker, who "became Pettigrew's and Trimble's Douglas Southall Freeman,"[65] though it appears that the name "Pickett's Charge" will remain with us forever.

Trimble passed through several weeks of uncertainty between his capture at Gettysburg and reaching his new home on Johnson's Island in Sandusky, Ohio. While in Pickett's Charge, a bullet passed through the same leg that had given Trimble so much trouble after he was wounded at Second Manassas. In his rather direct style he chastised the surgeon for not removing the leg when requested after Second Manasses, pointing out that

On the third day at Gettysburg, Trimble assumed command of Pender's division in time to participate in Pickett's Charge, though he preferred to call it "Longstreet's Charge." He paid the price for leading his men in the charge when he took another bullet in his leg and as a result had to stay behind and accept capture by the Union Army.

if the leg had been removed then he would not have been reduced to helplessness by the second bullet.[66] After amputation the surgeons warned that the leg would become inflamed by moving in the ambulance, and that erysipelas would ensue. Trimble accepted his fate and put himself in Union hands. On July 6 he went to the home of Mr. McCardy, "& there treated with the most tender kindness."[67] They removed him to a hospital at the Seminary two weeks later "where we were fairly treated — here we found Genl. Kemper, Col. Powel of Texas, Major Douglas of Jackson's staff & a few other Confederates."[68] Sentinels guarded the hospital doors and restricted visitors and food. Trimble complained of the lieutenant of the guard, a man named Rice, who took "every occasion to vex us & circumscribe our privileges. May the chances of war put him some day in our power."[69] The new commander, Col. Hopkinson of Philadelphia, removed the guard, to which Trimble said, "It is some relief to have the bayonets taken from our throats."[70]

Before the war Trimble had created a network of business and personal acquaintances that traversed state and regional boundaries, and after being wounded he utilized his connection with George Meade, commander of the Union forces at Gettysburg. Trimble's brother, when in Congress, rendered a service to Meade's merchant brother who had been thrown into a Spanish prison. The other Trimble proposed a resolution in Congress that three Spanish citizens living in the United States be arrested in retaliation for the imprisonment of the other Meade. The resolution passed, but the Spanish Minister intervened so that Meade's brother gained his freedom, and thus Meade felt an obligation to the Confederate general.[71] Trimble wrote a letter to General Meade on July 16: "Having been wounded on Friday last, suffered amputation of a foot within your lines I having long had acquaintance with your family ... respectfully apply for permission for some of my family to bring me from Baltimore such articles as my condition renders necessary."[72]

On August 20 they took him to Baltimore in "a miserable rough burden lime-car and laid on straw," and upon arrival placed him in a hospital on Lexington Street, which he found to be "clean and comfortable."[73] Fortunately for Trimble he did not spend long in the "West Hospital," which one fellow prisoner described as "originally a warehouse intended for the storage of cotton, now transformed into a hospital by the Federal government. It had not a single element of adaptation for the purpose to which it was applied."[74] On August 23 they moved him to Fort McHenry where he stated, "No one [is] allowed to see us or communicate with us."[75] While in the fort, they fitted his leg for an artificial one. The food was such that he commented, "But for ... [Baltimore] ladies we should starve or become skeletons by inches."[76] He passed the hours walking around the fort, and visiting the ladies who brought him food, the only visitors allowed by special orders from Washington.[77]

Despite his serious wound and being in the hands of the enemy, the general elicited fear from his captors. They said he took advantage of the liberal arrangements in McCardy's care and his extensive knowledge of the railroads in the area, and claimed that "he directed and superintended the burning of the bridges between Baltimore and Columbia, and York and Harrisburg." On July 11 Simon Cameron wrote to Abraham Lincoln and complained of the incidents, to which he added that "he is now living in comfort at the house of a rebel sympathizer in this town [Gettysburg]."[78] On July 11 Major General Robert C. Schenck wrote to the provost marshal of Gettysburg expressing concern about the location of Trimble, after revoking the parole of one of his staff, Major Hall, his assistant adjutant general, and finding another staff officer among their own wounded "disguised in the greatcoat of a Union soldier."[79] Upon hearing of plans to send Trimble to Baltimore, Cameron and General Turner Morehead telegraphed both President Lincoln and Secretary of War Edwin Stanton claiming that it would be dangerous to send him to Baltimore along with Lieutenant Granger, Major Hall, and Private Champion, and suggested that the party be sent instead to Harrisburg or Pittsburgh. General Schenck felt confident in handling them and assured Stanton that "he need have no fear that he will not be protected even at the scene of [Trimble's] traitorous and scoundrel acts"[80] of sabotage committed during his retreat from Baltimore in 1861.

It may be that they considered treating Trimble as a guerrilla fighter, though they did not use that word. In a letter dated August 15, 1863, W. W. Morris wrote to the post attorney "to proceed to investigate the title to any and all property belonging the Gen'l Trimble within [his] jurisdiction and to account for the same or any portion thereof belonging to him since the commencement of the rebellion." He continued by ordering to "proceed to confiscate said property."[81] This may have been in response to the U. S. War Department General Order No. 100, issued in April of 1863, which eventually became known as the Lieber Code, for the Columbia University law professor — Francis Lieber — who drafted it. The order covered noncombatants with the purpose of halting guerrilla activities. They may have considered Trimble to have fallen into that category when he blew up the bridges in Baltimore back in April of 1861.[82]

General Morris, the commandant of Fort McHenry and Trimble's former classmate, warned him that he would be tried by court-martial for his actions in 1861. They said that he had acted over some misunderstanding he had with the railroads prior to the war. He wrote a letter to the secretary of war defending his actions, and explained that he acted on the orders of the mayor of Baltimore and the governor of Maryland, and that they did so to avoid further bloodshed during the riots. The government must have concluded, perhaps influenced by Meade, that they had no case as the court-martial never materialized.[83] Trimble's volatile reputation sparked concern from the Confederate agent of exchange, Robert Ould, who wrote to the Union agent of exchange, Brigadier General S. A. Meredith, expressing concern about the condition of the aged general. Meredith assured him that Trimble received the same treatment as any other officer.[84]

On August 29, while in Fort McHenry, Trimble launched into a lengthy tirade to his diary in which he displayed extreme Southern nationalism he had never demonstrated prior to the start of the war; his statements suggest that the war itself had generated these feelings. Though he had demonstrated compassion toward the civilians in Pennsylvania, his "southernness" had grown. He responded to a statement that the North desired to restore the Union "as it was under the Constitution." He clearly stated, "She can never join the North in political hands much less in brotherly kindness." He utilized images of the war as he wrote:

> to the North she may say — If all the Southern blood shed by you in this unjust war were poured into the sources of the Potomac, that long, broad river would be incarnodined [sic] from its head spring to

After Gettysburg the Union Army sent Trimble to Ft. McHenry, and thus he saw Baltimore for the first time since he left his home. He managed to avoid court-martial for his actions in April of 1861.

> the capes of the ocean, with one deep red and do you expect! nay, can you ask us of the South to forget our wrongs, wade through this river of blood & clasp in friendship the hands of those who have just stricken us in death? But lately desecrated & made our homesteads— hollowed for centuries by every sacred tie & tender memory — scenes of desolation —can you think us so lost to every manly virtue as to believe we would aid you to reconstruct a Union and cement its fabric with the purple current of our children.[85]

He spoke of honor and virtue and manliness, but constantly fell back on the descriptions of the horrors of war. "For like the fabled sort of antiquity the blood shed on Southern fields, will spring up in dragons teeth to revenge hereafter your wrongs & tyranny, and guard her borders from future desecration, long after you have carried out your boastful schemes of conquest or extermination." He exaggerated his claims when he said "there are now no union men in the south & never have been in any numbers to claim notice," but he obviously felt that the men he fought with remained dedicated to their cause. Though he had not spoken of regional patriotism prior to the war, he wrote that "our connection with you never had, from the early settlement of the colonies till now, any bond but that of political interest." He then delved into his belief that northern "bigotry & hatred of every thing southern drove us from you — the Union was at variance with our feelings, tastes, pursuits, honorable aims & religion." Though he had traveled freely from state to state prior to the war he believed that "time instead of removing these, has strengthened them until on the great principles of self preservation and self respect, the Union has been sundered forever."[86]

He accepted the possibility of Confederate defeat, but consoled himself with the thought that "if she perish, she can go down to the grave of nations, with the proud boast that she has abundantly nourished with her blood the seeds of Liberty, which will spring up & bear fruit to bless mankind in coming time." He gave the Union a final curse, again calling upon images of the war freshly imprinted on his brain and nurtured by the pain of his wound:

> ... for in the still hours of darkness, the sighing winds shall bear to your ears the doleful wail of the widow & the orphan to disturb your midnight slumbers & sit heavy on your souls.
> Your women shall dream of bloody massacres and of pale faces hung with locks stiffened by gory blood, and innocent childhood shall take refuge in alarm on the mothers lap, flying from the imagined specters of some bloody spot where tradition marks the lone & hasty sepulcher of those slaughtered in the defense of homes, that shall know them no more forever. The whole land shall be to you a curse and the favor of a just God shall rest upon it; never.[87]

On August 28 his captors sent Trimble, along with 35 other Confederate officers, to Johnson's Island. They took them by the Northern Central Railway from the Calvert Station, through Pittsburgh to Sandusky, Ohio. One fellow officer described Trimble as "the foremost soldier of Maryland in the Confederate service, who was in a state of almost absolute helplessness."[88]

Johnson's Island, where Trimble spent most of his captivity, is located near Sandusky, Ohio, at the mouth of Sandusky Bay on Lake Eire.[89] The 16-acre "Bull Pen" was an irregular four-sided area which narrowed on one end. Twelve whitewashed barracks ran down the middle of the yard with a quagmire between them. A thirteenth barrack lay at the end near the stockade. The poorly drained privies behind the blocks filled the air with their aroma. Toward the bay was a large open area where the men played baseball and tried to get water from the often frozen pumps. A smaller building became home to those singled out for special punishment. The green lumber used in construction shrank as it dried allowing the already fierce elements easy access to the inhabitants, though in the summer the prisoners expanded the openings by punching out the knotholes in an effort to increase ventilation. Each block had a stove at the end which served as the kitchen, though so small the men took meals in shifts. They slept on bunks, no more than rough shelves, stacked three high. In addition to the cook stove each block had a potbelly stove intended to warm all of the residents, but of course it proved to be insufficient on the coldest winter days.[90] The larger rooms contained more than 60 men, and during winter they could not all fit around the stove. While one shift warmed themselves, the remainder lay covered in their bunks or danced about the room to keep from freezing. By the time that Trimble arrived, the island housed primarily officers; on September 28, 1863, he reported 1,500 officers and 600 privates.[91]

Trimble immediately assumed his position as the ranking Confederate officer. He did not yield to the depressing conditions, but used his natural skills to make the best of his situation. He stood up for the rights of his fellow prisoners, made plans for escape, and found various other ways to look after his subordinates. He considered their individual needs and participated in their attempts to find amusement.

The general fulfilled a primary responsibility as the commanding officer of prisoners of war, which was to see that the men received fair treatment. On January 26, 1864, he composed a letter to Brigadier General Terry, commander of the post at Sandusky, in which he identified five problems. He tactfully presented his request and stated, "that an officer of rank who has seen active service in the field may not think such treatment the best or most honorable way of subduing an enemy."[92] He mentioned first that the officers had "been required to dig sinks, remove privies, and load piles of kitchen garbage in Johnson's carts ... contrary to the usages of war among civilized nations, and not inflicted on Federal officer prisoners in Richmond."[93] He next complained about the fuel supplied, being green and of such types that are not normally used by the army when in garrison. He also claimed that the men had been "'fired on' by day and night."[94] He observed that though surrounded by fresh water, the men had to draw deficient water from the wells in the yard. Lastly he stated that "the meat supplied ... with a few exceptions, [was] composed of necks, shanks, pieces of thin ribs, and other refuse parts never in 'quarters' of beef as should be done, thus doubtless defrauding ... [the U. S.] Government."[95] He also felt that the men should be able to make purchases with their own money and that the condition of the hospital needed reform.[96]

In general the conditions at Johnson's Island may have been better than most prisoner of war camps, north or south, but nevertheless they proved difficult for those who had to endure the drab surroundings. The purpose here is not to evaluate the treatment of the prisoners of Johnson's Island, but it does require consideration. It serves to understand the conditions under which General Trimble lived and lends credibility to the complaints he lodged, especially considering that Trimble often reacted to what he considered bad conditions. No one disputed the hardships caused by the location, best described as "the place to convert visitors to the theological belief of the Norwegian that Hell has torments of

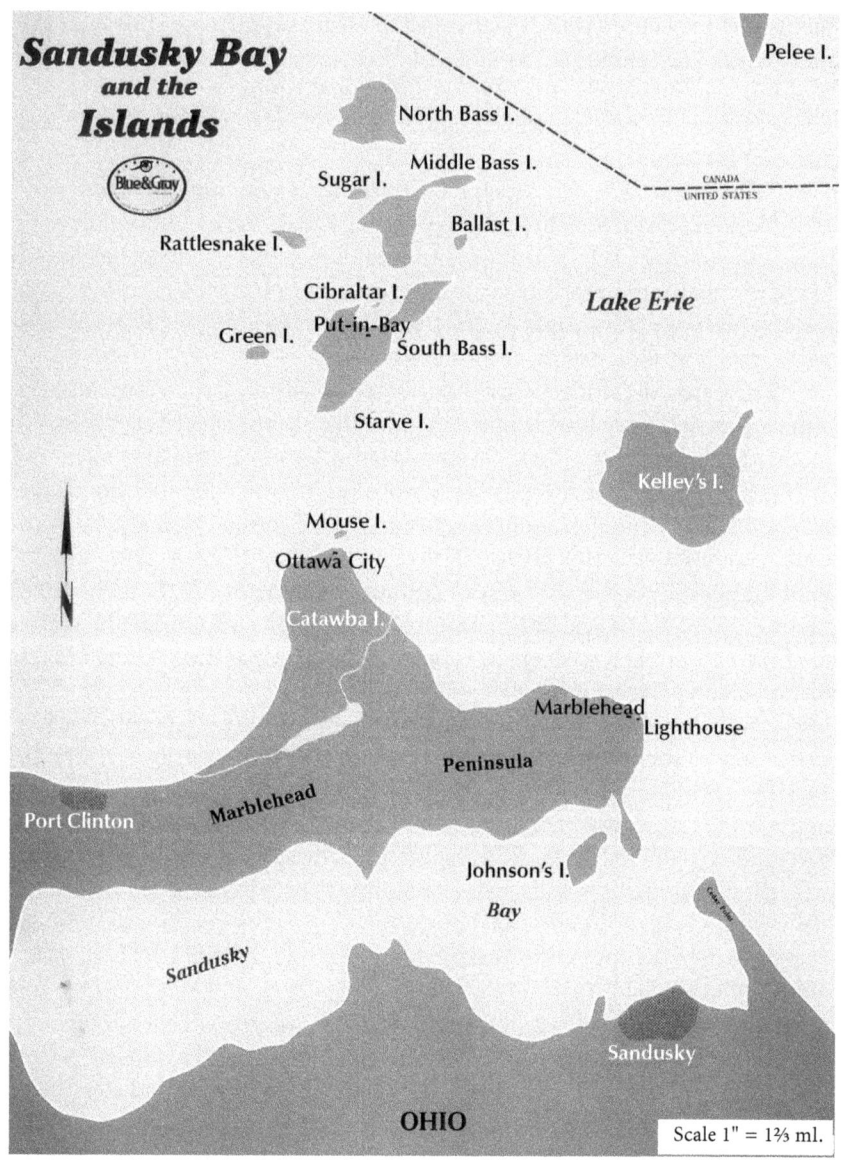

In September of 1863 Trimble arrived at the prison camp on Johnson's Island, Ohio, where he would spend more than a year of his life. The location on Lake Erie offered little promise for escape from the Union soldiers or the northern winters. Courtesy *Blue & Gray* Magazine, Columbus, Ohio.

cold instead of heat."[97] Frost or near freezing weather appeared as early as August and as late as May;[98] of the prisoners, "many were from the extreme South, and some had never seen a fall of snow."[99] Even with the harsh weather, one prisoner wrote in a letter published in the *Memphis Appeal*, "Altogether Sandusky is the least disagreeable prison I ever saw or heard of."[100] One of the guards, claimed "Everything is satisfactory to the 'rebs' with the exception of the cold weather which keeps them in the buildings most of the time."[101] A report on the treatment of the prisoners filed with the Congress of 1868–9 claimed that the prisoners had comfortable accommodations, plenty of blankets, and a good stove with sufficient wood. They had an exercise yard where they could sing Southern songs, praise Jeff Davis, or play games. They received the same rations as the garrison with fresh beef, sugar, coffee, and a supply of soap and candles. They could receive gifts of clothing and edibles as well as money that could be spent at the sutler's store inside the prison.[102] The death rate for Johnson's Island does lend credibility to the positive reports; only two percent (127 of 6,410 prisoners) died between April 1862 through December 1864, contrasted with 8.4 percent for Fort Delaware or 4.5 percent at Point Lookout, and the 1864–5 period produced only 94 more deaths.[103] One must consider the possibility that the extreme cold may have contributed to the low death rate, considering that disease caused most of the deaths during the Civil War and that bacteria thrive better in warm climates.

Not everyone agreed with the descriptions of good conditions, and many confirmed the specific complaints listed by Trimble. After the editor of the Sandusky *Register* boasted of the good conditions at the prison, one Confederate recorded in his diary, "The kind treatment he speaks of is being shot down by a villainous Yankee sentinel without any provocation whatever; and barely enough gun-waddling bread with flyblown beef and tainted pork to keep soul and body together."[104] Another described the rations as "one-half loaf of hard bread, and a piece of salt pork, in size not sufficient for an ordinary meal. In taste the latter was almost nauseating, but it was devoured because there was no choice other than to eat it, or endure the tortures of prolonged starvation."[105]

In addition to the lack of respect for officers, demonstrated by calling them "Mister" instead of by their rank, they also faced taunting by the local residents on their way into the prison as well as boatloads of tourists sitting offshore studying the men as if they had been assembled there for their amusement.[106] Trimble believed some of the disrespect began with the attitude of politicians who "retain their existence by false & scandalous tales of Southern people."[107] Other prisoners confirmed his complaints of

The barracks at Johnson's Island were made of green wood. The resulting cracks between the planks provided ventilation in the summer but made it more difficult to keep out the cold in winter. Courtesy *Blue & Gray* Magazine, Columbus, Ohio.

the inadequacy of the equipment and of the firewood provided to protect the men from the cold.[108]

It could be argued that the North picked the frigid location for the prison because of its strategic value, but the accusation of "murder" of prisoners is not so easy to defend. It is difficult to evaluate their motivation, but it is clear that the guards frequently fired upon the prisoners. The guards justified the shots by claiming that the men had been outside their rooms after nine o'clock, at the well after dark, or lighting a candle so that some aid could be rendered to a fellow prisoner who had the misfortune of being sick in the middle of the night. Some prisoners claimed to have heard the word "halt" immediately before the crack of a musket, so that they concluded that guards used the word "to stop the victim in order for the typically inexperienced guard to make a more sure fire."[109] Such shootings gained praise from the local press, and in at least one case a prisoner blamed the "authorities ... [as] accessories to the crime for justifying the sentinel instead of punishing him."[110] It is difficult to determine the frequencies of the shootings or how many men the guards wounded or killed, but several diaries confirmed them, such as Col. Inzer who recorded, "The Yankees here guarding us have been keeping up a regular fire on us a large portion of the time since we came here. For the last two weeks [entry dated July 24, 1864] the fire has been awful."[111] In addition to the shootings, many of the men, probably because of their officers' status, believed that they would be hung. They had no evidence confirming their fears; however, six colonels and lieutenant colonels felt the threat serious enough that they drew lots with each other to determine which would be hung first.[112]

The prisoners often complained about a lack of the basics of life: water and food. The men had two wells in the enclosure from which they drew their requirements for drinking, washing, and cooking. When it was not frozen the men would often spend hours in line waiting for the water, which rose at the rate of one full bucket per half hour.[113] In the beginning food did not seem to be a problem for the prisoners, and in fact they confirmed the boasting of the Union authorities. A sudden change took place in the spring of 1864 when the sutler moved out of the prison, taking with him the opportunity to supplement the ration provided. The same prisoner who once called the food "abundant," later wrote, "I do know that it was sufficient to satisfy the cravings of hunger, and left us each day with a little less life and strength with which to fight the battle of the day to follow."[114] Many of the men believed the cut in rations came in response to rumors in the northern press that their Union soldiers starved in southern prisons such as Richmond's Libby or Georgia's Andersonville. Regardless of the reasoning, the men inside the stockade on Johnson's Island reduced the rat population considerably in an attempt to supplement their diet, while those in the nearby town of Sandusky threw away scraps that the Confederate soldiers would have gladly accepted in place of their rodent side dishes.[115] Even in the earlier days of the sutler's presence the prisoners often complained that the guards took the little money they had with them.[116] Trimble later claimed the total amount to be in excess of 3,000 dollars.[117]

Trimble criticized the medical facilities. On a mortuary list of 200 deaths, at least one half of them resulted from lack of clean beds, medicines, and proper attention, and "many cases are known where persons died of fever, & delirious, who had nothing but a log of wood for a pillow." He went on to say "the hospital was filthy & overrun with vermin."[118] One prisoner described the hospital and medical care as good,[119] but another confirmed Trimble's impression. He stated "I am told by the surgeons that it is often impossible to get such medicine as is absolutely necessary to check a disease and save a patient's life, and thus many valuable lives are lost that might be saved."[120] Another prisoner claimed that "the sick and wounded in the prison hospital had no especial provision made for their comfort. They received the prescribed rations, and were cared for in their helplessness, as in their dying hours, by other prisoners detailed as nurses."[121] The previously stated mortality statistics suggest that the conditions could not have been too bad since the death rate remained lower than in other prisons. It may also be that the conditions did not remain the same throughout, explaining why some called them good while others called them bad.

It does appear that the North made an attempt to respond to at least some of General Trimble's complaints. His connection with General George Meade may have earned him some respect from the high command. Trimble admitted that the conditions at the hospital improved after Dr. Everman took over and he saw "new equipments supplied in full, and cleanliness produced."[122] The water problem had been solved by January 27, 1864, with a plan that allowed regular calls, from ten to twelve a.m. and from two to four p.m., in which squads of 50 prisoners at a time could, under guard, draw water from the lake.[123] In February of 1864 Terry wrote to Col. William Hoffman, commissary general of prisoners, stating that "as far as possible the real evils are being remedied, such as the water drainage problem."[124] He also added, "Some, indeed most, of the complaints are without substantial foundation."[125]

Trimble did not limit his responsibilities to those of military importance, nor of a serious nature. Several of the prisoners recorded the great snowball fight in which the old general assumed command of the six upper blocks who attacked the six lower blocks under the command of Colonel Maxwell of Florida. The half-day battle left many wounded, sore heads and black eyes, and several prisoners taken, all paroled.[126] He filled a paternalistic role with some of the men. One prisoner recorded his gratitude for the favors received from General Trimble, as well as Captain Chichester and Colonel W. J. Greene.[127] Another collected Trimble's words, along with other Confederate generals, in his notebook.[128]

An island in the far northern country of Ohio offered little hope of escape for those unfortunate enough to find themselves within the walls, but some had to try. The middle of winter froze the water so hard that one could easily make it by foot to the mainland, but most knew the difficulties would begin with trying to find food and shelter in the middle of a frozen enemy land while looking for passage home. At least one man jumped the wall in the middle of January and achieved his goal, and another passed himself off as an ardent Union sympathizer.[129] Some tried tunneling, but not successfully. One man went outside the walls with a party sent to bring in hay for bedding. He hid under a pile of the hay and remained concealed until dark, constructed a small raft to get off the island but abandoned that plan after he found the raft unseaworthy. He waited until morning and walked down to the wharf, boarded a boat for Sandusky and eventually made it back to Dixie. Another made a blue uniform out of scraps of cloth and a dummy gun out of wood, silvering the barrel with tobacco wrappings, and warned the commander of a tunnel being dug, make-believe of course, and then attempted to follow the troops out of the gate. The officer in command caught him because he lacked the formal Yankee training and did not hold his gun correctly.[130] In January of 1864 prisoner Boyd succeeded in getting out, but turned himself in when overcome by the cold. He offered encouragement when he observed that once outside no one was on the lookout. The 27 degrees below zero weather kept the guards inside long enough for three of the prisoners to get away, though they stopped a fourth. The success prompted others to follow suit which resulted in some claiming success, while others suffered frostbite or recapture.[131] One prisoner claimed, "since our capture we have devised a thousand ways and means of escape and discussed them over and over."[132] Another emphasized the risk involved with attempted escape: they "were subjected to the most degrading punishments in the form of servile labor, scarcely adapted to the status of convicts."[133]

Unknown to the men in captivity, plans for their rescue had been in progress since February of 1863, leading to a thwarted attempt in early November of the same year. Lieutenant William H. Murdaugh, of the Confederate navy, proposed capturing the *Michigan*, the only Union man-of-war in the Great Lakes, and using the contraband to free the officers confined on Johnson's Island. Captain Robert D. Minor pursued the objective through to the end, gaining support of the Confederate government on the way. He deferred command of the operation to his friend lieutenant John Wilkinson. After giving initial approval President Jefferson Davis requested that they delay the plan out of fear of upsetting the British, who might put a halt to the completion of the ironclad and other vessels being constructed for the Confederacy in England.[134]

Finally, Davis gave the orders to proceed and in October a party of 22 headed for Canada, arriving in Montreal on the 21st. They sent first word to the prisoners through a Baltimore lady, Mrs. P. C. Martin, then residing in Montreal. She received a letter from Beverly Saunders, Esq. of Baltimore, in which General James Jay Archer of Maryland advised them to use the personal columns of the New York *Herald* to communicate with the men inside the prison. Archer, who had been captured at Chancellorsville, must have communicated with his fellow Marylander, General Trimble, though no mention of this plan is found in Trimble's diary or papers. On November 4 a personal ad appeared which said that "a carriage would be at the door," referring to the *Michigan*. With final plans completed and arms purchased, the Confederates prepared for the final assault when Secretary of War Edwin Stanton sent a telegram to the mayors of the lake cities to be on their guard against a Confederate raid. Minor later learned that a compatriot, McQuaig, betrayed them to a Mr. Holden, a member of the Canadian provincial Cabinet, who then communicated the information to the governor general, Lord Monck. Desirous to keep on good terms with the United States he informed that government and thus ended the dramatic plans to rescue the prisoners of Johnson's Island.[135]

Trimble, in his usual fashion, took charge of the situation within his control and orchestrated an attempted mass escape from inside. Recalling the conditions of imprisonment previously described, he claimed that in the winter of 1863-4 "our treatment was so bad that we determined to make an organized effort to escape."[136] He took advantage of the extensive knowledge he acquired of the topography of the lakes during his service in the Army, thinking it an easy matter to cross the ice all the way to Canada. He saw an advantage over the guards, who had not been in combat, and felt confident in being able to frighten and demoralize them with a night assault. He had a conference with the leading officers who agreed to make the attempt with Trimble in command. They perfected a thorough and systematic organization with companies and regiments. They had a supply of revolvers, axes, hatchets, and other weapons smuggled in and hid away. They also made pikes from the bottom of the bunks with knives mounted on the ends.[137]

In December of 1863 Captain Allen devised the plan of escape adopted by Trimble's group. No doubt, they became encouraged by the successful escapes of the following January. The plan had four phases. They had two options for the first phase, which called for getting out of the enclosure, either storming or bribing. Perhaps the most dangerous phase, capturing the garrison, demanded 1,500 to 2,000 men to capture 800 to 1,000 armed men. The third phase, escape from the island, had three possibilities: crossing on the ice to the mainland, securing a steamer to Sandusky and from there procuring other transportation, or being furnished transportation from friends on the outside. The fourth and final phase, returning to the South, had three options. For the first, they would reach the mainland and procure horses and march through Ohio to Pittsburgh or Wheeling, or through Kentucky to Virginia, Tennessee, or Georgia. For the second option, they would reach the mainland and go toward Toledo, or the straits, to Canada. The third involved simply crossing the lake to Canada.[138]

The board of officers reached several conclusions. They needed at least 1,200 or 1,500 of the "truest and most trusty" of the prisoners, with each block having at least 100 men sworn to attempt any plan sanctioned by the board, and that they "will succeed or die in the attempt." They also decided that liberal use of money should be made in attempts to bribe, with one or two discreet men entrusted to the task. The details of the plan should be at the arrangement and execution of the commander, General Trimble. Someone should be sent to Richmond to secure government help. If the escape were successful all would remain under control of the board of officers until they reach the South. If the time or circumstances arose for escape, they would do so rather than await government aid.[139]

The men did not dread winter this time, as the cold solidified the lake and their plans for escape. The lake froze solid enough to carry men, but not wagons, with perfect safety. They armed the men and had good organization. They decided to break the stockade in several different locations, thus dividing the enemy troops. Once the guards were overpowered, the prisoners would cross the ice to Canada. The governor general of Canada received intelligence of the plan and informed Lord Lyons in Washington, who in turn informed Secretary of State William Seward.[140] The Army fortified the garrison and at the same time spread rumors that the officers would be exchanged as soon as possible. After the release of a trainload of prisoners Trimble became convinced that no more would be exchanged, but only Colonel Shannon of Texas supported him in his pleas to continue with the plan. No more officers left the island, and they later learned that those who did depart had been sent to Point Lookout, not home. By the time the other officers realized Trimble had been correct, the ice had broken up and the best opportunity for escape had passed.[141]

The most ambitious of the escape plans originated from outside the walls and included the 8,000 Confederate prisoners at Camp Douglas, near Chicago, 8,000 more at Camp Chase in Columbus, Ohio, the 4,000 at Camp Morton near Indianapolis, and the 3,200 at Johnson's Island. If completed, the plan would have produced an army of more than 20,000 men strategically placed behind Union lines as well as a small navy which would have posed at least a temporary threat to trade on the Great Lakes. In 1864 Jake Thompson, former secretary of the interior under President Buchanan, led the "Conspiracy of 1864," attempting to capitalize on the Northern discontent with the war effort. At first they hoped to begin the attack during the Democratic convention to be held in Chicago, while General Jubal Early distracted the Union army by attacking Washington. Thompson put Major C. H. Cole in charge of making the arrangements in Sandusky, where he established himself as a wealthy oil speculator from Titusville, Pennsylvania. On Monday, September 19, 1864, Major Cole "was to capture the *Michigan,* release the prisoners on the island, cut all the telegraph wires, seize a train, run down to Columbus, help release the prisoners at Camp Chase, return to Sandusky and establish temporary headquarters of the Confederate Department of the Northwest"[142] under the command of General Trimble.

The "Conspiracy of 1864" involved the capture of the Union ship *Michigan*. A successful plan would have left Trimble in command of a division made up of escapees from Camp Douglas, Camp Chase, and Camp Morton in addition to those from Johnson's Island. Courtesy *Blue & Gray* Magazine, Columbus.

Though Trimble would be given command of the new department, he had minimum knowledge of the events taking place outside. They first got word to him of some government plans for their release in April of 1864, at which time they told him to again use the New York *Herald* personals as a channel of communications. The ads would be written so that only those in on the secret would know the hidden meaning of certain words. Trimble learned only general facts and nothing about the greater scheme, including the position of command to be given to him. The *Herald* first told them to expect release in July with the final signal coming with the opening of fire upon the island from a boat in the bay, but beyond that they knew only that the plan depended upon the capture of the *Michigan*. As the day arrived the threat of spies forced the men to keep their excitement hidden, but they could read the joy in each other's eyes. Their hope faded with the setting sun. Their disappointment subsided the next day when they read in the personals that the plan had only been delayed, not canceled. They finally received word of the September 19 date, and again they anxiously awaited their release. This time their anxieties reached a higher peak as they saw the ferry *Philo Parsons* approach the island, the boat now in Confederate hands. As they watched the vessel offshore "every moment seemed a day and every second to be laden with lead."[143] The hours passed and then the ferry steamed away, taking their hopes with it. This time the *Herald* informed them of failure with no future plans. A few days later the guards moved Trimble and the other general officers to Fort Warren in Boston Harbor.[144]

Trimble and the men on the island did not learn of what happened outside until after the war. Cole, who had become acquainted with the commander of the *Philo Parsons*, Captain Atwood, boarded the ferry with the other conspirators, covered Atwood with a revolver and officially took over. His men quickly recovered the hidden weapons and placed the former crew below the hatches and replaced the Stars and Stripes with the Stars and Bars. They then captured the steamer *Island Queen*, bound for Cleveland with 300 passengers. After returning the captured ship to shore, Cole then boarded the *Michigan*. He delayed too long and the entire plan collapsed rather undramatically as an officer from Johnson's Island entered the wardroom, patted Cole on the shoulder and said, "Major, I arrest you as a Confederate Spy."[145]

Trimble played a significant role in trying to resolve some of the problems with supplies for prisoners. The plan negotiated by Colonel Robert Ould, Confederate commissioner of exchange, and Lieutenant General Ulysses S. Grant called for an exchange of 1,000 bales of cotton to be sent out of Mobile on a Federal ship in exchange for "shoes, blankets, &c."[146]

for the Confederates in Union hands. Ould notified General Grant in November of 1864 that Trimble should be the Confederate to "make the necessary and proper arrangements for the sale of the cotton, and the purchase of the articles needed by our prisoners,"[147] with General William N. R. Beall as an alternate. This prompted the message by the secretary of war, Stanton, to Grant less than a week later stating that "it is objectionable on several grounds to let General Trimble have any parole, or trust, or indulgence in relation to supplies for prisoners, or any other purpose." Obviously fearing the aged warrior, Stanton added, "he cannot be trusted, and is the most dangerous rebel in our hands."[148] Later that year Trimble and Beall from the South and General Hays and Colonel Wild for the North all received paroles to enable them to carry out their duties, although the final details are unclear.[149]

Trimble gained his freedom from Fort Warren on March 5, 1865, and after a brief period of recuperation he headed toward Virginia to join his commander, Robert E. Lee. Upon reaching Lynchburg he learned that Lee had surrendered the day before. He was paroled in Lynchburg, Virginia, April 16, 1865. He returned to Baltimore, where he lived until his death January 2, 1888.[150]

While in Pennsylvania Trimble solidified his Southern identity, yet recognized being part of a larger community, whether that be called mankind or Christendom. He became the leader of a new community while on Johnson's Island; however, this could not be seen as anything but a temporary situation. While a prisoner in Fort McHenry he recorded his thoughts on the possibility of restoring the Union and clearly confirmed his dedication to his new nation. His extensive use of war images indicate that the war had served to deepen his new Southern identity, an identity which he had not even hinted at prior to 1861.

Trimble had not changed. He possessed the same personality traits that he had before the war. He had always been a resourceful man, and had a keen ability to recognize opportunity and respond quickly before it disappeared; this proved beneficial in business and war. His contentious aggressive behavior served him well at times, though he paid the price by making enemies; however, even his enemies respected his abilities. What changed the most was his new national identity. He was no longer an American, but a Southerner. Despite the fact that his home state of Maryland had remained in the Union, in the eyes of Trimble his Maryland was Confederate, and no other Confederates disputed his claims.

9

Unreconstructed Rebel

In April of 1882 an interviewer sat in the home of Isaac Trimble and recorded the retired general's responses to questions asked about the role he played in the "Conspiracy of '64." The interviewer, identified only by the initials F. A. B., displayed considerable respect for the man he had been talking to:

> The old General as he told his story grew warm with his theme and seemed to be again in the midst of the scenes he was describing. He is still the very picture of a soldier—fully up to medium height, a full round, well-knit frame and a carriage as erect and soldierly as if he were but forty. His face is full and round and fringed with a full suit of gray whiskers cut in Burnside fashion. His eyes are sharp and piercing, but have a kindly expression. He has a genial manner and a straightforward convincing way of speaking. He is a man of means and position. He has crowded much that is useful and eventful into the eighty years he has lived. It is not often that a man survives the amputation of a leg after he is sixty years of age. And instances are still rarer where they ever live to see active military service after such an ordeal. This man planned the escape to Canada while on crutches, and would have led the night attack upon the fifteen hundred soldiers guarding the camp, and then started to hobble a half hundred miles to reach the Dominion line.[1]

During his final years Trimble had two purposes in his life, both central stories in Southern history. First, he had to support his family and rebuild his fortune, but not in the "New South" imagined by Henry Grady. Like most of the returning Confederate officers he came home to a significantly reduced estate. He did not recover his financial losses with new enterprises but rather returned to the same endeavors he had actively pursued before the war. Second, though he had not been a planter nor a slave owner, he worked endlessly in defending the name of the Confederate soldier; he became a "Redeemer." He did not become a Redeemer in the true sense of the word, such as his friend and associate Wade Hampton, but rather by dedicating much of his time to defending the Confederate cause.

In a way Trimble did not return to the same local community he had been part of before 1861. Baltimore, like other large cities, had been a collection of several smaller communities even before the war. When Trimble returned to Baltimore, he became part of a new and distinctive community within the city—those who had been supporters of the Confederacy. He once again accepted his national identity but remained a part of the former Confederate leaders and emerged from the war as a "Southerner." The fact that he lived in Baltimore and not in one of the occupied military districts of the Reconstruction South did not exempt him from being accepted as a "real Southerner." He had different experiences from his comrades, but there is no doubt that they accepted him as one of their own. Several Confederate leaders served with him on various committees, but he bonded especially well with the famous South Carolina Redeemer Wade Hampton and the former Confederate president Jefferson Davis. Since Union troops did not occupy Maryland he did not have enemies to eject from his homeland; however, he felt compelled to defend not only his actions but those of his comrades from Maryland who also fought for the Confederacy.

This new identity became critical in Trimble's achievement of the highest level in Maslow's hierarchy of needs. The first two levels had been satisfied while still a young man, though he found them threatened at times under the stress of warfare. He had firmly established a community identity among the local leaders of Baltimore and Maryland, but in the spring of 1861 these state and local communities found themselves divided along the same lines as the nation as a whole. Trimble took the path chosen by the defenders of a new national identity. He found it necessary to work after the end of hostilities, but whereas he sought self-actualization in his career before the war, by the end it had become merely a means of making a living. He had achieved a form of self-actualization in being recognized as a Confederate general and hero, and he fought to defend the honor of the soldiers who had served under him and with him. The war had forged his Southern identity which had become intertwined with his self-esteem and pursuit of self-actualization.

Trimble returned to Ravenshurst in the Dulaney Valley near Baltimore. He built the 38-room mansion in 1854 as an expansion of a stone farmhouse that had been standing since 1800. The 52-foot front exemplified the Gothic revival ideas of William H. Ranlett, New York architect and publisher of a monthly architectural journal. The house had two outstanding features: first, a dramatic domed cupola in an octagon format which offered a view of the bay; second, a pair of openings or wells, one elliptical and one octagonal, cut into the floors below the lantern and equipped with balustrades which led to the cupola. The house and his fortune both showed the neglect of a four-year absence. He would have to restore the latter in order to maintain the former. He spent the warm summers at Ravenshurst, but passed the winters in his cozier quarters on Maryland Street in Baltimore.²

In the 1880s Trimble attempted to rebuild his fortune, but also worked hard to preserve the history of the Confederate soldier. Courtesy the Virginia Historical Society.

Twenty years after the war Trimble saw a prosperous South, but he did not see it as a "New South." He described the post-war Southern land as a place with "Agriculture flourishing, cities rebuilt, new ones springing up, manufactories established and prosperous, valuable mines discovered and developed, old railroads repaired, thousands of miles of new ones constructed, commercial interests vastly extended." He did not see this as the product of a new society, but rather something that came from the nature of the Southern people themselves, "all the sturdiest and noblest traits inherited from their English ancestry; among them, fortitude in adversity, endurance under hardships, perseverance under failures, self-reliance and courage to struggle against difficulties however formidable, and, above all, never to abandon the hope of a better future."³

Trimble did not pursue new economic ventures to restore his wealth but rather immediately returned to his old career as an engineer. In 1868 he worked as a consultant for the City of Baltimore on the Druid Lake Reservoir as well as the Jones Falls project. In the case of the latter he

Ravenshurst was built by Trimble in 1854. By the early 1980s the home had been ravaged by time and vandals to the point that it faced demolition. While restoration was being done it burned to the ground. Courtesy the Hearst Corporation.

served as a member of the board of engineers, along with his old friend Benjamin H. Latrobe. His reputation did not suffer in the community as a result of his serving the Confederacy.[4]

With some difficulty Trimble was able to recover his former lifestyle. He still had his real estate and his engineering skills. He managed to land consulting jobs and his inventions produced possibilities in manufacturing similar to those he started before the war. Two new companies were founded based on his inventions. In both of these the former Confederate general Wade Hampton served as president, probably because of assistance in raising the needed financing. Trimble owned stock in the Baltimore Concentric Engine Company which he purchased in 1872. Hampton was president of the company, which had capital stock of $400,000. Trimble also owned stock in the Baltimore Fire Extinguisher Works. He purchased this stock in 1873, and Hampton was president of the company which had $35,000 in capital stock.[5]

Trimble did enter a new business when he became a stockholder and general agent for the Carolina Insurance Company. This enterprise not only involved Wade Hampton, but also Jefferson Davis. Davis had been recruited as the president in October of 1869 and Trimble bought stock in the company in 1871. This business venture came about as the result of Trimble's association with a network of Confederate leaders from across the South who had not only worked together in preserving the honor of the Southern soldier, but worked together in rebuilding the vast fortunes they had before the war.[6]

Trimble knew Davis and Hampton before 1865, but became more involved with them during Reconstruction. He described himself as "a warm friend to Mr. Davis" at the time of the "Conspiracy of 1864," but the name of the Confederate president does not appear elsewhere in the documents left by Trimble.[7] Their relationship appears to have expanded after the war. It is known that Davis went to Trimble's home to convalesce upon his release from prison in 1867. Davis visited Baltimore on several occasions during his tenure as president of the Carolina Insurance Company, and even had a personal ambition to see the company relocate from Memphis to Baltimore. He brought his family on several occasions; his daughter Winnie Davis planted a tree in the front yard of Ravenshurst. Wade Hampton also frequented Trimble's home, and on one occasion gave a member of the family a "Martha Washington" cup and saucer. Trimble recruited him to speak to the Baltimore Society of Confederate Soldiers and Sailors in 1871. In addition to the previously mentioned business ventures, Hampton also became involved with the Carolina Insurance Company when he accepted the position of vice president in charge of the branch office in Baltimore in September of 1872.[8]

Davis had been a planter before the war and replaced John C. Calhoun as the primary advocate of States' rights; however, he resembled Trimble in that he initially resisted secession and had a relatively modern attitude toward business. To have defended a particular interpretation of the Constitution does not mean that an individual desired to see the demise of the Union. Davis resented the Northern attempts to limit Southern expansion in the territories and became the South's spokesman in the Senate, but remained guarded at the suggestion of secession if Lincoln became president. As a planter he ranked among those known as "improving planters," running his plantation as a business and seeking scientific ways to increase production. He urged Southerners to find economic independence from the North by developing manufacturing and encouraging immigration. He did not develop a modern attitude toward business as part of a "New South," but rather tried to rebuild his depleted fortune by continuing along the same lines he had started before the war. He accepted the presidency of the Carolina Insurance Company in an attempt to revive his wealth.[9] Davis agreed with Trimble; he said, "there is no New South! No, it is the Old South rehabilitated, and revivified by the energy and virtues of Southern men."[10]

Hampton too had resisted secession and promoted modern business. He believed Northern extremists to be the chief cause of ill feeling between the sections, but did not want disunion regardless of whose fault it might be, and at one point called Governor Pickens a fool for his secessionist policies. Like Trimble, after four years of war his attitude changed to the point that he supported Davis in his attempt to defend the Confederacy even after Lee had surrendered. Like Trimble and Davis, the once wealthy Hampton returned home from the war to find little of his estate intact except for his debts. Hampton became a "Redeemer," but not in some cavalier attempt to restore the old South nor even with a desire to keep the black man in a subservient role.[11] He wrote, "They [Southerners] are willing to treat the negro with kindness, giving to him every civil right, and, I think, to accord him such political privilege as he is fitted to enjoy." He went on to define what Southerners did want, "that their states should be restored to their old place in the Union, 'with all their rights, dignity, and equality unimpaired.'"[12] He declared, "It is full time that some voice from the South should be raised to declare that, though conquered, she is not humiliated; that though she submits, she is not degraded; that she has not lost her self-respect, that she has not laid down her arms on dishonorable terms." Hampton went on to clarify his intentions, "she has observed these terms with the most perfect faith, and that she has a right to demand the like observance of them on the part of the North."[13] It is in this last respect that Trimble became a Redeemer; he sought to preserve the honor and memory of those who had fought for South.

The insurance network of former Confederate leaders brought Trimble into indirect contact with slave-trading, Fort Pillow "butcher," Ku Klux Klan founder Nathan Bedford Forrest. Forrest and John B. Gordon both had been representatives of the Southern Insurance Company, which absorbed the Carolina Insurance Company in 1873. Wade Hampton too had been involved with the Southern Insurance Company. Klan activities by nature had been secretive, and thus it has been speculated that Forrest used the cover of insurance company business to conduct Klan business. When he went to meet with Gordon, the Georgia branch head of the Southern Insurance Company, it is reasonable to assume that the two men also discussed Klan business since Gordon held the title of grand dragon for the Georgia Klan.

Trimble became indirectly involved with the founder of the Ku Klux

Klan, and more directly associated with some of its other leaders such as John B. Gordon. There is no evidence to suggest that Trimble had any involvement in Klan activities. Forrest may have founded the Klan, but he also had business enterprises. Though Forrest traded in an unusual commodity, he still had been a businessman before the war and had no trouble resuming a business career without the slave trade. He had encouraged railroad development in the Memphis area both before and after the war. Like the other Confederate leaders he found it necessary to expend significant energy in rebuilding his fortune. In so doing he also became involved with the network of Confederate businessmen, many of whom had continued the struggle to preserve the honor of the Confederate soldiers. Again, there has been no evidence found suggesting that Trimble conducted anything but financial business with the Klansmen.[14]

Trimble never relied upon slave labor and suffered no losses with the passage of the Thirteenth Amendment, yet he did agree with at least some of the beliefs of the Redeemers relating to this issue. He never defended slavery nor did he have a reason to cultivate rationalizations. He felt that the state of Southern labor contributed to the problems in the region, and that white Southerners should have the right to control racial affairs and to seek solutions. No record has been found indicating that he saw the labor problem as a racial issue, though it is most likely that many, if not most, of his fellow Southerners did. He saw slavery as "an institution forced upon them by the policy of their Mother-England — an institution not then repugnant to the moral sentiment of nations, and perpetuated beyond their control."[15] He believed that the accomplishments during the 20 years after the war came about despite "uncontrolled and uncontrollable labor" that existed in many states in the South. There is little doubt that Trimble's views toward labor would have been more traditional compared to twenty-first century standards; however, he had a record of treating his workers with respect. Back when he laid off a worker on the PW&B he boasted of his sensitivity regardless of how high or low a position the man held. He personally nursed his men in Cuba and Virginia, and in his wartime reports he often praised the enlisted men. He did not have a condescending attitude towards those who labored but rather felt that the labor relations in the South should be left to Southerners. He said, "The strife between labor and capital is not confined to the South; it is growing into an importance so vital to the peace of the land, that the calmest wisdom of statesmen everywhere must be evoked to solve the problem safely for all sections, each in its own sphere."[16] He believed that all the people of the South "ask is the same privilege that other States enjoy — of regulating their own concerns."[17]

As previously stated, Trimble felt compelled to defend the name of the Confederate soldier. He said, "in this great land one great truth was established by the inexorable logic of the sword, namely: That we are and shall be one people; that this continent, broad as it is, cannot contain two republics or two nations." He went on to add, "the Southern States accepted the results of the war without mental reservations, and the terms which General Grant, at Appomattox, generously offered and to which General Lee acceded. The former made a pledge, and the latter accepted and gave a 'parole.'"[18] Trimble even stated that the people of the South had become convinced that the result of the conflict "was for the best." Nonetheless he believed that they deserved respect, and that most Union soldiers offered it. "When the men of Lee and of Johnston laid down their arms, they were, in one sense victors; for they had, by the skill of their general, and the bravery of their soldiers, conquered the respect of every officer and man in the Federal Armies."[19]

He struggled to see that history properly recorded the role played by the men from Maryland. In January of 1866 he accepted the position of founding president for the Society of the Army and Navy of the Confederate States in Maryland, and in 1886 was elected honorary president of that organization for life. He claimed that during the war Lee boasted of Marylanders as "unrivaled soldiers," and that with an army of 20,000 such men they could have marched to New York. Trimble became the Maryland representative and vice president of the Southern Historical Society. In 1871 he served as vice president-general from Maryland with the Lee Memorial Association, again working with John B. Gordon and Wade Hampton. He attended the West Point reunions of 1884 and 1887, making a speech at the former in which he praised the Confederate soldier. He also helped to establish the Confederate Home of Maryland which gave a place for the older soldiers to spend their final days.[20]

Even in death he became a symbol of the role Maryland played in fighting for the South. In 1897 Confederate Veteran Camp No. 1025 became known as the Isaac R. Trimble Camp, with "one of its worthy purposes to prepare and perpetuate a memoir of the life and distinguished services of Maj. Gen. Isaac Ridgeway Trimble."[21] His great-granddaughter, Miss Margaret Lloyd Trimble, participated in the dedication ceremony for the 1903 monument to Maryland Confederates built by the United Daughters of the Confederacy.[22]

Most of his final decade he spent alone. His second wife, Ann, died in 1879. An 1879 letter from the secretary of state requested an accounting of any possible debts owed by Trimble, along with several other retired U. S. officers. The letter does not specify the reason for the investigation

By the beginning of World War II much of the President Street station had collapsed. The main entrance still stands in a recently revitalized section of the city and today is the home of the Baltimore Civil War Museum.

but it seems likely that these men had requested pensions. In December of 1887 he visited relatives in Ohio and caught cold. As his condition worsened he decided to head home for Baltimore. On December 30 he took to his bed and finally went into a coma. He did not suffer but quietly passed his final hours at the home of his grandson, Dr. Isaac R. Trimble of 1123 North Eutaw St., Baltimore. He spent his last moments as a ghost on the battlefield and cried out, "Hold there steady — same — steady." At 5:15 p.m. on January 2, 1888, he expired.[23]

The city of Baltimore mourned the loss of their Confederate hero; Congressman W. H. F. Lee commented that Trimble personified "the able soldier and gallant gentleman."[24] On the morning of January 4 his casket lay in the parlor of his grandson's home. It bore a simple design, with a silver plate attached giving his name, date of birth and date of death, with a flower pillow and cross constituting the only decoration. The pallbearers wore the badge of the Society of the Army and Navy of the Confederate States and black crape on their left arms as they walked on either side of the hearse. They had a service at Emanuel Church, and then the procession moved on to Greenmount Cemetery where they laid Trimble to rest. Several Confederate generals attended the services, including Cadmus M. Wilcox, John W. Daniel, Alfred M. Scales, George G. Stuart, and Joseph E. Johnston. The last two would eventually join him in eternity at Greenmount along with four other Confederate generals: Benjamin Huger, Arnold Elzey, John H. Winder, and Henry Little.[25]

Trimble returned to his Baltimore home after the war, but he became a member of a new community of former Maryland Confederates. During the next 20 years he saw an increase in prosperity across the South, but he did not attribute this to a "New South" but rather to a continuation of advances made between 1840 and 1860. In his case he continued in the progressive economy that he had participated in prior to the war. He entered one new industry, insurance, but only because he became part of a network of former Confederate leaders. He had no direct involvement with slaves before the war nor the freemen after the war, but he still stood up for the right of the South (probably the white South) to manage its own affairs including its unique flavor of labor problems. In his mind the South could best resolve its labor issues. He accepted Lee's surrender at Appomattox as a reality, and softened his stand toward the possibility of reunification; however, he did not accept the notion that he or his fellow Confederate soldiers had made a mistake. Though they suffered defeat he felt that they still deserved respect. He committed a great deal of time during his last years to trying to see that the soldiers occupied a noble place in American history. This activity did not arise as the result of any nostalgic longing for the cavalier antebellum days of the South, but rather came about defending their memory. He accepted the reality of military defeat, but never agreed with the notion that the South had been wrong. His self-esteem and self-actualization revolved around his southern identity and the role he played in defending the Confederacy. His personal identity and self-worth had become intertwined with the lost cause.

The fact that he came from Maryland instead of one of the Deep South states subject to the military districts of Reconstruction did not exempt him from membership in the band of Confederate leaders who struggled to preserve what remained of their Southern identity. He became part of a network of former Confederate generals and dignitaries who worked together in their business ventures as well as in their efforts to preserve the history of their short-lived nation. He became a leader among those who lived in Baltimore and Maryland who had fought for the South. Marylanders could have easily faded into the tapestry of industrialized America but instead stepped forward boldly boasting of the role they had played in the recent struggle, and honoring the memory of those from their state who had fallen wearing the gray. Though Trimble had never described himself as a Southerner before the war, he became a defender of the Southern nation that continued long after Appomattox. Trimble and those involved in the network of Confederate leaders contributed to strengthening southern identity during the Reconstruction years.

10

Conclusion

The life of one man, Isaac Trimble, cannot serve as proof of any historical question. Biography can enhance history by serving as an example of the complexities faced by the individual during historical events. For Trimble the most critical event came when he made the decision to join the Confederacy rather than remaining loyal to the Union. The fact that he came from a border state enhances his value as a subject worthy of investigation. He was but one man among millions, and he came from one of many communities that existed in the South. He was unique, but exemplified the diversity of people who supported the CSA. None of those that he served under treated him or other Marylanders as any less Confederate than those from the Deep South, either during the war or during Reconstruction.

Like most individuals, Trimble lived his life in pursuit of his individual goals. These have been classified by the psychologist Abraham Maslow as the hierarchy of needs. The first two of five levels described by Maslow are rather basic, the first being food and water and the second to acquire a sense of safety. During the war Trimble had times in which he felt these needs threatened but during most of his life he, like most Americans, did not spend much energy on them. The most critical level of personal fulfillment is one that takes the individual and brings him or her into the group environment, the fulfillment of what Maslow called the belongingness needs. On the more basic level this leads the individual to establish a family unit. On a grander scale this is what creates the urge to belong to a community.

It is the desire to be part of a community which relates most to the questions of interest to historians, since they study the events in which large numbers participated. Primitive men had little trouble with their group identity or with their role within that group. They usually belonged to a tribe or village and had a function within that community. What we see in the case of Trimble is that in the modern world men can belong to more than one community. For Trimble this included his family, both nuclear and extended, his city, his state and his nation; it is the question of national identity that relates to the study of the Civil War. Trimble also belonged to the communities of West Point graduates, professional railroad men, and Confederate veterans. At times these various communities produced personal crises; Trimble fought against some of his fellow West Point graduates over the question of national identity. This only serves to demonstrate the complexity of identity in the modern world; it was this observation that led Maslow to recognize the problem of identity as a major source of maladjustment for the individual in the modern world.

One of the most fascinating aspects of this biography is how easily Trimble traded his citizenship in the United States and joined the Confederate States. This might suggest that the feelings of national identity are more shallow than some of the other group belongings. Since Trimble came from a border state the question may have been more difficult since Marylanders fought equally fiercely for the blue and for the gray. It is even more interesting when we see that Trimble never expressed any strong regional identity prior to the war. The events that led to the war forced Trimble to decide on which side he belonged. For this reason the study of a man like Trimble offers no insight on the causes of the initial hostilities, but rather an understanding of how many such as he found themselves trapped by events totally beyond their control.

Trimble had grown quite comfortable with his American citizenship and during most of his life drifted freely across local and state borders as if he truly felt that he belonged to the nation. A number of variables led to his final decision, but the point of no return came in April of 1861 when it became clear that he would have to choose sides. Though he had lived in northern states both as a child and as an adult he seemed to find greater identity with the place of his birth, even though he spent very little time in the Old Dominion state of Virginia. His wife's family had much stronger ties to the South than did his own and there is little doubt that this contributed to his feelings that he belonged more with that region than the northern one. His personal conflict with the New Englander Samuel Felton could very well have aggravated his belief that Northerners hated "every thing Southern." He may have projected hostilities he felt toward Felton to all Northerners. It seems quite possible that Felton's strong and swift support for the Union contributed in some degree to Trimble's stand for the opposing side.

The issue of slavery and its spread in the territories may very well have been the major variable that started the chain reaction that quickly became more powerful than any single individual; however, it had nothing to do with Trimble's decision. He never expressed any hatred for slavery; the strongest statement he made against owning another human being came from the fact that he never owned any himself. He did make use of slave labor early in the war when he was assigned to building fortifications; this indicates that he had no great feelings of outrage over its morality. During Reconstruction he did express his belief that the South should have the right to settle its own labor problems. At this point the question of slavery had been resolved and to Trimble the laboring class in the South was no different from that in the North. He was raised by Quakers, a people who neither gave nor expected deference. Through the years he had demonstrated a sympathetic attitude towards those farther down the social ladder, though it may have been somewhat paternalistic. The main issue to Trimble was the right for the individual states to solve their own problems.

Trimble serves as a good example of the role of aggression in the relationship between individuals within a community. Maslow described two basic types of aggression, that between groups and that within groups. As a general officer Trimble had plenty of opportunity to be aggressive toward another group, the Federal soldiers; however, what is more fascinating are his acts of internal aggression. Both the Union and the Confederate armies had problems because of internal bickering. Trimble quite often became involved in squabbles with his compatriots. Before the war his conflict with Samuel Felton led to a long and hotly contested hearing. While in military service with the Confederacy he became deeply involved in conflict with other officers including Richard Ewell and Jeb Stuart. This internal aggression is generally less costly than aggression between groups. It is related to the two higher levels of needs described by Maslow, self-esteem and self-actualization. Individuals within a community often compete for social position as a means for achieving these higher level needs, but generally do so in a way that does not jeopardize their need to belong to the group. Some, such as artists, are less dependent on rivalry and pecking order such as can be found among military, economic, or political leaders; however, even these people quite often become jealous of each other's successes.

It is clear in the case of Isaac Trimble the he did not fight for the South in order to preserve a premodern way of life; he was in the vanguard of American modernization. He began his life in a typical pioneer family but he sought social and economic advancement by seizing the opportunities that he saw in a growing and developing nation. He did not attend West Point for military training but rather as a means to earn an education. He worked hard to become an engineer, no doubt recognizing that the new land would need engineers. Chance introduced him to railroads but he quickly saw that he had a bright future in that line of work. Though his marriage did more to draw him into the community of Baltimore, he and his new home struggled to maintain a leadership role in the search for progress. It could be argued that he was atypical since he lived in the border state of Maryland; however, many of the Confederate leaders that he became associated with also had progressive attitudes toward the development of commerce and industry in the South. This included such men as Wade Hampton, Jefferson Davis, and Nathan Bedford Forrest. Unlike Trimble, these three men all owned slaves, but they were also businessmen who wanted to see the South compete with the North and not simply remain a nation of planters. As individuals, self-interest may have been the main motivation.

This causes one to question the notion of the "New South." Since the idea was popularized by C. Vann Woodward, historians have debated the existence of the "New South." In recent years the trend has been against Woodward. Trimble's life certainly confirms this point of view. He did not enter new business enterprises upon his return from the war but rather continued along the same lines as before he joined the Army. He worked as a civil engineer, started manufacturing companies, and continued to make new inventions. He became involved in a new field when he joined the Carolina Insurance Company, but that was the result of his association with the network of former Confederates who looked to that industry as a means to restore their lost wealth. Trimble claimed that it was the nature of the Southern people that allowed for the economic progress that the region saw after the war, the same industrious people who lived there before. The South may have lagged behind the North, but they began the process of modernization before 1861 and not during Reconstruction.

Trimble did not become a true Redeemer in that he did not have to recover his homeland from the Union army and Carpetbaggers, but he did work tirelessly in defending the honor of his fellow Confederates. Even in this task his state received recognition for the part it played in the lost cause. He represented Maryland in the Southern Historical Society, served on the Robert E. Lee Memorial Committee, and became one of the senior and most respected among the ex-Confederates of his state. When he passed away they laid him to rest with other Confederate generals buried in the city of Baltimore.

Isaac Trimble was one among many. His background was unique and he was unique; however, he did not appear to be that much different from the other men that he served with. He was not a fire-eater and thus the study of his life offers little in trying to understand the events that caused the Civil War. He was one of the millions who joined the Confederacy after the South started down the road to a separate national existence. Trimble, like others from the four Upper South states of Tennessee, Arkansas, Virginia, and North Carolina, did not follow the leaders down that road until after the firing on Fort Sumter and the subsequent demand for 75,000 men by the president of the United States. These four states accounted for 43 percent of the Confederate population and provided some of the most talented military commanders, such as Robert E. Lee, Thomas J. Jackson, and Joseph E. Johnston. In addition, several regiments were raised from Maryland, Kentucky, Missouri, West Virginia and Indian Territory. The war could not have gone on so long without the Upper South and border states. Isaac Trimble serves as an example of how these people were simply trying to live their private lives neither advocating slavery nor threatening resistance to a changing nation; they became caught up in the whirlpool of events created by others. Many on both sides struggled to keep from being consumed by the flames of radicalism but to no avail. Men who wanted the same thing, to see the nation remain together and in peace, ended up facing each other on the battlefield. After it was over Trimble had an identity he never displayed before the war; he was a Southerner.

Bibliographic Essay

The life of Isaac Trimble touches on several aspects of Southern history. As stated in the introduction a biography can not serve as proof for any particular point of view on any of these topics but it can be useful as a case study. The most pressing question is: why did this man join the Confederacy? Related to this question is: did modernization have anything to do with his decision? Isaac Trimble came from a border state; did this make any difference? This in turn brings up the question of how to define the South. What made him identify with the South, and what is Southern distinctiveness? When the war ended did Trimble change because of the "New South"? Or, was there such a thing as the "New South"?

Most histories explaining causes of the war fit into one of three categories: ideological, political, or economic. Many of the ideological explanations focused on various aspects of slavery, often overlapping with political or economic explanations.[1] Others have focused on the Southern concerns about republicanism.[2] Political interpretations have looked at failures in the party system or other ways in which the balance of powers between slave and free states collapsed just before the start of hostilities.[3] Some have offered an economic interpretation based on differences of private property,[4] while others have postulated a conflict between the Northern and Southern class structures.[5] Several economic interpretations are related to the question of modernization. Trimble and most Southern sympathizers in Baltimore did not give their support to the Confederacy until they realized that they would have to choose sides. They saw no major conflict over slavery since they had a society where slavery and modernization coexisted.

A favorite theme among economic interpretations has been to consider the South resistant to modernization.[6] There is evidence that even though the South lagged behind the North in industrialization they nonetheless adopted modernizing practices.[7] Some authors have found centers of Southern manufacturing and participation in the world economy.[8] Others have looked at individual Southern leaders and demonstrated that the South was in the process of modernization.[9] Both Isaac Trimble and the city of Baltimore not only participated in modernization but they occupied a role of leadership.

The question of Southern distinctiveness has been brought up in seeking the causes of the Civil War and has usually been related to ideological explanations.[10] The Celtic fringe theory states that ethnic differences divided the regions, the New Englanders coming from the predominantly Anglo-Saxon southeast part of England and those in the South descending from the Celtic fringes in the west and north of the island.[11] Some have seen the South as growing distinctive after the formation of the United States, largely because of its dependence on slavery.[12] Recently it has been suggested "that their increased distinctiveness was, in fact, a *product* of the war."[13] Trimble's case supports this latter point of view. Even though he claimed in his diary that the two regions had been different from the start, he did not reveal any regional identity until after the war commenced, and then these feelings intensified as the war progressed.

Related to the question of Southern identity is the definition of the "real South." The question of definition overlaps with the concept of community (which will be discussed in more detail later). Over the years many have looked at Southern history as the study of the white population only, while some have focused primarily on the planter class. Only recently has the diversity of Southern culture been emphasized.[14] This becomes critical in a study of Isaac Trimble because his background does not match the traditional view of the Confederate elite; Trimble lived most of his life in the border states and on both sides of the Mason-Dixon line. The problem of defining "the South" also relates to the issue of modernization, since diversity is often one of the characteristics of a modern society. Historians have identified numerous communities existing within individual states of the South, let alone the region as a whole.[15] Even the stereotype of Southern evangelicalism has been questioned, thus explaining why Judah Benjamin of the Confederacy became the first Jew to hold a cabinet post in America.[16] Some have assumed that the non-white Southerners contradicted the image of the Confederate; however, recent studies have even explored Confederates of color including African Americans, both slave and free.[17]

A belief in the "New South" assumes the view that the antebellum South was a premodern world and that a new breed of men led the way to industrialization. In *Origins of the New South*, C. Vann Woodward saw the Redeemers as the "new men" who rejected agrarianism in favor of modernization.[18] Some authors have questioned the origins of these new men, suggesting that those making money after the war were the same as those who were making money before the war.[19] One interpretation holds that the "New South" was the product of Southern mythology,[20] and the trend currently has been toward rejecting the concept of a "New South." Nonetheless, some historians have continued to support Woodward's views.[21] In the case of Trimble there was nothing new about the economy after the war; he simply returned to the same enterprises that he had been involved in before. Some might make the point that Baltimore was an exception from the rest of the South; however, Trimble networked with other leaders from the former Confederacy. They, too, attempted to rebuild their lost fortunes, their most significant difference from Trimble being that they had to find a new source of labor.

Chapter Notes

Preface

1. "Ravenhurst," *The Sun Magazine*, (May 31, 1981): 6–7.

Introduction

1. Robert Hollinger, *Postmodernism and the Social Sciences: A Thematic Approach* (London: Sage Publications, 1994), xiii, 2.
2. W. W. Rostow, *The Stages of Economic Growth: A Non-Communist Manifesto* (Cambridge: The University Press, 1971), 38.
3. Richard D. Brown, *Modernization: The Transformation of American Life 1600–1865* (New York: Hill and Wang, 1976), 9–12.
4. *Ibid.*, 94–95.
5. Edward Quinn, Robert Lilienfield, and Rodman Hill, eds., *Interdiscipline: A Reader in Psychology, Sociology, and Literature* (New York: The Free Press, 1972), xix.
6. *Ibid.*
7. Anthony J. Sutich and Miles A. Vich, eds., *Readings in Humanistic Psychology* (New York: The Free Press, 1969), 1–4.
8. *Ibid.*, 1.
9. *Ibid.*, 7.
10. Andrea Gabor, *The Capitalist Philosophers: The Geniuses of Modern Business— Their Lives, Times, and Ideas* (New York: Time Business, 2000), 155.
11. Abraham H. Maslow, *Motivation and Personality* (New York: Harper & Row, Publishers, 1970), xviii.
12. *Ibid.*, xii–xiii.
13. *Ibid.*, 35.
14. *Ibid.*, 41.
15. *Ibid.*, 43.
16. *Ibid.*, 44.
17. *Ibid.*, 45–46.
18. *Ibid.*, 47.
19. *Ibid.*, 54.
20. Abraham H. Maslow, *New Knowledge in Human Values* (New York: Harper & Brothers, Publishers, 1959), 124.
21. *Ibid.*, 127.
22. Louis Breger, *From Instinct to Identity: The Development of Personality* (Englewood Cliffs, NJ: Prentice-Hall, Inc., 1974), 45–46, 350–351.
23. Maslow, *Motivation*, xix.
24. Abraham H. Maslow, *Dominance, Self-Esteem, Self-Actualization: Germinal Papers of A. H. Maslow* (Monterey, CA: Brooks/Cole Publishing Company, 1973), 16, 50, 56, 67.
25. Breger, *From Instinct*, 333, 338, 340, 347, 348, 350.
26. Brown, *Modernization*, 15.
27. *Ibid.*, 95.
28. Ruth Benedict, *Patterns of Culture* (New York: Houghton Mifflin Company, 1934), 253–254.
29. Thomas Bender, *Community and Social Change in America* (New Brunswick, NJ: Rutgers University Press, 1978), 5.
30. For books dealing with the definition of community as well as the conflicts produced by industrialization see Rene König, *The Community* (London: Rutledge & Kegan Paul, Ltd., 1968); Robert Redfield, *The Little Community* (Chicago: University of Chicago Press, 1956);

Martin Buber, *Paths to Utopia* (Boston: Beason Press, 1958); Peter Laslett, *The World We Have Lost* (London: Methuen & Co., 1965); David J. Russo, *Families and Communities: A New View of American History* (Nashville: The American Association for State and Local History, 1974); Bender, *Community and Social Change*.

31. Barbara Hanawalt and Henry Pirenne have demonstrated that the nuclear family has been the basic family structure in western Europe since the Middle Ages. Barbara Hanawalt, *The Ties That Bound: Peasant Families in Medieval England* (New York: Oxford University Press, 1986); Henry Pirenne, *Economic and Social History of Medieval Europe* (London: K. Paul, Trench, Truber & Co. Ltd., 1936)

32. Breger, *From Instinct*, 75.

33. David J. Russo, *Families and Communities*, 15, 34–35. Several studies of New England towns have debated when the decline of the New England town community began and ended. Page Smith, *As A City Upon a Hill: The Town in American History* (New York: Alfred A. Knopf, Inc., 1966); Michael Zuckerman, *Peaceable Kingdoms: New England Towns in the Eighteenth Century* (New York: Alfred A. Knopf, Inc., 1970); Kenneth Lockridge, *A New England Town — The First Hundred Years: Dedham, Massachusetts, 1636–1736* (New York: William Norton & Co., Inc., 1970); Sumner Chilton Powell, *Puritan Village: The Formation of a New England Town* (New York: Anchor Books, 1965); Paul Boyer and Stephen Nissenbaum, *Salem Possessed: The Social Origins of Witchcraft* (Cambridge, MA: Harvard University Press, 1974).

34. Alexis de Tocqueville, *Democracy in America*, trans. and ed., Phillips Bradley (New York: Vintage Books, 1945), 1:61–86.

35. Bender, *Community and Social Change*, 89–96.

36. *Ibid.*, 84–86.

37. Breger, *From Instinct*, 81.

38. Several works have shown the existence of market economy in medieval England. Marianne Kowaleski, *Local Markets and Regional Trade in Medieval Exeter* (Cambridge: Cambridge University Press, 1995); Christopher Dyer, *Standards of Living in the Later Middle Ages* (Cambridge: Cambridge University Press, 1989); Sylvia Thrupp, *The Merchant Class of Medieval London: [1300–1500]* (Chicago: The University of Chicago Press, 1976); A. Macfarlane, *The Origins of English Individualism* (Oxford: Oxford University Press, 1978); R. H. Hilton, "Lords, Burgesses and Hucksters." *Past and Present*, 97 (Spring, 1982), 3–15.

39. Several of the books mentioned in the previous note speak of the increased demand for labor after the great plague, but one of the best to demonstrate how this affected the average peasant is by Barbara Hanawalt, *The Ties That Bound* (New York: Oxford University Press, 1986).

40. Jonathan I. Israel gave a good account of the development of the world market. Jonathan I. Israel, *Dutch Primacy in World Trade, 1585–1740* (Oxford: Oxford Clarendon Press, 1989). The development of a common culture built around commerce, which allowed the development of nationalism and the Dutch Republic is traced by Simon Schama. Simon Schama, *The Embarrassment of Riches: An Interpretation of Dutch Culture in the Golden Age* (New York: Alfred A. Knopf, 1988).

41. Two books that tried to show the relationship between the colonies and England and how they helped to lead to revolution are Lawrence A. Harper, *The English Navigation Laws: A Seventeenth Century Experiment in Social Engineering* (New York: Cornell University Press, 1939); Thomas C. Barrow, *Trade and Empire: The British Customs Service in Colonial America, 1600–1775* (Cambridge, MA: Harvard University Press, 1970). George R. Taylor took the position that the colonies did quite well despite English policy; George R. Taylor, "Economic Growth Before 1840: An Exploratory Essay," *Journal of Economic History*, 24 (Winter, 1964), 427–444.

42. Louis Dumont, *From Mandeville to Marx: The Genesis and Triumph of Economic Ideology* (Chicago: The University of Chicago Press, 1977): 42–43, 52, 59–60.

43. Drew R. McCoy, *The Elusive Republic: Political Economy in Jeffersonian America* (Chapel Hill: The University of North Carolina Press, 1980), 6, 17, 46, 68–69, 104, 116–119, 135, 165, 185, 235.

Chapter 1. From the Wilds of Kentucky to West Point

1. Isaac R. Trimble, "Memoirs," unpublished manuscript in possession of William C. Trimble, Baltimore, MD.

2. Hollinger, *Postmodernism and the Social Sciences*, xiii, 2; Brown, *Modernization*, 9–12.

3. William Wade Hinshaw, *Encyclopedia of American Quaker Genealogy*, 6 volumes (Ann Arbor, MI, 1936–1950); reprint, (Baltimore: Genealogical Publishing Co., Inc., 1991–1994). Some might be tempted to dismiss this set of books as a poor primary source because of the word "Genealogy" in the title; however, they are nothing more than a fairly complete set of the monthly meeting records of all of the Quaker congregations prior to the Civil War

and some after. Hinshaw did miss a few of the meetings formed in Virginia prior to the establishment of Penn's Colony. Volume I on North and South Carolina has more than 1,100 pages and Volume V on Virginia has more than 1,000 pages. Volume II, Pennsylvania, has about 1,100 pages. It is difficult to get an exact count since many of the families are listed in more than one volume. A particular family might have came from Pennsylvania, then moved to Virginia, and then North Carolina and would thus appear in all three volumes. Nonetheless, the margin of data is so great that it is quite clear that more Quakers lived in the South than in Pennsylvania. Shortly after the turn of the nineteenth century the Quakers from the South exceeded those from Pennsylvania in the exodus to Ohio and Indiana; however, many such as the Trimble family left the Society of Friends at about the same time and thus Trimble had many former Quaker kinsmen who remained in the South and eventually fought for the Confederacy. The development of the Society of Friends in the South, including Virginia, is also covered by Stephen B. Weeks, *Southern Quakers and Slavery* (New York: Bergman Publishers, 1968).

4. Weeks mentions the fact that many of the Southern Quakers went west. The Encyclopedia of Quaker Genealogy had two volumes of Ohio records alone and Willard Heiss compiled six volumes, though much smaller sized books, on the Quaker records of Indiana. One of the records recorded in the monthly meetings was transfer of membership, with many coming from Pennsylvania. This also suggests that the rich farmlands of the Ohio valley provided as much of an incentive as the desire to escape slavery.

5. These statistics are based on the unpublished research, Randy Beeson, "Roll of Honor, 1861–1865;" Thomas A Valentine, *The Mendenhall Family: Descendants of Thomas Mendenhall and Joan Stroade.* (n.p.: Published by Author, 1994). It is common for genealogies to be self-published but this does not mean they are inaccurate. Even if an error or two was made this still serves as an example of how the old Quaker families left a number of descendants who served on both sides during the Civil War including these two families related to Trimble.

6. Isaac Trimble, "Memoirs,"; John Farley Trimble, *Trimble Families of America* (Parsons, WV: McClain Printing Co., 1973): 159–161; Joint Committee of Hopewell Friends, *Hopewell Friends History 1734–1934: Frederick County, Virginia* (Strasburg, VA: Shenandoah Publishing House, 1936. Reprint, Baltimore: Genealogical Publishing Co., Inc., 1993): 291; William Wade Hinshaw, *Encyclopedia of Quaker Genealogy*, 1:452.

7. Trimble, "Memoirs," 6–7; Hinshaw, *Encyclopedia of Quaker Genealogy*, 4:112, 6:589; Trimble, *Trimble Families*, 162–163.

8. Jean R. Soderlund, *Quakers & Slavery: A Divided Spirit* (Princeton, NJ: Princeton University Press, 1985), 11, 12, 173, 176–177, 185–187; Weeks, *Southern Quakers and Slavery*, 1–12; see also, Thomas Edward Drake, *Quakers and Slavery in America* (New Haven, CN: Yale University Press, 1950).

9. Ray Allen Billington and Martin Ridge, *Westward Expansion: A History of the American Frontier* (New York: Macmillan Publishing Co., Inc., 1982), 262–266.

10. Capt. George W. Cullum, Comp., *Register of the Officers and Graduates of the U. S. Military Academy at West Point, N. Y.* (New York: J. F. Trow, Printer, 1850), 108; *Nineteenth Annual Reunion of the Association of Graduates of the United States Military Academy, at West Point June 11, 1888* (East Saginaw, MI: Evening News Printing and Binding House, 1888), 64; 11, Box 548, Appointment, Commission, and Personnel Branch Document File, National Archives, 1879; RG94, David Trimble to Col. Johnson, March 13, 1818, Records Relating to the U.S. Military Academy, Application Papers of Cadets, 1805–1866, Isaac Trimble; Isaac Trimble to George W. Cullum, July 22, 1855, U. S. Military Academy, Isaac Ridgeway Trimble Papers; Hinshaw, *Encyclopedia of Quaker Genealogy*, 4: 112. Several Sources give May 15, 1802, as the birth date for Isaac Trimble. The primary source for this error is probably from the memorial biography printed in the 1888 West Point Reunion book. Trimble himself usually gave 1804 as the year of this birth, though in the 1855 letter to George Cullum he said 1806. The 1804 date is confirmed by the *Register of the Officers* which shows Trimble to have been aged 14 years six months when he enrolled at West Point in November of 1818. The source for this information no doubt came from the 1818 letter of David Trimble which stated that he was aged 14 years and six months. This is probably the most reliable of all the sources since it was written in 1818. Also, the exact place of his birth has been disputed with some sources saying Culpepper, Virginia, and others giving Pennsylvania. The above mentioned Register gives Virginia as the birthplace. The Quaker records at Redstone, Pennsylvania, shows the family of John Trimble arriving on April 2, 1802, and as of that date Isaac was not yet born. This would lead one to conclude that he was born after they arrived, and thus he was born in Pennsylvania. The Redstone meeting did have members from

what is today Manongalia County, West Virginia, but which at the time was part of the state of Virginia. I have concluded that Trimble was not born in Culpepper County, which is south of even the Hopewell meeting, but that he probably was born in Virginia, which is where he states he was born and which appeared in the West Point Register in 1818.

11. Hinshaw, *Encyclopedia of Quaker Genealogy*, 5:266; Trimble, *The Trimble Families*, 162–163; Trimble, "Memoirs," 17.

12. Trimble, "Memoirs," 17–18.

13. *Ibid.*, 8–9, 14; Francis R. Heitman, *Historical Register and Dictionary of the United States Army* (Washington: Government Printing Office, 1903), 970. According to the Historical Register David Trimble held the rank of 3rd lieutenant in 1814. It may have been that this is a different David Trimble or it may have been that the rank of major was in the State militia and the rank of lieutenant was in the United States Army. The third possibility is that Isaac Trimble was mistaken in claiming that his brother was a major.

14. Isaac Trimble to John A. Trimble, October 1880, in possession of William C. Trimble.

15. Trimble, "Memoirs," 11–13.

16. Will of David Trimble, September 1, 1832; codicil added August 13, 1836, copy in possession of William C. Trimble.

17. Trimble, "Memoirs," 18–19; West Point application of Isaac Trimble.

18. *Ibid.*, 14–16.

19. Stephen E. Ambrose, *Duty, Honor, Country: A History of West Point* (Baltimore: The Johns Hopkins Press, Baltimore, 1966): 3.

20. *Ibid.*, 4.

21. *Ibid.*, 5.

22. *Ibid.*, 22–31.

23. *Ibid.*, 87–89; *Reports of the Course of Instruction in Yale College* (New Haven, 1828); George P. Schmidt, *The Old Time College President* (New York, 1930), 130.

24. *The Debates and Proceedings in the Congress of the United States, Seventh Congress, First Session* (Washington, 1834), 1312, Library of Congress. Ambrose, *Duty, Honor, Country*, 22; Thomas J. Fleming, *West Point: The Men and Times of the United States Military Academy* (New York: William Morrow & Company, Inc., 1969): 15–16; Sidney Forman, *West Point: A History of the United States Military Academy* (New York: Columbia University Press, 1950): 24–25.

25. Fleming, *West Point: The Men and Times*, 20–22; Forman, *West Point: A History*, 36; Ambrose, *Duty, Honor, Country*, 38–39.

26. James Monroe to Alden Partridge, January 3, 1815; Joseph Gardner Swift, *Memoirs* (Privately Published, 1890), 139–140; Ambrose, *Duty, Honor, Country*, 44–45; Forman, *West Point: A History*, 40–41; Fleming, *West Point, The Men and Times*, 4–6.

27. Thayer to Academic Board, August 1, 1817; Thayer to Secretary of War, August 4, 1817; Thayer to Secretary of War, September 27, 1817; Thayer to Secretary of War, August 19, 1817, West Point Military Academy, Sylvanus Thayer Papers. Ambrose, *Duty, Honor, Country*, 70, 89–90, 97; Fleming, *West Point: A History* 30–32, 37.

28. Trimble, "Memoirs," 19; Latrobe, *Eighteenth Annual Reunion of the Association of the Graduates of the United States Military Academy at West Point*, 2–3; Isaac R. Trimble, *15th Annual Reunion of the Association of the Graduates of the United States Military Academy* (E. Saginaw, MI: Courier Printing Co., 1884), 30–31. Trimble claimed to travel the distance in 10 hours on his steam boat, whereas Latrobe said he landed 24 hours after leaving New York. Apparently the steamboat trip was faster.

29. Trimble, *Reunion*, 23.

30. Latrobe, *Eighteenth Annual Reunion of the Association of the Graduates of the United States Military Academy at West Point*, 4–5, 21, 25.

31. *Ibid.*, 5–6.

32. *Ibid.*, 12.

33. *Ibid.*, 18, 22, 25, 28. Unfortunately the records of Delinquencies, Registrar of Merit books, or Register of Punishments for the years in which Trimble attended West Point do not exist.

34. *Ibid.*, 27–28, 33–34.

35. William Henry Harrison to David Trimble, February 14, no year, in possession of William C. Trimble.

36. Latrobe, *Eighteenth Annual Reunion*, 25.

37. Papers of Jefferson Davis, Vol. I, pp. 17–19; William C. Davis, *Jefferson Davis: The Man and His Hour* (New York: Harper Collins Publishers, 1991): 28.

38. *Ibid.*, 9.

39. In the Trimble genealogy the only evidence of a relationship between Isaac Trimble and Senator William A. Trimble is the memoirs of the former in which he recalled this visit. The exact relationship is based on family oral tradition.

40. Trimble, "Memoirs," 20–21.

41. *Ibid.*, 21–22.

42. *Ibid.*, 22–25.

43. *Ibid.*, 25–26; Cullum, *Register of the Officers and Graduates*, 108; Heitman, 970; Isaac R. Trimble to George W. Cullum, October 16, 1859, United States Military Academy, Isaac Ridgeway Trimble Papers.

44. Maslow, *The Farther Reaches*, 48

Chapter 2. Army Life: Toward a New Identity

1. *Detailed and Correct Account of the Grand Civic Procession, in the City of Baltimore, of the Fourth of July, 1828; in Honor of the Day, and in Commemoration of the Commencement of the Baltimore and Ohio Rail-Road* (Baltimore: Thomas Murphy, 1828): 3–4.
2. John F. Stover, *History of the Baltimore and Ohio Railroad* (West Lafayette, IN: Purdue University Press, 1987), 27.
3. *Grand Civic Procession*, 9.
4. Albert Gallatin, "Report on Roads and Canals," presented to the Senate by the secretary of the treasury, April 4, 1808, American State Papers, Miscellaneous, I, 724–921; Annals, 4th Congress, 2nd Session, pp. 2052–2041; Carter Goodrich, *Government Promotion of American Canals and Railroads 1800–1890* (New York: Columbia University Press, 1960), 3, 19, 28, 37; Forest G. Hill, *Roads, Rails & Waterways: The Army Engineers and Early Transportation* (Norman: University of Oklahoma Press, 1960), 4–5, 37; James D. Dilts, *The Great Road: The Building of the Baltimore & Ohio, The Nation's First Railroad, 1828–1853* (Stanford, CA: Stanford University Press, 1993), 18.
5. Isaac Trimble, "Memoirs," 27; "Report on the Topographical Engineers," December 25, 1822, Bulky File, No. 114, pp. 11–12, National Archives, Washington D.C., Engineer Department, War Records Division; Hill, *Roads, Rails & Waterways*, 26–27, 45;
6. George Rogers Taylor, *The Transportation Revolution 1815–1860* (New York: Rinehart and Winston, 1951), 21
7. Charles Henry Ambler, *A History of Transportation in the Ohio Valley* (Glendale, CA: The Arthur H. Clark Company, 1932), 211–212; Taylor, *The Transportation Revolution*, 21–22.
8. Abert to S/W Porter, February 12, 1829, Topographical Bureau, National Archives, Washington, D.C.; Hill, *Roads, Rails & Waterways*, 75–77.
9. Commission of Isaac Trimble, William C. Trimble, Baltimore, Maryland, Isaac Ridgeway Trimble Papers; Trimble to Cullum, July 22, 1855, United States Military Academy at West Point Library, Isaac Ridgeway Trimble Papers; Trimble to Cullum, October 16, 1859, United States Military Academy at West Point Library, Isaac Ridgeway Trimble Papers; M617, National Archives and Records Administration, Roster of Officers and Enlisted Men, First U.S. Artillery; M727, National Archives and Records Administration, Monthly Post Returns, 1800–1916; Heitman, *Historical Register*, 970; Cullum, *Biographical Register*, 228.
10. Trimble to Cullum, July 22, 1855, United States Military Academy at West Point Library, Isaac Ridgeway Trimble Papers; Trimble to Cullum, October 16, 1859, United States Military Academy at West Point Library, Isaac Ridgeway Trimble Papers; Heitman, *Historical Register*, 970; Cullum, *Biographical Register*, 228.
11. Trimble, "Memoirs," 27; Trimble to Cullum, July 22, 1855, United States Military Academy at West Point Library, Isaac Ridgeway Trimble Papers; Trimble to Cullum, October 16, 1859, United States Military Academy at West Point Library, Isaac Ridgeway Trimble Papers; Engineering Department, National Archives, Washington, D.C., Letters Received, I, No. E1709; Taylor, *The Transportation Revolution*, 34, 49–51; Hill, *Roads, Rails & Waterways*, 45, 52.
12. Trimble, "Memoirs," 27; Trimble to Cullum, July 22, 1855, United States Military Academy at West Point Library, Isaac Ridgeway Trimble Papers; Trimble to Cullum, October 16, 1859, United States Military Academy at West Point Library, Isaac Ridgeway Trimble Papers Taylor, *The Transportation Revolution*, 22; Goodrich, *Government Promotion*, 69;.
13. Trimble, "Memoirs," 27; Hill, *Roads, Rails & Waterways*, 53; Dilts, *The Great Road*, 49; Taylor, *The Transportation Revolution*, 48–49.
14. Trimble, "Memoirs," 27–28.
15. Trimble to Cullum, July 22, 1855, United States Military Academy at West Point Library, Isaac Ridgeway Trimble Papers; Trimble to Cullum, October 16, 1859, United States Military Academy at West Point Library, Isaac Ridgeway Trimble Papers; Stephen H. Long, "A Report Upon ... A National Road From Washington to Buffalo," 1827, House Report, 19th Congress, 2nd Session, Report no. 105; Dilts, *The Great Road*, 52–53, 57; Stover, *History of the Baltimore and Ohio Railroad*, 21.
16. Majority Report of Committee on Internal Improvements, 1832; J. M. Vincent, J. H. Hollander, and W. W. Willoughby, eds., *Johns Hopkins University Studies in Historical and Political Science*, Vol. 25, *International and Colonial History* (Baltimore: Johns Hopkins Press, 1907), 72–73.
17. Gary Lawson Browne, *Baltimore in the Nation, 1789–1861* (Chapel Hill: The University of North Carolina Press, 1980), 8.
18. Browne: xi.
19. *Ibid.*, 9–12, 17.
20. *Ibid.*, 40.
21. *Ibid.*, 40–45.

Notes—Chapter 2

22. *Pennsylvania Archives*, Fourth Series, IV, 198; *Pennsylvania Gazette*, February 6, 1828, March 14, 1828; James Weston Livingood, *The Philadelphia-Baltimore Trade Rivalry 1780–1860* (New York: Arno Press, 1970): iii, 21, 39–41, 54, 120.

23. Browne, 69.

24. *Ibid.*; Taylor, *The Transportation Revolution*, 8.

25. *Niles Register*, March 17, 1827, June 23, 1827, July 7, 1827, October 27, 1827; *Baltimore Gazette*, February 23, 1827, February 28, 1827, March 2, 1827, March 6, 1827; *Baltimore American*, March 2, 1827; "An Act to Incorporate the Baltimore and Ohio Rail Road Company," Laws and Ordinances, B&O RR, p. 24 and passim; John H. B. Latrobe, Baltimore and Ohio Railroad Personal Recollections, A Lecture (Baltimore: Sun Book and Job Printing, 1868), 6; Stover, *History of the Baltimore and Ohio Railroad*, 15–20; Dilts, *The Great Road*, 26, 37–38, 42–46; Ambler, *A History of Transportation*, 213; *Grand Civic Procession*, 9.

26. *Baltimore Gazette*, February 23, 1827; *Niles Register*, March 17, 1827; Dilts, *The Great Road*, 42; Stover, *A History of the Baltimore & Ohio*, 18.

27. Latrobe, *The Baltimore and Ohio Railroad*, 6.

28. *Ibid.*; Dilts, *The Great Road*, 45–46.

29. Latrobe, *The Baltimore and Ohio Railroad*, 4–6.

30. Thomas to Kennedy, July 3, 1828, Phillip E. Thomas Letterbooks, B&O Archives, Baltimore, Maryland; Dilts, *The Great Road*, 11.

31. Trimble to Cullum, July 22, 1855, United States Military Academy at West Point Library, Isaac Ridgeway Trimble Papers; Trimble to Cullum, October 16, 1859, United States Military Academy at West Point Library, Isaac Ridgeway Trimble Papers; B&O Minute Books, July 2, 1827; Thomas to Long, McNeill, and Howard, July 2, 1827, Thomas Letterbooks, Baltimore and Ohio Archives; Macomb to McNeill and Long, June 22 and July 2, 1827, Engineering Department, Letters to Officers of Engineers, III, 84, 87, National Archives, Washington, D.C.; *Niles Register*, July 7, 1827; Dilts, *The Great Road*, 2, 26, 52–56; Hill, *Roads, Rails & Waterways*, 44, 100–102; Stover, *History of the Baltimore & Ohio*, 11, 20–21.

32. Thomas to Long, McNeill and Howard, July 2, 1827, Thomas Letterbooks, B&O Archives; Dilts, *The Great Road*, 54.

33. McNeill and Howard, July 2, 1827, Thomas Letterbooks, B&O Archives; Dilts, *The Great Road*, 54.

34. Trimble, "Memoirs," 28–29; Dilts, *The Great Road*, 57–61; Stover, *History of the Baltimore and Ohio*, 22–23.

35. B&O Minute Books, November 5, 1827, B&O Archives, Baltimore, Maryland; *Report of the Engineers on the Reconnaissance and Surveys* (Baltimore: William Woody, 1828); Dilts, *The Great Road*, 68.

36. Trimble, "Memoirs," 29; B&O Minute Books, May 23, 1828, B&O Archives, Baltimore, Maryland; *The Early Correspondence of Alex. Brown and Sons With Regard to the Building of the Baltimore and Ohio Railroad* (Baltimore, 1927), 7; Dilts, *The Great Road*, 63.

37. Trimble, "Memoirs," 29; J. Knight and Benj. H. Latrobe, *Report Upon the Locomotive Engines and the Police and Management of Several of the Principal Rail Roads in the Northern and Middle States* (Baltimore: Lucas & Deaver, 1838): 35–36.

38. Hill, *Roads, Rails & Waterways*, 77–78, 146–147.

39. M617, Monthly Post Returns, 1800–1916; Trimble to Cullum, July 22, 1855, United States Military Academy at West Point Library, Isaac Ridgeway Trimble Papers; Trimble to Cullum, October 16, 1859, United States Military Academy at West Point Library, Isaac Ridgeway Trimble Papers.

40. David Trimble to Isaac Trimble, May 26, 1828, William C. Trimble, Baltimore, Maryland, Isaac Trimble Papers.

41. Trimble, "Memoirs," 29.

42. William Cattell Trimble, *The Presstman Family of Baltimore* (Baltimore: J. H. Furst Co., 1989): 1.

43. William Trimble, *The Presstman Family of Baltimore*, 1–2.

44. William Cattell Trimble, *The Cattells of South Carolina* (Baltimore: J. H. Furst Co., 1988): 7–8. Family tradition recalled the romantic meeting of the two Cattell sisters, but William Trimble thought that this story might be false. He said that the meeting occurred "more likely, in Maryland." In either case this marriage is an example of how the wealthy families established relationships along the coast as the result of extensive trade networks.

45. Trimble, "Memoirs," 30–31.

46. Trimble, "Memoirs," 32; "Diary of Maria Presstman Trimble," William C. Trimble, Baltimore, Maryland.

47. *Ibid.*

48. Trimble, "Memoirs," 35.

49. Trimble to Cullum, July 22, 1855, United States Military Academy at West Point Library, Isaac Ridgeway Trimble Papers; Trimble to Cullum, October 16, 1859, United States Military Academy at West Point Library, Isaac Ridgeway Trimble Papers; Cullum, *Biographical Register*, 109.

Chapter 3. A New Profession: Railroad Man

1. "Diary of Maria Trimble," np, in possession of William C. Trimble.
2. Browne, *Baltimore in the Nation*, 114.
3. *Ibid.*
4. *Ibid.*, 115; *Baltimore Gazette*, December 9–30, 1833, January 3–March 22, 1834; *Baltimore Patriot*, February 16, 1839; September 27, 1842, March 31, 1843, July 11, 1843.
5. *Ibid.*, 139.
6. Taylor, *The Transportation Revolution*, 207.
7. Browne, *Baltimore in the Nation*, 139–140.
8. *Ibid.*, 141; *Baltimore Gazette*, July 2, 1832, September 3–December 12, 1834, March 4–September 13, 1836.
9. Browne, *Baltimore in the Nation*, 155.
10. *Ibid.*, 155–157; Mayors Annual Message, January 5, 1835; Ordinances March 9, 1841, May 23, 1838, February 12, 1839, February 9, 1841, February 26, 1842, Register, Baltimore City Hall, Baltimore Department of Legislative Reference.
11. Browne, *Baltimore in the Nation*, 158.
12. Trimble to Reeves, November 1, 1847, United States Military Academy Library, West Point, Isaac Ridgeway Trimble Papers.
13. Trimble, "Memoirs," 35; Trimble to Cullum, July 22, 1855; Trimble to Cullum, October 16, 1859; Cullum, *Biographical Register*, 109.
14. Trimble, "Memoirs," 35–36; Trimble to Cullum, October 16, 1859.
15. Diary of Maria Trimble, np.
16. Trimble, "Memoirs," 38.
17. Benton, William, Publisher, *Encyclopedia Britannica* (Chicago: Encyclopedia Britannica, Inc.): 21: 387.
18. The General's collection consisted of 47 volumes when the collection was donated by two of his great-grandsons to the United States Military Academy Library between 1972 and 1985. A special bookplate was affixed to each.
19. Trimble, "Memoirs," 41.
20. Diary of Maria Trimble, np.
21. *Ibid.*
22. *Ibid.*
23. Trimble, "Memoirs," 42.
24. Taylor, *The Transportation Revolution*, 98.
25. *Ibid.*, 79; *Hunt's Merchants Magazine*, XXV (September, 1851); Henry V. Poor, *Manual of the Railroads of the United States for 1868–69* (New York: H. V. and H. W. Poor, 1868), 20–21;
26. Taylor, *The Transportation Revolution*, 88–89, 240.
27. Livingood, *The Philadelphia Baltimore Trade Rivalry*, 118.
28. *Ibid.*, 118; *York Gazette*, August 21, November 6, December 25, 1827.
29. Taylor, *The Transportation Revolution*, 88.
30. Livingood, *The Philadelphia Baltimore Trade Rivalry*, 118–119.
31. *Ibid.*, 118–120; *Baltimore and Susquahanna Railroad Annual Report*, 1828; *Pennsylvania Gazette*, January 12 – February 25, 1828; *Niles Weekly Register*, XXXIII, 331; MS Petition from Philadelphia County to the Senate and House, 1828, Archives Division, Pennsylvania Historical Society, Philadelphia.
32. *Pennsylvania Gazette*, March 14, 1828; *York Gazette*, December 16, 1828, January 27, 1829; Livingood, *The Philadelphia Baltimore Trade Rivalry*, 120–122.
33. *Pennsylvania Gazette*, March 13, 1828; *The York Gazette*, December 2 and 16, 1828, January 27, 1829; The Pennsylvania Register, January 30, 1829; *Niles Weekly Register*, XXXVIII, 107, 125, 205; Livingood, *The Philadelphia Baltimore Trade Rivalry*, 123–130.
34. *Niles Weekly Register*, XLVIII, 121; Livingood, *The Philadelphia Baltimore Trade Rivalry*, 130–131.
35. Maryland Laws, 1837, Chapter 30L; Maryland Laws, 1838, Chapter 395; Maryland Laws, 1839, Chapter 20; J. M. Vincent, J. H. Hollander, and W. W. Willoughby, eds., *A Financial History of Maryland (1789–1848)* (Baltimore: The Johns Hopkins Press, 1907): 91; Goodrich, *Government Promotions*, 83–84.
36. Trimble to Cullum, October 16, 1859; *York Gazette*, July 7, 1835, August 18, 1835, April 19, March 22, July 26, August 9, September 6, September 26, September 27, 1835; Livingood, *The Philadelphia Baltimore Trade Rivalry*, 132–133.
37. *8th Annual Report of the President & Directors to the Stockholders of The Baltimore & Susquehanna Railroad Co., January 1836* (Baltimore: Lucas & Deaver, 1836): 22; *9th Annual Report of the President & Directors of The Baltimore & Susquehanna Railroad Co.* (Lucas & Deaver, 1837): 18–19.
38. *8th Annual Report of the B&S*, 11–13; *9th Annual Report of the B&S*, 16.
39. *The York Gazette*, March 29, 1836; *Baltimore & Susquehanna Annual Report*, 1836; Livingood, *The Philadelphia Baltimore Trade Rivalry*, 131.
40. *9th Annual Report of the B & S*, 14; Trimble, "Memoirs," 42–43; Dilts, *The Great Road*, 258, 434. The Baltimore & Ohio was able to pull a grade of 80 feet per mile in 1839, but even this was less than Trimble accomplished a year earlier.

41. *9th Annual Report of the B&S*, 14–15; Taylor, *The Transportation Revolution*, 289.
42. *8th Annual Report of the B&S*, 11–13; *9th Annual Report of the B&S*, 19; John A. Garraty and Mark C. Carnes, *American National Biography* (New York: Oxford University Press, 1999): 208–209; Anne W. Chapman, "Benjamin Stoddert Ewell: A Biography" (Ph.D. diss., The College of William and Mary, 1984): 42–45.
43. Donald C. Phanz, *Richard S. Ewell: A Soldier's Life* (Chapel Hill: The University of North Carolina Press, 1998): 1–10; Chapman, "Benjamin Stoddert Ewell," 18–32; Folders 22 and 23, Benjamin Stoddert Ewell Papers, Manuscript Division, College of William and Mary, Williamsburg, Virginia; Biographical Sketch of Thomas Ewell, folder 23, Manuscript Division, College of William and Mary, Williamsburg, Virginia; Harriot Stoddert Turner, "Ewells of Virginia," 1–18, Manuscript Division, College of William and Mary, Williamsburg, Virginia
44. Trimble, "Memoirs," 42.
45. *Ibid.*, 43–44; Isaac Ridgeway Trimble, Report of the Engineer Appointed by the Commissioners of the Mayor and City Council of Baltimore, on the Subject of the Maryland Canal (Baltimore: Lucas & Deaver, 1837), University of Virginia Libraries. It should be noted that the adoption of his mother's maiden name, Ridgeway, during this time did not reflect any burst of family pride, but rather came about as an attempt to reduce confusion between himself and others with the same name.
46. *The Pottsville Emporium and Colliers Democratic Register*, January 25, 1840.
47. Diary of Maria Trimble, np; Trimble, "Memoirs," 44–45; Trimble to Cullum, July 22, 1855.

Chapter 4. Becoming a Modern Businessman

1. Maria's brother, Stephen Wilson Presstman, had just died.
2. William McClintick to Charity McClintick, September 1848, letter in possession of William C. Trimble.
3. Breger, *From Instinct to Identity*, 45–46, 350–351.
4. Maslow, *Motivation and Personality*, 44.
5. Brown, *Baltimore and the Nation*, 162–163.
6. *Charleston Courier*, October 24, 1837; *DeBow's Review*, XIII, 483–484; John G. Van Deusen, *The Ante-Bellum Southern Commercial Conventions* (Durham, NC: The Seeman Printery, Inc., 1926): 9, 99.
7. *DeBow's Review*, I, 9; *Richmond Enquirer*, November 21, 1845; Van Deusen, *Ante-Bellum Southern Commercial Conventions*, 9, 21, 99.
8. *Charleston Courier*, June 4, 1853; Van Deusen, *Ante-Bellum Southern Commercial Conventions*, 9–10.
9. *DeBow's Review*, XXVI, 713, XXVII, 94–103, 205–220, 360–365, 469–471, XVII, 95–98; Van Deusen, *Ante-Bellum Southern Commercial Conventions*, 62, 67, 101.
10. *Richmond Enquirer*, October 23, 1849, October 30, 1849; *DeBow's Review*, VIII, 217; Van Deusen, *Ante-Bellum Southern Commercial Conventions*, 26–27.
11. *DeBow's Review*, XVIII, 377; *Baltimore Sun*, December 20, 1852; *Richmond Enquirer*, December 24, 1852; *Charleston Courier*, December 22, 1852; *National Intelligencer*, December 20, 1852; Van Deusen, *Ante-Bellum Southern Commercial Conventions*, 39.
12. *DeBow's Review*, XVIII, 353–355; Van Deusen, *Ante-Bellum Southern Commercial Conventions*, 50.
13. *Richmond Enquirer*, December 21, 1852, April 14, 1854; Van Deusen, *Ante-Bellum Southern Commercial Conventions*, 39–41.
14. *Baltimore American*, June 2–5, 1857; *Baltimore Clipper*, June 2–5, 1857; John H. Baker, *Ambivalent Americans: The Know-Nothing Party in Maryland* (Baltimore: The Johns Hopkins University Press, 1977): 3.
15. John H. Baker, *Ambivalent Americans*, xvi–xvii.
16. *Baltimore Clipper*, January 14, 1853, March 8, 1853; *Baltimore Sun*, August 8, 1853; John H. Baker, *Ambivalent Americans*, 7, 17–20, 23, 39.
17. John H. Baker, *Ambivalent Americans*, 8–14.
18. Charles P. Dare, *Philadelphia, Wilmington and Baltimore Railroad Guide: Containing a Description of the Scenery, Rivers, Towns, Villages, and Objects of Interest Along the Line of Road* (Philadelphia: Fitzgibbon & Van Ness, 1856): 13–16.
19. *Ibid.*, 16.
20. *Ibid.*, 17.
21. *Ibid.*
22. *Ibid.*
23. *Ibid.*, 18.
24. Trimble, "Memoirs," 45.
25. Dare, *Philadelphia, Wilimington and Baltimore Railroad Guide*, 18.
26. *Ibid.*, 19.
27. John A. Garraty and Mark C. Carnes, eds., *American National Biography* (New York: Oxford University Press, 1999): 21:211.

28. Dare, *Philadelphia, Wilmington and Baltimore Railroad Guide*, 19.
29. Allen Johnson and Dumas Malone, eds., *Dictionary of American Biography* (New York: Charles Scribner's Sons, 1931): 6: 318–319; Wheeler Preston, *American Biographies* (New York: Harper & Brothers, 1974): 309.
30. Dare, *Philadelphia, Wilmington and Baltimore Railroad Guide*, 20; *Thirteenth Annual Report of the Philadelphia, Wilmington & Baltimore Railroad Company* (Philadelphia: John C. Clark, 1852): 19.
31. Dare, 20.
32. Alfred D. Chandler, Jr., *The Railroads: The Nation's First Big Business* (New York: Harcourt, Brace & World, Inc., 1965): 97–98; Alfred D. Chandler, Jr., *The Visible Hand: The Management Revolution in American Business* (Cambridge, MA: The Belknap Press, 1977): 8–9.
33. *Fifth Annual Report of the Philadelphia, Wilmington & Baltimore Railroad Company* (Philadelphia: United States Book and Job Office, 1843): 15, 17; *Fourteenth Annual Report of the Philadelphia, Wilmington & Baltimore Railroad Company* (Philadelphia: John C. Clark, 1852): 20.
34. Matthew Carey, *Address to the Wealthy of the Land* (Philadelphia: W. F. Geddes, 1831), 6; *Niles Weekly Register*, XL, 338–339; Taylor, *The Transportation Revolution*, 289–290.
35. *Fifth Annual Report of the PW&B*, 16
36. *Ibid.*, 11.
37. *Ibid.*, 10–17.
38. Dare, *Philadelphia, Wilmington and Baltimore Railroad Guide*, 20–21.
39. *Eleventh Annual Report of the Philadelphia, Wilmington & Baltimore Railroad Company* (Philadelphia: John C. Clark, 1850), 16.
40. *Fifth Annual Report of the PW&B*, 10.
41. *Eleventh Annual Report of the PW&B*, 12.
42. *Seventh Annual Report of the Philadelphia, Wilmington & Baltimore Railroad Company* (Philadelphia: John C. Clark, 1845), 6.
43. *Eighth Annual Report of the Philadelphia, Wilmington & Baltimore Railroad Company* (Philadelphia: John C. Clark, 1847), 9–10.
44. Dare, *Philadelphia, Wilmington and Baltimore Railroad Guide*, 19.
45. *Investigation Into the Late Superintendent of the Philadelphia, Wilmington and Baltimore Railroad Co.* (Philadelphia: James H. Bryson, 1854), 1: 3.
46. *Ibid.*, 1: 272–274.
47. *Ibid.*, 1: 275–276.
48. *Ibid.*, 2: 225–227.
49. *Ibid.*, 1: 3–4.
50. *Ibid.*, 1: 724–725.
51. *Ibid.*, 2: 227–228.
52. *Ibid.*, 1: 4.
53. *Ibid.*, 1: 726–730.
54. *Ibid.*, 2: 228.
55. *Ibid.*, 1: 4.
56. *Ibid.*, 1: 730–731.
57. *Ibid.*, 2: 228.
58. *Ibid.*, 1: 4.
59. *Ibid.*, 1: 731.
60. *Ibid.*, 2: 229.
61. *Ibid.*, 1: 5.
62. *Ibid.*, 1: 731.
63. *Ibid.*, 2: 229.
64. *Ibid.*, 1: 1033.
65. *Ibid.*, 1: 1031.
66. *Ibid.*
67. *Ibid.*, 1: 1031–1032.
68. *Ibid.*, 1: 1028–1032.
69. *Ibid.*, 1: 1.
70. *Ibid.*, 1: 2.
71. *Ibid.*, 1: 7–8.
72. Pratt to Felton, May 26, 1854, Box 1, Folder 2, Felton Family Papers, Pennsylvania Historical Society, Philadelphia.
73. John Farley Trimble, *Trimble Families of America*, 171.
74. Trimble to Cullum, October 16, 1859; Cullum, *Biographical Register*, 228.
75. United States Patent, 1855 (Copy in possession of William C. Trimble); *Wilmington City Directory* (Wilmington, DE: Joshua T. Healed, Bookseller and Stationer, 1857), 120; *Boyds' Delaware State Directory* (Wilmington, DE: Joshua T. Healed, 1859), 24; *The Wilmington Directory for the Year 1853* (Wilmington, DE: Joshua T. Healed, 1853), 151; *The National Cyclopedia of American Biography* (Ann Arbor, MI: University Microfilms, 1967), 15: 376.
76. William C. Trimble, "Trimble Outline" (np, nd), 4
77. *Copy of Mortgage of the Baltimore and Potomac Rail Road Co.* (Baltimore: Lucas Brothers, 1871), 1.
78. "Trimble Outline," 4; Trimble to Cullum, October 16, 1859; Cullum, *Biographical Register*, 228.
79. Isaac Trimble, *Baltimore and Potomac Railroad: Report of I. R. Trimble, Esq.* (Baltimore: James Young's Steam Printing Establishment, 1855), 15.
80. *Ibid.*
81. *Ibid.*, 25.
82. *Ibid.*, 19.
83. *Ibid.*, 20–21.
84. *Ibid.*, 22.
85. *Ibid.*, 28–29.
86. *Ibid.*, 29.
87. *Ibid.*, 5.
88. *Ibid.*, 23.
89. *Ibid.*, 24.
90. *Ibid.*, 15.

91. *Ibid.*, 16.
92. *Ibid.*, 24–25.
93. *Ibid.*, 24.
94. *Ibid.*, 21.

Chapter 5. A Time for Decision

1. *Compilation of the Official Records of the Union and Confederate Armies*, 128 volumes (Washington, DC: 1880–1901), ser. 1, 2, 740 (Cited hereafter as O. R.); Harry Wright Newman, *Maryland and the Confederacy* (Annapolis, MD: Harry Wright Newman, 1976), 228.
2. *Nineteenth Annual Reunion of the Association of Graduates of the United States Military Academy*, 68.
3. Charles Reagan Wilson & William Ferris, *Encyclopedia of Southern Culture* (Chapel Hill: The University of North Carolina Press, 1989), 534.
4. John Shelton Reed, *The Enduring South: Subcultural Persistence in Mass Society* (Lexington, MA: Lexington Books, 1972), 14.
5. The *Daily Oklahoman*, June 4, 1999; reporting The Southern Focus Poll, conducted by the Institute for Research in Social Sciences at the University of North Carolina.
6. William J. Evitts, *A Matter of Allegiances: Maryland From 1850 to 1861* (Baltimore: Johns Hopkins University Press, 1974), 25. Evitts made the statement, "While most Marylanders habitually referred to Maryland as a Southern state, they seldom called themselves Southerners. Most Northerners thought that Baltimore was Southern." Several contemporaries referred to the city as appearing to be more Southern during the crisis period, including Mayor Brown. Many probably experienced the same process that Trimble did; they did not express strong regional identity, but when forced to decide what they were, they concluded that they were Southerners.
7. William A. Blair, "Maryland, Our Maryland." In *The Antietam Campaign*, ed. Gary W. Gallagher (Chapel Hill: The University of North Carolina Press, 1999), 74.
8. Blair, "Maryland, Our Maryland," 74–100. Blair believed that Maryland played a role in the Southern view that they were fighting the tyranny of Lincoln and the North and that this view began to change after the Antietam campaign.
9. William W. Freehling, *The Road to Disunion: Volume I, Secessionists at Bay 1776–1854* (New York: Oxford University Press, 1990), vii–viii. Freehling makes reference to the fact that a unified South did not exist in 1854, but "that before and after the mid–1830s in the South, as well as the North, change was omnipresent, varieties abounded, visions multiplied." He also referred to other historians who promoted this idea of "many Souths," including: David Potter, *The South and the Sectional Conflict* (Baton Rouge: Louisiana State University Press, 1968); Carl Degler, *The Other South: Southern Dissenters in the Nineteenth Century* (New York: Harper & Row, 1974); Michael Holt, *The Political Crisis of the 1850s* (New York: John Wiley & Sons, 1978); Daniel W. Crofts, *The Reluctant Confederates: Upper South Unionists in the Secession Crisis* (Chapel Hill: University of North Carolina Press, 1989). These sources generally focused on the Southerners who did not support the Confederacy rather than the effect Lincoln's policies had on driving the four states of the Upper South out of the Union, as well as those in the Lower South who might have changed their views for the same reason.
10. Summarized from: Donald B. Dodd and Wynelle S. Dodd, *Historical Statistics of the South 1790–1970* (University, AL: The University of Alabama Press, 1973), 1–85.
11. *Ibid.*; Freehling, *The Road To Disunion*, 19.
12. Population information is summarized from: Donald B. and Wynelle S. Dodd, *Historical Statistics of the South*; voting statistics: Dwight Lowell Dumond, *The Secession Movement 1860–1861* (New York: Macmillan Company, 1931): 271; United States Census Records, 1850 & 1860, National Archives, Washington, D.C.
13. Dumond, *The Secession Movement*, 271.
14. Baker, *The Politics of Continuity*, 11, 14, 15; George William Brown, *Baltimore and The Nineteenth of April, 1861* (Baltimore: Johns Hopkins University Press, 1887), 30; James M. McPherson, *Battle Cry of Freedom: The Civil War Era* (New York: Oxford University Press, 1988), 285; Freehling, *The Road to Disunion*, 18, 32.
15. *Niles Weekly Register*, July 12, 1845, 293; *Niles Weekly Register*, July 26, 1845, 332; Brown, *The Nineteenth of April*, 30–31; Baker, *The Politics of Continuity*, 10–15; Daniel Carroll Toomey, *The Civil War in Maryland* (Baltimore: Toomey Press, 1983), 6; Matthew Ellenberger, "Whigs in the Streets? Baltimore Republicans in the Spring of 1861," *Maryland Historical Magazine* 86 (1991), 25.
16. Brown, *The Nineteenth of April*, 31.
17. Ellenberger, "Whigs in the Streets," 23. Matthew Ellenberger's article focused on the Whigs on the streets of Baltimore despite the demise of that party, using the argument that the Whig philosophy was a major cause for the riots in Baltimore on April 19.
18. Ellenberger, "Whigs in the Streets," 25;

Baker, *The Politics of Continuity*, xvi; Brown, *The Nineteenth of April*, 34; Evitts, *A Matter of Allegiances*, 25–26. Evitts claimed that Maryland was consistent with the tradition of the border states and the Whigs in the spirit of compromise, but this does not take into account the violence in the 1850s. It seems more likely that Brown and his reformers gained support on the promise of ending the violence that the general population had grown tired of.

19. Baker, *The Politics of Continuity*, 19; Evitts, *A Matter of Allegiances*, 59–60.

20. *Baltimore Sun*, October 5, November 7, 1860, July 26–August 1, 1853; *Port Tobacco Times*, August 1, October 8, November 18, December 1, 1853; L. F. Schemeckebier, *History of the Know-Nothing Party in Maryland, Economic History—Maryland and the South*, Vol. 17 (Baltimore: Johns Hopkins Press, 1899), 112–113; Brown, *The Nineteenth of April*, 34; Ellenberger, "Whigs in the Streets," 26. Some secondary sources say that Brown and his reform party were elected in 1859, but Brown himself said that he won the election a few weeks before Lincoln was elected.

21. Evitts, *A Matter of Allegiances*, 152. Evitts calculated the coefficient of correlation between Brown and Breckinridge to be +0.844. Evitts stated, "business and civic leaders of Baltimore were later uniformly conservative and cautions in the secession crisis and supported the Unionist stand of American Governor Thomas H. Hicks." He went on to say, "the answer to this puzzle and to Breckinridge's victory in Maryland, was the reform issue, which swept away the former American Bell on a wave of indignation." It is clear from Brown's actions that he did not encourage the secessionist during the time of civil unrest.

22. Browne, *Baltimore in the Nation*, 214; Brown, *The Nineteenth of April*, 30.

23. Brown, *The Nineteenth of April*, 30.

24. Allen Johnson, ed. *Dictionary of American Biography* (New York: Charles Scribner's Sons, 1929), 1: 118–119.

25. Garraty and Carnes, *American National Biography*, 10: 747–748; Malone, *Dictionary of Nation Biography*, Vol. 9, pp. 8–9.

26. *The National Cyclopedia of American Biography*, Vol. 5, p. 398.

27. Dummond, *The Secession Movement*, 271; Courtney B. Wilson and Shawn Cunningham, *The Baltimore Civil War Museum: President Street Station* (Baltimore: The Civil War Museum, 1997), 11.

28. Brown, *The Nineteenth of April*, 32.

29. Isaac Trimble, *Our Infantry* (Baltimore: np, 1883), 3.

30. Wilson and Cunningham, *The Baltimore Civil War Museum*, 17; Toomey, *The Civil War in Maryland*, 14.

31. James Ryder Randall, *Maryland My Maryland* (Baltimore: Miller & Beacham, 1861).

32. Brown, *The Nineteenth of April*, 11.

33. *Ibid*.

34. *Ibid*., 13; Wilson & Cunningham, *The Baltimore Civil War Museum*, 11; Felton Family Papers, Box 1, folders 3 & 4, Pennsylvania Historical Society, Philadelphia, Pennsylvania.

35. Brown, *The Nineteenth of April*, 15.

36. *Ibid*., 19.

37. Brown, *The Nineteenth of April*, 11–13; Wilson & Cunningham, *The Baltimore Civil War Museum*, 11; McPherson, *Battle Cry of Freedom*, 262.

38. Brown, *The Nineteenth of April*, 19.

39. *Ibid*., 12.

40. *American*, April 19, 1861; *Republican*, April 19, 1861; Ellenberger, "Whigs in the Streets," 27, 35; Toomey, *The Civil War in Maryland*, 9; Clark, *The Civil War*, 39, 56.

41. Brown, *The Nineteenth of April*, 35.

42. O. R. 1 3, 79–80; Maryland House and Senate Documents, Document A, Laws of Maryland, Maryland Historical Society, Baltimore ; Ellenberger, "Whigs in the Streets," 26–28; Clark, *The Civil War*, 40; Brown, 33–36; O. R., Ser. 1, 6 Part 1 328–329; "April 19, 1861: A Record of the Events in Baltimore, Md. On that Day," *Southern Historical Society Papers*, 29 (1901), 253.

43. O. R. 1 3, 79–80; Maryland House and Senate Documents, Document A; Clark, *The Civil War*, 40.

44. O. R., 1 6 part 1, 327–328.

45. Brown, *The Nineteenth of April*, 36.

46. *Southern Historical Society*, "April 19, 1861," 253.

47. *Ibid*., 252.

48. Brown, *The Nineteenth of April*, 37.

49. *Ibid*., 40.

50. *Ibid*., 41.

51. *Ibid*.

52. Frank H. Taylor, *Philadelphia in the Civil War 1861–1865* (Philadelphia: City of Philadelphia, 1913), 44.

53. Brown, *The Nineteenth of April*, 43; *Southern Historical Society*, "April 19, 1861," 255–256; Clark, *The Civil War*, 48; "Baltimore in 1861," *Southern Historical Society Papers*, 38 (1910), 319.

54. *Southern Historical Society*, "April 19, 1861," 261.

55. Horace Greeley, *The American Conflict: A History of the Great Rebellion in the United States of America, 1860–1865*, (Hartford, CN, 1867), I, 468; Edward A. Robinson, "Some

Recollections of April 19, 1861," *Maryland Historical Magazine*, 27 (1932), 274–279; Clark, *The Civil War*, 65, 67, 69.
56. *O.R.* Series 1, 2, 17.
57. *Southern Historical Society*, "April 19, 1861," 258.
58. *O.R.* Series 2, 1, 658.
59. Brown, *The Nineteenth of April*, 56.
60. *Baltimore Sun*, April 20, 1861; *Baltimore American*, April 20, 1861.
61. *O.R.* Series 2, 1, 629–630.
62. Isaac R. Trimble, "Statement on April 19th, 1861, Riot and Events Thereafter," Trimble Papers, Maryland Historical Society.
63. Brown, *The Nineteenth of April*, 81.
64. *Southern Historical Society*, "April 19," 255.
65. Ellenberger, "Whigs in the Streets," 29.
66. Ellenberger, "Whigs in the Streets," 30; McPherson, *Battle Cry of Freedom*, 285; *O.R.*, series 1, 2, 12.
67. F. A. B., "The Conspiracy of '64: The Attempt to Relieve Rebel Prisoners in the West," (n.p., n.p., 1882). This is an unpublished manuscript of an interview of Isaac Trimble by F. A. B. (no further identity) found in the papers of Isaac Trimble now in possession of William C. Trimble of Maryland. This document is dated April 29, 1882.
68. *O.R.* Series 1, 2, 12.
69. *Ibid.*, 12–14.
70. F. A. B., "Conspiracy of '64," 2. Trimble said that the government believed that "I had willfully burned the bridges because of some misunderstanding I had with the railroads prior to the war," clearly referring to his dismissal and subsequent hearing.
71. Trimble, "Statement of April 19."
72. *Ibid.*
73. *O.R.*, Series 1, 6, Part 1, 330–331; Series 1, 27, Part 3, 646; Series 2, 1, 618; Series 1, 2, 578; Clark, *The Civil War*, 54–55.
74. Charles McHenry Howard, "Baltimore and the Crisis of 1861," *Maryland Historical Magazine*, 16 (December 1946), 259, 261, 262, 278, 280–281. This order was dated April 22, 1861, and was one of several such orders reproduced in this article submitted from the "papers of Isaac Trimble," with an introduction written by the grandson of the president of the Baltimore Police Board; Brown, *The Nineteenth of April*, 63; Newman, *Maryland and the Confederacy*, 37; Trimble, "Statement on April 19th;" Richard Walsh and William Lloyd Fox, eds., *Maryland: A History 1632–1974* (Baltimore: Maryland Historical Society, 1974), 344.
75. Howard, "Baltimore and the Crisis of 1861," 261.
76. Howard, "Baltimore and the Crisis of 1861," 280–281; Brown, *The Nineteenth of April*, 63; *Southern Historical Society*, "Baltimore in 1861, 319; *Southern Historical Society*, "April 19," 262; *The Sun*, November 22, 1861.
77. Ellenberger, "Whigs in the Streets," 29; Brown, *The Nineteenth of April*, 63; Trimble, "Statement of April 19."
78. Howard, "Baltimore and the Crisis of 1861," 268.
79. *O.R.*, Series 2, 1, 625.
80. Brown, *The Nineteenth of April*, 71–74.
81. *Ibid.*, 74.
82. *Ibid.*, 75.
83. Clark, *The Civil War*, 71; Howard, "Baltimore and the Crisis of 1861," 264–265.
84. Howard, "Baltimore and the Crisis of 1861," 267.
85. *Ibid.*, 274.
86. Brown, *The Nineteenth of April*, 77.
87. *Ibid.*, 34.
88. *Ibid.*, 77.
89. Toomey, *The Civil War in Maryland*, 13–14; McPherson, *Ordeal by Fire*, 286.
90. Brown, *The Nineteenth of April*, 84–85; Malone, *Dictionary of American Biography*, 9: 9.
91. Brown, *The Nineteenth of April*, 85.
92. *Ibid.*, 86.
93. *O.R.*, Series 1, 6, Part 1, 331.
94. *Ibid.*, 337.
95. Bowman, John S., Ed., *The Civil War Almanac* (New York: World Almanac Publications, 1983), 54–55; Ellenberger, "Whigs in the Streets," 32–33; Toomey, *The Civil War*, 17–19.
96. "April 19," 268.
97. Brown, *The Nineteenth of April*, 84.
98. Wilson & Cunningham, 20; Brown, *The Nineteenth of April*, 84, 97, 104; *O.R.*, Series 2, 1, 621; McPherson, *Battle Cry of Freedom*, 289.
99. *O.R.*, Series 2, 2, 792.
100. James I. Robertson, ed., *Proceedings of the Advisory Council of the State of Virginia, April 21–June 19, 1861* (Richmond: Virginia State Library, 1977), 115–116; Trimble Records, National Archives, M331, Role #250; Trimble, "Statement;" George Yellott, "A Delayed Letter to the Editor," *History Trails* (Spring 1977), 16–17. This letter gave an account of the raid on Trimble's home. It was never published in the *Baltimore County Advocate*, but was found in their files.
101. *O.R.*, Series 1, 52, Part 2, 129.
102. *O.R.*, Series 2, 1, 647.
103. *Ibid.*, 647.
104. *Ibid.*, 667.
105. Isaac Trimble, "The Civil War Diary of General Isaac Ridgeway Trimble," *Maryland Historical Magazine*, 17 (March 1922), 15.
106. Trimble, *West Point Reunion*, 28.

107. Isaac Trimble, "The Southern Cross," *Collection of the Virginia Historical Society*, New Series 6 (1887), 334.
108. Trimble, "Infantry," 4–5.
109. Ibid., 4.
110. Trimble, "Address," *West Point Reunion*, 27.
111. Trimble, "Civil War Diary," 15.
112. Brown, *The Nineteenth of April*, 27.
113. Howard R. Floan, *The South in Northern Eyes 1831 to 1861* (Austin: University of Texas Press, 1958), viii, 54–55; Anne Norton, *Alternative Americas: A Reading of Antebellum Political Culture* (Chicago: The University of Chicago Press, 1986), 5–7.
114. Floan, *The South in Northern Eyes*, 16–19, 34, 40, 51–53, 62, 71–75, 83, 89–91, 111, 181–184.
115. Levi Coffin, *Reminiscences of Levi Coffin* (Cincinnati: Clarke Company, 1898; reprint, New York: Arno Press, 1968), 505–506.
116. Grant, Susan-Mary, *North Over South: Northern Nationalism and American Identity in the Antebellum Era* (Lawrence: University of Kansas Press, 2000), 17.
117. Joan Pastor, "Who's Afraid of a Little Conflict? Part I: 'The Three stages of Conflict and Resolution in the Warning Stage," *The CPA Letter* 3 (April 2000), D2. Joan Pastor is head of Joan Pastor and Associates, International. A psychotherapist, she offers consulting services to resolve organizational conflict. Her firm is paid for practical application of psychology and not just for theory.
118. Trimble, "statement."
119. Brown, *The Nineteenth of April*, 116.

Chapter 6. Into the Valley

1. Capt. B. F. Wyly, "Repulse of Federal Raid on Knoxville July, 1863," *Southern Historical Society Papers*, 4 (October, November, December, 1881), 485–486. This report did refer to "Army of the Potomac," which would normally mean the Union Army; however, it is clear in this case that the author was referring to the Army of Northern Virginia. Though this article is about a raid in 1863 this particular incident occurred earlier.
2. Rowland Dunbar, ed., *Jefferson Davis, Constitutionalist, His Letter, Papers, and Speeches*, (Jackson, MS, 1923), V 209, 248; Quote from James M. McPherson, *Battle Cry of Freedom: The Civil War Era* (New York: Oxford University Press, 1988), 428.
3. Isaac Ridgeway Trimble Service records, M331, National Archives; "General Trimble Obituary," The Baltimore *Sun*, January 3, 1888; Charles C. Jones, "Confederate Roster," *Southern Historical Society Papers*, 1 (December, 1876), 390. James I. Robertson, Jr., ed. *Proceedings of the Advisory Council of the State of Virginia: April 21–June 19, 1861* (Richmond: Virginia State Library, 1977), 115–116
4. *O. R.*, Ser. 1, 51, Part 2, 129–130.
5. Ibid., Ser. 1, 5, 851, 853, 883, 959–960, 6. Ibid., 853.
7. Ibid., 967, 1031.
8. William C. Oates, *The War Between the Union and the Confederacy* (New York: The Neale Publishing Company, 1905), 80–81; Stewart Sifakis, *Compendium of the Confederate Armies: North Carolina* (New York: Facts On File, 1992), 114–115; Stewart Sifakis, *Compendium of the Confederate Armies: Alabama* (New York: Facts on File, 1992), 75–77.
9. Trimble to Adjutant, September 20, 1861, Letters Received by the Confederate Adjutant and Inspector General, National Archives, Washington, DC, M474.
10. Oates, *The War Between the Union and the Confederacy*, 80.
11. Weymouth T. Jordon, Jr. *North Carolina Troops 1861–1865: A Roster* (6 vols; Raleigh, NC: Division of Archives and History, 1977), VI, 530.
12. Jeb Stuart to his wife, January 24, 1862, Stuart Papers, Virginia Historical Society; *Macon Daily Telegraph*, June 16, 1862; Ewell to Lizinka Campbell Brown (Ewell), June 8 & 11, 1865, Brown-Ewell Family Papers, Manuscript Department, Filson Club, Louisville, KY; Ewell to Thomas, April 24, 1861, M619, National Archives, Washington, DC; Harriot Stoddert Turner, "Ewells of Virginia," Manuscript Department, College of William and Mary, Williamsburg, VA; Jackson to Ewell, April 28, 1862, Autobiography File, Chicago Historical Society; Pfanz, *Richard S. Ewell*, 121, 150; McPherson, *Battle Cry of Freedom*, 454; James I. Robertson, Jr., *Stonewall Jackson: The Man, The Soldier, The Legend* (New York: Macmillan Publishing, 1997), 367, 389.
13. Edward Alexander Moore, *The Story of a Cannoneer Under Stonewall Jackson* (New York: Neale, 1905), 77; David French Boyd, *Reminiscences of the War in Virginia* (Austin, TX: Jenkins, 1989), 13; John Cheve Haskell Memoir, Duke University; *Southern Historical Society Papers*, 7 (1879), 345; 20 (1892), 33; Robertson, *Stonewall Jackson*, 389; Dumas Malone, *Dictionary of American Biography*, vol. 18 (New York: Charles Scribner's Sons, 1936), XVIII, 340–341; *The National Cyclopedia of American Biography*, IV, 331.
14. Allen Johnson and Dumas Malone, *Dictionary of American Biography*, vol. (New York: Charles Scribner's Sons, 1931), 123–124; The

National Cyclopedia of American Biography, VI, 217.

15. T. T. Munford, "Reminiscences of Jackson's Valley Campaign, *Southern Historical Society Papers* 11 (November 1879), 523.

16. *Ibid.*, 530.

17. *O. R.*, 12 (3) 32, 50, 80, 845, 849, 851; Mark M. Boatner III, *The Civil War Dictionary* (New York: David McKay Company, Inc., 1959), 739–740; McPherson, *Battle Cry of Freedom*, 454–455; Pfanz, *Richard S. Ewell*, 158; Shelby Foote, *The Civil War A Narrative: Fort Sumter to Perryville* (New York: Random House), 451.

18. *Richmond Daily Dispatch*, April 19, 1861; *Lexington Gazette*, May 30, 1861; McPherson, *Battle Cry of Freedom*, 454–455; Robertson, *Stonewall Jackson*, 1–23, 205–212; Burke Davis, *They Called Him Stonewall: A Life of Lt. General T. J. Jackson, C. S. A.* (New York: The Fairfax Press, 1988), 88–96, 129–130, 132–134; Mary Anna Jackson, *Memoirs of Stonewall Jackson* (Dayton, OH: Morningside Bookshop, 1976), 139–140, 142–143, 287.

19. Munford, "Reminiscences of Jackson's Valley Campaign," 523.

20. Boyd, *Reminiscences*, 12; Pfanz, *Richard S. Ewell*, 172.

21. Ewell to Lee, May 13, 1862, Folder 3, Heartt-Wilson Papers, Southern Historical Collection, University of North Carolina, Chapel Hill; Ewell to Stuart, JEB Stuart Papers, Huntington Library; Richard Ewell to Elizabeth Ewell, May 13, 1862, Richard Stoddert Ewell Papers, Manuscript Division, Library of Congress, Washington, DC; Pfanz, *Richard S. Ewell*, 172, 174; McPherson, *Battle Cry of Freedom*, 455; Robertson, *Stonewall Jackson*, 382–383.

22. *O. R.* Ser. 1, 12, Part 3, 845–846, 848–851; Ewell to Jackson, Richard Stoddert Ewell Letterbook, Manuscript Department, William R. Perkins Library, Duke University, Durham, NC; Jones, *Personal Reminiscences*, 187; Dabney, *Life and Campaigns*, 337; Munford's, On the Life of Elzey, 4, Miscellany, box 3, Munford-Ellis Papers, Duke University; Pfanz, *Richard S. Ewell*, 159–161; Robertson, *Stonewall Jackson*, 367.

23. *O. R.*, Ser. 1, 12, Part 3, 868–871; Jackson to Ewell, April 26, 1862, Milligan Papers, Maryland Historical Society; Pfanz, *Richard S. Ewell*, 164.

24. Samuel D. Buck, *With Old Confederates: Actual Experiences of a Captain in the Line* (Baltimore: H. E. Houck, 1925), 28; Douglass, *I Rode With Stonewall*, 55; *O. R.*, Ser. 1, 12, Part 3, 876–877, 881; Boyd, *Reminiscences*, 8–10; Pfanz, *Richard S. Ewell*, 165–166.

25. John William Jones, "Port Republic," 364–365; Pfanz, *Richard S. Ewell*, 166–167.

26. Jones, "Port Republic," 364–365; Pfanz, *Richard S. Ewell*, 167.

27. *O. R.*, Ser. 1, 12 Part 3, 887–892; Pfanz, *Richard S. Ewell*, 174–176; McPherson, *Battle Cry of Freedom*, 456; Robertson, *Stonewall Jackson*, 386–387.

28. *O. R.*, Ser. 1, 12, Part 1, 702, 778; Pfanz 180–182, 186; Robertson, *Stonewall Jackson*, 398.

29. Campbell Brown Memoirs, Brown-Ewell Papers, Manuscripts Division, Tennessee State Library and Archives; Pfanz, *Richard S. Ewell*, 190.

30. *O. R.*, Ser. 1, 12, Part 1, 702–704, 779.

31. *Ibid.*, 704.

32. *Ibid.*, 704, 779, 794.

33. *Ibid.*, 794.

34. *Ibid.*

35. *Ibid.*, 780.

36. *Ibid.*, 794.

37. *Ibid.*, 706.

38. John W. Fravel, "Jackson's Valley Campaign," *Confederate Veteran* 9 (September, 1898), 418.

39. General B. T. Johnson, "Memoir of the First Maryland Regiment," *Southern Historical Society Papers* 10 (March 1882), 99.

40. *O. R.*, Series 1, 12 Part 1, 707–708; Pfanz, *Richard S. Ewell*, 198–200; Robertson, *Stonewall Jackson*, 413–415; McPherson, *Battle Cry of Freedom*, 457.

41. Robertson, *Stonewall Jackson*, 415.

42. *O. R.*, Ser. 1, 12, Part 1, 708; Johnson 101–102; William Allan, "History of the Campaign of Gen. T. J. (Stonewall) Jackson in the Shenandoah Valley of Virginia," *Southern Historical Society Papers* 43 (August 1920), 247; Pfanz, *Richard S. Ewell*, 200–204; Boatner, *Civil War Dictionary*, 210; McPherson, *Battle Cry of Freedom*, 458, 462; Robertson, *Stonewall Jackson*, 428.

43. John A. Harman to Asher W. Harman, June 8, 1862, Reel 39, Jedediah Hotchkiss Papers, Library of Congress; *O. R.*, Ser. 1, 12, Part 1, 18, 652, 783; Munford Ms., Miscellany Box 1, Munford-Ellis Papers; George Campbell Brown, "Notes on Ewell's Division in the Campaign of 1862," *Southern Historical Society Papers* 10 (1882), 257; Johnson Ms., Miscellany, box 5, p. 134, Johnson Papers, Duke University, Durham, NC; Robertson, *Stonewall Jackson*, 428; Pfanz, *Richard S. Ewell*, 204–207; Foote, *The Civil War*, 459.

44. *O. R.*, Ser. 1, 12, Part 1, 782, 795; Pfanz, *Richard S. Ewell*, 208–209

45. *O. R.*, Ser. 1, 12, Part 1, 796.

46. *Ibid.*

47. *Ibid.*, 796–797.

48. *Ibid.*, 797.

Notes — Chapter 6

49. *Ibid.*
50. *Ibid.*
51. *Ibid.*
52. *Ibid.*
53. *Ibid.*, 798.
54. *Ibid.*
55. *Ibid.*
56. *Ibid.*; 786.
57. *Ibid.*, 798.
58. *Ibid.*
59. *Ibid.*, 783.
60. *Richmond Daily Enquirer*, June 18, 1862; John William Jones, "Reminiscences," 118; Jackson, *Memoirs*, 287; Pfanz, *Richard S. Ewell*, 220.
61. *Southern Historical Society Papers*, 7 (1879), 530; Thomas T. Munford Manuscript, Munford-Ellis Family Papers; Robertson, *Stonewall Jackson*, 438.
62. *New York Times*, June 16, 1862; McPherson, *Battle Cry of Freedom*, 460; Foote, *The Civil War*, 464–465; Davis, *They Called Him Stonewall*, 192–193; Robertson, *Stonewall Jackson*, 446.
63. James Harvey Wood, *The War: "Stonewall" Jackson, His Campaigns and Battles, The Regiment as I Saw Them* (Gaithersburg, MD: Butternut Press, 1984), 63–64; Douglass, *I Rode with Stonewall*, 94; Robertson, *Stonewall Jackson*, 447; Boatner, *The Civil War Dictionary*, 324; Douglas Southall Freeman, *Lee's Lieutenants: A Study in Command* (New York: Charles Scribners Sons, 1943), 2, 259.
64. George Washington Nichols, *A Soldiers Story of His Regiment*, (Jessup, GA: Privately Published, 1898), 41; Hotchkiss to Chase, March 28, 1892, Reel 9, Hotchkiss Papers, Library of Congress; Hotchkiss Memo of June 17 Activities, Reel 39, Hotchkiss Papers, Library of Congress; Robertson, *Stonewall Jackson*, 456–457; McPherson, *Battle Cry of Freedom*, 464; Foote, *The Civil War*, 469–470; *O. R.*, Ser. 1, 11, Part 2, 552.
65. Dabney to Hotchkiss, December 28, 1896, Reel 13, Hotchkiss Papers, Library of Congress; McPherson, *Battle Cry of Freedom*, 466; Robertson, *Stonewall Jackson*, 484, 497–498.
66. Fravel, "Jackson's Valley Campaign," 420.
67. *Ibid.*
68. *Ibid.*
69. *Ibid.*
70. *O. R.*, Ser. 1, 7, Part 2, 552; Pfanz, *Richard S. Ewell*, 222–223; Davis, *They Called Him Stonewall*, 199, 208; Robertson, *Stonewall Jackson*, 460–466; Foote, *The Civil War*, 475.
71. *O. R.*, Ser. 1, 7, Part 2, 552.
72. *Ibid.*, 614.
73. *Ibid.*, 553, 614.
74. *Ibid.*, 605, 614.
75. *Ibid.*, 614.
76. *Ibid.*, 606.
77. *Ibid.*
78. John C. Stiles, "In the Years 1861–62," *Confederate Veteran* 25 (1917), 318.
79. *Ibid.*; Charles R. Hyde, "The Father of Woodrow Wilson," *Confederate Veteran*, 35 (1927), 334.
80. *O. R.*, Ser. 1, 7, Part 2, 614–615.
81. *Ibid.*, 615.
82. "Flag of the 16th Mississippi Regiment," *Confederate Veteran* 26 (1918), 75.
83. *Ibid.*
84. *Ibid.*, 75–76.
85. *Ibid.*, 76.
86. *O. R.*, Ser. 1, 7, Part 2, 615.
87. *Ibid.*
88. *Ibid.*, 615–616.
89. *Ibid.*, 616.
90. *O. R.*, Ser. 1, 11, Part 2, 974–975, 975–977; William J. Seymour, The Civil War Memoirs of Captain William J. Seymour, edited by Terry L. Jones (Baton Rouge: Lousiana State University Press, 1991), 74; Wood, *The War*, 73–75; Dabney, *Life and Campaigns*, 452; Pfanz, *Richard S. Ewell*, 228; Boatner, *Civil War Dictionary*, 321; Foote, *The Civil War*, 490; Robertson, *Stonewall Jackson*, 483.
91. *O. R.*, Ser. 1, 7, Part 2, 607, 617.
92. *Ibid.*
93. *Ibid.*, 556.
94. *O. R.*, Ser. 1, 11, Part 2, 494–495, 556–557; Charles Brown to Lizinka Campbell Brown (Ewell), July 3, 1862, Polk-Brown-Ewell Papers, Southern Historical Collection, University of North Carolina, Chapel Hill; *Ibid.*, 556–557; Pfanz, *Richard S. Ewell*, 230; Foote, *The Civil War*, 501.
95. Foote, *The Civil War*, 499–501; Boatner, *Civil War Dictionary*, 504–506.
96. *O. R.*, Ser. 1, 7, Part 2, 618.
97. *Ibid.*
98. *Ibid.*
99. Washington Hands Memoir, Manuscript Department, University of Virginia, Charlottesville; *O. R.*, Ser. 1, 11, Part 2, 607, 619; Richard S. Ewell to Elizabeth Ewell, July 20, 1862 & May 13, 1862, Richard Stoddert Ewell Papers, Library of Congress, Washington, DC; Benjamin S. Ewell, "Jackson and Ewell," *Southern Historical Society Papers* 20 (1892), 30; Boyd, *Reminiscences*," 8–10; Taylor, "Destruction," 38; Pfanz, *Richard S. Ewell*, 236–237; McPherson, *Battle Cry of Freedom*, 470; Foote, *The Civil War*, 513; Robertson, *Stonewall Jackson*, 503–504; Davis, *They Called Him Stonewall*, 264.

Chapter 7. The Second Round at Manassas

1. *Confederate Veteran*, (1897), 613.
2. Stephen W. Sears suggested that the success of the Army of Northern Virginia was due more to the internal strife in the Army of the Potomac than to Confederate fighting abilities. Stephen W. Sears, *Controversies and Commanders: Dispatches from the Army of the Potomac* (Boston: Houghton Mifflin, 1999).
3. Brown, *Modernization*, 95; Hollinger, *Postmodernism and the Social Sciences*, xiii.
4. John J. Hennessy, *Return to Bull Run: The Campaign and Battle for Second Manassas* (New York: Simon & Schuster, 1994), xi–xii.
5. O. R., Ser. I, 12, 473–474; Hennessy, *Return to Bull Run*, xi–xii; Boatner, *Civil War Dictionary*, 101–103; Foote, *The Civil War*, 602–618; Pfanz, *Richard S. Ewell*, 238.
6. Richard S. Ewell to Elizabeth Stoddert Ewell, August 14, 1862, Richard S. Ewell Papers, Library of Congress, Washington, DC; Pfanz, *Richard S. Ewell*, 244.
7. Terry L. Jones, *Lee's Tigers: The Louisiana Infantry in the Army of Northern Virginia* (Baton Rouge: Louisiana State University Press, 1987), III; Taylor, *Destruction*, 93; Robertson, *Stonewall Jackson*, 526; Pfanz, *Richard S. Ewell*, 230, 237–238.
8. Jubal Anderson Early, *Lieutenant General Jubal Anderson Early: Autobiographical Sketch and Narrative of the War Between the States* (Philadelphia: J. B. Lippincott Company, 1912), 1–30, 77; Pfanz, *Richard S. Ewell*, 230; Boatner, *Civil War Dictionary*, 254; *The National Cyclopedia of American Biography*, 506; Johnson and Malone, *Dictionary of American Biography*, 598; Robertson, *Stonewall Jackson*, 526;
9. Campbell Brown, "Gaines Mills," Tennessee State Library, Nashville; O. R., Ser. I, 2, 2, 605–606; Howard, *Recollections*, 137; William A. McClendon, *Recollections of War Times* (Montgomery, AL: Paragon Press, 1909), 77; Boatner, *Civil War Dictionary*, 473; Pfanz, *Richard S. Ewell*, 227; Dumas Malone, ed., *Dictionary of American Biography* (New York: Charles Scribner's Sons, 1933), 11: 61–62; *Cyclopedia of American Biography*, 2: 148–149.
10. Early, *Autobiographical Sketch*, 115; Campbell Brown, "Notes on Ewell's Division in the Campaign of 1862," *Southern Historical Society Papers*, 10 (June, 1882), 259; Isaac Trimble, "General I. R. Trimble's Report of Operations of his Brigade from 14th to 29th of August, 1862," *Southern Historical Society Papers*, 8 (June & July, 1880), 309.
11. John Purifoy, "Gen. Robert E. Lee, The Peerless Soldier—I," *Confederate Veteran*, 34 (1926), 304; Boatner, *Civil War Dictionary*, 102; Robertson, *Stonewall Jackson*, 513–514.
12. Taliaferro to wife, July 14, 1862, William B. Taliaferro Papers, College of William and Mary, Williamsburg, VA; Robertson, *Stonewall Jackson*, 514.
13. Robertson, *Stonewall Jackson*, 514.
14. Boatner, *Civil War Dictionary*, 102; Robertson, *Stonewall Jackson*, 514; Trimble, "Civil War Diary," 2–3.
15. Hotchkiss, Journal, August 9, 1862, Reel 1, Jedediah Hotchkiss Papers, Library of Congress, Washington, DC; O. R., Ser. I, 12, 2, 182–183; Robertson, *Stonewall Jackson*, 523–527.
16. Trimble, "Civil War Diary," 3; O. R., Ser. 1, 16, 235–236; Brown, "Notes on Ewell's Division," 260.
17. Robertson, *Stonewall Jackson*, 537–538; O. R., Ser. 1, 16, 236.
18. Trimble, "Civil War Diary," 4; Robertson, *Stonewall Jackson*, 539, 541; Trimble, "General I. R. Trimble's Report," *Southern Historical Society Papers*, 306.
19. Robert U. Johnson and C. C. Buel, eds., *Battles and Leaders of the Civil War*, 4 vols.. (NY: Century Company, 1887–88), 2: 405; Thomas C. Elder to Anna Elder, August 15, 1862, Thomas Claybrook Elder Papers, Virginia Historical Society; Robertson, *Stonewall Jackson*, 540; Davis, *They Called Him Stonewall*, 285–286.
20. Douglas Southall Freeman, *Lee's Lieutenants: A Study in Command* (New York: Charles Scribners Sons, 1943), 2: 259.
21. Dr. J. William Jones, "The Career of General Jackson," *Southern Historical Society Papers*, 35 (1907), 92.
22. Ibid.
23. O. R., Ser. 1, 16, 718.
24. Ibid.
25. Ibid.
26. Ibid.
27. Ibid., 718–719.
28. O. R., Ser. I, 12, 2, 554, 642–643, 650; Hotchkiss Journal, March 4, 1863, Reel I; Boatner, *Civil War Dictionary*, 103; Davis, *They Called Him Stonewall*, 289; Robertson, *Stonewall Jackson*, 547.
29. Trimble, "Report of Operations," 306.
30. O. R., Ser. 1, 12, Part 2, 643, 734; Trimble, "Report of Operations," 306; Robertson, *Stonewall Jackson*, 552; Davis, *They Called Him Stonewall*, 291; Hennessy, *Return to Bull Run*, 112.
31. Foote, *The Civil War*, 617–618; Davis, *They Called Him Stonewall*, 291.
32. O. R., Ser. 1, 12, Part 2, 643.
33. Hennessy, *Return to Bull Run*, 113.
34. *The Baltimore Sun*, January 3, 1888.

35. *O. R.*, Ser. 1, 12, Part 2, 643.
36. *Ibid.*, 720–721.
37. *Ibid.*, 721; Trimble, "Report of Operations," 306.
38. Thomas J. Jackson to Isaac R. Trimble, August 27, 1862, Trimble Papers, Maryland Historical Society, Baltimore.
39. *O. R.*, Ser. 1, 12, Part 2, 721.
40. John N. Ware, "Second Manassas—Fifty-Eight Years Afterwards," *Confederate Veteran*, 30 (February, 1922), 60; Campbell Brown Memoirs; Johnson & Buell, *Leaders*, 505; James B. Sheeran, *Confederate Chaplain: A War Journal of Rev. James B. Sheeran, c. ss. r., 14th Louisiana, C.S.A.*, ed. By Joseph T. Durkin (Milwaukee: Bruce Pub. Co., 1960), 11; Robertson, *Stonewall Jackson*, 557; Davis, *They Called Him Stonewall*, 292; Hennessy, *Return to Bull Run*, 129; Pfanz, *Richard S. Ewell*, 253.
41. Ware, "Second Manassas," 60.
42. *Ibid.*
43. Edward McGrady, Jr., "Gregg's Brigade of South Carolinians in the Second Battle of Manassas," *Southern Historical Society Papers*, 13 (1885), 11.
44. *Ibid.*, 12.
45. *O. R.*, Ser. I, 12, 2, 710–711; Early, *Autobiographical Sketch*, 119; Charles Campbell Brown Memoirs, Nashville; McClendon, *Recollections*, 106; Trimble, "Report of Operations," 307; Pfanz, *Richard S. Ewell*, 253–254
46. Boatner, *Civil War Dictionary*, 102–103.
47. Ware, "Second Manassas," 61.
48. *Ibid.*
49. Trimble, "Report of Operations," 307–308; Robertson, *Stonewall Jackson*, 561; Boatner, *Civil War Dictionary*, 104; Hennessy, *Return to Bull Run*, 179–183; Early, *Lieutenant General Jubal A. Early*, 119–121; *O. R.*, Ser. 1, 12, Part 2, 704; Pfanz, *Richard S. Ewell*, 257–258.
50. William C. Oates, *The War Between The Union and the Confederacy: History of the 15th Alabama Regiment and the Forty-Eight Battles in Which It Was Engaged* (New York: The Neale Publishing Company, 1905), 141; Campbell Brown Memoirs, Nashville; *The Medical and Surgical History of the War of the Rebellion*, 6 vols.., Comp. By George A. Otis and D. L. Huntington (Washington, DC: Government Printing Office, 1883), 3 (2): 242; Charles A. Evans, Ed., *Confederate Military History: A Library of Confederate States History ... Written by Distinguished Men of the South*, 13 vols. (Atlanta: Confederate Pub. Co., 1889), 8: 596; Pfanz, *Richard S. Ewell*, 257–258.
51. Trimble, "Report of Operations," 308.
52. *O. R.* , Ser. 1, 12, Part 2, 704; Trimble, "Report of Operations,"1 308; Pfanz, *Richard S. Ewell*, 257–258.
53. Oates, *The War Between The Union and the Confederacy*, 143.
54. *Ibid.*
55. Trimble, "Report of Operations," 309.
56. *Ibid.*; Records of Isaac R. Trimble, M331, National Archives.
57. *O. R.*, Ser. 1, 12, Part 2, 712.
58. Mss3 Ea764 a 555–570, Jubal Early Papers, Virginia Historical Society, Richmond, VA; Mss3 Ea 764 a 516–537, Jubal Anderson Early Papers, Virginia Historical Society, Richmond, VA.
59. Trimble, "Civil War Diary," 5.
60. *Ibid.*, 6–7.
61. Freeman, *Lee's Lieutenants*, 2: 414–417.
62. Trimble to Cooper, MS, December 22, 1862, Trimble MSS, quoted in *Lee's Lieutenants*, 2: 416.
63. Trimble to Seddon, MS, December 22, 1862, 437, Letters Received by the Confederate Secretary of War, 1861–1865, National Archives, Washington, DC.
64. Isaac R. Trimble to Richard S. Ewell, n.d., Vol. 4, Ewell Papers, Library of Congress.
65. Pfanz, *Richard S. Ewell*, 270.
66. Thomas J. Jackson to Isaac R. Trimble, January 1, 1863, Maryland Historical Society, Baltimore.
67. Trimble, "Civil War Diary," 7.
68. Trimble, "Civil War Diary," 6–7; Civil War Records of Isaac Trimble, M331, National Archives; *O. R.*, Ser. 1, 19, Part 2, 683–684; Freeman, *Lee's Lieutenants*, 2: 417.
69. Alvy L. King, *Louis T. Wigfall, Southern Fire-Eater* (Baton Rouge: Louisiana State University Press, 1970), 158–159.
70. Trimble, "Civil War Diary," 8.
71. *Southern Historical Society Papers*, 1 (1876), 18–19.
72. Isaac R. Trimble, "Address to the 1st Division, 2nd Corps on Shooting of Deserters," March 2, 1863, William C. Trimble, Baltimore; *O. R.*, Ser. I, 25, 2, 658; Trimble, "Civil War Diary," 8; William M. Grace, "Isaac Ridgeway Trimble: The Indefatigable and Courageous" (Masters Thesis: Virginia Polytechnic Institute and State University, 1984), 104–110.
73. *O. R.*, Ser. 1, 25, Part 2, 812.
74. *Ibid.*, 830.
75. *O. R.*, Ser. 1, 12, Part 2, 721–722.
76. *Ibid.*, 722–723.
77. *Ibid.*, 742–743.
78. *Ibid.*, 723.
79. *Ibid.*, 743.
80. James Longstreet, *From Manassas to Appomattox: Memoirs of the Civil War in America* (Secaucus, NJ: The Blue and Grey Press, n.d.), 167; Jackson to Stuart, April 14, 1863, Letters of Confederate general Robert E. Lee, Stonewall Jackson, Jeb Stuart and Joseph E.

Johnston [manuscript], 1861–1884, University of Virginia Library, Charlottesville.
81. *O. R.,* Ser. 1, 12, Part 2, 720.
82. Trimble, "Civil War Diary," 4.
83. *Ibid.,* 6.
84. Jackson's MS Letter Book, p. 42, quoted in *Lee's Lieutenants,* 2: 259.
85. *O. R.* Ser. 1, 12, Part 2, 741.
86. *Ibid.,* 742.
87. Trimble, Civil War Diary, 6.
88. *O. R.,* Ser. 1, 12, Part 2, 719.
89. *Ibid.,* 721.
90. Trimble, "Report of Operations," 308.

Chapter 8. From Gettysburg to Surrender

1. Trimble, "Civil War Diary," 10.
2. *Ibid.,* 9.
3. *Ibid.,* 10.
4. *O. R.,* Ser. 1, 25, part 2, 801–802.
5. Robert E. Lee to Isaac R. Trimble, May 20, 1863, Trimble Papers, Maryland Historical Society.
6. *O. R.,* Ser. 1, 25, part 2, 822.
7. *Ibid.,* 837.
8. *Ibid.,* 830.
9. Isaac R. Trimble, "The Campaign and Battle of Gettysburg," *Confederate Veteran,* 25 (1917), 209.
10. *Ibid.;* Isaac R. Trimble, "The Battle of Gettysburg," *Southern Historical Society Papers,* 26 (December 1898), 118.
11. *O. R.,* Ser. 1, 27, Part 3, 923.
12. Trimble, "The Battle of Gettysburg," 118.
13. *Ibid.*
14. *Ibid.,* 118–119. Donald Pfanz, in his book about Ewell, made the statement, "Lee had no delusions that Trimble could raise a regiment north of the Potomac, much less a division, but he agreed to let him come along. Trimble joined Lee in Maryland and promptly made a nuisance of himself," 300. Pfanz must have been trying to make Ewell look better by making it appear that his main critic was an unwanted troublemaker. From the letters written to Trimble by Lee it is clear that he sincerely wanted to see Trimble raise the troops in Maryland, and from the greeting recorded here it does not appear that Lee considered him a "nuisance." If anything, the letters quoted suggest that the delusion resided with Lee, not Trimble. It is possible that Trimble was simply unaware of being intrusive; however, on at least two occasions, as will be seen, Lee tried to take advantage of Trimble's experience as an engineer and his knowledge of the terrain.

On the first two days of the battle Trimble had been a general without a command, but on the third day Lee did not hesitate in putting him in place of the fallen General Pender.
15. Trimble, "The Battle of Gettysburg," 119.
16. *Ibid.*
17. *Ibid.*
18. *Ibid.*
19. Frans de Waal, *Good Natured: The Origins of Right and Wrong in Humans and Other Animals* (Cambridge, MA: Harvard University Press, 1996), 213–214.
20. Isaac Trimble to John B. Bachelder, February 8, 1883, Bachelder Papers, New Hampshire Historical Society. Bachelder had attempted to record the history of the Battle of Gettysburg and had requested the stories of those who were there. This no doubt served as the basis for Trimble's version that was posthumously published in the *Southern Historical Society Papers* (1898) and the *Confederate Veteran* (1917).
21. *Ibid.*
22. *Ibid.*
23. *Ibid.*
24. *Ibid.*
25. Trimble, "The Battle of Gettysburg," 120; Trimble, "The Campaign of Gettysburg," 210.
26. Trimble, "The Campaign of Gettysburg," 210.
27. *Ibid.*
28. *Ibid.*
29. *Ibid.*
30. *Ibid.*
31. Trimble, "The Battle of Gettysburg," 121.
32. *Ibid.,* 121–122.
33. *Ibid.,* 122–123.
34. *Ibid.,* 123.
35. *Ibid.*
36. *Ibid.*
37. *Ibid.*
38. *Ibid.*
39. Trimble, "The Campaign of Gettysburg," 211.
40. Trimble to Bachelder, February 8, 1883, John B. Bachelder Papers, New Hampshire Historical Society.
41. *Ibid.*
42. *Ibid.*
43. *Ibid.*
44. *Ibid.* This conversation was recorded in slightly different variations in the *Confederate Veteran* and *Southern Historical Society Papers,* both based on manuscripts written by Trimble. In the latter version Trimble simply stated, "General Ewell made some impatient reply, and the conversation dropped." A more color-

ful version was reported by Randolph H. McKim, "The Gettysburg Campaign," *Southern Historical Society Papers*, 40 (September, 1915), 273. According to McKim, Trimble said "Give me a division and I will engage to take that hill." When refused he said, "Give me a good regiment and I will engage to take that hill." When Ewell refused that too, Trimble threw down his sword and left Ewell's headquarters saying that "he would not serve longer under such an officer!" Since McKim was not actually present during the conversation I have reported it as given to us by Trimble.

45. Walter H. Taylor, *Four Years with General Lee* (New York: Appleton, 1877), 95; *O. R.* Ser. I, 27, part 2, 445, 317–318, 470; Early, "A Review," 255; Campbell Brown Memoirs, Tennessee State Library; Campbell Brown note in Box 2, Folder 41, Polk-Brown-Ewell Papers, Southern Historical Collection, University of North Carolina, Chapel Hill; Thomas Turner, "Gettysburg," Vol. 4, Early Papers, Library of Congress; Pfanz, *Richard S. Ewell*, 308–314.

46. Percy Gatling Hamlin, *"Old Bald Head" (General R. S. Ewell): The Portrait of a Soldier* (Strasburg, VA: Shenandoah Publishing House, Inc., 1940), 199–200; Edwin B. Coddington, *The Gettysburg Campaign: A Study in Command* (New York: Charles Scribner's Sons, 1968), 319; Pfanz, *Richard S. Ewell*, 311–314.

47. John B. Gordon, *Reminiscences of the Civil War* (New York: Charles Scribners Sons, 1904), 153–154.

48. Douglas Southall Freeman, *Lee* (New York: Charles Scribner's Sons, 1991), 326.

49. Trimble, "The Battle of Gettysburg," 117.

50. Trimble to Bachelder, February 8, 1883, John B. Bachelder Papers, New Hampshire Historical Society.

51. Trimble, "Civil War Diary," 11.

52. Trimble, "The Campaign of Gettysburg," 212.

53. *Ibid.* John Purifoy did not hear the conversation, but he did verify Trimble and Lee climbing the cupola. John Purifoy, "The Battle of Gettysburg, July 2," *Confederate Veteran*, 31 (1923), 252.

54. Trimble, "The Battle of Gettysburg," 125.

55. Trimble, "The Campaign of Gettysburg," 212.

56. *Ibid.*

57. Isaac Trimble, "Letter From General Trimble: Baltimore, October 15th, 1875," *Southern Historical Society Papers*, 9 (January, 1881), 33.

58. *Ibid.*

59. *Ibid.*, 35.

60. *Ibid.*

61. *Ibid.*

62. Walter Clark, ed., *Histories of the Several Regiments and Battalions from North Carolina in the Great War, 1861–1865*, 5 vols. (Raleigh, NC: E. M. Uzzell, 1901), V, 564.

63. F.A.B., "Conspiracy," 1.

64. Trimble, "Letter from General Trimble," 32.

65. Carol Reardon, *Pickett's Charge in History and Memory* (Chapel Hill: The University of North Carolina Press, 1997), 206. Reardon gives good coverage to the images of the charge in both its role in Southern history and history of the Civil War. Generally, Pickett and his Virginians received good press shortly after the war, reflected in the name given to the attack. Reardon would probably be in agreement with the statement made by Trimble in his letter of 1881.

66. McHenry Howard, *Recollections of a Maryland Confederate Soldier and Staff Officer Under Johnson, Jackson, and Lee* (Dayton, OH: Morningside Bookstore, 1975), 416.

67. Trimble, "Civil War Diary," 13.

68. *Ibid.*

69. *Ibid.*

70. *Ibid.*

71. F. A. B., "Conspiracy," 2.

72. Isaac R. Trimble to George G. Meade, July 16, 1863, War Department Collection of Confederate Records, Record Group 109, National Archives.

73. Trimble, "Civil War Diary," 13.

74. Henry E. Shepherd, *Narrative of Prison Life at Baltimore and Johnson's Island, Ohio* (Baltimore: Commercial Ptg. & Sta. Co., 1917), 6.

75. Trimble, "Civil War Diary," 13.

76. *Ibid.*, 16.

77. *Ibid.*, 16.

78. *O. R.*, Ser. 1, 27, part 3, 646.

79. *O. R.*, Ser. 2, 6, 103.

80. *Ibid.*, 107–108.

81. Morris to Thayer, August 15, 1863, M619, Letters Received by the Office of the Adjutant General (Main Series), 1861–1870, National Archives, Washington, DC.

82. Adjutant General's Office, General Orders Affecting the Volunteer Force, 1863 (Washington, DC, 1864), 64–87; *O. R.* Ser. III, 2, 301–309; Daniel E. Sutherland, "Guerrilla Warfare, Democracy, and the Fate of the Confederacy, *The Journal of Southern History*, 48 2 (May, 2002), 288.

83. F. A. B., "Conspiracy," 2.

84. *O. R.*, Ser. 2, 6: 387, 451, 486.

85. Trimble, "Civil War Diary," 14.

86. *Ibid.*, 15–16.

87. *Ibid.*, 16.

88. Shepherd, *Narrative of Prison Life*, 8.

89. Trimble, "Civil War Diary," 17.
90. Roger Long, "Johnson's Island Prison," *Blue and Gray* [Special Issue] (March 1987), 8.
91. Trimble, "Civil War Diary," 17, 20.
92. *O. R.*, Ser. 2, 6, 901.
93. *Ibid.*
94. *Ibid.*
95. *Ibid.*, 902.
96. *Ibid.*
97. Henry Kyd Douglas, *I Rode With Stonewall: Being Chiefly the War Experience of the Youngest Member of Jackson's Staff from the John Brown Raid to the Hanging of Mrs. Surratt* (Chapel Hill: The University of North Carolina Press, 1945), 260.
98. John Washington Inzer, *The Diary of a Confederate Soldier*, ed. Mattie Lou Teague Crow (n.p.: Mattie Lou Teague Crow, 1977), 77, 97.
99. Horace Carpenter, "Plain Living at Johnson's Island," *Century Magazine*, 31 (March, 1891), 710.
100. Hewson L. Peeke, "Johnson's Island," *Ohio Archaeological and Historical Publication*, 26 (October, 1917), 472.
101. *Ibid.*, 472–473.
102. *Ibid.*, 475–476.
103. Edward T. Downer, "Johnson's Island," *Civil War History*, 77 (June, 1962), 209.
104. Andrew Jackson Campbell, *The Civil War Diary of Andrew Jackson Campbell*, ed. Jill Knight Garrett (Columbia, TN: Jill Knight Garrett, n.d.), 53.
105. Shepherd, *Narrative of Prison Life*, 14.
106. Trimble, in his diary, wrote "Officers addressed at all times in a disrespectful or insulting tone." Trimble, "Civil War Diary," 19. Ultimus Barziza wrote, "Col. Pierson did not recognize rank in our officers, but addressed all as Mr." Ultimus Barziza, *The Adventures of a Prisoner of War, 1863–1864*, ed. R. Henderson Shuffler (Austin: University of Texas Press, 1964), 100. Among those who confirmed the taunting by residents: Edmund DeWitt Patterson, *Yankee Rebel: The Civil War Journal of Edmund DeWitt Patterson*, ed. John G. Barrett (Chapel Hill, University of North Carolina Press, 1966), 124, 168; William Henry Asbury Speer, "A Confederate Soldier's View of Johnson's Island Prison," ed., James B. Murphy, *Ohio History*, 79 (Spring, 1970), 109.
107. Trimble to Davis, October 23, 1886, Davis Family Collection, Box 21, Eleanor S. Brockenbrough Library, The Museum of the Confederacy, Richmond, VA.
108. Inzer, *Diary*, 64; Campbell, *Diary*, 35.
109. Campbell, *Diary*, 56.
110. *Ibid.*, 42.
111. Inzer, *Diary*, 89. Other sources indicating the shooting of prisoners: Campbell, *Diary*, 37–39, 50, 56; Horace, "Plain Living," 711, 714; Speer, "Confederate Soldier's View," 107, 110; Trimble, "Civil War Diary," 89; Douglas, *I Rode with Stonewall*, 263–264; Barziza, *Prisoner*, 78.
112. Speer, "Confederate Soldier's View," 110.
113. Barziza, *Prisoner*, 77–78; John Dooley, *Confederate Soldier: His War Journal*, ed. John T. Durkin (Georgetown: Georgetown University Press, 1945), 145.
114. Carpenter, "Plain Living," 714–715.
115. It is not the purpose here to evaluate the claims that have often been made that the North intentionally tried to punish the Confederate prisoners by cutting rations and generally increasing mistreatment of the prisoners. For discussion of this subject see William Best Hesseltine, *Civil War Prisons: A Study in War Psychology* (New York: Drederick Ungar Publishing Co., 1930), 191–197. Numerous accounts confirm the scarcity of food after the sutler pulled out in 1864, and also the consumption of rats, clearly out of necessity and not desire. For confirmation of the food situation by prisoners see also: Downer, "Johnson's Island," 206–207; Campbell, *Diary*, 53; Inzer, *Diary*, 49, 63, 96; Douglas, *I Rode with Stonewall*, 263; Confederate, 163; Patterson, *Yankee Rebel*, 194–195; Barziza, *Diary*, 77; Shepherd, *Narrative of Prison Life*, 13.
116. Trimble, "Civil War Diary," 19.
117. Trimble to Davis, October 23, 1886, Davis Family Collection, Box 21, Eleanor S. Brockenbrough Library, The Museum of the Confederacy, Richmond, VA,
118. *Ibid.*
119. Douglas, *I Rode With Stonewall*, 263
120. Patterson, *Yankee Rebel*, 148.
121. Shepherd, *Narrative of Prison Life*, 16–17.
122. Trimble, "Civil War Diary," 19.
123. *O. R.*, Ser. 2, 6: 902–903.
124. *Ibid.*, 899.
125. *Ibid.*, 900.
126. Barziza, *Prisoner*, 101; Patterson, *Yankee Rebel*, 157; Dooley, *Confederate Soldier*, 158.
127. Norman, *A Portion*, 204.
128. Civil War Notebook of John Peter Jones, 1862–1863, MSS 11095, University of Virginia Libraries, Charlottesville, VA.
129. Shepherd, *Narrative of Prison Life*, 11.
130. Howard, *Recollections*, 400–402.
131. Dooley, *Confederate Soldier*, 154–158; L. W. Allen, "A Plan To Escape," *Southern Historical Society Papers*, 19 (January, 1891), 283.
132. Campbell, *Diary*, 44.
133. Shepherd, *Narrative of Prison Life*, 11.
134. Allen, "A Plan to Escape," 283–290.

135. *Ibid.*
136. F. A. B., "Conspiracy," 3.
137. *Ibid.*
138. Allen, "A Plan to Escape," 284–285.
139. *Ibid.*, 286–288.
140. Did the governor general of Canada inform the United States government of both the November 1863 planned attack on the *Michigan* and the later January 1864 plans under Trimble's command? Allen claimed that the news of the escape had been received from the Governor-General of Canada. Captain Minor made the same claim about his November plans for an assault on the *Michigan*. It is possible that the governor-general informed the United States of only one of these plans and the two men each believed their plans to be the ones reported. If this is the case then it was probably the earlier plans that the Union learned about and they were still on their guard for the second attempt.
141. Allen, "A Plan to Escape," 288; F. A. B., "Conspiracy," 4.
142. "Johnson's Island: Thrilling Story a Visit Thereto Recalls," *Southern Historical Society Papers*, 30 (1902): 257–259. For more details on the Conspiracy of 1864 see Long, "Johnson's Island," 44–57; Charles E. Frohman, *Sandusky's Yesterdays* (Columbus: The Ohio Historical Society, 1965), 72–114.
143. F. A. B., "Conspiracy," 6.
144. *Ibid.*, 6–7.
145. "Johnson's Island, Thrilling Story," 260–261.
146. *O. R.*, Ser. 2, 7: 1132.
147. *Ibid.*, 1117.
148. *Ibid.*, 1131.
149. Robert Ould, "Captain Irving and the Steamer Convoy — Supplies for Prisoners," *Southern Historical Society Papers*, 10 (July, 1882), 327.
150. *Baltimore Sun*, January 23, 1886; Records of Isaac R. Trimble, M331, National Archives, Washington, DC.

Chapter 9.
Unreconstructed Rebel

1. F. A. B., "Conspiracy of '64," 8.
2. American News, March 17, 1985; Carleton Jones, "Ravenhurst," *The Sun Magazine* (May 31, 1981), 6–7, 19.
3. Trimble, *15th Annual Reunion, West Point*, 28.
4. Consulting Engineers, *Report on Condition of Druid Lake Reservoir* (Baltimore: John Cox, Book and Job Printer, 1868); Board of Engineers, *Report Upon Changing the Course of Jones Falls, With a View to Prevent Inundations* (Baltimore: John Cox, Book and Job Printer), 1868.
5. Stock certificate, Trimble Papers in possession of William C. Trimble of Baltimore.
6. Stock certificate, Trimble Papers in possession of William C. Trimble of Baltimore; Isaac R. Trimble to Ira Hotchkiss, 1870, Issac R. Trimble Papers, in possession of William C. Trimble, Baltimore, MD; Trimble to Davis, December 1, 1871, Davis Family Collection, Box 21, Eleanor S. Brockenbrough Library, The Museum of the Confederacy, Richmond, VA; Hudson Strode, *Jefferson Davis: Tragic Hero: The Last Twenty-Five Years, 1864–1889* (New York: Harcourt, Brace & World, Inc., 1964), 355.
7. F. A. B., "Conspiracy of '64," 7.
8. Strode, *Jefferson Davis*, 355, 357, 363, 379; "Ravenhurst," 6; Manly Wade Wellman, *Giant in Gray: A Biography of Wade Hampton of South Carolina* (New York: Charles Scribner's Sons, 1949), 230; William C. Davis, *Jefferson Davis: The Man and his Hour* (New York: Harper Collins Publishers, 1991), 660.
9. Clement Eaton, *Jefferson Davis* (New York: The Free Press, 1977), 71; Davis, *Jefferson Davis*, 205–206, 208, 663–664, 681; Strode, *Jefferson Davis*, 355, 357, 363, 379, 382–383.
10. Davis, *Jefferson Davis*, 681.
11. Wellman, *Giant in Gray*, 34–35, 47, 184, 194–195, 210.
12. Wade Hampton to G. L. Park, October 17, 1868, as published in: Hampton M. Jarrell, *Wade Hampton and the Negro: The Road Not Taken* (Columbia: University of South Carolina Press, 1950), 167. There is no disputing that many Southerners had the ambition of preventing the social and economic rise of blacks in the South; however, researchers continue to show that Hampton meant what he said in this quote and that he had a certain appeal to the African American population in South Carolina. See Edmund L. Drago, *Hurrah for Hampton! Black Red Shirts in South Carolina During Reconstruction* (Fayetteville: University of Arkansas Press, 1998).
13. Wellman, *Giant in Gray*, 210.
14. Jack Hurst, *Nathan Bedford Forrest: A Biography* (New York: Alfred A. Knopf, 1993), 26–28, 55, 58, 281–282, 294–295.
15. Trimble, *15th Annual Reunion, West Point*, 28.
16. *Ibid.*, 30.
17. *Ibid.*
18. *Ibid.*, 29.
19. *Ibid.*, 30.
20. Trimble, "Our Infantry," 13; *Baltimore Sun*, January 23, 1886; "Editorial Paragraphs," *Southern Historical Society Papers*, 1 (January–

June, 1876), 43; "Editorial Paragraphs," *Southern Historical Society Papers*, 9 (July–August, 1881),48; "Editorial Paragraphs," *Southern Historical Society Papers*, 9 (October–December, 1881), 574–575; "Editorial Paragraphs," *Southern Historical Society Papers*, 10 (January & February, 1882), 55, 66; "Sketch of the Lee Memorial Association," *Southern Historical Society Papers*, 11 (August–September, 1883), 388–391; "The Southern Historical Society: Its Origin and History," *Southern Historical Society Papers*, 18 (January–December, 1890), 349–365; "The Confederate Home of Maryland," *Confederate Veteran*, 19 (1921), 176.

21. "Isaac R. Trimble Camp No. 1025," *Confederate Veteran*, 7 (1899), 85.

22. "Unveiling of Maryland Monument," *Confederate Veteran*, 11 (1903), 268.

23. *The Sun*, January 4, 1888; 11ACP, Box 548, Appointment Commission and Personnel Branch Document File, 1879, National Archives, Washington, DC; David Trimble to Davis, January 2, 1888, Davis Family Collection, Box 21, Eleanor S. Brockenbrough Library, The Museum of the Confederacy, Richmond, VA; Nineteenth Annual Reunion of the Associated Graduates, 63–68.

24. Ibid.

25. *The Sun*, January 4 and 5, 1888; "Where Confederate Generals are Buried," *Confederate Veteran*, 8 (1910), 427.

Bibliographic Essay

1. William J. Cooper, *The South and the Politics of Slavery, 1828–1856* (Baton Rouge: Louisiana State University Press,1978); J. Mills Thornton, III, *Politics and Power in a Slave Society: Alabama, 1800–1860* (Baton Rouge: Louisiana State University Press, 1978), xv; David M. Potter, *The Impending Crises, 1848–1861* (Baton Rouge: Louisiana State University Press, 1976); Anthony Gene Carey, *Parties, Slavery, and the Union in Antebellum Georgia* (Athens: The University of Georgia Press, 1997), xi–xx; Jonathan M. Atkins, *Parties, Politics, and the Sectional Conflict in Tennessee, 1832–1861* (Knoxville: The University of Tennessee Press, 1997); Richard J. Carwardine, *Evangelicals and Politics in Antebellum America* (New Haven, CN: Yale University Press, 1993); Don Edward Fehrenbacher, *Sectional Crisis and Southern Constitutionalism* (Baton Rouge: Louisiana State University, 1995).

2. Lacy Ford, *Origins of Southern Radicalism: The South Carolina Upcountry, 1800–1860* (New York: Oxford University Press, 1988); Kenneth S. Greenberg, *Masters and Statesmen: The Political Culture of American Slavery* (Baltimore: Johns Hopkins University Press, 1985); Michael A. Morrison, *Slavery and the American West: The Eclipse of Manifest Destiny and the Coming of the Civil War* (Chapel Hill: University of North Carolina Press, 1997).

3. Michael F. Holt, *The Political Crisis of the 1850s* (New York: John Wiley & Sons, 1978); John H. Aldrich, *Why Parties?: The Origin and Transformation of Political Parties in America* (Chicago: The University of Chicago Press, 1995); Maizlish, Stephen E., *The Triumph of Sectionalism: The Transformation of Ohio Politics 1844–1856* (Kent, OH: Kent State University Press, 1983).

4. Gavin Wright, *The Political Economy of the Cotton South: Households, Markets, and Wealth in the Nineteenth Century* (New York: W. W. Norton & Company, Inc.); Roger L. Ransom, *Conflict and Compromise: The Political Economy of Slavery, Emancipation, and the American Civil War* (New York: Cambridge University Press, 1989); Gerald Gunderson, "The Origin of the American Civil War," *The Journal of Economic History*, 34 (December, 1974), 915–950; James L. Huston, "Property Rights in Slavery and the Coming of the Civil War," *The Journal of Southern History*, 65 (May, 1999), 249–286.

5. John Ashworth, *Slavery, Capitalism and Politics in the Antebellum Republic* (New York: Cambridge University Press, 1996); Bruce Levine, *Half Slave and Half Free: The Roots of Civil War* (New York: Hill and Wang, 1992); Michael P. Johnson, *Toward a Patriarchal Republic: The Secession of Georgia* (Baton Rouge: Louisiana State University Press, 1977).

6. Eugene Genovese. *The Political Economy of Slavery: Studies in the Economy & Society of the Slave South* (New York: Columbia University Press, 1960). Bertram Wyatt-Brown looked at the social values of the premodern society of the South. Bertram Wyatt-Brown, *Southern Honor: Ethics and Behavior in the Old South* (New York: Oxford University Press, 1982). John Hope Franklin and several others have agreed that the mythology of Southern history enabled the region to resist modernization. See Charles Grier Sellers, ed., *The Southerner as American* (Chapel Hill: University of North Carolina Press, 1960).

7. Herbert Collins, "The Southern Industrial Gospel Before 1860," *Journal of Southern History*, 12 (Fall, 1946), 386–402; Robert Russell, *Economic Aspects of Southern Sectionalism, 1840–1861* (New York: Russell & Russell, 1960).

8. Ernest M. Lander, Jr. concluded that "After 1840 Charleston civic leaders worked vigorously to stimulate industry in and near

the port city." Ernest M. Lander, Jr., "Charleston: Manufacturing Center of the Old South," *Journal of Southern History,* 26 (August, 1960), 330–351, quote p. 351. George D. Green showed that the bankers may not have loaned great sums for manufacturing, but they were not dominated by the planters and they did finance New Orleans commerce and internal improvements as well as small agricultural endeavors. George D. Green, *Finance and Economic Development in the Old South: Louisiana Banking, 1804–1861,* (Stanford, CA: Stanford University Press, 1972).

9. Broadus Mitchell, *William Gregg: Factory Master of the Old South,* (Chapel Hill: University of North Carolina Press, 1928).

10. Wesley Frank Craven identified distinctive regions within the South in the early days of colonialism. Wesley Frank Craven, *The Southern Colonies in the Seventeenth Century.* (Baton Rouge: Louisiana State University Press, 1949). Though T. H. Breen dealt only with the Chesapeake colonies he saw a distinctive culture originating in the planter society. T. H. Breen, *Tobacco Culture: The Mentality of the Great Tidewater Planters on the Eve of the Revolution* (Princeton, NJ: Princeton University Press, 1985).

11. Grady McWhiney, *Cracker Culture: Celtic Ways in the Old South* (Tuscaloosa: University of Alabama Press, 1989); Grady McWhiney and Perry D. Jamieson, *Attack and Die: Civil War Military Tactics and the Southern Heritage* (University: University of Alabama Press, 1982).

12. Edmond S. Morgan claimed that since the slaves occupied the lower rungs of the social ladder this allowed the poor and middle class whites to elevate their status, thus promoting democracy among whites. Edmond S. Morgan, *American Slavery American Freedom: The Ordeal of Colonial Virginia,* (New York: W. W. Norton & Company, 1975). See also John McCardell, *The Idea of a Southern Nation: Southern Nationalists and Southern Nationalism, 1830–1860* (New York: W. W. Norton & Company, 1979).

13. Peter A. Coclanis, "Tracking the Economic Divergence of the North and the South," *Southern Cultures,* 6 (Winter, 2000), 99. See also Rollin G. Osterweis, *The Myth of the Lost Cause, 1865–1900* (Hamden, CN: Archon Books, 1973).

14. C. Vann Woodward, *The Burden of Southern History* (Baton Rouge: Louisiana State University Press, 1950); Larry J. Griffin, "Southern Distinctiveness, Yet Again, or, Why America Still Needs the South," *Southern Cultures,* 6 (Fall, 2000), 47–72.

15. Robert Kenzer studied Orange County, North Carolina, and identified several different communities within a single county. Robert Kenzer, *Kinship and Neighborhood in a Southern Community: Orange County, North Carolina, 1849–1881* (Knoxville, University of Tennessee Press, 1987). William Shade focused on the numerous communities within the state of Virginia. William Shade, *Democratizing the Old Dominion: Virginia and the Second Party System, 1824–1861* (Charlottesville: University of Virginia Press, 1996).

16. Religion has played a key role in Southern identity, but a collection of essays in *Religion in the South,* edited by Charles Reagan Wilson, explored some of the less traditional southern religious communities, including the often persecuted Catholics and Jews. Charles Reagan Wilson, ed., *Religion in the South* (Jackson: University Press of Mississippi, 1985). See also Robert N. Rosen, *The Jewish Confederates* (Columbia: University of South Carolina, 2000).

17. John W. Blassingame described the influence the slave community had on the white population; John W. Blassingame, *The Slave Community: Plantation Life in the Antebellum South* (New York: Oxford University Press, 1979). Mechal Sobel emphasized the African American influences on the slave owners; Mechal Sobel, *The World They Made Together: Black and White Values in Eighteenth Century Virginia* (Princeton, NJ: Princeton University Press, 1987). James H. Brewer covered the African American contribution to the Confederate cause with their labor; James H. Brewer, *The Confederate Negro: Virginia's Craftsmen and Military Laborers, 1861–1865* (Durham, NC: Duke University Press, 1969). J. K. Obatala, an African author, was one of the first to cover actual combat of black Confederates; J. K. Obatala, "The Unlikely Story of Blacks Who Were Loyal to Dixie," *Smithsonian,* 9 (March, 1979), 94–101. There have been a few books written about black Confederates since then. Richard Rollins, *Black Southerners in Gray: Essays on Afro-Americans in Confederate Armies* (Murfreesboro, TN: Southern Heritage Press, 1994); Charles Kelly Barrow, J. H. Segars, and R. B. Rosenburg, eds., *Forgotten Confederates: An Anthology About Black Southerners* (Atlanta: Southern Heritage Press, 1995); Ervin L. Jordan, Jr., *Black Confederates and Afro-Yankees in Civil War Virginia* (Charlottesville: University Press of Virginia, 1995). John O'Donnell-Rosales compiled a list of more than 3,000 Hispanics who fought for the Confederacy; John O'Donnell-Rosales, *Hispanic Confederates* (Baltimore: Clearfield, 1998). Many books have been written about the Five Civilized Tribes of Indian Territory,

but other tribes joined them in fighting for the South. Two of the best books on the subject are by the same author, Annie Heloise Abel. They are old but gave a very thorough account. Annie Heloise Abel, *The American Indian as Slaveholder and Secessionist* (Cleveland: Arthur H. Clark; reprint, Lincoln: University of Nebraska Press, 1992); Annie Heloise Abel, *The American Indian in the Civil War, 1862–1865* (Cleveland: Arthur H. Clark; reprint, Lincoln: University of Nebraska Press, 1992). Kenny Franks wrote a book that delved into the relationship between full bloods and mixed bloods in the Cherokee nation; Kenny Franks, *Stand Waite and the Agony of the Cherokee Nation* (Memphis: Memphis State University Press, 1979).

18. C. Vann Woodward, *Origins of the New South, 1877–1913* (Baton Rouge: Louisiana State University Press, 1951).

19. Dwight B. Billings, Jr. in *Planters and the Making of a "New South": Class, Politics and Development in North Carolina, 1865–1900*, (Chapel Hill: University of North Carolina Press, 1979); Jonathan Wiener, *Social Origins of the New South: Alabama, 1860–1880* (Baton Rouge: Louisiana State University Press, 1978).

20. Paul M. Gaston, *The New South Creed: A Study in Southern Mythmaking*, (New York: Alfred A. Knopf, 1970).

21. David L. Carlton, *Mill and Town in South Carolina, 1880–1920* (Baton Rouge: Louisiana State University Press, 1982); Michael Wayne, *Reshaping of Plantation Society* (Urbana: University of Illinois Press, 1983).

Bibliography

Primary Sources

MANUSCRIPTS AND COLLECTIONS

Baltimore and Ohio Railroad Archives, Baltimore and Ohio Railroad Museum, Baltimore, Maryland
    Baltimore and Ohio Annual Reports to Stockholders
    Baltimore and Ohio Minute Books
    Philip E. Thomas Letterbooks
Baltimore City Hall, Department of Legislative Reference, Baltimore, Maryland City Register, Ledgers
Chicago Historical Society
    Thomas J. Jackson Papers
College of William and Mary
    Benjamin Stoddert Ewell Papers
    William B. Taliaferro Papers
    Harriot Stoddert Turner, "The Ewells of Virginia, Especially of Stony Lonesome"
Duke University, William R. Perkins Library, Manuscript Department, Durham, North Carolina
    Bradley Tyler Johnson Papers
    John Cheeves Haskell Memoir
    Munford-Ellis Family Papers
    Richard Stoddert Ewell Letterbook
Eleanor S. Brockenbrough Library, The Museum of the Confederacy, Richmond, Virginia
    Davis Family Collection
Huntingdon Library, San Marino, California
    J. E. B. Stuart Papers
Library of Congress,
    Jedediah Hotchkiss Papers
    Richard S. Ewell Papers
    Jubal Anderson Early Papers
Maryland Historical Society, Baltimore, Maryland
    Baltimore and Susquehanna Railroad Annual Reports to the Stockholders
    Baltimore and Potomac Railroad Annual Reports to Stockholders
    Laws of Maryland, Published in biennial volumes by the General Assembly, 1763–1861

Isaac R. Trimble Papers
Milligan Papers
Philadelphia, Wilmington, & Baltimore Railroad Annual Reports to the Stockholders
National Archives, Washington D. C.
   1790–1860 Census Records
   Appointment, Commission, and Personnel Branch Document File, Box 548
   Compiled Service Records of Confederate and Staff Officers, and Nonregimental Enlisted Men, M331, Isaac R. Trimble Papers
   Corps of Engineers Reports, 1812–1823, 1 vol.
   Engineer Department, Bulky File
   Letters Received by the Confederate Secretary of War, 1861–1865, M474
   Letters Received by the Office of the Adjutant General (Main Series), 1861–1870, M619
   Returns from U.S. Military Posts, 1800–1916, M617
   Roster of Officers and Enlisted Men, First U.S. Artillery, 1814–1855
   Topographical Bureau, Internal Improvement Letters Issued
   U.S. Military Academy Cadet Application Papers, 1805–1866, M688
New Hampshire Historical Society
   John B. Bachelder Papers
Pennsylvania Historical Society, Philadelphia, Pennsylvania
   Felton Family Papers
   Petition from Philadelphia County to the Senate and House
Tennessee State Library and Archives, Nashville, Tennessee
   Brown-Ewell Papers, "Military Reminiscences of Maj. Campbell Brown, 1861–1865," I-A-5; Box 2-5.
William C. Trimble, Jr. Collection, Baltimore, Maryland
   Journal of Maria Trimble
   Isaac Ridgeway Trimble Papers
   Isaac R. Trimble, "Address to the 1st Division, 2nd Corps on the Shooting of Deserters," March 2, 1863
   Isaac R. Trimble, "The Conspiracy of 1864: The Attempt to Relieve Rebel Prisoners in the West" (n.p., n.d.)
   Isaac R. Trimble, "Memoirs," unpublished
   William C. Trimble, Sr., "Trimble Outline"
   David Trimble Papers
United States Military Academy Library, Special Collections, Manuscript Collection, West Point, New York
   Isaac Ridgeway Trimble Papers
   Official Register of the Officers and Cadets of the U.S. Military Academy, 1818–1827
   Register of Delinquencies
   Register of Merit
   Register of Punishments
   West Point Letters (the Sylvanus Thayer collection)
University of North Carolina, Southern History Collection, Chapel Hill, North Carolina
   Heartt-Wilson Papers
   Polk-Brown-Ewell Papers
   Henry E. Shepherd, Narrative of Prison Life at Baltimore and Johnson's Island, Ohio, Electronic Edition
University of Virginia Libraries, Manuscript Department, Charlottesville, Virginia
   Isaac Ridgeway Trimble, *Report of the Engineer Appointed by the Commissioners of the Mayor and City Council of Baltimore, on the subject of the Maryland Canal*
   Letters of Confederate generals Robert E. Lee, Stonewall Jackson, Jeb Stuart and Joseph E. Johnston [manuscript], 1861–1884
   Civil War Notebook of John Peter Jones, 1862–1863, MSS 11095
Virginia Historical Society
   Visual Resources
   Jubal Anderson Early Papers
   James Ewell Brown Stuart Papers
   Thomas C. Elder Papers

Newspapers, Periodicals, Brochures, and Others

American News (Baltimore)
Baltimore American
Baltimore Clipper
Baltimore County News
Baltimore Gazette
Baltimore Patriot
Baltimore Sun
Charleston Courier
DeBow's Review
Hunt's Merchants Magazine
Lexington Gazette
New York Times
Niles Weekly Register
Oklahoma City Daily Oklahoman
Pennsylvania Gazette
Port Tobacco Times (Maryland)
The Pottsville Emporium and Colliers Democratic Register
Randall, James Ryder. *Maryland My Maryland*. Baltimore: Miller & Beacham, 1861.
Republican (Baltimore)
Richmond Daily Dispatch
Richmond Enquirer
The South (Baltimore)

Unpublished Manuscripts

Beckman, Thomas. "Wilmington Cameo Stamps," n.d.
Beeson, Randy. "Roll of Honor, 1861–1865: The Beeson/Beason Family," n.d.
Chapman, Anne W. "Benjamin Stoddert Ewell: A Biography." Ph. D. Dissertation: William and Mary, 1984.
Grace, William M. "Isaac Ridgeway Trimble, the Indefatigable and Courageous." Masters Thesis: Virginia Polytechnic Institute and State University, 1984.

Published Letters, Recollections, and Other Primary Sources

Adjutant General's Office, General Orders Affecting the Volunteer Force, 1863 (Washington, DC, 1864).
Allen, L. W. "History of the Campaign of Gen. T. J. (Stonewall) Jackson in the Shenandoah Valley of Virginia." *Southern Historical Society Papers* 43 (August 1920): 113–295.
———. "A Plan to Escape." *Southern Historical Society Papers* 19 (January 1891): 283–289.
Annals of the Congress of the United States, 1789–1825. Washington: Gales and Seaton, 1834–1856.
"April 19, 1861: A Record of the Events in Baltimore, Maryland on that Day." *Southern Historical Society Papers* 29 (1901): 251–269.
Barziza, Ultimus. *The Adventures of a Prisoner of War*. Edited by R. Henderson Sheffler. Austin: University of Texas Press, 1964.
Boyd, David French. *Reminiscences of the War in Virginia*. Austin, TX: Jenkins, 1989.
Boyds' Delaware State Directory. Wilmington: Joshua T. Heald, 1859.
Brown, Campbell. "Notes on Ewell's Division in The Campaign of 1862." *Southern Historical Society Papers* 10, No. 6 (1882): 254–261.
Brown, George William. *Baltimore and the Nineteenth of April, 1861: A Study of the War*. Baltimore: Johns Hopkins University, 1887.

———. "Notes on Ewell's Division in the Campaign of 1862." *Southern Historical Society Papers* 10 (1882): 255–61.
Buck, Samuel D. *With the Old Confeds: Actual Experiences of a Captain in the Line.* Baltimore: H. E. Houck, 1925.
Campbell, Andrew Jackson. *Civil War Diary of Andrew Jackson Campbell.* Edited by Jill Knight Garrett. Columbia, TN: Jill Knight Garrett, 1965.
Carey, Matthew. *Address to the Wealthy of the Land.* Philadelphia: Gaddes, 1831.
Carpenter, Horace. "Plain Living at Johnson's Island." *Century Magazine* 41 (March 1891): 705–718.
Charter and Ordinances of the Baltimore and Potomac Railroad Company. Baltimore: T. Newton Jurtz, 1870.
Clark, Walter, ed. *Histories of the Several Regiments and Battalions from North Carolina in the Great War, 1861–1865.* 5 vols. Raleigh, NH: E. M. Uzzell, 1901.
Coffin, Levi. *Reminiscences of Levi Coffin.* Cincinnati: The Robert Clarke Company, 1898; reprint, New York: Arno Press, 1968.
Compilation of the Official Records of the Union and Confederate Armies. 128 vols. Washington, D.C.: United States Government Printing Office, 1880–1901.
"The Confederate Home of Maryland." *Confederate Veteran* 19 (1921): 176–178.
Confederate Veteran. 40 vols. Nashville, TN: Confederate Veteran Association, 1893–1932.
Consulting Engineers. *Report on the Condition of Druid Lake Reservoir.* Baltimore: John Cox, Book and Job Printer, 1868.
Cullum, George W. *Biographical Register of the Officers and Graduates of the U.S. Military Academy, at West Point, New York, from Its Establishment March 16, 1802, to the Army Reorganization of 1866–67.* 2 vols. New York: Houghton & Mifflin Co., 1868.
Dabney, Robert L. *Life and Campaigns of Lieut.-Gen. Thomas J. Jackson (Stonewall Jackson).* New York: Blelock, 1866.
Dare, Charles P. *Philadelphia, Wilmington and Baltimore Railroad Guide: Containing a Description of the Scenery, Rivers, Towns, Villages, and Objects of Interest Along the Line of Road.* Philadelphia: Fitzgibbon & Van Ness, 1853.
Debates and Proceedings in the Congress of the United States Seventh Congress, First Session. Washington, 1834.
Detailed and Correct Account of the Grand Civic Procession, in the City of Baltimore on the Fourth of July, 1828; In Honor of the Day, and in Commemoration of the Commencement of the Baltimore and Ohio Rail-Road. Baltimore: Thomas Murphy, 1828.
De Tocqueville, Alexis. *Democracy in America.* 2 vols. New York: Vintage Press, 1945.
Dooley, John. *Confederate Soldier, His War Journal.* Edited by Joseph T. Durkin. Georgetown: Georgetown University Press, 1943.
Douglas, Henry Kyd. *I Rode with Stonewall: Being Chiefly the War Experiences of the Youngest Member of Jackson's Staff from the John Brown Raid to the Hanging of Mrs. Surratt.* Chapel Hill: University of North Carolina Press, 1940.
Dunbar, Rowland, ed. *Jefferson Davis, Constitutionalist: His Letters, Papers, and Speeches.* 10 vols. Jackson, MS: 1923.
Early, Jubal A. *Autobiographical Sketch and Narrative of the War Between the States.* Philadelphia: J. B. Lippincott Company, 1912.
———. "A Review by General Early." *Southern Historical Society Papers* 4 (1877): 241–281.
———. *War Memoirs.* Bloomington, Indiana University Press, 1960.
"Editorial Paragraphs." *Southern Historical Society Papers* 1 (January–June 1876): 43.
"Editorial Paragraphs." *Southern Historical Society Papers* 9 (July–August 1881): 48.
"Editorial Paragraphs." *Southern Historical Society Papers* 9 (October, November, December 1881): 51–53.
"Editorial Paragraphs." *Southern Historical Society Papers* 10 (January & February 1882): 94–95.
The Eighth Annual Report of the Philadelphia, Wilmington & Baltimore Railroad Company:

With the Report of the Chief Engineer and the Proceedings of the Stockholders' Meeting. Philadelphia: John C. Clark, 1846.

The Eighth Annual Report of the President and Directors to the Stock Holders of the Baltimore and Susquehanna Rail Road Co. Baltimore: Lucas and Deaver, 1836.

The Eleventh Annual Report of the Philadelphia, Wilmington & Baltimore Railroad Company: With the Report of the Chief Engineer and the Proceedings of the Stockholders' Meeting. Philadelphia: John C. Clark, 1849.

Evans, Clement A., ed. Confederate Military History: A Library of Confederate States History ... Written by Distinguished Men of the South. 13 vols. Atlanta: Confederate Pub. Co., 1889.

Ewell, Benjamin S. "Jackson and Ewell." Southern Historical Society Papers 20 (1892): 26–33.

The Fifth Annual Report of the Philadelphia, Wilmington & Baltimore Railroad Company: With the Report of the Chief Engineer and the Proceedings of the Stockholders' Meeting. Philadelphia: United States Book and Job Office, 1843.

The First Annual Report of the President and Directors to the Stock Holders of the Baltimore and Susquehanna Rail Road Co. Baltimore: Lucas and Deaver, 1828.

"Flag of the 16th Mississippi Regiment." Confederate Veteran 26 (1918): 75–76.

The Fourteenth Annual Report of the Philadelphia, Wilmington & Baltimore Railroad Company: With the Report of the Chief Engineer and the Proceedings of the Stockholders' Meeting. Philadelphia: John C. Clark, 1852.

Fravel, John W. "Jackson's Valley Campaign." Confederate Veteran 6, no. 9 (1898): 418–420.

Freeman, Douglas Southall. R. E. Lee: A Biography. 4 vols. New York: Charles Scribner's Sons, 1934–35.

_____. Unpublished Letters of General Robert E. Lee, C. S. A. to Jefferson Davis and the War Department of the Confederate States of America, 1862–65. New York: G. P. Putman's Sons, 1957.

Gordon, John B. Reminiscences of the Civil War. New York: Charles Scribner's Sons, 1904.

Greeley, Horace. The American Conflict: A History of the Great Rebellion in the United States of America, 1860–1865. Hartford, 1867.

Hamlin, Percy G., ed. The Making of a Soldier: Letters of General R. S. Ewell. Richmond, VA: Whittet & Shepperson, 1935.

Heitman, Francis R. Historical Register and Dictionary of the United States Army. Washington: Government Printing Office, 1903.

Hinshaw, William Wade. Encyclopedia of American Quaker Genealogy. 6 volumes. Ann Arbor, MI: 1936–1950. Reprint, Baltimore: Genealogical Publishing Co., 1991–94.

Howard, Charles McHenry. "Baltimore and the Crises of 1861." Maryland Historical Magazine 16 (December 1946): 259–281.

_____. Recollections of a Maryland Confederate Soldier, 1861–1865. Baltimore: Williams & Wilkins Co., 1914.

Hyde, Charles R. "The Father of Woodrow Wilson." Confederate Veteran 25 (1927): 334.

Inzer, John Washington. The Diary of a Confederate Soldier: John Washington Inzer 1834–1928. Edited by Mattie Lou Teague Crow. n. p.: Mattie Lou Teague Crow, 1977.

"Isaac R. Trimble Camp NO. 1025." Confederate Veteran 7 (1899): 85.

Jackson, Mary A. Memoirs of Stonewall Jackson. Louisville, KY: Courier Journal Job Printing Co., 1895; reprint, Dayton, OH: Press of Morningside Bookshop, 1976.

Johnson, Bradley T., General. "Memoir of the First Maryland Regiment: Paper No. 3." Southern Historical Society Papers 10 (January & February 1882): 46–57.

Johnson, Robert Underwood and Clarence Clough Buel, eds. Battles and Leaders of the Civil War. 4 vols. New York: Century Co., 1887–88.

"Johnson Island: Thrilling Story a Visit Thereto Recalls." Southern Historical Society Papers 30 (1902): 256–266.

Joint Committee of Hopewell Friends, Comp. Hopewell Friends History, 1734–1934: Records of Hopewell Monthly Meetings and Meetings Reporting to Hopewell. Strasburg, VA: Shenandoah Publ. House, 1936; reprint, Baltimore: Genealogical Publishing Co., 1993

Jones, J. William. "The Career of General Jackson." *Southern Historical Society Papers* 35 (1907): 79–98.

———. "Reminiscences of the Army of Northern Virginia." *Southern Historical Society Papers* 9 (April 1881): 185–189.

Jones, Terry L. *Lee's Tigers: The Louisiana Infantry in the Army of Northern Virginia.* Baton Rouge: Louisiana State University Press, 1987.

Knight, J., and Benjamin H. Latrobe. *Report Upon the Locomotive Engines and the Police and Management of Several of the Principal Rail Roads in the Northern and Middle States.* Baltimore: Lucas & Deaver, 1838.

Latrobe, John H. B. *Personal Recollections. A Lecture, Delivered Before the Maryland Institute March 23d, 1868.* Baltimore: The Sun Book and Job Printing, 1868.

———. "West Point Reminiscences," in *Eighteenth Annual Reunion of the Association of the United States Military Academy, at West Point, New York.* East Saginaw, MI: Evening News Printing and Binding House, 1887.

Longstreet, James. *From Manassas to Appomattox: Memoirs of the Civil War in America.* New York: The Blue and Grey Press, n.d.

McClendon, William A. *Recollections of War Times.* Montgomery, AL: Paragon Press, 1909.

McGrady, Edward, Jr. "Gregg's Brigade of South Carolinians in the Second Battle of Manassas." *Southern Historical Society Papers* 13 (1885): 3–40.

McKim, Randolph H. "The Gettysburg Campaign." *Southern Historical Society Papers* New Series, No. 2 (September 1915): 253–300.

———. *A Soldier's Recollections.* New York: Longmans, Green, 1911.

The Medical and Surgical History of the War of the Rebellion. 6 vols. Compiled by George A. Otis and D. L. Huntington. Washington, DC: U.S. Government Printing Office, 1883.

Moore, Edward Alexander. *The Story of a Cannoneer Under Stonewall Jackson.* New York: Neale, 1905.

Munford, T. T., General. "Reminiscences of Jackson's Valley Campaign." *Southern Historical Society Papers* 7 (1879): 523–535.

Nichols, George W. *A Soldier's Story of His Regiment.* Jessup, GA: Privately Published, 1898.

Nineteenth Annual Reunion of the Association of Graduates of the United States Military Academy, at West Point, New York, June 11th, 1888. East Saginaw, MI: Evening News Printing & Binding House, 1888.

The Ninth Annual Report of the President and Directors to the Stock Holders of the Baltimore and Susquehanna Rail Road Co. Baltimore: Lucas and Deaver, 1836.

Oates, William C. *The War Between the Union and the Confederacy and Its Lost Opportunities, with a History of the 15th Alabama Regiment and Forty-eight Battles in Which It Was Engaged.* Dayton, OH: Morningside Press, 1974.

Ould, Robert, Judge. "Captain Irving and the 'Steamer Convoy'—Supplies for Prisoners." *Southern Historical Society Papers* 10 (July 1882): 320–328.

Patterson, Edmund DeWitt. *Yankee Rebel Civil War Journal of Edmund DeWitt Paterson—9th Alabama Infantry.* Chapel Hill: University of North Carolina Press, 1966.

Paxton, John G., ed. *The Civil War Letters of Frank "Bull" Paxton, C.S.A.* Hillsboro, TX: Hill Junior College Press, 1978.

Poor, Henry V. *Manual of the Railroads of the United States for 1868–1869.* New York: H. V. and H. W. Poor, 1868.

Proceedings of the Sundry Citizens of Baltimore. Baltimore: William Woody, 1827.

Purifoy, John. "The Battle of Gettysburg." *Confederate Veteran* 31 (1923): 252.

———. "Gen. Robert E. Lee, The Peerless Soldier—I." *Confederate Veteran* 34 (1926): 304.

Report on the Course of Instruction in Yale College. New Haven, 1828.

Robertson, James I., Jr., ed. *Proceedings of the Advisory Council of the State of Virginia, April 21–June 19, 1861.* Richmond: Virginia State Library, 1977.

Robinson, Edward A. "Some Recollections of April 19, 1861." *Maryland Magazine of History* 27 (1932): 274–279.

Schmidt, George P. *The Old Time College President*. New York, 1930.
The Seventh Annual Report of the Philadelphia, Wilmington & Baltimore Railroad Company: With the Report of the Chief Engineer and the Proceedings of the Stockholders' Meeting. Philadelphia: John C. Clark, 1845.
Seymour, William J. *The Civil War Memoirs of Captain William J. Seymour*. Edited by Terry L. Jones. Baton Rouge: Louisiana State University Press, 1991.
Sheeran, James B. *Confederate Chaplain: A War Journal of Rev. James. B. Sheeran, c. ss. r., 14th Louisiana, C.S.A.* Edited by Joseph T. Durkin. Milwaukee: Bruce Pub. Co., 1960.
Shepherd, Henry E. (Elliot). *Narrative of Prison Life, At Baltimore and Johnson's Island, Ohio.* (Baltimore: Commercial Ptg. & Sta. Co., 1917).
"Sketch of the Lee Memorial Association." *Southern Historical Society Papers* 11 (August & September 1883): 388–391.
"The Southern Historical Society. Its Origin and History." *Southern Historical Society Papers* 18 (1890): 349–365.
Southern Historical Society Papers. 52 vols. Richmond: Southern Historical Society Association, 1876–1959.
Speer, William Henry Asbury. "Johnson's Island." Edited by James B. Murphy. *Ohio History* 79 (Spring 1970): 101–111.
Stiles, John C., comp. "In the Year 1862." *Confederate Veteran* 25 (1917): 368.
_____. "In the Years 1861–62." *Confederate Veteran* 25 (1917) 317.
Swift, Joseph Gardner. *Memoirs*. Privately published, 1890.
Taylor, Richard. *Destruction and Reconstruction*. New York: Appleton, 1879.
Taylor, Walter H. *Four Years with General Lee*. New York: Appleton, 1879.
The Thirteenth Annual Report of the Philadelphia, Wilmington & Baltimore Railroad Company: With the Report of the Chief Engineer and the Proceedings of the Stockholders' Meeting. Philadelphia: John C. Clark, 1851.
Trimble, Issac R. "Address," in *Fifteenth Annual Reunion of the Association of the Graduates of the United States Military Academy at West Point, New York*. E. Saginaw, MI: Corier Printing Co., 1884.
_____. *Baltimore and Potomac Railroad: Report of I. R. Trimble, Esq., Containing Result of Surveys and Estimates made June 1, 1855*. Baltimore: James Young Steam Printing Establishment, 1855.
_____. "The Battle of Gettysburg." *Southern Historical Society Papers* 26 (1898): 116–128.
_____. "The Campaign and Battle of Gettysburg." *Confederate Veteran* 25 (1917): 209–213.
_____. "The Civil War Diary of General Isaac Ridgeway Trimble." *Maryland Historical Magazine* 17 (March 1922): 1–20.
_____. "Gallant Lieut.-Col. Fulton, of N.C." *Confederate Veteran* 4 (1896): 27.
_____. "General I. R. Trimble's Report of Operations of His Brigade From 14th to 29th of August, 1862." *Southern Historical Society Papers* 8 (June & July 1880): 306–310.
_____. *Investigation into the Alleged Official Misconduct of the Late Superintendent of the Philadelphia, Wilmington, and Baltimore Railroad Company*. 2 vols. Philadelphia: Press of J. H. Bryson, 1854–55.
_____. "Letter from General Trimble." *Southern Historical Society Papers* 9 (January 1881): 29–35.
_____. *Our Infantry*. Baltimore: n.p., 1883.
_____. *The Replies of I. R. Trimble to the Inquiries Propounded to Him, by Samuel M. Felton, Esquire, Before the Committee of Investigation, of the Philadelphia, Wilmington, and Baltimore Railroad Company, Appointed Under a Resolution of the Board of Directors, Together with the Report of the Committee*. Baltimore: F. A. Hanzsche, 1854.
_____. *Report of the Engineer [Isaac Trimble] Appointed by the Commissioners of the Mayor and City Council of Baltimore, On the Subject of the Maryland Canal*. Baltimore: Lucas & Deaver Printers, 1837.

_____. *Report of the Engineers on the Reconnaissance and Surveys Made in Reference to the Baltimore and Ohio Railroad.* Baltimore: W. Woody Printer, 1828.

_____. "The Southern Cross." *Collections of the Virginia Historical Society*, New Series 6 (1887): 334–336.

_____, B. H. Latrobe, and John H. Tegmeyer. *Report of the Board of Engineers Upon Changing the Course of Jones Falls, With a View to Prevent Inundation to the Mayor and City Council of Baltimore.* Baltimore: John Cox, Book and Job Printer, 1868.

"Unveiling of Maryland Monument." *Confederate Veteran* 11 (1903): 368–369.

Ware, John N. "Second Manassas—Fifty-Eight Years Afterwards." *Confederate Veteran* 30, no. 2 (1922): 60–62.

The Wilmington Directory. Wilmington, DE: Joshua T. Heald, Bookseller and Stationer, 1857.

The Wilmington Directory for the Year 1853. Wilmington, DE: Joshua T. Heald, Book-Seller, Stationer, Binder, and Blank Book Manufacturer, 1853.

Wood, James Harvey. *The War: "Stonewall" Jackson, His Campaigns and Battles, the Regiment as I Saw Them.* Gaithersburg, MD: Butternut Press, 1984.

Wyly, B. F., Capt. "Repulse of Federal Raid on Knoxville." *Southern Historical Society Papers* 9 (October–December 1881): 479–488.

Yellott, George. "A Delayed Letter to the Editor." *History Trails* (Spring 1977): 16–17.

Secondary Sources

BOOKS

Abel, Annie Heloise. *The American Indian as Slaveholder and Secessionist.* Cleveland: Arthur H. Clarke, 1915. Reprint, Lincoln: University of Nebraska Press, 1992.

_____. *The American Indian in the Civil War, 1862–1865.* Cleveland: A. H. Clark, 1919. Reprint, Lincoln: University of Nebraska Press, 1992.

Aldrich, John H. *Why Parties?: The Origin and Transformation of Political Parties in America.* Chicago: The University of Chicago Press, 1995.

Ambler, Charles Henry. *A History of Transportation in the Ohio Valley.* Glendale, CA: The Arthur H. Clark Company, 1932.

Ambrose, Stephen E. *Duty, Honor, Country: A History of West Point.* Baltimore: Johns Hopkins Press, 1966.

Ashworth, John. *Slavery, Capitalism and Politics in the Antebellum Republic.* New York: Cambridge University Press, 1996.

Atkins, Jonathan M. *Parties, Politics, and the Sectional Conflict in Tennessee, 1832–1861.* Knoxville: The University of Tennessee Press, 1997.

Baker, Jean H. *Ambivalent Americans: The Know-Nothing Party in Maryland.* Baltimore: Johns Hopkins University Press, 1977.

Barrow, Charles Kelley, J. H. Segars, and R. B. Rosenburg, eds. *Forgotten Confederates: An Anthology About Black Southerners.* Atlanta: Southern Heritage Press, 1995.

Barrow, Thomas C. *Trade and Empire: The British Customs Service in Colonial America, 1600–1775.* Cambridge, MA: Harvard University Press, 1970.

Bender, Thomas. *Community and Social Change in America.* New Brunswick, NJ: Rutgers University Press, 1978.

Benedict, Ruth. *Patterns of Culture.* New York: Houghton Mifflin Company, 1934.

Beringer, Richard E., et al. *Why the South Lost the Civil War.* Athens: The University of Georgia Press, 1986.

Billings, Dwight B., Jr. *Planters and the Making of a "New South:" Class, Politics and Development in North Carolina, 1865–1900.* Chapel Hill: University of North Carolina Press, 1979.

Billington, Ray Allen, and Marti Ridge. *Westward Expansion: A History of the American Frontier.* New York: Macmillan, 1982.

Blassingame, John W. *The Slave Community: Plantation Life in the Antebellum South.* Rev. ed., New York: Oxford University Press, 1979.
Boatner, Mark Mayo, III. *The Civil War Dictionary.* New York: David McKay Company, 1959.
Bowman, John S. *The Civil War Almanac.* New York: World Almanac Publications, 1983.
Boyer, Paul, and Stephen Nissenbaum. *Salem Possessed: The Social Origins of Witchcraft.* Cambridge, MA: Harvard University Press, 1974.
Breen, T. H. *Shaping Southern Society: The Colonial Experience.* New York: Oxford University press, 1976.
Breger, Louis. *From Instinct to Identity: The Development of Personality.* Englewood Cliffs, NJ: Prentice-Hall, 1974.
Brewer, James H. *The Confederate Negro: Virginia's Craftsmen and Military Laborers, 1861–1865.* Durham, NC: Duke University Press, 1969.
Brown, Richard D. *Modernization: The Transformation of American Life, 1600–1865.* New York: Hill and Wang, 1976.
Browne, Gary Lawson. *Baltimore in the Nation, 1789–1861.* Chapel Hill: The University of North Carolina Press, 1980.
Buber, Martin. *Paths to Utopia.* Boston: Beacon Press, 1958.
Carey, Anthony. *Parties, Slavery, and the Union in Antebellum Georgia.* Athens: University of Georgia Press, 1997.
Carlton, David L. *Mill and Town in South Carolina, 1880–1920.* Baton Rouge: Louisiana State University Press, 1982.
Carwardine, Richard J. *Evangelicals and Politics in Antebellum America.* New Haven, CN: Yale University Press, 1993.
Chandler, Alfred D., Jr. *The Railroads: The Nation's First Big Business, Sources and Readings.* New York: Harcourt, Brace & Wold, Inc., 1965.
_____. *The Visible Hand: The Managerial Revolution in American Business.* Cambridge: Harvard University Press, 1977.
Coddington, Edwin B. *The Gettysburg Campaign: A Study in Command.* New York: Charles Scribner's Sons, 1988.
Cooper, William J. *The South and the Politics of Slavery, 1828–1856.* Baton Rouge: Louisiana State University Press, 1978.
Craven, Wesley Frank. *The Southern Colonies in the Seventeenth Century.* Baton Rouge: Louisiana State University Press, 1949.
Crofts, Daniel W. *Reluctant Confederates: Upper South Unionists in the Secession Crises.* Chapel Hill: The University of North Carolina Press, 1989.
Davis, Burke. *They Called Him Stonewall: A Life of Lt. General T. J. Jackson, CSA.* New York: The Fairfax Press, 1954.
Davis, William C. *Jefferson Davis: The Man and His Hour.* New York: Harper-Collins Publishers, 1991.
Degler, Carl N. *The Other South: Southern Dissenters in the Nineteenth Century.* New York: Harper & Row, 1974.
De Waal, Frans. *Good Natured: The Origins of Right and Wrong in Humans and Other Animals.* Cambridge, MA: Harvard University Press, 1996.
Dilts, James D. *The Great Road: The Building of the Baltimore & Ohio, the Nation's First Railroad, 1828–1853.* Stanford, CA: Stanford University Press, 1993.
Dodd, Donald B., and Wynelle S. *Historical Statistics of the South, 1790–1970.* AL: University of Alabama Press, 1973.
Drago, Edmund L. *Hurrah for Hampton! Black Red Shirts in South Carolina During Reconstruction.* Fayetteville: University of Arkansas Press, 1998.
Drake, Thomas Edward. *Quakers and Slavery in America.* New Haven, CT: Yale University Press, 1950.
Dummond, Dwight Lowell. *The Secession Movement 1860–1861.* New York: Macmillan, 1931.
Dumont, Louis. *From Mandeville to Marx: The Genesis and Triumph of Economic Ideology.* Chicago: The University of Chicago Press, 1977.

Dyer, Christopher. *Standards of Living in the Later Middle Ages.* Cambridge: Cambridge University Press, 1989.
Eaton, Clement. *Jefferson Davis.* New York: The Free Press, 1977.
Encyclopædia Britannica. London: Encyclopædia Britannica, Inc., 1961.
Evitts, William J. *A Matter of Allegiances: Maryland from 1850 to 1861.* Baltimore: Johns Hopkins University Press, 1974.
Fehrenbacher, Don Edward. *Sectional Crisis and Southern Constitution.* Baton Rouge: Louisiana State University Press, 1995.
Fleming, Thomas J. *West Point: The Men and Times of the United States Academy.* New York: William Morrow, 1969.
Floan, Howard R. *The South in Northern Eyes, 1831–1861.* Austin: University of Texas Press, 1958.
Foote, Shelby. *The Civil War: A Narrative.* 3 vols. New York: Random House, 1958.
Ford, Lacy. *Origins of Southern Radicalism: The South Carolina Upcountry, 1800–1860.* New York: Oxford University Press, 1988.
Forman, Sidney. *West Point: A History of the United States Military Academy.* New York: Columbia University Press, 1950.
Franks, Kenny A. *Stand Watie and the Agony of the Cherokee Nation.* Memphis: Memphis State University Press, 1979.
Freehling, William W. *The Road to Disunion: Volume I, Secessionists at Bay 1776–1854.* New York: Oxford University Press, 1990.
Freeman, Douglas Southall. *Lee,* an abridgement of the four-volume *R. E. Lee,* by Richard Harwell. New York: Charles Scribner's Sons, 1991.
_____. *Lee's Lieutenants: A Study in Command.* 5 vols. New York: Charles Scribner's Sons, 1943.
Frohman, Charles E. *Sandusky's Yesterdays.* Columbus: Ohio Historical Society, 1965.
Gabor, Andrea. *The Capitalist Philosophers: The Geniuses of Modern Business — Their Lives, Times, and Ideas.* New York: Times Business, 2000.
Gallagher, Gary W., ed. *The Antietam Campaign.* Chapel Hill: University of North Carolina Press, 1999.
Garraty, John A., and Mark C. Carnes, editors. *American National Biography.* New York: Oxford University Press, 1999.
Gaston, Paul. *The New South Creed: A Study in Southern Mythmaking.* New York: Alfred A. Knopf, 1970.
Genovese, Eugene. *The Political Economy of Slavery: Studies in the Economy & Society of the Slave South.* New York: Pantheon Books, 1965.
Goodrich, Carter. *Government Promotion of American Canals and Railroads 1800–1890.* New York: Columbia University Press, 1960.
Grant, Susan-Mary. *North Over South: Northern Nationalism and American Identity in the Antebellum Era.* Lawrence: University of Kansas Press, 2000.
Green, George D. *Finance and Economic Development in the Old South: Louisiana Banking, 1804–1861.* Stanford, CA: Stanford University Press, 1972.
Greenberg, Kenneth S. *Masters and Statesmen: The Political Culture of American Slavery.* Baltimore: Johns Hopkins University Press, 1985.
Hamlin, Charles B. *"Old Bald Head" (General R. S. Ewell): The Portrait of a Soldier.* Strasburg, VA: Shenandoah Publishing House, 1940.
Hanawalt, Barbara A. *The Ties That Bound: Peasant Families in Medieval England.* New York: Oxford University Press, 1986.
Harper, Lawrence A. *The English Navigation Laws: A Seventeenth Century Experiment in Social Engineering.* New York: Cornell University Press, 1939.
Hennessy, John J. *Return to Bull Run: The Campaign and Battle of Second Manassas.* New York: Simon & Schuster, 1994.
Hesseltine, William B. *Civil War Prisons: A Study in War Psychology.* New York: Frederick Ungar, 1962.

Hill, Forest G. *Roads, Rails, & Waterways: The Army Engineers and Early Transportation.* Norman: University of Oklahoma Press,
Hollinger, Robert. *Postmodernism and the Social Sciences: A Thematic Approach.* London: Sage Publications, 1994.
Holt, Michael F. *The Political Crisis of the 1850s.* New York: John Wiley & Sons, 1978.
Hurst, Jack. *Nathan Bedford Forrest: A Biography.* New York: Alfred A. Knopf, 1993.
Israel, Jonathan I. *Dutch Primacy in World Trade, 1585–1740.* Oxford: Clarendon Press, 1989.
Jarrell, Hampton M. *Wade Hampton and the Negro: The Road Not Taken.* Columbia: The University of South Carolina Press, 1950.
Johnson, Allen, ed. *Dictionary of American Biography.* New York: Scribner's Sons, 1929.
Johnson, Michael P. *Toward a Patriarchal Republic: The Secession of Georgia.* Baton Rouge: Louisiana State University Press, 1977.
Jordan, Ervin L., Jr. *Black Confederates and Afro-Yankees in Civil War Virginia.* Charlottesville: University Press of Virginia, 1995.
Jordon, Weymouth T., Jr. *North Carolina Troops 1861–1865: A Roster.* 6 vols. Raleigh, NC: Division of Archives and History, 1977.
Kenzer, Robert C. *Kinship and Neighborhood in a Southern Community: Orange County, North Carolina, 1849–1881.* Knoxville: The University of Tennessee Press, 1987.
King, Alvy L. *Louis T. Wigfall, Southern Fire-eater.* Baton Rouge: Louisiana State University Press, 1970.
König, Rene. *The Community.* London: Rutledge & Kegan Paul, Ltd., 1968.
Kowaleski, Marianne. *Local Markets and Regional Trade in Medieval Exeter.* Cambridge: Cambridge University Press, 1995.
Laslett, Peter. *The World We Have Lost.* London: Methuen, 1965.
Levine, Bruce. *Half Slave and Half Free: The Roots of Civil War.* New York: Hill and Wang, 1992.
Livingood, James Weston. *The Philadelphia-Baltimore Trade Rivalry 1780–1860.* New York: Arno Press, 1970.
Lockridge, Kenneth. *A New England Town—The First Hundred Years: Dedham, Massachusetts, 1636–1736.* New York: William Norton, 1970.
Macfarlane, A. *The Origins of English Individualism.* Oxford: Oxford University Press, 1978.
Maizlish, Stephen E. *The Triumph of Sectionalism: The Transformation of Ohio Politics 1844–1856.* Kent, OH: Kent State University Press, 1983.
Malone, Dumas, ed. *Dictionary of American Biography.* New York: Charles Scribner's Sons, 1932.
_____. *Dictionary of American Biography.* New York: Charles Scribner's Sons, 1933
_____. *Dictionary of American Biography.* New York: Charles Scribner's Sons, 1936.
_____, and Allen Johnson. *Dictionary of American Biography.* New York: Charles Scribner's Sons, 1931.
_____. *Dictionary of American Biography.* Vol. 5. New York: Charles Scribner's Sons, 1930.
_____. *Dictionary of American Biography.* Vol. 1. New York: Charles Scribner's Sons, 1933.
Maslow, Abraham H. *Dominance, Self-Esteem, Self-Actualization: Germinal Papers of A. H. Maslow.* Monterey, CA: Brooks/Cole Publishing Company, 1973.
_____. *Motivation and Personality.* New York: Harper & Row, 1970.
_____, ed. *New Knowledge in Human Values.* New York: Harper & Brothers, 1959.
McCardell, John. *The Idea of a Southern Nation: Southern Nationalists and Southern Nationalism, 1830–1860.* New York: W. W. Norton, 1979.
McCoy, Drew R. *The Elusive Republic: Political Economy in Jeffersonian America.* Chapel Hill: The University of North Carolina Press, 1980.
McPherson, James. *Battle Cry of Freedom: The Civil War Era.* New York: Oxford University Press, 1988.
McWhiney, Grady. *Cracker Culture: Celtic Ways in the Old South.* Tuscaloosa: University of Alabama Press, 1988.

_____, and Perry D. Jamieson. *Attack and Die: Civil War Military Tactics and the Southern Heritage.* Tuscaloosa: University of Alabama Press, 1982.

Mitchell, Broadus, Ph.D. *William Gregg: Factory Master of the Old South.* Chapel Hill: The University of North Carolina Press, 1928.

Morgan, Edmund S. *American Slavery American Freedom: The Ordeal of Colonial Virginia.* New York: W. W. Norton & Company, 1975.

Morrison, Michael A. *Slavery and the American West: The Eclipse of Manifest Destiny and the Coming of the Civil War.* Chapel Hill: The University of North Carolina Press, 1997.

The National Cyclopedia of American Biography. Ann Arbor, MI; University Microfilms, 1967.

Norton, Ann. *Alternative Americas: A Reading of Antebellum Political Culture.* Chicago: The University of Chicago Press, 1986.

O'Dell, Cecil. *Pioneers of Old Frederick County, Virginia.* Marceline, MO: Walsworth Publishing Company, 1995.

O'Donnell-Rosales, John. *Hispanic Confederates.* Baltimore: Clearfield, 1998.

Osterweis, Rollin G. *The Myth of the Lost Cause, 1865–1900.* Hamden, CT: Archon Books, 1973.

Pfanz, Donald C. *Richard S. Ewell: A Soldier's Life.* Chapel Hill: University of North Carolina Press, 1998.

Pirenne, Henry. *Economic and Social History of Medieval Europe.* London: K. Paul, Trench, Truber & Co. Ltd., 1936.

Potter, David M. *The Impending Crises 1848–1861.* New York: Harper & Row, 1976.

_____. *The South and the Sectional Conflict.* Baton Rouge: Louisiana State University Press, 1968.

Powell, Sumner Chilton. *Puritan Village: The Formation of a New England Town.* New York: Anchor Books, 1965.

Preston, Wheeler. *American Biographies.* New York: Harper & Brothers, 1974.

Quinn, Edward, ed. *Interdiscipline: A Reader in Psychology, Sociology, and Literature.* New York: Free Press, 1972.

Ransom, Roger L. *Conflict and Compromise: The Political Economy of Slavery, Emancipation, and the American Civil War.* New York: Cambridge University Press, 1989.

Reardon, Carol. *Pickett's Charge in History & Memory.* Chapel Hill: University of North Carolina Press, 1997.

Redfield, Robert. *The Little Community.* Chicago: University of Chicago Press, 1956.

Reed, John Shelton. *The Enduring South: Subcultural Persistence in Mass Society.* Lexington, MA: Lexington Books, 1972.

Robertson, James I., Jr. *Stonewall Jackson: The Man, the Soldier, the Legend.* New York: Macmillan, 1997.

Rollins, Richard, ed. *Black Southerners in Gray: Essays on Afro-Americans in Confederate Armies.* Murfreesboro, TN: Southern Heritage Press, 1994.

Rosen, Robert N. *The Jewish Confederates.* Columbia: University of South Carolina Press, 2000.

Rostow, W. W. *The Stages of Economic Growth: A Non-Communist Manifesto.* Cambridge: The University Press, 1971.

Russell, Robert Royal. *Economic Aspects of Southern Sectionalism, 1840–1861.* New York: Russell & Russell, 1960.

Russo, David J. *Families and Cummunities: A New View of American History.* Nashville: The American Association for State and Local History, 1974.

Schama, Simon. *The Embarrassment of Riches: An Interpretation of Dutch Culture in the Golden Age.* New York: Alfred A. Knopf, 1988.

Schmeckebier, Laurence F. *History of the Know Nothing Party in Maryland.* Vol. 17, *Johns Hopkins University Studies in Historical and Political Science.* Baltimore: Johns Hopkins University Press, 1899.

Sears, Stephen W. *Controversies and Commanders: Dispatches from the Army of the Potomac.* Boston: Houghton Mifflin, 1999.

Sellers, Charles Grier, ed. *The Southerner as American*. Chapel Hill: University of North Carolina Press, 1960.
Sewell, Richard H. *A House Divided: Sectionalism and the Civil War, 1848–1865*. Baltimore: Johns Hopkins Press, 1988.
Shade, William G. *Democratizing the Old Dominion: Virginia and the Second Party System 1824–1861*. Charlottesville: University of Virginia Press, 1996.
Shepherd, James F., and Gary M. Walton. *The Economic Rise of Early America*. New York: Cambridge University Press, 1979.
Sifakis, Stewart. *Compendium of The Confederate Armies: Alabama*. New York: Facts on File, 1992.
Smith, Page. *As a City Upon a Hill: The Town in American History*. New York: Alfred A. Knopf, 1966.
Sobel, Mechal. *The World They Made Together: Black and White Values in Eighteenth Century Virginia*. Princeton, NJ: Princeton University Press, 1987.
Soderlund, Jean R. *Quakers & Slavery: A Divided Spirit*. Princeton, NJ: Princeton University Press, 1985.
Stover, John F. *History of the Baltimore and Ohio Railroad*. West Lafayett, IN: Purdue University Press, 1987.
Strode, Hudson. *Jefferson Davis: A Tragic Hero, the Last Twenty-Five Years, 1864–1889*. New York: Harcourt, Brace & World, 1964.
Sutich, Anthony J., ed. *Readings in Humanistic Psychology*. New York: Free Press, 1969.
Taylor, Frank H. *Philadelphia in the Civil War, 1861–1865*. Philadelphia: Dunlap Printing Company, 1913.
Taylor, George Rogers. *The Transportation Revolution 1815–1860*. New York: Holt, Rinehart and Winston, 1951.
Thornton, J. Mills, III. *Politics and Power in a Slave Society: Alabama, 1800–1860*. Baton Rouge: Louisiana State University Press, 1978.
Thrupp, Sylvia. *The Merchant Class of Medieval London: [1300–1500]*. Chicago: The University of Chicago Press, 1948.
Toomey, Daniel Carroll. *The Civil War in Maryland*. Baltimore: Toomey Press, 1983.
Trimble, John Farley. *Trimble Families of America*. Parsons, WV: McClain Printing Co., 1973.
Trimble, William Cattell. *The Cattell Family of South Carolina*. Baltimore: J. H. Furst Co., 1988.
_____. *The Presstman Family of Baltimore*. Baltimore, J. H. Furst Co., 1989.
Valentine, Thomas A. *The Mendenhall Family: Descendants of Thomas Mildenhall and Joane Strode*. n.p.: Published by author, 1994.
Van Deusen, John G. *The Ante-Bellum Southern Commercial Conventions*. Durham, NC: The Seeman Printing, 1926.
Vincent, J. M., J. H. Hollander, and W. W. Willoughby, eds. *A Financial History of Maryland (1789–1848)*. Baltimore: Johns Hopkins University Press, 1907.
_____, _____, and _____, eds. *Johns Hopkins International and Colonial History and Political Science*. Baltimore: Johns Hopkins University Press, 1907.
Walsh, Richard, and William Lloyd Fox, eds. *Maryland: A History 1832–1974*. Baltimore: Maryland Historical Society, 1974.
Weeks, Stephen B. *Southern Quakers and Slavery: A Study in Institutional History*. New York: Bergman, 1968; reprint, Baltimore: Johns Hopkins Press, 1868.
Wellman, Manly Wade. *Giant in Gray: A Biography of Wade Hampton of South Carolina*. New York: Charles Scribner's Sons, 1949.
Wiener, Jonathan M. *Social Origins of the New South: Alabama, 1860–1885*. Baton Rouge: Louisiana State University Press, 1978.
Wilson, Charles Reagan, ed. *Religion in the South*. Jackson: University Press of Mississippi, 1985.

———, and William Ferris, eds. *Encyclopedia of Southern Culture*. Chapel Hill: The University of North Carolina Press, 1989.
Wilson, Courtney, and Shawn Cunningham. *The Baltimore Civil War Museum President Street Station: A Visitor's Guide*. Baltimore: The Baltimore Civil War Museum, 1997.
Woodward, C. Vann. *Origins of the New South, 1877–1913*. Baton Rouge: Louisiana State University, 1951.
Wright, Gavin. *Old South, New South: Revolutions in the Southern Economy Since the Civil War*. New York: Basic Books, 1986.
———. *The Political Economy of the Cotton South: Households, Markets, and Wealth in the Nineteenth Century*. New York: W. W. Norton, 1978.
Wyatt-Brown, Bertram. *Southern Honor: Ethics and Behavior in the Old South*. New York: Oxford University Press, 1982.
Zuckerman, Michael. *Peaceable Kingdoms: New England Towns in the Eighteenth Century*. New York: Alfred A. Knopf, Inc., 1970.

ARTICLES

Coclanis, Peter A. "Tracking the Economic Divergence of the North and the South." *Southern Cultures* 6 (Winter 2000): 82–103.
Collins, Herbert. "The Southern Gospel Before 1860." *The Journal of Southern History* 12 no. 3 (Fall, 1946): 386–402.
Downer, Edward T. "Johnson's Island." *Civil War History* 8 (1962): 202–217.
Ellenberger, Matthew. "Whigs in the Streets? Baltimore Republicanism in the Spring of 1861." *Maryland Historical Magazine* 86 (1991): 23–38.
Griffin, Larry J. "Southern Distinctiveness, Yet Again, or, Why America Still Needs the South." *Southern Cultures* 6 (Fall 2000): 47–72.
Gunderson, Gerald. "The Origin of the American Civil War." *The Journal of Economic History* 34 (December 1974): 915–950.
Hilton, R. H. "Lords, Burgesses and Hucksters." *Past and Present* 97 (Spring, 1982): 3–15.
Huston, James L. "Property Rights in Slavery and the Coming of the Civil War." *The Journal of Southern History* 65 (May 1999): 249–286.
Jones, Carleton. "Ravenhurst." *The Sun Magazine*, May 31, 1981.
Lander, Ernest M., Jr. "Charleston: Manufacturing Center of the Old South." *The Journal of Southern History* 26 (August 1960): 330–351.
Long, Roger. "Johnson's Island Prison." *Blue and Grey* Special Issue (March 1987): 6–58.
Obatala, J. K. "The Unlikely Story of Blacks Who Were Loyal to Dixie." *Smithsonian* 9 (March 1979): 94–101.
Pastor, Joan. "Who's Afraid of a Little Conflict? Part I: 'The Three Stages of Conflict and Resolution in the Warning Stage.'" *The CPA Letter* 80 (April 2000): D2–D3.
Peeke, Hewson L. "Johnson's Island." *Ohio Archaeological and Historical Publications* 26 (October 1917): 470–476.
Sutherland, Daniel E. "Guerrilla Warfare, Democracy, and the Fate of the Confederacy." *Journal of Southern History* 48 (May, 2002): 259–292.
Taylor, George R. "Economic Growth Before 1840: An Exploratory Essay." *Journal of Economic History* 24 (Winter, 1964): 427–444.

Index

Adams, Abigail 65
Adams, John 26, 65
Adams, John Quincy 26, 35, 36
Adelphi Hotel 58
Alabama 42, 104
Albert, Major 39
Alexandria, Virginia 155, 157
Alleghenies 127
Allen, Captain 192
American (Baltimore) 46
American Institute of Certified Public Accountants 78
American Party *see* Know-Nothing Party
American Philosophical Society 26
American Railroad Journal 46
Andersonville 189
Andrew's Battery 124
Annapolis, Maryland 43, 104, 111–2
Anne Arundel County, Virginia 88
Antietam, Battle of *see* Sharpsburg, Battle of
Appleton, Mr. 58
Appomattox 204, 206–7
April 19 (Baltimore Riot) 106–8, 111, 119
Archer, James J. 191
Arkansas 95, 212
Army of Northern Virginia 137–8, 143–4, 171
Army of the Potomac 121, 126, 143
Army of Virginia 147
Articles of War 165
Ashby, Turner 133, 137
Ashland, Virginia 138

Atrim County, Ireland 22
Atwood, Captain 195
Augusta and Savannah Railroad 148
Augusta, Georgia 88, 126

Back River 91
Balthis's Battery 138
Baltimore 14, 35–7, 40, 42–8, 50, 51–3, 55–7, 59, 60–3, 66–7, 69–73, 77, 81–2, 87–8, 91–114, 119, 173–4, 181–3, 191, 196, 198–9, 201, 206, 211–2
Baltimore & Ohio Railroad 16, 35, 37, 39, 42, 45–6, 49–50, 55, 60–2, 64, 72, 80, 84, 87, 102, 106, 112
Baltimore and Potomac Railroad 86–7
Baltimore & Susquehanna RR 16, 59–60, 62–4, 66–7, 80, 87, 90
Baltimore Concentric Engine Company 200
Baltimore Fire Extinguisher Works 200
Baltimore Society of Confederate Soldiers and Sailors 201
Baltimore Water Company 57
Bank of Maryland 100
Bank of the United States 38
Banks, Nathaniel 110, 127–30, 143, 147
Barbour, James 45
Barney, Joshua 47
Beall, William N. R. 196
Beeson, Charity 22–3
Beeson, Edward 22
Beeson Family 22
Bell, John 96

Berkshires 64
Bernard, General 41
Berryville 172
Bethesda Church 139
Bickersteth, Dr. 59
Biddeford, Maine 76
Blood Tubs 98
Blue and Gray Magazine 186, 188, 194
Blue Ridge Mountains 42
Board of Internal Improvements 39
Bonaparte, Napoleon 41
Bonifant, Washington 113
Boston and Lowell Railroad 49, 58, 77
Boston and Providence Railroad 49, 77
Boston, Massachusetts 52, 58, 195
Boston, Massachusetts, and Providence, Rhode Island, Railroad 52, 58
Boteler 162–3
Bottom's Brigade 141
Bowman, Jane 91–2
Bowman, Mr. 91, 109
Boyd, prisoner 191
Breckinridge, John C. 96, 99, 101
Bristoe, Virginia 153
British Corn Laws 70
Brockenbrough's Battery 130
Brooks, Joseph 81–3
Brown, Campbell 130
Brown, George W. 45, 97–102, 104–13, 115, 117, 119
Brown, Governor 149
Brown, John C. 108
Brown, Richard D. 6, 11, 20, 146
Brown, William 22
Brune, John C. 110
Brunswick 51
Buchanan, James 193
Buckley, M. Brooke 73, 75
Buffalo, New York 42
Burr, Aaron 65
Bush River 91
Butler, Benjamin F. 94, 111–5

Calhoun, John C. 13, 38–40, 201
Calhoun, William 51
Calvert Street Station 102, 184
Camden Station 102 106
Cameron, Simon 104–5, 109–10, 181
Camp Chase 193–4
Camp Douglas 193–4
Camp Morton 193–4
Campbell, Mr. 84
Canada 191–3, 197
Canadian provincial Cabinet 192
Canton Company 83

Carlisle 174
Carolina Insurance Company 201–2, 211
Carpetbaggers 211
Carroll, Charles 35
Cashtown, Pennsylvania 175
Cattell, Anne Ferguson 50–1
Cattell, Benjamin 50
Cattell, Lydia 51
Cecil County, Maryland 127
Cedar Mountain, Battle of 149–51
Cemetery Hill 176–8
Centerville, Virginia 121, 124, 157
Champion, Private 181
Champlain Canal 40
Chancellorsville, Battle of 163, 191
Charles City Road 142
Charleston Convention 126
Charleston, South Carolina 50–1, 71, 88, 94
Charlottesville, Virginia 161, 164
Chesapeake and Ohio Canal 35, 38, 40–1, 45, 49, 53, 66
Chesapeake Bay 43
Chester County, Pennsylvania 74
Chester, Pennsylvania 74
Chicago, Illinois 193
Chichester, Captain 190
Chickahominy, Virginia 140–1
Chillicothe, Ohio 19, 24
Choptank River 100
Clarke, J. W. 163, 170
Clark's Mountain 151
Clay, Henry 25
Cloud Family 160
Cloud, Mrs. 160
Coddington, Edwin B. 177
Coffin, Levi 118
Cold Harbor, Battle of *see* Gains Mill, Battle of
Cole 195
Cole, C. H. 193
Coles, Governor 35
Columbia 181
Columbia University 182
Columbus, Ohio 40, 186, 188, 193–4
Confederate Congress 170
Confederate Home of Maryland 204
Confederate States 209
Confederate Veteran Camp No. 1025 204
Connecticut 34
Conrad's Store, Virginia 128
Conspiracy of '64 197, 201
Cooper, Samuel 143, 161
Corps of Engineers 36, 49, 52
Courtney's Artillery 124, 130

Crawford, A. 74
Crittenden's brigade 124
Crooked Run, Virginia 22
Cross Keys, Battle of 133–4, 136, 140, 145, 162
Crown, Captain 160
Cuba 86–7, 124, 203
Culpeper Road 150
Culpeper, Virginia 149
Culps Hill 176–8
Cumberland 47, 49
Cumberland, Maryland 40
Cumberland River 47
Curtin, Andrew G. 104

Dabney, Robert L. 138
Dale, Edward D. 75
Daniel, John W. 206
Darbytown Road 142
Dartmouth College 28, 42, 100
Davidson, Colonel 171
Davies, Charles 28
Davis, Jefferson 32, 121, 126–7, 137, 141, 161–2, 187, 191, 201–2, 211
Davis, Winnie 201
Declaration of Independence 35–6
Delaware 13, 86, 94, 104, 112
Delaware and Maryland Railroad Company 73
Democratic Convention 193
Democratic Party 99, 112, 126
Department of the Northwest 193
Department of the Shenandoah 127
DeTocqueville, Alexis 13
Devereux, General 35
Dispatch Station, Virginia 141
Dobbin, George W. 110
Dorchester County 100
Doudel, Emmett M. 62
Douglas, Henry K. 128
Douglas, Major 180
Douglas, Stephen 96
Dover, England 59
Druid Lake Reservoir 199
Drurary Lane Theater 59
Dulaney Valley 1, 198
Dumfries 163

Early, Jubal 125, 148, 150, 160–1, 175–6, 178, 193
Early, Thomas 148
Eastern Shore (Maryland) 97
Ecole Militaire 26
Edinburgh, Scotland 126
Eighth Brigade 139

Eighth Massachusetts 111
Eliason 166
Elkton, Maryland 74
Elzey, Arnold 121, 125–6, 129–30, 133–4, 140, 148, 161, 206
Elzey's Brigade 141
Emanuel Church 206
Emerson, Ralph Waldo 117
Emmitsburg, Pennsylvania 177
Emmitsburg Road 178
Emory University 173
England 59, 72, 203
Erie Canal 40
Eutaw House 66
Evensport, Virginia 124
Everman, Dr. 190
Ewell, Benjamin 64–5, 125
Ewell, Elizabeth *see* Stoddert, Elizabeth
Ewell, Richard S. 65, 124–32, 134–7, 139, 141–3, 145, 147–9, 151, 153, 158–9, 161–2, 169, 173–8, 210
Ewell, Thomas 65
Ewell Family 64–5
Ewell's Division 125, 133, 139, 141, 148–50, 152

Fairfield, Ohio 23–4
Faulkner, O. J. 164
Fayette County, Pennsylvania 22
Federalists Party 17
Felton, Samuel M. 75–6, 79, 84–6, 90, 93, 102–3, 106, 119, 168, 209–10
Fifteenth Alabama Infantry 124, 130, 133–4, 139, 140–1, 150, 152, 157, 159
Fifth Louisiana Infantry 148
Fillmore, Millard 100
Financial Accounting Standards Board 78
First Artillery, US 34, 39
First Battalion of North Carolina Sharpshooters 125
First Manassas, Battle of 126–7
First Maryland Infantry (Confederate) 126, 130, 132
First Volunteer Regiment 148–9
Floan, Howard 118
Florida 190
Foote, Mr. 160
Forest, Nathan B. 202, 211
Forno, Henry 148. 150, 153, 158
Fort Delaware 187
Fort La Fayette 40, 114
Fort McHenry 111, 181–3, 196
Fort Monroe, Virginia 50
Fort Pillow 202
Fort Pulaski 149

Fort Sumter 95, 104, 126
Fort Warren 195–6
Fourth Division 126
Fourth Virginia Infantry 149
France 59, 126
Franklin, Benjamin 27
Franklin Gazette 25
Fravel, John W. 131, 138
Frederick County, Virginia 22
Frederick, Maryland 112, 174
Frederick Pike 40
Fredericksburg, Virginia 128–9, 132
Freeman, Douglas Southall 177, 179
Fremont, John C. 127, 132–3, 135, 138, 143, 147
Front Royal, Virginia 129–32, 160
Fulton, General 168
Fulton, Robert 26

Gains Mill, Battle of 138–9, 141, 148, 162
Gallatin, Albert 37, 46
Garnett, Dr. 161
Garrison, William L. 117
General Assembly of Maryland 82
General Order No. 100 182
General Survey Act of 1824 38, 40
George II 26
Georgetown, Maryland 35
Georgia 42, 95, 104, 149, 189, 192, 202
Georgia House of Representatives 148
Gettysburg, Battle of 1, 94, 109, 116, 135, 169, 177, 179–80, 183
Gettysburg, Pennsylvania 63, 174–6
Glover, Thomas C. 165
Godwin, Thomas 149
Gordon, John B. 176–7, 202–4
Gordonsville, Virginia 149
Grady, Henry 197
Granger, Lieutenant 181
Grant, Ulysses S. 195–6, 204
Grapevine Bridge, Virginia 141
Gray's Ferry 73
Great Britain 56
Great Lakes 191, 193
great snowball fight 190
Greene, W. J. 190
Greenmount Cemetery 206
Grenier, Colonel 35
Grogan, Charley 178–9
Groveton, Virginia 158
Gunpowder River 91, 109
Gwynn's Falls, Maryland 35

habeas corpus 112
Hagerstown, Maryland 47, 174

Hall, Major 181
Hamlin, Percy 177
Hampton, Wade 5, 198, 200–2, 204, 211
Hanover Junction, Virginia 149
Harman, John 132, 137
Harpers Ferry, Virginia 47, 132
Harrisburg, Pennsylvania 68, 102, 174, 181
Harrison, William Henry 23–4, 32
Harrisonburg, Virginia 133
Harvard University 27, 76, 126
Havana, Cuba 87
Havre de Grace, Maryland 74, 77, 82
Hawthorn, Nathaniel 118
Hays, General 196
Hays, Harry T. 148, 176
Heath, Harry 161
Heidelburg, Pennsylvania 175
Henry House Hill 158
Hicks, Thomas J. 91, 99–100, 104–10
Highland County, Ohio 23
Hill, Ambrose P. 138, 142, 144, 149, 151, 174–5, 178
Hill, D. Harvey 138, 142
Hill, General 139, 143
Hillsboro, Ohio 24
Holden, Mr. 192
Holiday Street 113
Hollinger, Robert 6, 20, 146
Holmes, Oliver W. 118
Holmes Division 142
Hood, John B. 138, 152
Hopewell, Virginia 22
Hopkinson, Colonel 180
Howard, Charles 110, 110–1
Howard, William 47
Huger, Benjamin 206
Huger's Division 142
Hundley's Corner, Virginia 139
Hunt, H. J. 177
Huston, William 86

Illinois 71
Indian Territory 212
Indiana 35, 71
Indianapolis, Indiana 193
Inzer, Colonel 188
Iowa 71
Ireland 59
Isaac R. Trimble Camp of Sons of Confederate Veterans 204
Island Queen 195

Jackson, Andrew 25, 41
Jackson, Thomas J. (Stonewall) 123, 125,

127–32, 135–9, 141–3, 145, 147, 149–55,
  157–9, 161–4, 166–7, 170, 180, 212
Jacksonians 57
James River 141, 143
Jefferson, Thomas 17–8, 26–7, 65
Jefferson, Virginia 153
Jenkins, General 171
Jenny 178–9
Johnson 1
Johnson, Edward 161, 176
Johnson, General 131
Johnson, Richard Mentor 25
Johnson's Division 178
Johnson's Island 116, 179, 184–6, 188–9,
  191–6
Johnston, Joseph E. 124, 128–9, 204, 206,
  212
Jones, J. William 151–2
Jones Falls 199

Kane, George P. 91, 100, 102, 105–8, 113–5
Keezletown Road 134
Kemper, General 180
Kentucky 13, 20, 24–5, 32, 34, 94, 96, 104,
  192, 212
Kernstown, Virginia 128, 137
Kinikonick River 24
Kirby-Smith, General 124
Kirkland, Colonel 131
Knight, Jonathan 47, 49
Know-Nothing Party 71, 98, 100
Knoxville 42
Ku Klux Klan 202–3

Lake Erie 41, 184
Lamon, Colonel 102
Lancaster, Massachusetts 126
Land Act of 1800 22
Lane, J. H. 178–9
Latimer's Battery 150
Latrobe, Benjamin 26
Latrobe, Benjamin H. 84, 87, 200
Latrobe, John H. B. 29, 30, 34, 46, 49, 97
Lawton, Alexander R. 148, 158–9
Lee, Henry 65
Lee, Robert E. 94, 114, 123–4, 127–8, 137–
  8, 141, 143, 146–7, 149, 152–3, 161–3,
  170–77, 196, 202, 204, 206, 212
Lee, W. H. F. 205
Lee Memorial Association 204
Leeds, England 58
Lehigh River 46
Lewis and Clark 42
Lexington Street 181
Liberty Mills, Virginia 149, 151

Libby prison 189
Lieber, Francis 182
Lieber Code 182
Lincoln, Abraham 92–3, 96, 101–4, 106,
  108, 110–2, 114, 119, 127, 132, 146, 153,
  181, 201
Lindsley, Philip 27
Little, Henry 206
Little Kanawha River 46–7, 49
Liverpool and Manchester Railway 63
Liverpool, England 56, 58
Locke, John 17
London, England 59
Londonderry, Ireland 50
Long, Stephen H. 42, 47, 49, 53
Longfellow, William W. 117
Longstreet, James 138, 143–4, 147, 151–2,
  158, 177–8
Louis XIV 26
Louis XV 26
Louisiana 89, 95, 126, 148, 153
Louisville, Kentucky 41, 126
Lowe, E. Louis 108
Lowell Manufacturing 58
Lynchburg, Virginia 196

Madison, James 26
Madison, Indiana 39
Maine 88
Malvern Hill, Virginia 141–2
Manassas Junction 153–4, 155, 157–8, 160,
  163–6, 168
Marshall, John 26
Martin, Mrs. P. C. 191
Martinsburg Turnpike 131
Maryland 1, 13, 21, 32, 43, 45, 53, 57,
  61–3, 65, 71–2, 91–7, 99–102, 104–5,
  107–14, 123–4, 126, 129, 132, 151, 163,
  171–2, 184, 191, 196, 199, 204, 206–9,
  211–2
Maryland Assembly 87, 108
Maryland Battalion 171
Maryland Colonization Society 97
Maryland Heights 132
Maryland My Maryland 101–2
Maryland Street 199
Maslow, Abraham 7–10, 14, 34, 69, 121,
  198, 208–10
Massachusetts 49, 102
Massachusetts and Western Railroad
  59–9, 64, 75
Mauch Chunk, Pennsylvania 46
Maxwell, Colonel 190
May, Henry 113
Mayer, Brantz 71

260   Index

McCardy, Mr. 180–1
McClellan, George B. 124, 126–7, 132, 137, 141–3, 146–7, 149, 158
McClintick, Charity *see* Trimble, Charity
McClintick, James 19, 24
McClintick, William 69, 86
McDaniel 25
McDowell 127–8, 132, 147
McDowell's Department 126
McGehee's farm 139–40
McGrady, Edward 158
McGregor, Douglas 7
McGuire, Hunter 151
McNeill, William G. 47, 49, 64, 87
McQuaig 192
Meade, George 180–1, 190
Mechanicsville 139
Memphis Appeal 187
Memphis, Tennessee 71, 94, 203
Mendenhall, Martha 22
Mendenhall family 22
Meredith, S. A. 182
Merryman, John 113–4
Mexican War 126–7, 148
Miami, Ohio 23
Michigan 71
Michigan (ship) 191, 193–5
Middletown, Pennsylvania 175
Mifflin, Governor 44
Minor, Robert D. 191
Mississippi 42, 95, 104
Missouri 96, 104, 212
Missouri River 42
Mobile, Alabama 71, 88
Mohawk and Hudson Railroad 51
Monacacy Valley 47
Monck, Lord 192
Monroe, James 26, 38
Montreal, Canada 88, 191
Morehead, Turner 181
Morris, W. W. 182
Moundsville, Virginia 39
Mount Sterling Academy, Kentucky 24–5
Mountain Department 127
Mummasburg Road 175
Munford, T. T. 126
Murdaugh, William H 191
Muscle Shoals 41

Nashville, Tennessee 42
National Intelligence 25
National Road 37, 40–2, 45, 53
National Survey Act of 1824 52
Neponset River 46
New England Magazine 118

New Hampshire 32
New Market Road 142
New Market, Virginia 128
New Orleans 40–2, 45, 47, 71, 88–9
New York 13, 34, 39, 53, 71, 114, 118, 204
New York City 29, 40, 45, 51, 54, 56, 58, 63, 65
New York Herald 191, 195
Newbury, Massachusetts 76
Newcastle-on-Tyne, England 58
Newkirk, Matthew 73
Newport 51
Newport, Rhode Island 67
Niles Register 46
Niles Weekly 35
Norfolk, Virginia 123
North American Review 118
North Carolina 21, 42, 66, 65, 170, 173, 178–9, 212
North Eutaw St. 205
Northern Central Railroad 108, 184
Northern Ireland 100
Notre Dame de Paris 59

Oates, William 159
Ohio 13, 22–3, 32, 34, 71, 190, 192, 205
Ohio River 41, 47
Ohio to Alabama Road 47
Ohio Valley 21, 40
Oklahoma 94
Opie, Mr. 161
Orange and Alexandria Railroad 125, 153–4
Ould, Robert 182, 195–6

Palais du Luxembourg 59
Palais Royal 59
Panic of 1819 56
Pantheon 59
Paris, France 59
Parkersburg, Virginia 39
Partridge, Alden 27–8
Pastor, Joan 118–9
Patterson, Robert 112
Patton, Colonel 136
Pender's Division 178, 180
Pennsylvania 13, 21–3, 32, 34, 39–40, 43–4, 60–3, 71, 87, 105, 112, 171–2, 182, 196
Pennsylvania Canal 46
Pennsylvania Gazette 61–2
Pennsylvania House of Representatives 62
Pennsylvania State Works 62
Pennsylvania Yearly Meeting 22
Pepperell Manufacturing 76

Pettigrew, J. J. 178-9
Philadelphia 14, 44-6, 51, 53, 60-1, 63, 65-7, 72-4, 77, 102-3, 174, 180
Philadelphia and Baltimore Central Railroad 86
Philadelphia and Delaware County Railroad Company 72
Philadelphia and Reading Railroad 66, 77
Philadelphia, Wilmington, and Baltimore Railroad 64, 66-7, 70, 72-7, 79-80, 86-7, 90-1, 93, 103, 106, 203
Phillips, Wendell 117
Philo Parsons 195
Pickens, Governor 202
Pickett's Charge 1, 170, 179-80
Pickett's Division 178
Pike, Zebulon 42
Pinckney, Thomas 28
Pittsburgh, Pennsylvania 39, 49, 181, 184, 192
Plug Uglies 98
Point Judith 51
Point Lookout 187, 193
Pope, John 147, 149-50, 153-5, 158
Port Republic, Virginia 133-6, 148
Potomac River 40-1, 47, 87, 173-5
Potomac River Valley 47
Pottsville, Pennsylvania 66
Powel, Colonel 180
Pratt Street 102, 106
President Street Station 55, 73, 75, 102, 106
Presstman, Ann Calhoun 86, 204
Presstman, George McDougall 86
Presstman, Georgiana 50
Presstman, Lydia 66
Presstman, Maria 50-4, 58-9, 66-8, 86, 90
Presstman, Stephen Wilson 52
Presstman, William 50-1
Presstman family 56, 65
Princeton University 27
Proclamation Line of 1763 14

Quakers *see* Society of Friends
Quesnay 17
Quigley, Philip 80
Quincy, Massachusetts 46

Randall, James R. 101
Ranlett, William H. 199
Rapidan River 151, 161
Rappahannock River 124, 126, 128
Ravenshurst 1, 114, 198-201
Reading Railroad 80

Red Necks 98
Redeemers 198, 202-3, 211
Redstone, Pennsylvania 22-3
Reilly's Battery 138
Relay, Maryland 112
Rensselaer Polytechnic Institute 29
Republican Party 17, 96
Reynolds, Minna 1
Reynoldsville, Virginia 142
Rice, Lieutenant 180
Richmond Enquirer 25, 71
Richmond, Virginia 24, 88, 94, 124, 128-9, 137-8, 144, 147, 149, 170, 189
Ridgely, Mrs. 82
Ridgeway, Josiah 23
Ridgeway, Rachel 22-4
Rip Raps 98
Robert E. Lee Memorial Committee 211
Robertson, General 165
Robespierre 114
Rockfish Gap 42
Rodes, Robert E. 176, 178
Rodes' Division 175
Rose Cottage 67
Rostow, W. W. 6
Royal Military Academy of Woolrich 26
Rush, Benjamin 65

St. Etienne-du-Mont Church 59
St. Louis, Missouri 71
St. Mary's, Virginia 39
St. Paul's Church 58
St. Roch Church 59
Salem, Virginia 153
Sandusky Bay 184
Sandusky, Ohio 179, 184-5, 189-90, 193
Sandusky Register 187
Sandy Hook 54
Santiago, Cuba 87
Saunders, Beverly 191
Savage's Station, Virginia 142
Savannah, Georgia 148
Scales, Alfred M. 206
Schenck, Robert C. 181
Scioto River 19
Scotch-Irish 21, 44, 50
Scotland 59
Scott, Winfield 102, 101-1, 113
Second Bull Run *see* Second Manassas
Second Corps 162, 176-7
Second Manassas, Battle of 123, 145, 147-8, 159-60, 179
Second Seminole War 148
Securities and Exchange Commission 78
Seminary Ridge 175

Seminole War 126
Senate Military Committee 162
Seven Days Battles 137–8, 143, 151
Seventh New York 111
Seward, Mrs. 114
Seward, William 193
Seymour, Isaac G. 128
Shannon, Colonel 193
Sharpsburg, Battle of 160–1
Shenandoah River 42
Shenandoah Valley 125–6, 128–9, 132, 137–8, 143–4, 147, 147, 151, 163, 171
Shields, General 129, 133, 138, 143
Shocco Springs, North Carolina 169–70
Sigel, General 152
Sistersville, Virginia 39
Sixteenth Mississippi Infantry 124, 130–1, 134, 139, 149
Sixth Louisiana Infantry 128
Sixth Massachusetts 106–7, 112
Slaughter Mountain *see* Cedar Mountain
Smith, Adam 17
Smith, James P. 176
Smith, Mr. 91
Smith, Samuel 100
Society of Friends (Quakers) 20–3, 34, 44, 47, 55, 117–8, 210
Society of the Army and Navy of the Confederate States 204, 206
South Carolina 21, 28, 42, 50, 66, 101, 148, 198
South Mountain, Maryland 47
Southern Historical Society 204, 211
Southern Insurance Company 202
Southern Trade Conventions 70–1
Spring Dale, Pennsylvania 66
Stanton, Edwin 181, 191, 196
Staunton, Virginia 160–1, 163, 171
Stemmer's Run, Maryland 81
Stockton and Darlington Railroad 59
Stoddert, Elizabeth 65
Strasburg, Virginia 130
Straw, Major 114
Strawberry Hill, Virginia 149
Stuart, General 133
Stuart, George G. 206
Stuart, Jeb 125, 146, 154–5, 158, 163–6, 169, 173–4, 210
Susquehanna River 63, 73, 77–8, 106
Susquehanna Valley 44, 46, 57, 60–3, 95
Swann's Cavalry 124
Swift, Joseph Gardner 25, 64, 75
Swift, William H. 75, 84, 87

Taliaferro, W. B. 158, 162
Taliaferro's Division 149
Tanny, Roger B. 113
Tariff of 1828 25
Tariff of 1832 26
Taylor, Richard 125, 130, 133–4, 136–7, 148, 162
Taylor, Robert 121
Taylor, W. H. 163
Taylor, Zachary 125
Tecumseh Uprising 24
Temperance Party 99
Tennessee 95, 192, 212
Tenth Virginia Infantry 131, 138
Terry, General 185
Texas 139, 193
Texas Brigade 138
Thayer, Sylvanus 27–9, 31–3, 64
Third Artillery, US 34, 39
Thirteenth Amendment 203
Thirteenth Virginia Infantry 128, 134
Thomas, Francis J. 110
Thomas, Philip E. 49
Thompson, Jake 193
Thunderbolts 98
Ticknor, George 27
Tiger Rifles 121, 124
Titusville, Pennsylvania 193
Tomb of Abelard and Heloise 59
Trimble, Ann 22–4
Trimble, Ann Calhoun *see* Presstman, Ann Calhoun
Trimble, Catherine 22–4
Trimble, Charity 19, 23–4
Trimble, David 20, 22–6, 32, 50
Trimble, David Churchman 52, 58, 66
Trimble, Dr. Isaac R. 205
Trimble, John, Jr. 22–3
Trimble, John, Sr. 22–4
Trimble, Joseph 22–3
Trimble, Margaret Lloyd 204
Trimble, Maria *see* Presstman, Maria
Trimble, Rachel *see* Ridgeway, Rachel
Trimble, Samuel 22–3
Trimble, Sarah 22–3
Trimble, William 22–3, 147
Trimble, William A. 32
Trimble & Huston Company 86
Trimble's Brigade (7th Brigade) 130–3, 136, 145, 150, 157
Twelfth Georgia Infantry 149, 157, 159–60
Twenty-fifth Virginia Infantry 134
Twenty-first Georgia Infantry 124, 130–1, 134, 139–41, 150, 152, 154, 159, 165
Twenty-first North Carolina Infantry 124–5, 130, 133, 139, 150, 152–4, 159

Union Church, Virginia 134
Union 11th Corps 175
United Daughters of the Confederacy 204
United Kingdom 64
United States 209
United States Military Philosophical Society 26
United States War Department 182
University of Nashville 27
University of Pennsylvania 65
Upper Patapsco Valley 47

Valley Campaign (1862) 123, 136, 145
Vandalia, Illinois 40
Vinton 33, 45
Virginia 13, 19, 21–3, 34, 39, 41, 43, 46, 49, 53, 65, 92, 95–6, 101–2, 104, 106, 110–1, 114, 123–4, 126, 139, 141, 148, 151, 179, 192, 203, 212
Virginia Central Railroad 128, 149
Virginia House of Delegates 148
Virginia Military Institute 127, 129
Virginia Volunteers 123
Volck, Adalbert J. 103

Waal, Frans de 173
Wales 59
Walker, Colonel 128–9
Walker's Battery 124
Walker's Brigade of Infantry 124
Waller's Cavalry 124
Wallis, S. T. 110
War of 1812 24–5, 27, 44
Ware, John 158
Warren County, North Carolina 169
Warrenton 169
Warrenton Springs, Virginia 153
Washington, George 17, 26
Washington, Martha 201
Washington, D.C. 45, 53, 57, 65, 87, 89, 94, 102, 104, 106–7, 110, 112, 124, 126, 132, 147, 181, 193
Washington Gazette 25
Waugh, Samuel Bell 48
Waverly Magazine 118
Weaver, Casper 49

Wellford's Ford, Virginia 152
Wellsburg, Virginia 39
Wempe, Henry 82–3
West Point 1, 3, 15, 18, 20–1, 25, 27, 28–34, 36, 38–9, 42, 47, 50, 64–5, 90, 92–3, 125, 127, 148, 209, 211
West Virginia 94, 212
Westminster, Maryland 47, 62
Westover, Virginia 39, 192
Wheeling, West Virginia 39, 192
Whig Party 100, 126
White Oak Swamp, Virginia 141–2
Whiting, General 139–40, 142
Whiting's Division 138
Whitney, Eli 26
Wigfall, Louis T. 162–3
Wild, Colonel 196
Wilkinson, John 191
William and Mary University 24, 65
Williams, Jonathan 26–7
Williamsburg, Battle of 148
Wilmington and Susquehanna Railroad 72–3
Wilmington, Delaware 66, 72–3, 77, 88
Wilson, Katherine 22–3
Winans, Ross 110
Winchester, Virginia 22, 130–2, 144, 172
Winder, General 132, 137, 140, 150, 151
Wisconsin 71
Wolcott, Oliver 65
Woodrow, Ann *see* Trimble, Ann
Woodrow, Joshua 24
Woodward, C. Vann 211
Wrightsville, Pennsylvania 63
Wrightsville Railroad Company 63, 66
Wrightsville, York, and Gettysburg Rail Road Company 63
Wythe, George 24

Yale University 27, 29, 126
York and Maryland Line Railroad 62
York Gazette 61–2
York Haven, Pennsylvania 61
York, Pennsylvania 61–2, 66, 181
York Railroad 141

www.ingramcontent.com/pod-product-compliance
Ingram Content Group UK Ltd.
Pitfield, Milton Keynes, MK11 3LW, UK
UKHW041932140426